AFRICAN CHRISTIAN ETHICS

Samuel Waje Kunhiyop

HIPPOBOOKS

Africa · Christian · TextbookS

CONTENTS

PART ONE: ETHICAL FOUNDATIONS

PART TWO: CONTEMPORARY ETHICAL ISSUES

SECTION A. POLITICAL ISSUES

SECTION B. FINANCIAL ISSUES

SECTION C. MARRIAGE AND FAMILY ISSUES

SECTION D. SEXUAL ISSUES

SECTION E. MEDICAL ISSUES

FOREWORD

African Christian Ethics is a very important book. Many other works have attempted to deal with contemporary African ethical reality, but few have been as comprehensive, relevant and up-to-date as this one. I congratulate Professor Kunhiyop for providing a book for which Africa has long been waiting.

Professor Kunhiyop is an outstanding African scholar and authority in the field of Christian ethics, social ethics and theology. His thorough training in biblical studies, theology, ethics, ministerial formation, research and scholarship stands out as one reads this book. Some African scholars have been accused of being shallow and lacking sound scholarship, but not this author. He is deep, thorough, expansive, relevant and persuasive. Nor is he simply an academic: he is a scholar who writes with great passion and deep conviction.

The reader will find that the author is thoroughly at home with the material he is dealing with. He recognizes that failure to understand African traditional beliefs is the source of many failures to understand African ethical problems and to suggest appropriate solutions. Some authors have responded to this situation by advocating a return to these traditional values. Others, recognising the impact of modernity in contemporary Africa, have uncritically accepted Western traditions with their ethical relativism and pluralism. Dr Kunhiyop seeks to avoid both these extremes. He identifies the strengths and weaknesses of both African and Western ethical traditions and examines them critically in the light of his firm belief in the centrality and authority of Holy Scripture.

He applies this approach to a range of contemporary ethical issues. He often begins by presenting the traditional African approach to the issue and then the Western approach. Finally, he explains what the Bible has to say about it and discusses how African Christians should deal with it biblically, while also drawing on what is good in traditional and Western values.

This book shows that moral maxims for Christians are rooted neither in African traditional ethics nor in Western traditional ethics, but in the Holy Scriptures. Let me quote the author:

> We have a duty to obey God based upon his revelation. Men and women seek to obey God through a proper reading and interpretation of Scripture. Scripture properly read and interpreted is normative — binding on all peoples at all times and in every place. Ethics is not what the Christian seeks to do for his or her own purpose. A Christian must seek to do what pleases God.

I highly commend this book to all Africans who seek to deal with a variety of burning ethical issues on the continent of Africa. I also recommend it to all policy-makers and decision-makers in Africa, who would do well to espouse the moral and ethical norms and standards in this book if they are to practise good leadership and governance. Most importantly, I commend this book to students and teachers. It offers a sound introduction to Christian ethics and social ethics for students in Bible colleges, seminaries and universities across the continent of Africa. It may also be of interest to those in other parts of the world who want to know how some of the ethical issues that concern them are addressed in an African context.

Yusufu Turaki.

Professor of Theology and Social Ethics
Jos ECWA Theological Seminary (JETS)
Jos, Nigeria
19 September 2007

ACKNOWLEDGEMENTS

Without the sacrifice of many dedicated people, this book would not have seen the light of the day. Let me mention only a few.

First, I would like to thank the Langham Writers' Grant programme which encouraged me to review and enlarge my previous book, *African Christian Ethics* (Kaduna: Baraka Press, 2004). Their financial assistance enabled me to take short, productive writing retreats at the Miango Rest Home in Jos, Nigeria and at the Institute for the Study of African Realities (ISAR) at the Nairobi Evangelical Graduate School of Theology (NEGST) at Karen in Kenya. In particular, I would like to thank Chris Wright (Director of Langham Partnership International), Brad Palmer and Pieter Kwant, who encouraged me in this project. Sid Garland, the executive director of Africa Christian Textbooks (ACTS) also played a major role in promoting the writing of this book for Africa.

I also thank Isobel Stevenson and Jeremy Ng'ang'a, who have been able and encouraging editors, as well as Friday Nwaohamuo, who assisted in the typing, arranging and proofreading of the early manuscripts.

Dr Yusufu Turaki, who wrote the foreword to this book, has been one of my intellectual mentors. He and Dr John S. Feinberg introduced me to the study of ethics during my student days. Without learning at their feet, this book would not have come into existence in its present form.

The New Commandment Class at Arlington Heights Evangelical Free Church, Illinois, and the Good Shepherd Community Church, Boring, USA, provided moral and financial support as I wrote. I also received massive support from dear friends such as Stu Weber, Randy Alcorn, Stan and Ruth Guillaume, Dave and Joy Dawson, Ron and Carol Speer, Gary and Sue Ellen Griffin, Bob and Mary Rieck.

I am also grateful to the staff and students of Jos ECWA Theological Seminary, with whom many of the issues raised in the book were discussed. My thanks, too, to Stephen Kemp, who wrote most of the study questions.

I am very thankful to my wife, Yelwa, and my children, Zigwai, Babangida, Kauna and Abrak, for their support while I was writing this manuscript.

Finally, I want to express my deep appreciation to my current employers, the South African Theological Seminary (SATS), Rivonia, for giving me sufficient time to work on the final aspects of the book. I am particularly grateful to Drs. Reuben van Rensburg and Kevin Smith (Principal and Vice- Principal of SATS) for their encouragement while I worked on the manuscripts.

PREFACE

African Christian ethics is a vast subject, which cannot possibly be addressed in depth in one book. Nor is it ever possible for any one book to address every conceivable ethical issue that may arise. However, what this book can offer is an evangelical and biblical framework that African Christians can use to help them when dealing with ethical problems.

African ethics is intensely personal, communal and religious. It is personal in the sense that it is deeply rooted in the being of the person, affecting not only the mind, but also the heart, body and spirit. Any attempt to draw a distinction between theoretical (or spiritual) ethics and practical morality is wrongheaded and irrelevant to African Christians.

African ethics is communal in that it seldom thinks in terms of individual ethical decisions that do not affect other people. Whatever affects individuals also affects their immediate family as well as their distant relatives, both those who are living and those who are dead but still interested in the affairs of the living. This comprehensive community is critical to understanding African ethics. It also means that these ethics are developed in interaction with the past, the present and the future.

African ethics is also very religious. God, the spirits of the departed (the ancestors), and good and evil spirits have a pervasive influence on the morality of the people. For Christians, the Bible also serves as an authoritative moral influence. Thus in Africa there is no such thing as an abstract ethical system that has no practical and religious implications. The principles or rules that guide behaviour are intertwined with the practice of ethics. It is in doing what is right that one discovers the ethical rules underlying the behaviour.

This book is divided into two main parts. Part 1 sets out the basic presuppositions, principles and values of African Christian ethics. Since ethics do not exist in a vacuum, this part of the book also deals with the socio-cultural and philosophical beliefs, values and convictions that make up the basic African world view. This world view has been shaped by the external forces of Westernization and Christianization and so these ethical influences are also discussed.

Part 2 of the book offers an overview of some ethical issues affecting African Christians. It touches on some key socio-political and financial issues, as well as on issues relating to the family, sexual and medical ethics, and religion. Under each of these headings, it presents the general ethical principles that are relevant to this area of life, and applies them to particular ethical problems. Each section includes study questions to encourage further thought about the issues raised in this book.

PART ONE
ETHICAL FOUNDATIONS

1

INTRODUCTION TO THE STUDY OF AFRICAN CHRISTIAN ETHICS

Every society is influenced by its history, beliefs and values. We need to know something of Africa's history if we are to be able to understand and address its present political and economic condition. Similarly, we need to understand the ethical values and beliefs that guide moral action in Africa if we are to develop an ethical system that is both African and Christian. Without such an understanding, teaching Christian ethics is like pouring water on a duck's back. The water runs off without even wetting the duck! Failure to appreciate this important point has led to shallow Christian teaching that often has little impact on moral behaviour.

Part 1 of this book thus introduces the subject of ethics and presents the different streams, Traditional, Western and Christian, that combine to produce African Christian ethics. It lays the groundwork for the more detailed discussion of specific ethical issues in Part 2.

Some Definitions

Before we begin this study it is important to define a few of the key terms involved in any discussion of ethics.

Ethics and Morality

The terms "ethics" and "morality" are so closely related that the *Encarta Dictionary* can define ethics as a "system of moral principles governing the appropriate conduct of an individual or group". Some people use the terms as if ethics relates to the theoretical study of right and wrong, good and bad, while morality relates to actual behaviour, the "living out of what one believes to be right and good."[1] Thus James William McClendon writes:

> Morals and morality come from the Latin word, *mos*, meaning custom or usage, while ethics comes from the Greek word, *ethos*, whose meaning is roughly the same. So it is hardly surprising that today, as earlier, these two words are often used interchangeably. When a distinction is made, "morals" nowadays refers to actual human conduct viewed with regard to right and wrong, good and evil, "ethics" refers to a theoretical overview of morality, a theory or system or code. In this sense, our morality is the concrete human reality that we live out from day to day, while ethics is an academic view gained by taking a step back and analyzing or theorizing about (any) morality.[2]

I do not like this compartmentalization because it often blurs issues. People tend to assume that theoretical issues are good only for the scholar, teacher, student or professor in the classroom, while the practical is what is real, useful and true in life situations. Thus in this book I will use the words "morality" and "ethics" interchangeably. This approach matches the African understanding that ethics is not based on abstract principles but on behaviour in specific situations.

For the purposes of this book, ethics and morality are thus defined as the definitions, principles and motivations for conduct and behaviour.

Personal and Social Ethics

A distinction is often made between personal ethics and social ethics. Personal ethics deals with individuals' obligations or duties, or in other words, with what is required of them. Most Western societies emphasize personal ethics because in the West the individual's desires, satisfactions, decisions and accomplishments take precedence over those of the community. Social ethics, on the other hand, deals with

---

[1] Stanley J. Grenz, *The Moral Quest: The Foundations of Christian Ethics* (Leicester: Apollos, 1997), 23. Arthur H. Jentz observes that "morality refers to social orders; ethics is the intellectual scrutiny of such orders and of the reasonings which articulate, support, or oppose them." "Some Thoughts on Christian Ethics", *Reformed Journal* 30 (1976): 52.
[2] James William McClendon, *Systematic Theology. Vol. I: Ethics* (Rev. ed.; Nashville: Abingdon Press, 2002), 45–46.

community morality and emphasizes communal values and interpersonal relationships at the expense of the individual's desires and decisions.

In Africa the focus falls on social ethics rather than personal ethics, for African peoples emphasize the community rather than the individual. Individuals are not neglected, but they are expected to fulfil their roles in a way that fits with the ethos of their society. Communal morality regulates and controls their conduct. For example, a man may marry not because he wants to but because his parents want to have grandchildren.

Values and Ethics

Values are underlying, fundamental beliefs and assumptions that determine behaviour. In Africa, as in the West, these beliefs and assumptions often remain unchanged even after there has been a religious conversion. Thus many African societies may have converted to Christianity or Islam but they still cling to traditional beliefs and assumptions that determine how they act morally. It is therefore critical to know and appreciate the role of values in the study of moral actions.

African and Western Ethics

If this book is to deal with African ethics, we also need to define what we mean by the term "African". The African continent contains many different people groups and cultures. It would theoretically be possible to produce a sociological or anthropological study of the ethics within each group, but that is not the goal here. Rather, this book deals with some general principles of cultural and moral life that apply across a wide range of groups. Thus **chapter 2** presents general ethical principles and motives governing African morality and illustrates them with examples from various groups in Sub-Saharan Africa.

African ethical thinking did not develop in isolation, but has been richly influenced by the forces of Westernization, Christianization, and Islamization. Western influences have been particularly strong in Sub-Saharan Africa, and so **chapter 3** explores Western ethics with its deep Judeo-Greco-Christian roots. This chapter also examines how the humanistic and secular world views associated with the Enlightenment and the technological-electronic revolutions have shaped current Western ethical thinking in many areas.

African Christian Ethics

A cursory look at the syllabi in many Bible colleges and seminaries in Africa will show that Christian ethics is often packaged along with Western ethics as if they are one and the same thing. They are not. The two have become confused because Western missionaries did not bring a naked gospel but one dressed in their own clothes and shoes. Students who should be studying African Christian ethics are too often engaged in wrestling with teleological, deontological, utilitarian and relativistic ethical theories emanating from the West.

What should be taught in African theological colleges is an ethics that is African, biblical and Christian. That is what this book seeks to provide. Thus **chapter 4** presents a careful study of key elements in general Christian ethics, while **chapter 5** presents a brief outline of what an African Christian ethics should look like, a theme that will be the subject of the whole of Part 2 of this book. Before proceeding to address specific ethical questions, however, **chapter 6** offers a brief discussion of some of the problems involved in ethical decision-making, particularly in situations involving conflicting ethical principles.

Questions

1. Write your own one-sentence definitions of ethics and morality. Then ask some Christians and some non-believers in your community to give you their definitions of these terms. Compare these definitions to the definitions given in this chapter.

2. What words are used in your native language to express concepts like ethics and morality, or other concepts defined in this chapter? What nuances of meaning do these words emphasize?

3. Describe the relationship of personal and social ethics in your situation. How does your understanding of personal and social ethics assist (or inhibit) your ability to minister effectively?

2

FOUNDATIONS OF CONTEMPORARY AFRICAN ETHICS

Failure to understand key elements that regulate African morality led many Westerners to misinterpret African moral life. For example, when Western missionaries saw a Christian take a second wife, they assumed that he was committing adultery. The fact that his polygamy was public and endorsed by his society was taken to show that African peoples are very immoral and "quite without a European sense of shame."[1]

In making this judgment, the missionaries were looking only on externals and were assuming that the only factor at play was sexual desire. They failed to recognize the values intrinsic to the African view of marriage and procreation, sexuality and immortality that underlay the practice of polygamy. To the man involved, the important question was not whether he married a second wife, but whether the marriage would produce a child (especially a male child) who would continue his lineage and honour him as an ancestor.

If Westerners did get a glimpse of these values, they often dismissed them, finding "it ludicrous to apply any such terms as 'moral' to African beliefs and actions were perceived as 'perversely irrational and ghost-ridden'."[2]

But the Westerners were wrong. African behaviour was not irrational or lacking morality. Thus in this chapter, we will set out to answer the question, "What are the roots of African values and moral behaviour?"

---

[1] Basil Davidson, *The African Genius* (Boston: Little Brown and Company, 1969), 80.
[2] Davidson, *The African Genius*, 71.

The ethical principles explored in this chapter are not necessarily Christian, but they are the general principles that have shaped African behaviour. If we do not understand them, we will inevitably draw some wrong conclusions about African morality.

Sources for the Study of African Ethics

One of the problems in studying African ethics is that there was traditionally no written record and no one place where its principles were clearly spelled out: "Unlike modern Western ethics, African thought does not regard ethics as a separate discipline, because morality is indistinguishable from the rest of African social life. To set out to discover and understand African ethics via abstract moral principles is to embark on a journey of frustration."[3] Instead, to determine what constitutes moral behaviour one has to "observe and reflect upon the social life of the people—their rituals, customs, practices, events and relationships."[4] Our sources of knowledge of African ethics are thus not written records but customs and the rich African oral tradition.

It must be admitted that it is sometimes difficult to understand and interpret traditions correctly. But there are ways in which this can be done. Bolaji Idowu gives some helpful hints:

> First, it is necessary … to listen carefully and get at the inner meaning. Secondly, it is also necessary to remember that the African situation is one in which life is not divided artificially into the sacred and the secular, that it is one in which reality is regarded as one, and in which the things of earth (material things and man's daily doings and involvements) have meaning only in terms of the heavenly (the spiritual, reckoning with the Transcendent and that part of man which has links with the supersensible world). Thirdly, a doctrine is not necessarily unhistorical or merely imaginary simply because it is mythological.[5]

---

[3] Neville Richardson, "Can Christian Ethics Find Its Way, and Itself, in Africa?" *Journal of Theology for Southern Africa*, 95 (1996): 37.

[4] Ibid.

[5] Idowu, *African Traditional Religion*, 83–84.

I would add a fourth principle to the three listed by Idowu: Traditions must be interpreted within their own contexts. Interpreters of the Bible like to say that "a text without a context is only a pretext". The same principle applies to African customs and the African oral tradition.

Customs and Taboos

In Africa, ethical principles and rules of conduct have been preserved over the ages in various customs and traditions that provide explanations of the reasons, motivations, values and purpose of behaviour. They supply the moral code and indicate "what the people must do to live ethically."[6] Traditions that are passed on from generation to generation become the "Scriptures" of the people, that is, their source of knowledge about what God requires. This knowledge is maintained by the elders, who are the custodians of the rules and regulations that guide the whole community. Thus Africans will often enquire what the elders (and the ancestors) have to say about something, and the tradition they transmit has the force of law. If tradition forbids someone from marrying into a particular clan, he or she must abide by that rule. Failure to do so will bring problems for the whole community, which comprises not only the living but also all those who have died but are still a vital part of the community.

Although murder is prohibited, the tradition of some groups allows euthanasia for the very elderly who can no longer function in society. Thus among the Bajju of Nigeria, an old woman who is tired of living may request her relatives to permit her to die peacefully and join her ancestors instead of living in misery. She then dies, either because her relatives ask God to take her life or because they serve her poisoned food. Similarly, in some societies, tradition has also laid down that twins are to be murdered because they bring bad luck, and babies with Down's syndrome or deformities are to be killed immediately after birth.

Many traditions relate to women and sex. Sexual intercourse with one's wife before a hunting expedition is wrong because it will bring misfortune and an unsuccessful hunt. Husbands are forbidden to have sexual intercourse with their wives during their menstrual periods. Pregnant women are expected to treat children with respect. If they do

---

[6] E. Bolaji Idowu, *African Traditional Religion: A Definition* (Maryknoll, N.Y.: Orbis, 1975), 42.

not, they will endure a very difficult childbirth until they repent of their harsh attitude.

Some groups forbid husbands from beating their wives during the week of peace before the planting season in order to avoid angering the goddess of the earth.[7]

Whistling at night is also strongly forbidden because it invites evil spirits into the compound. And exposing the god the men worship to public view brings instant death

The Oral Tradition

The other major source of information about African ethics is the oral tradition, that is, the many stories and legends by which knowledge is transmitted across generations by way of the spoken, as opposed to the written, word. This tradition includes myths and stories, liturgies, songs and proverbs.

Western scholars have often looked down on oral traditions as being less valid and credible than written sources. Judaism, Christianity and Islam, for example, are often seen as valid and superior to other religions because they have written records. But these religions did not always have written documents. Many of the Hebrew Scriptures were transmitted orally for generations before they were committed to writing, and Christianity was transmitted by the spoken word before it was recorded in the written word. To say that early Christianity was invalid and inferior because there were no written documents is to completely misunderstand the place of oral and written records. Jesus' method of teaching was by oral instruction, and the apostles and the early church fathers employed oral tradition, which they passed on to later generations. John the Apostle himself states in 1 John 1:1: "we declare to you what was from the beginning, what we have heard, what we have seen with our eyes, what we have looked at and touched with our hands, concerning the word of life." The words "what we have heard" are repeated in 1 John 1:3 and 1:5. John is clearly referring to oral transmission of the message he and the other apostles received from Jesus.

---

[7] Chinua Achebe mentions this tradition in his novel *Things Fall Apart* (London: Heinemann, 1958).

There is thus no reason to despise the oral tradition. Just like the lived tradition, it must be carefully interpreted within its own context.

Myths and legends

Myths and legends are traditional stories about something that happened in the past which explains something in the present. They often involve gods and heroic figures. As pointed out above, it is important to take into account the context in which they are told if one is to interpret them correctly. Failure to do so will give a false and misleading meaning.

An Igbo story from Nigeria illustrates what this means in practice. The story says that in ancient times God used to live very close to human beings. However, one day a woman was pounding her yam so vigorously that her pole accidentally struck God on the forehead, and he retreated into the heavens. A careless reading of this story would suggest that the Igbo saw God as a human being. But the context and thrust of the tradition have nothing to do with God's physical nature. Rather, the story explains why we cannot see God, and thus deals with his transcendence. He exists, but is far removed from human beings.

Stories

Africans love stories and storytelling, and these are an important way of entrenching ethical values and motivation. All African children who grow up in traditional societies listen to stories after dinner and by the fireside. The storytellers, who are usually older women such as grandmothers, teach many values:

> The context in which young people learn [these values] is fellowship with older, wise persons. In a society in which the spoken word is more important than the written, fellowship with old, experienced persons is an essential task in life, since the young person who is growing up must not only learn how to master life, but must also acquire the art of speaking.[8]

Some of these stories are traditional myths; others are made up to teach some moral principle. Various animals like the jackal, hyena, hare, lion, cat, elephant, python, dog and he-goat are personified to teach

---

[8] Bénézet Bujo, *Foundations of an African Ethic: Beyond the Universal Claims of Western Morality* (trans. Brian McNeil; New York: Crossroad, 2001), 25.

moral truths. Specific animals often represent specific characteristics: the hare is clever and shrewd; the hyena is greedy, and the he-goat is very promiscuous. Thus a story is told about a he-goat who asked some passers-by whether they had possibly seen any women walking along the road. They told him that the only women they had seen were his mother and sisters. The goat replied that was fine: his mother and sisters were women, and so he could sleep with them too! The moral of this story is that failure to respect basic morality and the rules governing sexual relationships reduces a person to acting like an animal.

The category of stories can also include modern novels like Chinua Achebe's *Things Fall Apart*. It deals with many communal traditions regarding marriage, sex, funerals, suicide, capital punishment, fertility, work, dignity, honour, pride, courage, truth and falsehood, wealth and health.

Songs

Singing is part of everyday African life, and songs reveal much about the ethical motivations for action. There are special songs for particular groups to sing on special occasions. Wedding songs, for example, reveal the community's expectations when it comes to marriage. Virginity is highly prized in many African societies: "Chastity before marriage on the part of the woman is essential. A woman who is not virtuous at marriage is a disgrace both to herself and to her family. Chastity in married life is a woman's bounden duty."[9] If a girl is found to be a virgin on her wedding day, there is praise and dancing for her self-control and the family is proud. But if a girl loses her virginity before her wedding night, she brings shame and disgrace on her family – and this shame is recorded in songs that are sung for all to hear.

Songs also indicate the community's attitude to procreation. The following song is sung by a Dinka woman who is barren:

What misfortune has befallen me
O Abyor

---

[9] E. Bolaji Idowu, *Olódùmarè: God in Yoruba Belief* (New York: African Islamic Mission, 1988), 157. He goes on to explain that "Although the rule is rather loose as far as the man is concerned, nevertheless, it is forbidden that a man should seduce another man's wife on pain of paying a heavy penalty and, in addition, of having to face grievous consequences. It is realized that the basis of conjugal happiness is in the faithfulness of both parties; that is so, even in a polygamous community".

People of my father
Do not blame me
Is it not for a baby born
That a woman keeps her home?[10]

The song affirms that the purpose of marriage is child-bearing. When there are no children, the marriage is meaningless. This belief is shared by many in Africa.

Songs for warriors demonstrate correct conduct during battle and a warrior's responsibilities. In *Things Fall Apart* a special song is made for Okafo, who defeats a famous wrestler known as Amalinze the Cat in a wrestling match. As soon as Okafo swings his leg over his opponent's head, his supporters sing:

Who will wrestle for our village?
Okafo will wrestle for our village,
Has he thrown a hundred men?
He has thrown four hundred men.
Has he thrown a hundred Cats?
He has thrown four hundred Cats
Then send him word to fight for us.[11]

The song makes it clear that a warrior is expected to use his skills on behalf of his community.

Songs not only tell what people must do but also warn them about what they must not do, such as raping or stealing. Songs also celebrate the activities of daily life like hunting and fishing and events like puberty.

Proverbs, riddles and wise sayings

African proverbs, riddles and wise sayings are a record of beliefs, values and morality. The concept of fairness is enshrined in the saying, "the cooking pot for the chameleon is the cooking pot for the lizard", the African version of "what's good for the goose is good for the gander". Patience is taught by the Hausa proverb which says that with long, slow cooking one can even make soup from a stone. Endurance is the theme of the saying "The horns cannot be too heavy for the head of the cow

---

[10] Francis Mading Deng, *The Dinka and Their Songs* (Oxford: Clarendon Press, 1973), 23.
[11] Achebe, *Things Fall Apart*, 36

that must bear them", meaning that one should bear one's own burdens even if they are heavy.

Other proverbs offer warnings: The Hausa warn that "greed is the gateway to grief". The Yoruba warn against judging how someone is doing by how they look by saying "all red-necked lizards look healthy including the one that has a stomach ache". People are urged to be cautious about what they say by the warning, "until the rotten tooth is pulled, the mouth must chew with caution" – if a guilty person hears what you are saying, he may try to escape. "If you defecate in the shade you must stand in the sunshine" is a reminder that if you chose to leave a good situation because you hope for something better, you must endure the consequences of your choice.

Many proverbs deal with relationships. The Hausa say that kindness is elastic and can extend to many. If a husband and wife are very close, they are said to be like a needle and thread – the thread goes wherever the needle goes, just as it does when sewing. Bad or dictatorial leadership is referred to as "the leadership of the cocoa yam". A cocoa yam is a kind of root that has one big yam from which other little yams grow. However, the presence of the big yam prevents the little yams from ever growing to full size.

Proverbs and sayings like these are widely used without explanation and immediately communicate what virtues are admired, as well as moral truths about relationships, marriage, leadership, and the like.

Liturgy

African religion has a rich tapestry of invocations, prayers, rituals and sacrifices addressed to the gods, spirits and ancestors. Worshippers pray for a good hunting season, the birth of a child or protection from harm, or they give thanks that their prayers have been answered. The words they use reveal much about their beliefs, values and morality. In Achebe's *Things Fall Apart*, an elder prays to the ancestors:

> We do not ask for wealth because he that has health and children will also have wealth. We do not pray to have more money but to have more kinsmen. We are better than animals

because we have kinsmen. An animal rubs his itching flank against a tree, a man asks his kinsman to scratch him.[12]

This invocation demonstrates a strong sense of the value of community and of one's relationship to one's family or clan. Health and children take priority over wealth.

The Role of Religion in African Ethics

Clifford Geertz defines religion as "1) a system of symbols which acts 2) to establish powerful, pervasive and long-lasting moods and motivations in men by 3) formulating conceptions of a general order of existence and 4) clothing these conceptions with such an aura of factuality that 5) the moods and motivations seem uniquely realistic."[13] The stress on moods and motivations and on "the general order of existence" in this definition makes it clear that moral and religious values or beliefs are intimately related. Religious values and beliefs have a great impact on the way people live.

The above point holds strongly in Africa, for Africans are incurably religious and religion permeates all aspects of life. Writing about the Yoruba of Nigeria, Idowu notes, "In all things, they are religious. Religion forms the foundation and the all-governing principle of life for them."[14] He insists that "with the Yoruba, morality is certainly the fruit of religion. They do not make any attempt to separate the two; and it is impossible for them to do so without disastrous consequences."[15] Throughout Africa in fact, "God, the ancestors, and the spirits are all powers or forces that impinge on human life in one way or another. In that sense they are all moral agents."[16]

Thus in order to understand African morality or ethics, and African people's deep sense of right and wrong, it is important to understand African religious beliefs.

---

[12] Achebe, *Things Fall Apart*, 117.
[13] Clifford Geertz, *The Interpretation of Cultures* (New York: Basic, 1973), 90.
[14] Idowu, *Olódùmarè*, 5.
[15] Ibid., 145.
[16] Laurenti Magesa, *African Religion: The Moral Traditions of Abundant Life* (Nairobi: Pauline Publications Africa/ Maryknoll, N.Y: Orbis, 1997), 42.

God's existence and nature

Africans regard debate about the existence of God as ridiculous. They take it as a given.[17] God is the foundation and explanation of all creation and existence. If he did not exist, nothing else would exist.

In Africa, knowledge of God is never sought for theoretical reasons or to satisfy intellectual curiosity. He is sought for practical reasons, and the appropriate response to him is practical devotion shown by living in the way he prescribes. This is the moral path of life, for God is the ultimate source of all morality: "God made man; and it is He who implants in him the sense of right and wrong."[18]

God is known by special names among all African peoples.[19] He is called Olodumare among the Yoruba, Mrungu among the Digo, Lubanga among the Acholi, Umlungu among the Nyika, Kazah among the Bajju, Chukwu among the Igbos, Leve among the Mende, Mawu among the Ewe, Dagwi among the Birom, Ngai among the Kikuyu and Nkulunkulu among the Zulu. Most of these names can be translated as the Supreme Being, the Owner of the Sky, the Creator, or the One Above. However, among the Ngbaka he is know as Gale, the One Who Helps in Times of Difficulties. The name Naawuni, used by the Dagbani, literally means the King of the Gods, while the name Katonda, used by the Buganda, means the Lord of Creation, which means that he is superior to all and can be referred to as the father of the gods.

This Supreme Being, by whatever name he is known, has the attributes of being the creator, king and judge who is omnipresent, omnipotent, all-wise, all-knowing, all-seeing and immortal.[20] His moral attributes include goodness, mercy, holiness, governance, justice and love. He is the one who gives good harvests, children, protection and more. Because he is good, he also demands that his created beings be

---

[17] Magesa, *African Religion*, 45.

[18] Idowu, *Olódùmarè*, 145.

[19] A fuller list can be found in John Mbiti's *Introduction to African Religion* (London: Heinemann, 1975), 47–48.

[20] Idowu, *Olódùmarè*, 39–48. John Mbiti (*African Religions and Philosophy* [New York: Frederick A. Praeger, 1969] 29–38) even provides a classical systematic classification of the attributes of God in African thought: God is a spirit with eternal intrinsic attributes such as omniscience, omnipotence, transcendence, immanence, self-existence, pre-eminence and supremacy. In another work (*Introduction to African Religion*, 54–59) Mbiti explains that God is good, God is merciful, God is holy, God is all-powerful, God is all-knowing, God is present everywhere, God is self-existent, God is the first cause, God is spirit, God never changes, God is unknowable.

good in their relationships with one another. Without God, there would be no morality. Morality is therefore strongly tied to belief in God.

But although God is omnipotent and omnipresent, he is also ultimately unknowable (as explained in the Yoruba myth cited earlier). He has assigned responsibility for most of his daily dealings with men and women to intermediaries, such as the spirits and ancestors. Thus in *The Gods Are Not To Blame* the character Aderopo is sent to "the land of Orunmila, to ask the all-seeing god why they were in pain." [21] Orunmila is a deity who occupies a position below that of the Supreme God, Olodumare, but who exercises some of his functions in that he, too, is all-seeing.

The correct response to God is to do what he dictates. As far as the Yoruba are concerned, "the full responsibility of all the affairs of life belongs to the Deity; their own part in the matter is to do as they are ordered through the priests and diviners whom they believe to be the interpreters of the will of the Deity." [22]

John Mbiti points out that

> It is believed in many African societies that their morals were given to them by God from the very beginning. This provides an unchallenged authority for the morals. It is also believed or thought that some of the departed and the spirits keep watch over people to make sure that they observe the moral laws and are punished when they break them deliberately or knowingly. This additional belief strengthens the authority of the morals. [23]

African ethics are thus deontological, in that they focus on doing one's duty by being obedient to the demands posed by the gods or the spirits of the ancestors.

Since God is completely good and there is no evil in him, evil is associated with other deities, spirits and witches or sorcerers. Death, lightning strikes, sickness, miscarriages, suffering and all other human misery are the direct work of these malevolent spirits, with whom

---

[21] Ola Rotimi, *The Gods Are Not To Blame*, 12. Newell S. Booth observes that "this immanent aspect of the Divine is personalized in the 'lesser divinities'" ("God and the Gods in West Africa", in *African Religions: A Symposium* [New York: NOK Publishers, 1977], 166).

[22] Idowu, *Olódùmarè*, 3.

[23] John Mbiti, *Introduction to African Religion*, 174.

some human beings may be in league. In this sense, African religion is dualistic.

Spirits

A great variety of spirit beings form an important supernatural reality. Mbiti notes that "myriads of spirits are reported from every African people, but they defy description almost as much as they defy the scientist's test tubes in the laboratory."[24] For example, the Yoruba people of Nigeria have at least 1700 deities. These spirits, which form part of the invisible world, influence human life on a daily basis and humans have to deal with them. According to Idowu, spirits "are ubiquitous; there is no area of the earth, no object or creature, which has not a spirit of its own or which cannot be inhabited by a spirit."[25]

The spirits are powerful but they are not omnipotent like God and are subordinate to him. Some of them are benevolent and others malevolent. They can assist one to have children, to become wealthy, and to perform wonders such as flying in the skies, etc. Spirits can possess a person to help others, such as in the Bori dance in some parts of Nigeria. This dance involves a person (usually a woman) becoming possessed by a spirit so that she goes into a trance while drums are beaten in a certain rhythm. While in this trance, she can diagnose and prescribe medication for a sick person.

The spirits can also make people do evil things, such as a mother killing her children. They can strike a person with a sickness like madness or a severe fever. If they so desire, some spirits can even take female form and marry a man and have children with him. The Bajju of Nigeria believe that an epileptic attack is actually sexual intercourse with a spirit. Spirits often give justification for certain actions such as war.

Depending on their nature, different spirits have greater or lesser association with human morality. In *Things Fall Apart*, Achebe tells us that Ani, the earth goddess, was "the ultimate judge of morality and conduct" because "she was in close communion with the departed fathers of the clan whose bodies had been committed to earth."[26]

---

[24] Mbiti, *African Religion and Philosophy*, 78.
[25] Idowu, *African Traditional Religion*, 174.
[26] Achebe, *Things Fall Apart*, 26.

The "departed fathers" or ancestors are an important category of spirits. Mbiti calls them the "living dead" because although they have died they are still very active and interested in the affairs of their descendants. He describes them as

> the closest links that men have with the spirit world … [They] are bilingual: they speak the languages of men, with whom they lived until 'recently'; and they speak the language of the spirits and of God, to Whom they are drawing nearer ontologically. These are the 'spirits' with which African peoples are most concerned: it is through the living-dead that the spirit world becomes personal to men. They are still part of their human families, and people have personal memories of them.[27]

Ancestral spirits are omnipresent, affecting the affairs of men and women on a constant basis. Achebe notes:

> The land of the living was not far removed from the domain of the ancestors. There was coming and going between them, especially at festivals and also when an old man died, because an old man was very close to the ancestors. A man's life from birth to death was a series of transition rites which brought him nearer and nearer to his ancestors.[28]

Ancestors often reveal themselves to their descendants through dreams and visions in order to provide information, such as warning against bad behaviour or revealing how to cure some disease. They usually appear to the oldest in the family, who will communicate their message to the other members of the family. These appearances have revelatory authority and are binding upon all members of the family.

Great care is taken to give old people fitting burial with observance of all the appropriate rituals. Though my grandfather was a Christian, his firm belief in the ancestors led him to give specific instructions on how he was to be buried. He insisted that he must not be put in a coffin because he wanted there to be no obstacles to his meeting with his ancestors. He threatened to take revenge on the family if his wishes were not honoured.

---

[27] Mbiti, *African Religion and Philosophy*, 83.
[28] Achebe, *Things Fall Apart*, 85.

The memory of ancestors is kept alive through rituals, through telling and retelling their biographies to their descendants and, above all, by seeing that the living follow their teachings and instructions. Thus the ancestors are continually involved in the lives of their descendants. What the living do or do not do affects them greatly.

If the living disregard a tradition or break taboos like those against incest, the ancestors are displeased and bring punishment through barrenness, miscarriages, poor harvests, misfortune and war. On the other hand, if the descendants do what the traditions and customs require of them, the ancestors are pleased and bless them with abundant harvests, answered prayers, fertility, good health, prosperity and protection.[29] In this sense, ancestors in Africa regulate the moral lives of the living.

The Role of Community in African Ethics

One's grasp of African morality is dismal if one does not come to terms with the profound concept of community. Richardson believes that "community is the central concept in African ethics, the central experience of African morality."[30] The idea of "we" and "us" is entrenched in Africans right from childhood, so that as they grow they know that they belong to and must function within the community in which they are rooted. This understanding is supported by many proverbs that buttress the significance of community and relationships. Thus the Lube tribe of the Democratic Republic of Congo have a saying, "When you get meat, share it with your family, or no-one will share with you when you don't have any."[31]

The individual "I" and "me" is understood from the perspective of "we" and "us". Western individualism is abhorrent in traditional African society. Africans argue that if God had wanted human beings to live and

---

[29] Enumerating the functions of the living-dead, Mbiti specifies that they "enquire about family affairs, and may even warn of impending danger or rebuke those who have failed to follow their special instructions. They are the guardians of family affairs, traditions, ethics and activities. Offence in these matters is ultimately an offence against the forebearers who, in that capacity, act as the invisible police of the families and communities ... They know the needs of men, they have 'recently' been here with men, and at the same time they have full access to the channels of communicating with God directly" (*African Religion and Philosophy*), 83.

[30] Richardson, "Can Christian Ethics", 40.

[31] Quoted by Kasongo Munza. *A Letter to Africa About Africa* (Kempton Park, South Africa: Trans World Radio, 2008), 15.

function only as individuals, he would never have arranged for them to be born into families.

John Mbiti, who was probably the first to articulate the African concept of community, writes:

> In traditional life, the individual does not and cannot exist alone except corporately. He owes his existence to other people, including those of past generations and his contemporaries. He is simply part of the whole. The community must therefore make, create or produce the individual; for the individual depends on the corporate group ... Only in terms of other people does the individual become conscious of his own being, his own duties, his privileges and responsibilities towards himself and towards other people. When he suffers, he does not suffer alone but with the corporate group; when he rejoices, he rejoices not alone but with his kinsmen, his neighbors and his relatives whether living or dead. When he gets married he is not alone, neither does the wife "belong" to him alone. So also the children belong to the corporate body of kinsmen, even if they bear only their father's name. Whatever happens to the individual happens to the whole group, and whatever happens to the whole group happens to the individual. Therefore the individual can only say, "I am because we are, and since we are, therefore, I am."[32]

Another way of saying this is "I am because we are related." It is in accordance with this understanding of community thinking that Mbiti reasons:

> The greater number of morals has to do with social conduct, that is the life of society at large, the conduct of the individual within the group or community or nation. African morals lay a great emphasis on societal conduct, since a basic African view is that the individual exists only because others exist.[33]

---

[32] Mbiti, *African Religion and Philosophy*, 108–109.

[33] Mbiti, *Introduction to African Religion*, 174. Deng (*Dinka and their Songs*, 15) similarly observes that among the Dinka, "Good human relations appear in the demand for unity and harmony among men and all the attuning of individual interest to the interests of others. This goal is more than avoidance of conflict and violation of other people's rights; it imposes a positive obligation to foster a solidarity in which people cooperate in shaping and sharing values."

There is thus an interconnectedness in the African sense of community. Malidoma Somé, in *Remembering Our Purpose* notes:

> What's good about this is that the individual never feels isolated from the rest of the community. And nobody is higher than anybody else, so there is no class.
>
> There is something very interesting about a classless society; it's one that allows itself to be led by the spirit. There is a greater tendency to assist those who are older and slower, and it prevents people from feeling cut off or left out or off track.[34]

What the community says or believes is binding on the individual. Africans who have lived in the West see the absurdity and cruelness of individualism and the so called freedom which is at the core of Western culture. The African scholar, Somé states: "The sense of privacy people have in the West is a very lonely privacy; it is a very frightening privacy. The freedom that goes along with it is of pretty much the same nature; it is a freedom that is weighty, that is a burden."[35]

The African sense of community is sometimes perceived by Westerners as encouraging laziness and allowing people to act as parasites. This is not true. On the contrary, responsibility and hard work are encouraged. The Bajju of Nigeria, for example, say "if you eat, you must pay". Another common saying among them is, "who will grind while another is eating?" Traditionally, the Bajju and many other African peoples used stones to grind corn in order to get fine flour. Grinding corn is hard work. The saying means that it is not proper for one person to be working away at grinding, while another just sits around and eats.

In the same vein, Julius Nyerere commented,

> Those of us who talk about the African way of life and, quite rightly, take a pride in maintaining the tradition of hospitality

---

[34] Malidoma Somé quoted in Sarah van Gelder, "Remembering Our Purpose: The Teachings of Indigenous Cultures May Help Us Go Beyond Modernity – An Interview with Malidoma Somé", *In Context*, 34 (2003), 30. Cited 21 April 2008. Online: www.context.org/ICLIB/IC34/Some. htm. Somé goes on to note that "In the West, what I've noticed is that what is called a community is more a conglomeration of individuals who are so self-centered and isolated that there, is a kind of suspicion of the *other*, simply because there isn't enough knowledge of the *other* to remove that suspicion. So trust becomes the challenge to actual community. ... The community I am talking about is one in which respect for the person is based upon that person's irreplaceable position in the world."

[35] Ibid.

which is so great a part of it, might do well to remember the Swahili saying … "Treat your guest as a guest for two days; on the third day give him a hoe!" In actual fact, the guest was likely to ask for the hoe even before his host had to give him one – for he knew what was expected of him, and would have been ashamed to remain idle any longer.[36]

Of course, there is the danger that this strong sense of community may jeopardize individual creativity. But it is not as if there is no individuality among Africans. The African view of community includes a balance in which individuals are encouraged to be creative. As Benjamin C. Ray notes,

> African views of man strike a balance between his collective identity as a member of society and his personal identity as a unique individual. In general, African philosophy tends to define persons in terms of the social groups to which they belong. A person is thought of first of all as a constituent of a particular community, for it is the community which defines who he is and who he can become … But African thought also recognizes that each individual is a unique person endowed by the Creator with his own personality and talents, and motivated by his own particular needs and ambitions. To this extent, African thought acknowledges the transcendence of individuals over their own socio-cultural conditions. However, the emphasis upon a person's individuality is always balanced against the total social and historical context. [37]

Thus individual achievements are encouraged, acknowledged and interpreted in the context of the whole community. The successes, achievements, failures, frustrations and grief or sorrow of the individual are shared by the entire community at the same time as "the solidarity of the unit is stressed at the expense of the individual's private interest or loyalties".[38] Packer J. Palmer, writing for a different context, expresses

---

[36] Julius Nyerere, "Ujamaa: The Basis of African Socialism" in *Ujamaa: Essays on Socialism* (Dar es Salaam: Oxford University Press, 1967), 31. Cited 19 April 2008. Online: www.ccmtz.org/ujamaaeng.htm.

[37] Benjamin C. Ray, *African Religions: Symbol, Ritual, and Community* (Englewood Cliffs: Prentice-Hall, 1976), 132.

[38] Davidson, *The African Genius*, 71.

this relationship well: "In a healthy society the private and the public are not mutually exclusive, nor in competition with each other. They are, instead, two halves of a whole, two poles of a paradox. They work together dialectically, helping to create and nurture one another."[39]

The community defines the taboos and the rules of marriage, sex, war, farming, leadership and hunting for the community. In all cases the good of the community is to be sought and anything that would harm it rejected. The elders play a crucial role in this, for they are said to speak words of wisdom. For example, in cases of widow inheritance, they decide who is to inherit the wife of the deceased. In some societies, the elders can even decide that a son will inherit his father's wife (provided she is not his mother).

Because of this strong sense of community, the concept of shame is an important regulating factor in African morality. If an individual does something disgraceful such as committing theft or adultery or breaking a taboo, the whole tribe, village or clan shares his disgrace. Thus, for example, an Akan child who commits nine crimes will be punished for only five of them, for the clan shares responsibility for his misdeeds.[40] It is said among some tribes in Nigeria that the thief feels no shame; it is his brother who is ashamed. The Hausa also say that a good person belongs to everybody, but someone who is wicked can only be claimed by his own clan or people.

The strong concept of community means that the common good takes precedence over the individual good. Consequently, "an individual who is really a danger for the community, or threatens the clan with loss of life or goods, must be simply removed."[41] Thus some groups in Africa will kill anyone who has committed adultery with a relative.

It can thus be said that a major part of African morality is the "mutual obligations of human persons", in particular the "duties of children towards parents, and the connected obligations towards the ancestors".[42]

---

[39] Packer J. Palmer, *The Company of Strangers: Christians and the Renewal of America's Public Life* (New York: Crossroad, 1981), 31.

[40] Robert B. Fisher, *West African Religions: Focus on the Akan of Ghana* (Maryknoll, N.Y.: Orbis, 1998), 16.

[41] Bénézet Bujo, *African Theology in Its Social Context* (trans. John O'Donohue; Maryknoll, N.Y.: Orbis, 1992), 34.

[42] Ibid.

Conclusion

The most significant aspect of ethics in African societies is the intimate relationship between religion and morality or ethics. There is a firm belief that one cannot be moral without a strong belief in the supernatural, which includes belief in a supreme God and other deities such as spirits and ancestors, all of whom can interact with the living.

The other fundamental aspect of African morality is community. Africans emphasize interpersonal relationships more than individual satisfaction. The community shapes and regulates moral life and behaviour.

The religious and communal aspects of morality both reflect and create values, that is, deep-seated, entrenched belief systems that exercise a profound influence on African morality. These core moral truths are embedded in the oral traditions, liturgies, stories and proverbs that are the foundations, grounds and motivations of morality among African people.

The emphasis on values and motivation provides the answer to the question of whether African morality involves only external conformity or whether it also involves an internal attitude. Bujo declares, "African traditions make it plain that the people considered that thoughts and intentions, as well as external acts, had a moral character, and deserved to be considered 'good' or 'bad.'"[43]

The morality presented in this chapter is the traditional morality that exists independent of Christian influence. If, as is the goal of this book, we are not only to formulate an increasingly Christian African morality but persuade others to pursue it, we must seek to understand the values and beliefs motivating traditional morality.[44] But we will also need to understand the values and beliefs that are exerting great pressure on traditional African beliefs, namely Western ideas of morality and ethics. That will be the topic of the next chapter.

---

[43] Bujo, *African Theology*, 37.
[44] Geertz, *The Interpretation of Cultures*, 90.

Questions

1. Which sources of ethics (tradition, liturgy, songs, proverbs, stories) are most influential in your culture?

2. How are the concepts of God, spirits, community, and values understood in your culture? How are these concepts related (or unrelated)? What are the implications for ministry in the culture and for the development of Christian ethics?

3. Give one example of a tradition, a myth, a story, a proverb, a song and a liturgical element from your culture and for each explain what moral principle it teaches.

3

FOUNDATIONS OF WESTERN ETHICS

Whereas African ethics is rooted in custom and oral tradition, Western ethics is rooted in Western philosophy. This philosophy has, both consciously and unconsciously, had a great impact on modern Western Christian ethics, and thus also on the way Christian ethics is taught in Africa. Too often, ethical questions are framed in ways that reflect Western values rather than biblical or Christian values. Moreover, the questions addressed are often not those that concern African Christians: the ethics taught in churches in Africa do not scratch where the African is itching.

In order to remedy this situation, African students of ethics need to understand the philosophical principles and values that have exerted a profound influence on the development of ethics and morality in the West. Thus this chapter will present a brief overview of the major influences in Western ethics and of the various ethical systems that have emerged. It will also touch briefly on how these principles influence Christian ethics and morality in Africa, an issue that will be developed more in the chapters that follow.

Major Influences on Western Ethics

Three of the major influences on Western ethical thinking are the Greco-Judeo-Christian tradition, the Enlightenment and the revolutionary technological developments in the past century.

Greco-Judeo-Christian philosophy

Both the Greek philosophical tradition and Jewish and Christian
religious and ethical teachings have had enormous influence on Western
thinking about ethics. They were the primary forces in play until the
Enlightenment in the eighteenth century.

Greek philosophical positions influenced the theological systems and
methodologies developed in the West. It was from them that the Western
world learned to emphasize reason and distrust emotion. The Western
dualism between spiritual and material concerns can also be traced back
to Greek thinkers who regarded the material world as inherently evil, or
at least as vastly inferior to the spiritual world.

Africans are uncomfortable with this dualism and feel more at home
with the more holistic Judeo-Christian world view presented in the Old
and New Testament. It is from this tradition that we get the belief that
morality can be summed up as "Love the Lord your God with all your
heart and with all your soul and with all your strength and with all
your mind; and, love your neighbour as yourself" (Luke 10:27; see also
Deut 6:5; Lev 19:18). These words have influenced the long-standing
affirmation of the "objective goodness and rightness of love, generosity,
self-sacrifice and equality", and the condemnation of selfishness, hatred,
abuse, discrimination and oppression as "objectively evil and wrong".[1]

The influence of the Judeo-Christian tradition will be explored more
in the chapters that follow, and so it will not be dealt with in any depth
at this point.

The Enlightenment

The intellectual and political upheavals accompanying the Renaissance
and the Reformation shook people's confidence in certainties that had
previously been accepted unquestioningly by entire communities. The
result was that "values became a matter of personal choice rather than
adherence to a community standard".[2] By the eighteenth-century,
this trend had grown into the philosophical movement known as
the Enlightenment. Among the most famous contributors to the

---

[1] William Lane Craig, "The Indispensability of Theological Meta-Ethical Foundations for
Morality". Cited 16 Oct 2007. Online: www.leaderu.com/offices/billcraig/docs/meta-eth.html.
[2] Warren Ashby, *A Comprehensive History of Western Ethics: What Do We Believe?* (Amherst, N.Y.:
Prometheus Books, 1997), 5. Online: www.questia.com/PM.qst?a=oandd=96871849.

Enlightenment were David Hume (1711–1776) and Immanuel Kant (1724–1804).

David Hume set out his moral theory in Book 3 of his *Treatise of Human Nature* (1740) and in *An Enquiry Concerning the Principles of Morals* (1751). He argued that we cannot make any statement about what ought to be the case on the basis of what actually is the case. Thus we cannot argue that because there *is* great diversity in nature, we *ought* to introduce environmental legislation to protect that diversity. Nor can we argue that because God exists (*is*) we *ought* to act in certain ways.

Hume argued that our ethical system derives neither from God nor from reason, but is product of "our dislike of pain, our sympathy for others, [and] our feelings of benevolence."[3] Human beings decide what is moral on the basis of whether a certain type of action elicits approval or disapproval from those who observe it. Thus we derive our moral principles from the community in which we live.

The German philosopher **Immanuel Kant** was shaken when he read Hume's work. He felt as if his own mind had been soundly asleep, but had now awakened to a new world of ideas. He defined this new world of the Enlightenment as follows:

> Enlightenment is mankind's exit from its self-incurred immaturity [tutelage]. Immaturity is the inability to make use of one's own understanding without the guidance of another. ... *Sapere aude!* Have the courage to use your own understanding! is thus the motto of enlightenment.[4]

Kant's stress on the need to think for oneself led him to reject any suggestion that revelation (revealed truth) has any significance in moral thinking. Any appeal to religious authority is invalid because human reason must have precedence over external revelation.

Though Kant died more than two hundred years ago, the effects of his ideas are still present in Western individualism and rationalism and in the separation of religions and ethics.

---

[3] Brian Hebblethwaite, *Christian Ethics in the Modern Age* (Philadelphia: Westminster, 1982), 15.

[4] Immanuel Kant, "An Answer to the Question: What is Enlightenment?" In James Schmidt, *What is Enlightenment? Eighteenth-Century Answers and Twentieth-Century Questions* (Los Angeles: University of California Press, 1996), 58. I prefer the translation "tutelage" to "immaturity" because it better conveys Kant's emphasis on instruction and guidance.

We all live in a world shaped by the ambiguous legacy of the Enlightenment. The epochal development enlarged the scope of human freedom, prepared our minds for the scientific method, made man the measure of all things, and placed individual consent front and center on the political stage. By encouraging these views it strengthened the sense of sympathy and fairness. If man is the measure of all things and men generally must consent to whatever regime is to rule them, then each is entitled to equal rights and to respect proportional to his merit.[5]

The increased sense of "sympathy and fairness" mentioned above explains why it can be said that the Enlightenment laid the political foundations for democracy. But a further effect of this approach was that "the individual became the focus of all values".[6] Over time, this stress on individualism has led to a focus on an individual's rights rather than an individual's responsibilities. Consequently the individual becomes more important than the family of which he or she is a part.

The liberalization of laws pertaining to marriage and divorce arose of just such a view. Marriage, once a sacrament, has become in the eyes of the law a contract that is easily negotiated, renegotiated, or rescinded. Within a few years, no-fault divorce on demand became possible, after millennia in which such an idea would have been unthinkable. It is now easier to renounce a marriage than a mortgage; at least the former occurs much more frequently than the latter. Half of all divorced fathers rarely see their children, and most pay no child support. We can no longer agree even on what constitutes a family. Husbands and wives? Heterosexual lovers? Homosexual lovers? Any two people sharing living quarters?[7]

---

[5] James Q. Wilson, *The Moral Sense* (New York: Free Press, 1993), 244–245. He goes on to note that "If rights are all that is important, what will become of responsibilities? If the individual man is the measure of all things, what will become of the family that produces and defines man?" (p. 245).

[6] Ashby, *Comprehensive History*, 5.

[7] Wilson, *The Moral Sense*, 248–249. He goes on to state that in the areas of families, schools, and entertainment, "we have come face to face with a fatally flawed assumption of many Enlightenment thinkers, namely, that the autonomous can freely choose, or will, their moral life. Believing that individuals are everything, rights are trumps, and morality is relative to time and place, such thinkers have been led to design laws, practices, and institutions that leave nothing between the state and

A similar focus on the individual is evident when pro-abortionists argue that a woman has the right to do whatever she likes with her body. Her rights as an individual override the rights of the unborn child. This argument is accepted because individualism is a key factor in Western ethical decision making.

The Kantian emphasis on the individual has been exported from the West to places like South Africa and has even become accepted within some of the mainline churches. Yet, as was seen in the previous chapter, Africa traditionally takes a very different view of the relationship of the individual to the community. The African critique is that the Kantian approach to ethics stresses

> individual freedom and choice, or the moral sovereignty of the individual, to the exclusion of any consideration of the fact that individuals live with, learn from and interact with other individuals. The moral significance of this is evident in the fact that even a hermit lives in relation to society … Surely, we are inescapably communal creatures.[8]

Another key feature of the Enlightenment that has impacted Western ethics is rationalism – the belief that unaided reason is the only source of ethics or morality. Consequently all traditional social, religious and political ideas are rejected in favour of what is sometimes referred to as radical autonomy. Kant argued that the "distinctive moral character of the rational creature was the capacity to live by no other law than that of its own making".[9] Thus he discouraged people from relying too much on the ideas of others:

> If I have a book that has understanding for me, a pastor who has a conscience for me, a doctor who judges my diet for me, and so forth, surely I do not need to trouble myself. I have no need to think, if only I can pay; others will take over the tedious business for me.[10]

---

the individual save choices, contracts, and entitlements. Fourth-grade children being told how to use condoms is only one of the more perverse of the results" (p. 250).

[8] Richardson, "Can Christian Ethics Find Its Way, and Itself, In Africa". *Journal of Theology for Southern Africa* 95 (July 1996): 45.

[9] Stanley Hauerwas, *The Peaceable Kingdom* (Notre Dame, Ind.: University of Notre Dame Press, 1983), 11.

[10] Kant, "What is Enlightenment?", 58.

The leaders of the Enlightenment thus sought to separate religion from ethics. Their aim was to use reason to establish universal moral principles of conduct without any metaphysical foundations.

> Implicit in this quest was a sense of optimism, a sense that this best of all possible worlds could yet be made even better, that goodness was natural, and that there were principles, natural human rights, which were universal and could transcend political boundaries. But the inherent worth of the individual was the cornerstone.[11]

This attitude marked the beginning of the secularism advocated by many Western ethicists today who argue for a morality that is not based on religion.

The technological and electronic revolutions

Over the past century, Western countries have played a prominent role in the explosive development of science and technology. Such development has enormous potential for good and evil. This potential was underlined on September 11, 2001 when airplanes, the fastest and safest means of travel ever invented, were used not to transport people but to wreak havoc on the twin towers of the World Trade Center in New York.

Growing technological capacity means that we now have to debate ethical issues such as nuclear armament and the appropriate response to perceived threats such as that posed by weapons of mass destruction. Does the possible existence of such weapons justify launching a war against a state that may have them? Is such a war justifiable when it results in the death of thousands of innocent civilians and the loss of billions of dollars worth of property, destabilizes an entire region, and poisons the relationship between major powers such as France and the USA? Does it make a difference if the leader of the state being targeted is a cruel dictator like Saddam Hussein?

The technological revolution has not only raised new ethical problems, it has also had a profound effect on morality in general. The Internet is a powerful source of information, but it also provides new ways of experiencing dating and sex, and offers easy access to all kinds of pornography, lotteries and gambling. People are thus exposed to

---

[11] Ashby, *Comprehensive History*, 5.

all kinds of behaviours and this exposure, in combination with a belief in individualism, makes such activities seem acceptable. Responses to violence and tragedy may also be blunted by constant exposure to them on television.

Improvements in medical technology have also led to debate about the significance of human life and what it means to be human. Many who would once have died can now be kept alive – but should this be done in all cases? What about reproductive technologies – they give hope to many couples who for some reason or other cannot have children, but should couples be allowed to choose whether they have a son or a daughter? It is wonderful that there is hope for cure of some genetic diseases, but should parents be encouraged to end pregnancies where there is any risk of a defect in the baby? As Paul Ramsey says:

> There are profound anthropological and ethical issues raised by the possible future technical biological control and change of the human species just as there are profound anthropological and ethical issues raised by the challenge to individual human self-awareness by the prospect of keeping alive a wholly "spare-parts" or an "artificial" man.[12]

These technological changes result in what Ramsey refers to as the "increasing erosion of the human personality". At the same time as the West celebrates the individual, it fosters a form of dehumanization or depersonalization.

> [This] has happened so quickly, and so quietly that we may not be aware of how it has happened to us. But it is marked by such qualities as a denial of our responsibility and a tendency to blame other persons and other situations for what we have become. There is also a brutalization of life or sandpapering of our sensitivity; an unwillingness to engage in sharp self-criticism, lovelessness, both toward the self and toward others.[13]

---

[12] Paul Ramsey, *Fabricated Man: The Ethics of Genetic Control* (New Haven: Yale University Press, 1970), 105. Despite its age, this book remains one of the most incisive analyses of the ethics of genetic engineering.

[13] Ashby, *Comprehensive History*, 10.

Major Theories in Western Ethics

The vast literature on Western ethical theories is full of terms like absolutism, relativism, utilitarianism, principlist ethics, moral law, consequentialism, and teleological, deontological and virtue ethics. In this section, I will try to provide a brief introduction to these terms. Utilitarian, relativist and consequentialist approaches to ethics are discussed under the heading teleological theories, while absolutist and principlist approaches or moral law are discussed under deontological theories. Character/virtue ethics will be treated on its own.

Teleological theories

Teleological (or consequentialist) theories take their name from the Greek word *telos*, which means "end" or "purpose". Those who support such theories argue that ethical rules are not laid down by God and that there are no universal ethical principles. Instead, actions are to be judged right or wrong on the basis of the results they produce. In other words, the end justifies the means. Thus a politician may argue that it is right for him to rig an election because his views deserve to be heard in parliament. At the same time, he may condemn other politicians for doing the same thing, claiming that they have no need to resort to such tactics.

Over the centuries, there have been many different forms of teleological approaches, which differ mainly in terms of how they define the best or most acceptable "end". The Epicureans in ancient Greece said that the right action was the one that promoted a peaceful and happy life that was free from fear, while the Cyrenaics advocated bodily pleasure as the chief good. For them, whatever made you happy was moral.

Jeremy Bentham (1748–1832), who was influenced by Hume, introduced the modern principle of **utilitarianism** into Western ethics, proclaiming that "what is right is what produces the greatest amount of happiness in the greatest number of people".[14] His ideas were then expanded on by John Stuart Mill (1806–1873) who moved the stress from the mere quantity of happiness (that is, the number of people

---

[14] William Sweet "Jeremy Bentham (1748–1832)" in *the Internet Encyclopedia of Philosophy*. Cited 18 Oct 2007. Online: *www.iep.utm.edu*.

made happy) to the quality of that happiness. Thus, for him "the best life is that ordered to the realization of the highest pleasure, satisfaction, happiness, that human beings are capable of as this may be empirically discerned in the lives of those who have attained the greatest self-realizations."[15] Mill emphasized that 1) right and wrong are dependant on the desired end, 2) acts are morally right in the proportion that they tend to promote happiness, and wrong if they produce the reverse of happiness; 3) every ethical dilemma allows multiple courses of action. When choosing between these possible courses of action, one should choose the one that provides the most benefits for the greatest number of people.

The **situation ethics** advocated by Joseph Fletcher (1905–1991) is also utilitarian. [16] However, unlike other utilitarians, Fletcher does not say that there are no ethical absolutes. As an Episcopalian priest, he accepts one absolute: Love. He argues that in any situation, the most loving thing to do is the right thing to do. What exactly this is will vary from situation to situation. For example, he would argue that a woman may be doing the right and loving thing if she becomes a prostitute in order to provide food for her family. Any action can be justified if it is motivated by love.

Arguments like these have had a considerable influence on Western Christian ethics and are often advanced by those who support abortion and euthanasia.

The utilitarian theories described above have generally focused on the happiness of others. However, **ethical egoism** is a teleological theory that focuses almost exclusively on the happiness of the person performing an action. It argues that "one ought to do whatever will produce one's own highest good, determined by the amount of pleasures or happiness that the person will receive from the action."[17]

One important proponent of in ethical egoism is Adam Smith (1723–1790), who has been called the father of modern capitalism. In his *Theory of Moral Sentiments* and *The Wealth of Nations,* Smith argued that "in economic life each person should seek his or her own good, unfettered by governmental interference". According to Hollinger,

---

[15] Jentz, "Some Thoughts", 48–49.
[16] Joseph Fletcher, *Situation Ethics: The New Morality* (Philadelphia: Westminster Press, 1966).
[17] Dennis P. Hollinger, *Choosing the Good: Christian Ethics in a Complex World* (Grand Rapids Baker, 2002), 28.

"He believed that self-interest (not selfishness) was the highest good in economics because the world was structured in such a way that from it everyone would benefit."[18]

Ayn Rand (1905–1982), an atheist novelist and philosopher who rejected any transcendent source of ethics and knowledge, vigorously promoted this individualistic ethical theory: "The first right on earth is the right of the ego. Man's first duty is to himself. His moral law is never to place his prime goal with the persons of others. His moral obligation is to do what he wishes, provided his wish does not depend primarily upon other men."[19]

The tenets of ethical egoism can be summarized as follows: 1) "an individual's one and only basic obligation is to promote for himself the greatest possible balance of good over evil ... 2) even in making second- and third-person moral judgements an individual should go by what is to his own advantage."[20]

Rand believed that "society functions best when people pursue their own self-interests"[21] and that reason itself shows the superiority of individualism over collectivism and of egoism over altruism. She further argued that "the man who attempts to live for others is dependent. He is a parasite in motive and makes parasites of those he serves. The relationship produces nothing but mutual corruption. The creator is the egoist in the absolute sense, and the selfless man is the one who does not think, feel, judge or act."[22]

Rand holds up the USA as an example of the benefits produced by this egoistic-utilitarian ethic:

> Now observe the results of a society built on the principle of individualism. This, our country. The noblest country in the history of men. The country of greatest achievement, greatest prosperity, greatest freedom. This country was not based on selfless service, sacrifice, renunciation or any precept of altruism. It was based on a man's right to the pursuit of happiness. His own happiness. Not anyone else's. A private,

---

[18] Hollinger, *Choosing the Good*, 29.

[19] Ayn Rand, *For the New Intellectual: The Philosophy of Ayn Rand* (New York: Signet, 1961), 82.

[20] William K. Frankena, *Ethics* (Englewood Cliffs: Prentice-Hall, 1973), 18. Cited 23 April 2008. Online: www.ditext.com/frankena/e2.html.

[21] Hollinger, *Choosing the Good*, 30.

[22] Ayn Rand, *For the New Intellectual*, 80–81.

personal, selfish motive. Look at the results. Look at your own conscience.[23]

Such individualism is, indeed, at the heart of American culture: "We believe in the dignity, indeed the sacredness, of the individual. Anything that would violate our right to think for ourselves, judge for ourselves, make our own decisions, live our lives as we see fit, is not only morally wrong, it is sacrilegious."[24]

This tradition derives from the belief that "the individual is prior to society, which comes into existence only through the voluntary contract of individuals trying to maximize their own self-interest".[25]

At the opposite pole from ethical egoism with its focus on the individual is **utilitarian or ethical universalism**, which focuses on the greatest possible effect when determining what is good. As Frankena says,

> the ultimate end is the greatest general good – that an act or rule of action is right if and only if it is, or probably is, conducive to at least as great a balance of good over evil in the universe as a whole as any alterative would be, wrong if it is not, and obligatory if it is or probably is conducive to the greatest possible balance of good over evil in the universe."[26]

Deontological theories

Deontological theories take their name from the Greek word *deon*, which means "duty". In contrast to teleological ethical theories, which focus on the results or consequences of actions when determining whether an action is right or wrong, deontological theories insist that certain actions are inherently right or wrong, regardless of the consequences. "This is an ethic of rights, duties, and obligations that we know by virtue of moral principles or rules, which can come from various sources including reason, religion, or the accumulated wisdom of life experience."[27]

---

[23] Ibid., 83–84.

[24] Robert N. Bellah, Richard Madsen, William M. Sullivan, Ann Swidler, and Steven M. Tipton, *Habits of the Heart: Individualism and Commitment in American Life* (updated edition, Berkeley: University of California Press, 1985), 142.

[25] Bellah, *Habits of the Heart*, 143.

[26] Frankena, *Ethics*, 15–16.

[27] Hollinger, *Choosing the Good*, 36.

Socrates (470–399 BC), the great Greek philosopher who has been a major influence in the history of Western philosophy, insisted that "ethics cannot be built on results from actions, including good ones; rather, ethics must be rooted in the belief that things are intrinsically right or wrong."[28] What was right or wrong was to be determined by reason. He lived and died by this belief, for when he was condemned to death for allegedly corrupting the minds of the youth, he rejected a scheme to escape from prison as ethically wrong.

Immanuel Kant (1724–1804) shared Socrates' belief that reason should be the source of ethics and that "moral duties … are inherently obligatory simply because they are duties"[29] As discussed earlier in this chapter, he argued the importance of reason, human autonomy, and independence from religious authority. There are four elements in his ethical system: 1) Actions are intrinsically right or wrong, regardless of the consequences; 2) Moral laws are as rational as the laws of physics and science; 3) Reason should be our sole guide; 4) The test for whether an action is morally correct is whether you would be happy to see it become a universal law. Point 4 is sometimes referred to as "the categorical imperative". It implies that other people should never be treated simply as the means to achieve some end.

Kant would argue that

> our knowledge as to what we ought to do arises only out of situations in which what we desire to do conflicts with what we think our duty to be. The moral task then becomes one of inferring a universalizable rule which is validly derived from the idea of duty itself. By this purely formal non-empirical procedure we derive specific moral laws: and the moral life is the life lived according to laws, the laws conceived by autonomous reason, which procedure is a logical one.[30]

The British philosopher W. D. Ross (1877–1971) also argued for deontological ethics. He provides the following list of what he regarded as our fundamental duties:

Fidelity: the duty to keep promises.

---

[28] Ibid., 37.
[29] Ibid., 38.
[30] Jentz, "Some Thoughts", 49.

Reparation: the duty to compensate others when we harm them.

Gratitude: the duty to thank those who help us.

Justice: the duty to recognize merit.

Beneficence: the duty to improve the conditions of others.

Self-improvement: the duty to improve our virtue and intelligence.

Non-malfeasance: the duty to not injure others.[31]

Kant and Ross would be classified as **rule deontologists**, because they both hold that right and wrong can be determined on the basis of rules, which are valid regardless of the results of following them. Another group, known as **act deontologists**, argue that there are no universal rules, but that we need to determine what is the right or wrong action in every particular situation on the basis of our knowledge of the facts of the situation. They differ from situation ethicists in that their evaluation of what is right or wrong is not based on the result of the action, but on the details of the situation itself.

An example may clarify the difference between these positions. Let us think in terms of the ethics of divorce. A rule deontologist will insist that divorce is always wrong regardless of the context and any problems in the marriage. An act deontologist might work from a definition of marriage as a partnership intended to provide companionship and love, and argue that divorce is justifiable when fighting and unfaithfulness mean that there is no companionship. A situation ethicist might argue that when partners are fighting all the time, the loving thing to do is to divorce and so stop the fighting.

The major weakness of rule-based deontological ethics is its tendency to ignore the particular context in which an action takes place. An ethical norm is seen as binding on all peoples at all times and in every situation:

> The Enlightenment sought the universally human, some fundamental core that could be stripped of particularity and exist independently of differences generated by race, gender, class, and culture. Moral appeal could be made to the shared faculty of "reason" in a way that permitted universal moral

[31] James Fieser "Ethics", *The Internet Encyclopedia of Philosophy*. Cited 19 Oct 2007. Online: www. iep.utm.edu.

norms and procedures. But more than this, the provincialities of traditional communities and cultures were held in veiled contempt as tribal residents in a world verging on true cosmopolitanism … Particularistic commitments were suspect, as were local and traditional ties.[32]

This approach is unhelpful, especially when searching for a non-Western approach to ethical norms. Universality and particularity must go hand in hand. Bénézet Bujo is right on target when he notes that

theories with universal claims must be brought down to earth by particular practices which concretize the universal; more than this, they must also expose themselves to question and demonstrate their worth. On the other hand, the particular must allow itself to be questioned by a principle that has been justified in formal universal terms. African ethics does this in its own fashion, in that the community plays an active role in shaping a meaningful moral life.[33]

Virtue or character ethics

For both teleological and deontological ethicists, the key question to be answered is always "What ought we to do?" In other words, what would be the morally correct action in a particular situation? Supporters of virtue ethics argue that this is the wrong question. Instead, we should be asking "What ought we to be?" In other words, what do our responses to situations show about the kind of people we are? Thus virtue ethics focuses neither on the consequences of our actions nor on our duties but on our character.

The starting point for virtue ethics is the development of good character traits. A person is good if he or she has virtues and lacks vices. The cardinal virtues were traditionally defined as wisdom, courage, temperance, piety and justice, and these are seen as the source of all other virtues. The vices included cowardice, insincerity, injustice, and vanity.

---

[32] Larry Rasmussen, *Moral Fragments and Moral Community: A Proposal for Church in Society* (Minneapolis: Fortress, 1993), 74.

[33] Bénézet Bujo, *Foundations of an African Ethic: Beyond the Universal Claims of Western Morality* (trans. Brian McNeil; New York: Crossroad, 2001), 23.

The ancient Greek philosopher Aristotle (384–322 BC) was a strong proponent of virtue ethics as the source of true happiness. He distinguishes between intellectual virtues, which can be taught, and moral virtues, which are only learned by practising right living. Good deeds and right actions will produce right habits and lead to the development of a strong and good character. In pursuing such a character, one should strive for the golden mean, which is the just-right point between too much and too little. In contemporary terms, one should strive for moderation. For example, in response to fear one should strive not for foolhardiness but for courage, and the correct response to the temptation to lust is not an ascetic renunciation of sex but an aspiration to love.

Contemporary character or virtue ethicists include Alasdair MacIntyre, who approaches ethics from a secular standpoint.[34] Stanley Hauerwas, Glen H. Stassen and David P. Gushee work from a theological and biblical perspective and assert that the essence of the Christian life is really character or virtue. Stassen and Gushee explicitly state that their "purpose is to reclaim Jesus Christ for Christian ethics and for the moral life of the churches". They base their interpretation of Christian ethics on the "rock" – the teachings and practices of Jesus, and in particular on the Sermon on the Mount.[35] Their book is called *Kingdom Ethics* because their approach to Christian ethics focuses on God's reign. They claim to be providing a basis for Christian ethics

> which recognizes and affirms reasoning – with and through holistic character, which includes the virtues. Virtues are character traits that are stable, consistent and reliable. Virtues aim toward discerning and doing what is good for our purpose in life as humans. They are developed by training and practice. They need a community where they are engendered, fostered and refined.[36]

Of all the Western ethical systems presented in this chapter, the most attractive to African Christians is that of Stassen and Gushee. There are several reasons for this. First, they strive to ground their ethics in the

---

[34] For more details on MacIntyre's views, see *After Virtue* (Notre Dame: University of Notre Dame Press, 1981).

[35] Glen H. Stassen and David P. Gushee, *Kingdom Ethics: Following Jesus in Contemporary Context* (Downers Grove: IVP, 2003), xl.

[36] Stassen and Gushee, *Kingdom Ethics*, 60.

Scriptures in our age when most ethicists prefer to appeal to secular and liberal philosophical authorities. Second, they stress that Jesus is the model for Christian ethics, the one whom Christians are called to follow. This approach is refreshingly understandable to believers, who are often left confused by complicated explanations filled with philosophical jargon.

Another important reason for preferring this ethical system is that Stassen and Gushee emphasize the role of community in correcting the disconnected individualism of the West. Yet their discussion of community gives rise to some lingering questions. What kind of community are they referring to? Is it an organic community where members share the same roots, history, goals, aspirations and world view? How is it related to the African understanding of community? How do character ethics promote a vertical relationship with God and a horizontal relationship with our neighbours? These questions will be taken up in the next chapter.

Western Ethics and Christian Ethics

The various ethical systems discussed in this chapter have had a profound influence on Western understandings of morality, and thus, sometimes knowingly and many times unconsciously, on Western Christian ethics. There are many Christian ethicists today who are willing to identify themselves as Kantian Christian ethicists, while utilitarians or situationist ethicists will often provide proof-texts to support their claim that their ethical system is Christian and biblically based.

> For instance, both Utilitarians and Kantians have frequently considered themselves to be propounding "good Christian teachings" in their ethics. Does God not will the happiness of his creatures? Does he not want us to realize our potentialities? Surely God must be a Utilitarian, and an Upholder of the Utilitarian Principle. But on the other hand, does not God stand for universal righteousness? Is he not a God who awakens us to our duties to our fellow human beings? Does he not discriminate between vicious happiness and happiness which is deserved? Does he not speak the language of commands?

> Surely God must be a Kantian and an Upholder of the Categorical Imperative. While neither Mill nor Kant argue their positions on the basis of Scripture, they do not hesitate to quote scriptural passages in corroboration of their views.[37]

Modern Christian Kantians, Utilitarians and Situationists have joined with secular ethicists in expressing serious doubt about biblical revelation. Many do not hesitate to reject Scriptural authority. Ashby summarizes the position:

> What began then as a confidence in authority with the Greeks and the Hebrews has changed to doubting authority. What began with a confidence in reason has changed to a fear of the irrational. What began as a sense of unity with the universe has changed to a sense of alienation from the natural and the spiritual world. As we look around our modern terrain we seem to be living in the ruins of ancient beliefs, caught up in irreconcilable conflicts with no moral exemplars and no clearly defined responsibilities.[38]

Ashby makes the point that today there is no compelling moral consensus that provides an adequate social base for the construction of an ethical system. However, the history of Western ethics shows that this has not always been the case.

Conclusion

In this chapter we have examined some of the history of Western ethics and have seen how schools of thought that began in ancient Greece continue to influence Western moral reasoning up to the present. We have also seen how the Enlightenment's focus on the autonomy of reason, radical individualism and the separation of religion and ethics has displaced the theistic, revelatory nature of Christian ethics and challenged the basic theological presuppositions of the Jewish and Christian religion.

Western approaches to ethics do not always transfer well to the rest of the world, particularly when they stress universals and neglect any

---

[37] Jentz, "Some Thoughts", 53.
[38] Ashby, *Comprehensive History*, 7.

understanding of local contexts. Moreover, since the Enlightenment the focus has been on developing a secular ethic without God or religion. The assumption has been that "we could and would be good without God".[39] But this attitude is totally out of harmony with traditional African ethics, as shown in the previous chapter. Similarly, Western ethics is based on individualism or the self devoid of community. Individuals make their own decisions about what is right and wrong, without regard for the views of parents, relatives and the community. Such an approach is unthinkable in Africa. Finally, Western ethics is devoid of authority. It is not built not on any external authority but solely on the subjective authority of the individual. It is for this reason that there are so many different types of ethics.

In the next chapter, we will attempt to provide a Christian foundation for ethics that can be used to develop an ethical system which will be biblically rooted, theologically sound and relevant to the African situation.

Questions

1. How have Western ethics been imported to Africa? In what ways has this importation been successful or helpful? In what ways has it been unsuccessful or unhelpful?

2. Based on the information in this chapter, what are the best contributions Western ethics might make to African ethics?

3. Evaluate the ethical theories presented in this chapter with regard to their relevance and usefulness in the context of your ministry.

4. Is it morally justifiable for a student to bribe his or her teacher in order to get a higher grade? How would a deontologist, teleologist and situationist respond to this question?

---

[39] Rasmussen, *Moral Fragments and Moral Community*, 74.

4

FOUNDATIONS OF CHRISTIAN ETHICS

Modern Western ethics has long abandoned any supernatural element or external source of authority. Christian ethics, by contrast, is firmly grounded in Christian theology. Our ultimate goal in this book is to develop a system of African Christian ethics that will incorporate those features within African ethics that are biblical and Christian. But in order to be able to do this, we must first develop an understanding of some of the core principles that shape Christian ethical thinking.

Christian theology is critical to the development of Christian ethics. It is wrong to dismiss it as too abstract to be of any relevance to our lives today. As Alister E. McGrath notes: "To lose sight of the importance of doctrine is to lose the backbone of faith and to open the way to a spineless ethic."[1] Dorothy L. Sayers makes the same point:

> It is ... useless for Christians to talk about the importance of Christian morality, unless they are prepared to take their stand upon the fundamentals of Christian theology. It is a lie to say that dogma does not matter; it matters enormously. It is fatal to let people suppose that Christianity is only a mode of feeling; it is vitally necessary to insist that it is first and foremost a rational explanation of the universe.[2]

---

[1] Alister E. McGrath, "Doctrine and Ethics", in *Readings in Christian Ethics Vol. I: Theory and Method* (ed. David K. Clark and Robert V. Rakestraw; Grand Rapids: Baker, 1994), 83.
[2] D. L. Sayers, *Creed or Chaos* (New York: Harcourt, Brace, 1949), 28.

The Source of Knowledge: Revelation

Both Christian ethics and African ethics agree that all ethical norms ultimately come from God. Such norms are not based on human values and ideas, but derive their "content and sanction and dynamic and goal from God – not from some inference from anthropology or sociology".[3] But how do we know what these norms are? The Christian answer is that God has revealed them to us as part of his disclosure of himself through general and special revelation.

General revelation

General revelation is God's revelation of himself through nature, history and the human conscience. Creation testifies to his existence: "The heavens declare the glory of God; the skies proclaim the work of his hands. Day after day they pour forth speech; night after night they display knowledge. There is no speech or language where their voice is not heard" (Ps 19:1–3; see also Ps 147:8–9).

In the New Testament, Paul makes the same point when writing to the Christians in Rome: "What may be known about God is plain to them, because God has made it plain to them. For since the creation of the world God's invisible qualities – his eternal power and divine nature – have been clearly seen, being understood from what has been made" (Rom 1:19–20).

When preaching in Lystra, Paul told the people that they needed to turn to the God who made heaven and earth. This God had permitted nations to go their own ways, "yet he has not left himself without testimony" (Acts 14:15–17). These words seem to imply that God's witness can be seen both in nature and in history. Similarly, when preaching in Athens (Acts 17:22–31) Paul related the "unknown god" who was worshipped there to the God he was preaching and quoted an Athenian poet who had come to the right conclusion regarding God's existence without the benefit of special revelation.

The Bible also insists that natural revelation informs the human conscience so that people can make ethical decisions and judge between right and wrong. Paul points out that when "the Gentiles, who do not have the law, do by nature things required by the law" this proves

---

[3] Carl F. H. Henry, *Christian Personal Ethics* (Grand Rapids: Eerdmans, 1957), 188.

that "the requirements of the law are written on their hearts, their consciences also bearing witness, and their thoughts now accusing, now even defending them" (Rom 2:14–15).

However, the Bible also makes it clear that human beings have not bothered to pay attention to God's general revelation. Paul complains that "although they knew God, they neither glorified him as God nor gave thanks to him, but their thinking became futile and their foolish hearts were darkened" (Rom 1:21). People live in ways that deny God's existence and readily misinterpret what he has revealed to them.[4]

Special revelation

General revelation tells us about some of God's attributes, but it does not clearly reveal his will for creation, that is, what he wants it to become. There is thus a need for special revelation to supplement general revelation. This special revelation is both verbal and personal, as the writer of Hebrews reminds us when he says, "in the past God spoke to our forefathers through the prophets at many times and in various ways" (Heb 1:1). Though the "forefathers" referred to here are Abraham, Moses and David, these words can also be applied to all our human ancestors who received divine revelations. But God's supreme revelation of himself came when he spoke "to us by his Son, whom he appointed heir of all things, and through whom he made the universe" (Heb 1:2; see also John 1:18).

The record of God's special revelation is contained in Scripture, as Peter remind us when he says that "no prophecy of Scripture came about by the prophet's own interpretation. For prophecy never had its origin in the will of man, but men spoke from God as they were carried along by the Holy Spirit" (2 Pet 1:20–21). It was God who pushed all the authors of Scripture to write, and that is why Paul can state that "All Scripture is inspired by God" (2 Tim 3:16a, NASB).

God's revelation in Scripture not only tells us about who he is but also about how we should live. As Paul goes on to say, it "is useful for teaching, rebuking, correcting and training in righteousness, so that the

---

[4] Paul Helm, *The Divine Revelation* (Westchester, Ill.: Crossway, 1982), 17, summarizes John Calvin's understanding of Acts 17:28–9: "As soon as men begin to think about God they vanish away in wicked inventions. The picture that God presents of himself is willingly and willfully misinterpreted in a variety of different ways. There was no pure and approved religion, founded upon common understanding."

man of God may be thoroughly equipped for every good work (2 Tim 3:16–17). In the Bible, God clearly lays out what he regards as ethical behaviour: "to act justly and to love mercy and to walk humbly with your God" (Mic 6:8).

The importance of Scripture as the source of our ethics is also clear from the fact that the Hebrew Scriptures are constantly quoted in the New Testament as the final authority on issues early believers were struggling with. There is also abundant evidence from the early church that even before the New Testament books had been compiled in one volume and accepted as canonical, the "letters from the ancestral faith communities held a place unparalleled among religious and philosophical movements of the ancient world. Their community authority was 'a unique characteristic of the Jewish ethos."[5]

The trustworthiness of any Christian discussion of ethical issues thus hinges on whether or not Scripture, properly interpreted, justifies the conclusions. But what do we mean when we say "properly interpreted"? To help us answer this question, scholars have identified some key principles to be observed and pitfalls to be avoided when reading the Bible in order to derive ethical norms from it.[6]

➲ *Acknowledge the usual rules of grammar and interpretation*

The Bible is, in its unique way, a piece of literature. When reading it, we need to apply some of the same simple rules of grammar and interpretation that we would use when reading any work of literature. When we encounter something that is difficult to understand, we can consult different translations to help us clarify the meaning. What we must not do is ignore the surface meaning of the text and seek for some allegorical meaning or insist that we must read with a mystical attitude to discern a mystical meaning.

Some people justify the search for hidden meanings by interpreting the words "the letter kills but the Spirit gives life" (2 Cor 3:6) as meaning that the ordinary, literal meaning of Scripture is not useful or edifying

---

[5] Bruce C. Birch, and Larry L. Rasmussen, *Bible and Ethics in the Christian Life* (Minneapolis: Augsburg, 1989), 32.

[6] The following books supply more detailed information about the principles of biblical interpretation: Robert A. Traina, *Methodical Bible Study: A New Approach to Hermeneutics* (Grand Rapids: Francis Asbury Press, 1952); Bernard Ramm, *Protestant Biblical Interpretation: A Textbook of Hermeneutics* (Grand Rapids: Baker, 1970); Gordon D. Fee and Douglas Stuart, *How to Read the Bible for All It's Worth: A Guide to Understanding the Bible* (Grand Rapids: Zondervan, 1981); and A. Berkeley Mickelsen, *Interpreting the Bible* (Grand Rapids: Eerdmans, 1963).

and that the allegorical or spiritual meaning revealed to the reader by the Holy Spirit is to be preferred.[7] But this interpretation ignores the fact that what Paul is talking about in Corinthians is that we were all condemned to death under the Old Testament law and that Christ has given us life through his Spirit within us. Paul is not saying that we can ignore the actual words of Scripture.

The major problem with any allegorical or mystical method is that "it obscures the true meaning of the Word of God … The Bible treated as allegory becomes putty in the hand of the exegete. Different doctrinal systems could emerge within the framework of allegorical hermeneutics and no way would exist to determine which were the truth."[8]

➲ Read the whole Bible

Some people read the Bible selectively, preferring only the Old or New Testament or certain portions of Scripture. But casual or selective reading of the Scriptures will yield poor and often misleading interpretations, for it will be easy to "read one's own, completely foreign ideas into a text and thereby make God's Word something other than what God really said".[9] We see this type of problem when groups like the Cherubim and Seraphim Church and many African initiated churches (AICs) justify their ethical practices by appealing only to the Old Testament when considering issues like polygamy.

The corrective to selective reading is to examine everything that Scripture teaches about a particular topic and not just the passages that favour your position. For example, on the question of whether or not a Christian should participate in war, it would be incomplete to quote only passages such as "If someone strikes you on the right cheek, turn to him the other also" (Matt 5:39), or "All who draw the sword will die by the sword" (Matt 26:52). You must also consider passages such as Luke 22:36: "if you don't have a sword, sell your cloak and buy one." Old Testament passages which deal with war and present images of God as a warrior must also be discussed. All the relevant passages must be carefully studied before any conclusion can be drawn.

---

[7] Supporters of allegorical interpretation believe "that beneath the letter (*rhete*) or the obvious (*phanera*) is the real meaning (*hyponoia*) of the passage". Bernard Ramm, *Protestant Biblical Interpretation*, 24.

[8] Ramm, *Protestant Biblical Interpretation*, 30.

[9] Fee and Stuart, *How to Read the Bible*, 21.

The need to use the whole Bible (or canon) is well stated by Birch and Rasmussen:

> The canon helps prevent the selecting of texts for ethical use based on the predisposition of the selector. The canon's stress on the wholeness of Scripture means that moral judgments cannot be based on marshaling only those texts that bolster a position already reached on other grounds. Even when it presents us with difficult tensions and contradictions, attentions to the canon requires that the totality of the biblical witness be weighed in reaching moral judgments. To pick out some portions as relevant and to reject others is to create one's own canon. Ethical statements based on such a limited canon are more often than not misleading. To do Christian ethics is to enter dialog with the whole of the Christian canon recognized as Scripture throughout the history of the church.[10]

➲ *Take note of the historical and literary context*

Sound interpretation and relevant application requires taking into consideration the historical and literary context of each passage in the Bible. To appreciate the historical context, some understanding of the time and culture of the biblical author is required. To appreciate the literary context, it is important to recognize that the words, phrases, sentences and paragraphs in any book derive their meaning from their relationship to one another, for "thought is usually expressed in a series of related ideas."[11] It is important that we do not indulge in what is called proof-texting, that is, in trying to prove a point by quoting a scriptural text without any regard for its context.

➲ *Read the Bible reverently with a desire for obedience*

Scripture should not be read for the purpose of winning intellectual arguments but with an attitude of reverent obedience like that of the psalmist: "I have hidden your word in my heart that I might not sin against you" (Psalm 119:11). Ezra is also a role model for he "devoted himself to the study and observance of the Law of the Lord, and to

---

[10] Birch and Rasmussen, *Bible and Ethics*, 180.
[11] Mickelsen, *Interpreting the Bible*, 100.

teaching its decrees and laws in Israel" (Ezra 7:10). We must seek to apply the word studied to our own situations.

The Source of Ethics: The Triune God

Many years ago, Paul Ramsay wrote:

> The fact that God requires something of man, and stands ready to reward obedience and punish violation, is not nearly so important as the question to what sort of God man has obligations and what are his commandments. Religious conviction concerning God's dealing with man affects the basic meaning and content of biblical ethics. God has something to do with the very meaning of obligation; he is no merely external threat standing behind morality.[12]

In answering Ramsey's question about what sort of God has determined their ethical obligations, many people are content to cling to a vague theism, saying that they believe in "a God". But the essential reality which lies at the heart of Christian ethics is not just any god but the Triune God, that is, the God who has made himself known to us as the Father, the Son and the Spirit.

> Christians call God triune because this way of speaking accords with the biblical witness and with the experience of the Church rooted in this witness. The God known in Jesus Christ is God over us, God for us, and God in us – the loving God, the gracious Lord Jesus Christ, and the community-creating Spirit of God (2 Cor 13:14).[13]

Our Christian ethics must be rooted in our understanding of the nature and actions of this God. It is thus important to be clear what we mean when we speak of the Triune God (or the Trinity):

*   *There is only one God, not three gods.* Biblical Christianity insists on the unity of God as expressed in passages like Deuteronomy 6:4: "Hear, O Israel: The Lord our God, the Lord is one."

---

[12] Paul Ramsey, *Basic Christian Ethics* (New York: Charles Scribner's Sons, 1953), 1.
[13] Daniel L. Migliore, *Faith Seeking Understanding: An Introduction to Christian Theology* (Grand Rapids: Eerdmans, 1991), 61.

- *Each of the three persons in the Trinity is equally God.* The Father is God in the same sense as the Son is God and the Holy Spirit is God. Their equality is clearly expressed in passages like Matthew 28:19, which speaks of "baptising them in the name of the Father and of the Son and of the Holy Spirit," and in 2 Corinthians 13:14 where all three are invoked in the blessing, "May the grace of the Lord Jesus Christ, and the love of God, and the fellowship of the Holy Spirit be with you all."

- *Although each person of the Godhead has the same essence, they fulfil different roles.* The Father is not the same as the Son, nor the same as the Holy Spirit. It was the Son who died on the cross and it is the Holy Spirit who indwells believers to empower them for works of ministry. Because of their different roles, the persons of the Trinity often act as if one is subordinate to another. Thus during his earthly life Jesus stated that the "Father is greater than I" (John 14:28). It can be said that "Each of the three persons of the Trinity has had, for a period of time, a particular function unique to himself. This is to be understood as a temporary role for the purpose of accomplishing a given end, not a change in his status or essence."[14]

- *All the three persons in the Trinity are eternal.* None is older or younger than the other. Moses referred to God as "the eternal God" (Deut 33:27). Jesus refers to Himself as "I AM," the name used for God in the Old Testament (John 8:58; see Exod 3:14), and Isaiah the prophet testifies that Jesus' titles will include "Everlasting Father" (Isa 9:6). In Genesis 1:2 we are told that the "Spirit of God" was moving over the waters before the world was formed, and the writer of Hebrews refers to as this same Spirit as the "eternal Spirit" (Heb 9:14).

The above statements should not be dismissed as abstract theology with no relevance to the study of ethics. They have important ethical implications. For one thing, they give the lie to the idea that God is only interested in spiritual matters. God's revelation and participation in creation and his personal revelation in the incarnation of Jesus Christ demonstrate that he has a personal and intimate relationship with his own creation. The Holy Spirit's continuing work in creation and

---

[14] Millard K. Erickson, *Introducing Christian Doctrine* (Grand Rapids: Baker, 1992), 103. I am indebted to Erickson for the articulation of the four essential aspects of the Trinity.

especially in the life of the believer also shows God's an intimate role in his created order.

> We need a fuller doctrine of God. For we tend to forget that he is concerned for the whole of humankind and for the whole of human life in all its color and complexity … The Living God is the God of nature as well as of religion, of the "secular" as well as of the "sacred". … His concerns are all-embracing – not only the "sacred" but the "secular", not only religion but nature, not only his covenant people but all people, not only justification, but social justice in every community, not only his gospel but his law. So we must not attempt to narrow his interests. Moreover, ours should be as broad as his.[15]

The stress on the need to know God before we can understand his ethical laws is not something that was invented by theologians: it is already present in the Scriptures themselves. Before God gave the Ten Commandments, he stated who he was and gave his authority to speak: "I am the Lord your God, who brought you out of Egypt" (Exod 20:2). To stress the commandments without appreciating the God who gave them is to miss the main point. We see the same approach in the New Testament, where specific commands are often associated with the theology that explains them (see, for example, 1 John 4:7, 11, 19; 2 Cor 8:7–9; Eph 4:32).

God the Father, the norm for Christian ethics

An important reason for knowing our theology well is that our character should mirror God's character. In the Old Testament, we are told to "be holy to me because I, the Lord, am holy, and I have set you apart from the nations to be my own (Lev 20:26). In the New Testament, we are told to "be perfect, therefore, as your heavenly Father is perfect" (Matt 5:48). To be able to understand what these commands mean, and what it means to be holy and perfect, we have to know the God we serve.

---

[15] John Stott, *Human Rights and Human Wrongs: Major Issues for a New Century* (Grand Rapids: Baker, 1990), 31.

Jesus Christ, the model for Christian ethics

People are not Christians merely because they believe in God or some supernatural power; they are Christians because they believe that Jesus is the Son of God who died and rose from the grave and gives every believer the power to live a moral life. As the Son of God, Jesus is the most complete revelation of who God is. He is thus our ethical paradigm, in other words, our example of how we should live. Paul tells the Philippian Christians that "your attitude should be the same as that of Christ Jesus" (Phil 2:5) and he commends the Thessalonians for having become "imitators of us and of the Lord" (1 Thess 1:6). Peter also stresses that Christ is our example: "Christ suffered for you, leaving you an example, that you should follow in his steps" (1 Pet 2:21). Following in Christ's steps means demonstrating the same qualities that Jesus demonstrated in his earthly life. Paul regularly draws out the implications of Jesus' death and resurrection for our ethical conduct (Rom 6:1–14; 8:17, 29–30; 15:1–7; 1 Cor 10:2–11; 2 Cor 4:7 15; 12:9–10; Gal 2:19–20; 5:24; 6:14).

The Holy Spirit, the power for Christian ethics

Jesus' death and resurrection have put us in a right relationship to God and make it possible for us to become holy and perfect. Yet we are still sinful and need help if we are to live ethical lives. So Jesus promised us the Holy Spirit (John 14:16; Acts 1:8), who energizes us to seek to live the way God wants and helps us understand the truth about God, ourselves and our world. "The Spirit is the dynamic principle of Christian ethics, the personal agency whereby God powerfully enters human life and delivers man from enslavement to Satan, sin, death, and law… He is a main character whose role is crucial for the life of holiness in all its phases."[16]

Without the Holy Spirit's enablement, none of us could live a moral life. The Apostle Paul knew this from his own experience, for he states that "I do not understand what I do. For what I want to do I do not do, but what I hate I do" (Rom 7:15). The reason we struggle is because we are naturally sinful. We need "the Spirit of life" to set us "free from the law of sin and death" (Rom 8:2) and to lead us to live like children of God.

---

[16] Henry, *Christian Personal Ethics*, 437.

The Recipients of Ethics: Human Beings

We need to understand not only the God who is the source of our ethics but also the people to whom these ethics are given. This point is ignored by both teleological and deontological ethicists, who seem to think that "good games depend on good rules more than they depend on good players."[17]

There are two important points we need to remember about human nature. First, humans are created in the image of God. Second, humans are fallen and need salvation. No matter how good the rules are, we cannot play by them because we are limited and corrupted by sin.

Created in the image of God

Creation is the handiwork of God, and he declared all of it good (Gen 1:31). Nothing was created bad. Therefore we can reject those ethical views that argue that certain aspects of creation are inherently bad. When God commanded Adam and Eve to multiply and dominate the earth, he was affirming that sex is good. He was also endorsing politics, for any group that multiplies will need to set up some system of organization. John Stott sums up the implications of God's creation of human beings as follows:

> These human but godlike creatures are not just souls (that we should be concerned exclusively for their eternal salvation), not just bodies (that we should care only for their food, clothing, shelter, and health), nor just social beings (that we should become preoccupied with their community problems). They are all three. A human being might be defined from a biblical perspective as "a body-soul-in community." For that is how God has made us.[18]

Stott can describe human beings as "godlike" because we are unique in God's creation in that he has made us in his own image (Gen 1:26). Though these words have many possible meanings, one thing is clear: the fact that we are made in the image of God means that we are rational and moral beings. This point is made even clearer when God issues the

[17] Larry Rasmussen, *Moral Fragments and Moral Community: A Proposal for Church in Society* (Minneapolis: Fortress, 1993), 73.
[18] John Stott, *Human Rights and Human Wrongs*, 35.

specific command "You are free to eat from any tree in the garden; but you must not eat from the tree of the knowledge of good and evil, for when you eat of it you will surely die" (Gen 2:16–17). This command implies that God has given human beings responsibility for making right decisions and acting ethically. What Adam and Eve did not have, and what eating of the fruit of this tree gave them, was experiential knowledge of evil.

Because God created human beings with a conscience, the inherent capacity to know good from evil, right from wrong, we find that throughout the world there is a

> universal conviction that the distinction between right and wrong, good and bad, is a genuine one – and that it is not merely a matter of personal prejudice ... Human experience is by definition ethical, in the sense at least that questioning the rightness and wrongness of thoughts and deeds is universal and inescapable.[19]

Fallen and in need of salvation

Though created good and without sin, Adam and Eve disobeyed God. Their fall into sin affected not only themselves but also the environment and all aspects of human culture. Everything now needs salvation or redemption. This fact is often ignored by ethicists, including contemporary African ethicists, who may acknowledge that humans are limited but do not admit that they are fallen. Thus they do not face up to the reality of human sinfulness.

Another aspect of Christian ethics that is missing in all other ethical systems is forgiveness. It is not that other systems have no kindness or compassion towards those who fail, but these systems have no grounds for offering grace. It is only Christianity that provides a solid foundation for forgiveness through God's self-revelation as one who comes not to condemn the world but to save it. Christians need to have a firm grasp not only of the importance of God's moral order but also of the truth of God's saving grace that renews the moral offender, the sinner. Christians can share in God's activity whereby sinners are restored and take up their place in the congregation of the righteous.

---

[19] Henry, *Christian Personal Ethics*, 152.

God provided salvation in Jesus Christ and we receive this salvation solely through faith in him. Ephesians 2:8–9 states this clearly: "For it is by grace you have been saved, through faith – and this not from yourselves, it is the gift of God – not by works, so that no one can boast". As Hollinger points out, "all solutions to the problem of sin that bypass this redemption are only partial solutions that never get to the core problem of sin".[20]

Salvation is by faith, but it also has an impact on our moral life, as the very next verse in Ephesians makes clear: "For we are God's workmanship, created in Christ Jesus to do good works" (Eph 2:10). To understand this point, we need to distinguish justification and sanctification. Evangelical Christians emphasize the importance of justification, or entering into a right relationship with God, by accepting in faith the death and resurrection of Jesus Christ. But sanctification, which follows logically on justification, is an equally necessary part of salvation. It involves "continued transformation of moral and spiritual character so that the life of the believer actually comes to mirror the standing which he or she already has in God's sight."[21]

While justification is instantaneous, sanctification is a process that will continue throughout each believer's life and will affect their attitudes and their actions in every sphere of life, including their marriages, their politics and the use they make of technology. All this is related to the fact that Scripture does not teach that the spirit is more important than the body. A person is a unity and believers should see their faith affecting all areas of their life, including their material life and their community life.

The Redeemed Community

It can be said that the "idea of community is at the heart of biblical theology".[22] At creation, Adam's loneliness signalled his first awareness of the need for community, and the focus of biblical revelation from then on is the story of how God created the first human community and then formed a covenant people. When God called Abraham, the idea of a community was central to his call: "I will make of you a great nation,

---

[20] Dennis P. Hollinger, *Choosing the Good: Christian Ethics in a Complex World* (Grand Rapids: Baker, 2002), 82.

[21] Erickson, *Introducing Christian Doctrine*, 269.

[22] R. K. McCloughry, "Community Ethics", in *New Dictionary of Christian Ethics and Pastoral Theology* (Downers Grove: IVP, 1995), 111.

and I will bless you, and make your name great, so that you will be a blessing" (Gen 12:2). In the book of Exodus, the idea of a community is again stressed when God tells the newly liberated Israelites, "I will take you as my people, and I will be your God" (Exod 6:7).

The nature of community

Before we discuss the implications of God's interest in community in more detail, we should define what we mean by community:

> Communities … have a history – in an important sense they are constituted by their past – and for this reason we can speak of a real community as a "community of memory," one that does not forget its past. In order not to forget that past, a community is involved in retelling its story, its constitutive narrative, and in so doing, it offers examples of the men and women who have embodied and exemplified the meaning of the community. These stories of collective history and exemplary individuals are an important part of the tradition that is so central to a community of memory.
>
> The stories that make up a tradition contain conceptions of character, of what a good person is like, and of the virtues that define such character.[23]

Important features of a community thus include an awareness of past heroes of the community, of the virtues praised in the community, and of what constitutes a good character. These key features of the ethical thinking of a community are also found in Judaism and Christianity, both of which

> conceived of the moral life as the practical outcome of the community's faith, as shown in the sorts of lives members of the community, and the community as a whole, lived. The community's task was to socialize its members into forms of life which displayed the kind of conduct befitting the experience of God in community. To be a Jew was to learn the story of Israel and the rabbinic traditions well enough to

[23] Robert N. Bellah, Richard Madsen, William M. Sullivan, Ann Swidler, and Steven M. Tipton, *Habits of the Heart: Individualism and Commitment in American Life* (Berkeley: University of California Press, 1985), 153.

experience the world from within these stories, and to act in accord with that experience as a member of an ongoing faith community. Similarly, to be a Christian was to learn the story of Israel and of Jesus and the ongoing church traditions well enough to experience the world from within those stories, and to act in keeping with that experience, as a member of that community.[24]

Thus Christians and Jews, unlike later philosophers, were not so much interested in questions like "What is the universal good?" as in the question "What character and conduct is in keeping with who we are as a people of God?"[25]

The Old Testament describes God's building of the community of Israel. The New Testament describes how God worked through Jesus Christ to create a redeemed community, which is also called the body of Christ, a city set on a hill, the temple where the Spirit dwells. This is the community Jesus is speaking of when he says "I will build my church" (Matt 16:18). Beginning with a group of disciples, this redeemed community has over the ages come to mirror the life of Jesus Christ. It has become one community, no longer divided by ethnicity, social status or gender (Gal 3:28) and has been called in its corporate life, "to embody an alternative order that stands as a sign of God's redemptive purposes in the world."[26]

The formation of this new moral community raised many questions for the first believers:

How do we now embody the intense reality of the living Christ among us, in our day-to day life together? What will we do with our goods, our houses, our land? How will we organize fellowship with one another, locally and across great distances, i.e., how will we "break bread together" as members of the same body in different locales? What should be our form of governance and how do we recognize our leaders, by what

---

[24] Birch and Rasmussen, *Bible and Ethics,* 21.

[25] Ibid., 19.

[26] Richard B. Hays, *The Moral Vision of the New Testament: Community, Cross, New Creation. A Contemporary Introduction to New Testament Ethics* (San Francisco: HarperCollins, 1996), 196. Hays observes that "The church is a countercultural community of discipleship, and this community is the primary addressee of God's imperatives...The primary sphere of moral concern is not the character of the individual but the corporate obedience of the church."

measure? How will worship be conducted? How will the rituals and rites and festivals of our former life be treated? What shall we now say to Caesar, now that Jesus is our Caesar (Acts 17:8); and what should we do about service in the emperor's army? How do the relationships of parents and children, of husband and wife, of slave and slaveholder change now? What are the requirements of membership in the community? How should transgressors be treated? How should we treat those who take offense at the new gospel and persecute us?[27]

The early Christian communities sought the answers to these questions in the Hebrew Scriptures and in the letters they received from the apostles.

While this emphasis on community ethics is very familiar to Africans, it is harder for those steeped in the individualism of Western ethics to grasp.

In societies whose communities emphasize individualism and nurture the illusion that individuals exist apart from or prior to communities and community influences, we must underscore community's place. Such societies frequently define "freedom" as independence, meaning freedom from all obligations except those chosen in accord with individual's desires; and, indeed, freedom from the need for other human beings. North Americans especially seem to live without the assumption that our lives are cast together in an inescapable social interrelatedness. Rather, the majority seems to contend that we are independent individuals who may choose to be, or not be, related to others.[28]

Yet, whether human beings accept it or not, the idea of community is a necessary part of life, for as Archbishop William Temple observed, "everyone has needs which he cannot supply for himself ... Man is naturally and incurably social."[29]

Our existence within communities means that the community has an influence on our moral life:

---

[27] Birch and Rasmussen, *Bible and Ethics*, 27–28.
[28] Ibid., 18.
[29] William Temple, *Christianity and the Social Order* (Harmondsworth: Penguin, 1942), 64.

> We are not born into an undifferentiated schema of disconnected events and relations, but into corporate life already alive with communities which structure our social existence. The moral life cannot exist apart from these, and is only possible with a view to these communities. Whatever moral consciousness we possess does not exist prior to, apart from, or independent of social relatedness.[30]

The redeemed community should, therefore, play a decisive role in moulding the life of the believer. This is done as members of the community, or the fellowship of believers, share in the reading and interpretation of Scripture. It is not just the elders or trained pastors who do the reading and pass information on to uninformed members. Rather, the whole membership should read and hear the word. Individuals will also read and digest the word, but they will do this as part of the whole community.

Membership in the community

Just as children must be born into a family in order to belong to it, so every person must be born again to become part of the redeemed community (John 3:3, 5; Titus 3:5). "The individual act of faith by which we are born anew takes place in the context of the church, which proclaims the gospel, nurtures the converts, and shares the eternal blessings for which it was chosen by God."[31]

This church community consists not only of the believers alive in our time but also of all the believers who have already been glorified. These heroes of the Christian community include Abraham, Isaac, Jacob, David, Jeremiah, the Apostle Paul, Jonathan Edwards, James Hannington, Byang Kato, Janani Luwum, Johan Heyns and many others who proclaimed and lived out the Good News. They are the believing dead (Hebrew and Christian) who constitute the "cloud of witnesses". Their lives should exert a profound influence on our lives (Heb 12:1). We can debate whether or not they are physically watching believers on earth, but that is not the main point – what is important is that their commitment and devotion stands as a constant example and

---

[30] Birch and Rasmussen, *Bible and Ethics*, 19.
[31] Stephen Mott, *Biblical and Social Ethics* (Oxford: Oxford University Press, 1982), 129.

encouragement to believers still on their Christian pilgrimage here on earth.

Believers should not only be inspired by the lives of departed leaders but also by the lives of their present leaders. The Apostle Paul often appealed to his life and the lives of other believers as examples of right conduct. "Follow my example, as I follow the example of Christ" (1 Cor 11:1); "You became imitators of us and of the Lord; ... And so you became a model to all the believers in Macedonia and Achaia (1 Thess 1:6–7); "Join with others in following my example, brothers, and take note of those who live according to the pattern we gave you" (Phil 3:17); "Therefore I urge you to imitate me. For this reason I am sending to you Timothy, my son whom I love, who is faithful in the Lord. He will remind you of my way of life in Christ Jesus, which agrees with what I teach everywhere in every church" (1 Cor 4:16–17).

It is clear from these passages that elders should demonstrate the kind of lifestyle that is appropriate for believers. By living like this, the redeemed community will have a public witness to an unbelieving world, for "the presence of the church as a visible sign of the reign of God produces social change in the surrounding society".[32] We will be what we are intended to be "the light of the world" and "a city on a hill" that cannot be hidden" (Matt 5:14).

Eternal Perspectives

Christians are inspired by the past as they live in the present, but their ethics are also affected by their hope for the future:

> Though Christ brought redemption to the world through his death and resurrection, it is quite clear that redemption of the moral life is not yet fully evident, even in the redeemed community. The realities of sin and the fall are prevalent everywhere, including in those who by grace have received forgiveness and moral empowerment.[33]

---

[32] Mott, *Biblical and Social Ethics*, 133–134. "A Christianity community as a city shedding light in the world seems a fitting picture of the social impact of the church as an alternative social reality" (Ibid., 137).

[33] Hollinger, *Choosing the Good*, 83.

The only hope that sin will be finally and eternally removed lies in the *eschaton*, the end or consummation when Christ will set up his kingdom in which evil will be removed and there will be peace and righteousness. Jesus proclaimed this eschatological kingdom throughout his earthly life (Matt 4:23), often through parables. But the fact that we cannot fully achieve freedom from evil in the present is not an excuse not to strive to live ethically now. The Apostle John insists that "everyone who has this hope in him purifies himself, just as he is pure" (1 John 3:3). The Apostle Peter also appeals to the *eschaton* as a motivation for godliness: "Since everything will be destroyed in this way, what kind of people ought you to be? You ought to live holy and godly lives … So then, dear friends, since you are looking forward to this, make every effort to be found spotless, blameless and at peace with him" (2 Pet 3:11–14)

Because of their eternal perspective, believers should not be materialistic or focus on their physical possessions. Instead, an understanding of the end should shape their values so that they set their hearts "on things above, where Christ is seated at the right hand of God." (Col 3:1). After all, they know that "everything in the world – the cravings of sinful man, the lust of his eyes and the boasting of what he has and does – comes not from the Father but from the world. The world and its desires pass away, but the man who does the will of God lives for ever" (1 John 2:16–17).

Believers should focus on eternal things not only because worldly pleasures are transient but because all actions will be judged. "For we must all appear before the judgment seat of Christ, that each one may receive what is due to him for the things done while in the body, whether good or bad" (2 Cor 5:10). William Lane Craig notes

> God holds all persons morally accountable for their actions. Evil and wrong will be punished; righteousness will be vindicated. Good ultimately triumphs over evil, and we shall finally see that we do live in a moral universe after all. Despite the inequities of this life, in the end the scales of God's justice

will be balanced. Thus, the moral choices we make in this life are infused with an eternal significance.[34]

Yet it is "striking how seldom Paul uses eschatological judgment as a threat to motivate obedience".[35] It is our love and gratitude for what the Lord has done that should move us to obedience, not our fear of his punishment. "The sense of the imminence of the coming of the Lord heightens rather than negates the imperatives of ethical action. The community is called to pursue with urgency the tasks of love and mutual service."[36]

Conclusion

The general principles outlined in this chapter hold true for Christianity throughout the world. But the focus of this book is on African Christian ethics. What exactly does that mean? Is there a difference between African Christian ethics and the universal Christian ethics discussed so far? That question is addressed in the chapter which follows.

Questions

1. How well are your and your culture's ethics grounded in God's general and special revelation? What are the places where the grounding needs to be strengthened and how might you go about strengthening it?

2. In which area are you strongest: applying principles of interpretation, reading the whole Bible, knowing the historical and literary context, or reverence and obedience? In which area are you weakest? How could you improve in each area?

3. How well are your and your cultures ethics grounded in God's creation, salvation, and the redeemed community? What are the places where the grounding needs to be strengthened and how might you go about strengthening it?

---

[34] William Lane Craig, "The Indispensability of Theological Meta-Ethical Foundations for Morality" *Foundations* 5 (1977): 9–12.

[35] Hays, *Moral Vision of the New Testament*, 26.

[36] Ibid. Hays adds that Paul "is sharply critical not only of the old age that is passing away but also of those who claim unqualified participation already in the new age. To live faithfully in the time between the times is to walk a tightrope of moral discernment, claiming neither too much nor too little for God's transforming power within the community of faith" (p. 27).

5

FOUNDATIONS OF AFRICAN CHRISTIAN ETHICS

Ethical teachings are normative and universally binding, yet they must be lived out in a particular situation or context. As Paul Tillich reminds us,

> A theological system is supposed to satisfy two basic needs: the statement of the truth of the Christian message and the interpretation of this truth for every new generation. Theology moves back and forth between two poles, the eternal truth of its foundation and the temporal situation in which the eternal truth must be received. [1]

African Christian ethics deals with Africa's "temporal situation", that is, the unique African reality in which African Christians seek to apply the biblical and Christian principles outlined in the previous chapter. The discussion in this chapter will not be long because the entire rest of this book will be devoted to addressing the issue of what constitutes African Christian ethics.

African Ethics and Christian Ethics

Just as the Western understanding of ethics has affected the ethical thinking of Christians in the West, so the traditional African understanding of ethics affects the ethical thinking of Christians in Africa. And just as Western Christians have brought some principles of Western ethics to Africa, so African ethical thinking can feed back into Western thought, pointing out biblical principles that have been

---

[1] Paul Tillich, *Systematic Theology, Vol. I* (Chicago: University of Chicago Press, 1951), 3.

neglected in Western Christianity. One of the most important of these principles is community. But before discussing community at more length, it is important to assess where African Christian ethicists stand in relation to the major points of Christian ethics discussed in the last chapter.

Most Africans are happy to acknowledge that moral principles come from God. This was the standard position in traditional African ethics, although there are now those who, under the influence of Western philosophy, seek to ground all ethical discussion in human thinking. But when it comes to African Christian ethics, it is not enough to simply acknowledge God as a Supreme Being. The God who is the source of Christian ethics must be the triune God – the Father, Son and Holy Spirit.

If African Christian ethics fails to affirm its commitment to the triune God, the ethics taught will be merely an exposition of African morality. We have seen this in the work of some who have written about African Christian ethics but have paid only lip service to the fact that God the Father, God the Son, and God the Holy Spirit are one.

Most African Christians would also agree that Christian morality must be grounded in God's revelation of himself in his word, the Holy Scriptures. But there is an ever-present danger of turning back to oral tradition. Dreams, visions and other subjective sources often take the place of the written word in Scripture. Even when Christians do believe in the authority of the word of God, they sometimes fail to apply the correct principles of interpretation. As mentioned earlier, some choose to cite only those passages of Scripture that support their views on issues like polygamy and do not consider everything that the Scripture has to say about marriage.

When it comes to the status of humans as created beings, Africans have traditionally taken a holistic view and rejected the dualism that regards body and soul as separate entities. Unfortunately, this division has been introduced into most African churches, especially those that were established by Western missions. But this dualistic tendency is neither Jewish nor Christian but derives from those elements of Greek philosophy that despised matter and exalted the soul.

Though God created humanity perfect, Adam and Eve fell, affecting the whole of creation. The salvation Jesus Christ provides has restored us through faith to a right standing before God. Yet our salvation is not only spiritual; it is also intensely physical and emotional, as the African holistic approach emphasizes. God does not only desire the salvation of souls. He also desires that his children live happy and fulfilled lives. Jesus himself said, "I have come that they might have life and have it more abundantly" (John 10:10). The traditional understanding of this abundant life has always been eternal life, but it can legitimately also be understood as a fulfilled life in this world as well. Even when there are crises or difficulties, God's children can still trust that he is with them and has not abandoned them

When we in a right standing with God, we are also in a position to have good relationships with other human beings, and particularly with the redeemed community to which we now belong. This concept of community is particularly strong in African thinking on ethics, and so will be dealt with at some length.

The Role of Community in African Ethics

Many years ago, John Taylor summarized the importance of community in African life:

> Every man is born into a community. He is a member of a family and he grows up inheriting certain family characteristics, certain property, certain obligations; he learns certain family traditions, certain patterns of behavior, and certain points of pride. In the same way, also, he is a member of a particular clan, tribe, and nation, and these will give him a particular culture and history, a particular way of looking at things, probably a particular religion. It is in such ways that every human being belongs to his own environment. He has his roots in a particular soil; he cannot be transplanted to a different soil without feeling the change very deeply; and if he is left with his roots in no soil his personality will become weak and unhappy and sick. Men and women who do not live in a community and feel that they really belong to it are not completely human. Something essential is missing, something which God has ordained for them as necessary for their true life. 'It is not good for the man to be alone' (Gen 2:18).[2]

---

[2] John V. Taylor, *Christianity and Politics in Africa* (Harmondsworth: Penguin, 1957), 35.

Unfortunately, the church in Africa is being robbed of this traditional and biblical concept of community, for it is fast falling into the Western model of becoming a conglomerate of individuals who come to church for spiritual meetings but fail to appreciate the organic nature of the church.

Bénézet Bujo, a Roman Catholic scholar from the DRC, recommends that community should be the organising framework for African ethics. He stresses that Africa has always thought in terms of a "we" ethics, involving not only the present generation, but also the dead (ancestors) and future generations (those yet to be born).[3] In applying this model to African Christian ethics, he argues that Jesus should be seen as the Great Ancestor.[4]

There arc many merits to this approach. First, community is indeed a critical part of African reality, and failure to appreciate this fact leads to a wrong concept of African morality. In Africa, it is the community, living and dead, that sanctions morality. Second, this approach recognizes the centrality of relationships and the fact that in Africa ethical issues are seen and interpreted in terms of community relationships. It is for this reason that African ethics is social rather than personal. For example, human sexuality is not a private matter as it is in Europe and North America. Marriage, procreation, divorce, polygamy and death are communal events. Those who fail to marry will not reproduce and will endanger the continuity of the family, past and future. Third, this approach honours the principle of community decision-making, in which the whole community must deliberate on an issue before any decision is taken. In Africa, no one person has the final word when it comes to making ethical decisions.

However, closer scrutiny reveals some problems with presenting community on its own as an adequate category for African ethics. First, in emphasizing community Bujo downplays the traditional role of God

---

[3] Bénézet Bujo, *Foundations of an African Ethic: Beyond the Universal Claims of Western Morality* (trans. Brian McNeil; New York: Crossroad, 2001), 71.

[4] Bujo (*Foundations,* 35) states that "African ethics is articulated in the framework of anamnesis, which involves remembering one's ancestors. As a narrative community, fellowship here on earth renews the existence of the community of the ancestors … Consequently, ethical behavior in the Black African context always involves reestablishing the presence of one's ancestors; for one who takes the anamnesis seriously is challenged to confront the ethical rules drawn up by the ancestors, in order to actualize anew the 'protological foundational act' which first called the clan fellowship into life." It should be noted that the concept of ancestors plays a prominent part in his theological thinking and development.

and the spirits. Belief in God and spirits has also played a key role in ethical thinking in Africa. Africans can appeal to something beyond the ancestors and the community when it comes to ethical matters. For example, those who have been wronged or misjudged by a family or community can appeal to the Almighty God to intervene on their behalf. If speaking Nigerian Pidgin English, the person will simply say *God de,* meaning "God exists". These words express a profound belief that God not only exists but also takes vengeance on behalf of those who have been wronged.

Second, Bujo's concept of community is not related to the redeemed community as presented in Scripture. He makes no serious attempt to interact with the biblical material. Thus he ignores the fact that the traditional African community is fallen, like everything else human in this world, and therefore needs transformation by the redeemed community as presented in Scripture.

African Christian ethics should therefore "concentrate upon what ways of thinking and what ways of acting are appropriate to the Christian community of faith ... Within that community a distinctive way of thinking and acting exists, nourished by the gospel, sustained by the grace of God, oriented toward the glory of God."[5]

What we need to develop is an African community ethic that not only reflects the African existential situation but is also rooted in Scripture.

Biblical Guidelines for African Christian Community

Drawing on the points made about Christian community in the previous chapter, it is possible to set out some clear biblical guidelines that must shape our thinking about the intersection of African Christian ethics and the African Christian community.

• Jesus Christ must be understood as the founder and keeper of this community. He gave it life and continues to maintain it. Hebrews 12:2 refers to him as "the author and perfecter of our faith."

---

[5] Alister E. McGrath, "Doctrine and Ethics", in *Readings in Christian Ethics Vol. I: Theory and Method* (ed. David K. Clark and Robert V. Rakestraw; Grand Rapids: Baker, 1994), 90. The essay is available online at www.bmei.org/jbem/volume5/num3/mcgrath_doctrine_and_ethics.php.

- The Scriptures must play a normative role in guiding the life of this redeemed community. Christian communities must take the Scriptures seriously. They are a reliable guide as to what we should believe and how we should live.

- The Christian community .is organic and experiences a deep relationship with the "great cloud of witnesses" in Hebrews 12:1. As mentioned in chapter 4, these witnesses include all the believers from Old and New Testament times to today, all those who are alive at present, and those yet to be born spiritually. These witnesses come from the worldwide church, but each local community also has its own heroes of faith whom we should celebrate in songs and stories and in the many rich ways in which Africans remember the dead. Their names and achievements should be celebrated in funeral rites, naming ceremonies, annual festivals and on other occasions. The community should also celebrate new life when individuals or communities come to conversion or are baptised. Rites like baptism and Holy Communion can be celebrated with dancing and song.

- The entire redeemed community must talk and deliberate about issues affecting their lives. The discussion must involve not only the trained pastor or shepherd but also the elders who have lived and experienced what it means to follow Jesus. For example, the current AIDS epidemic needs to be discussed by each community openly and seriously. Bujo makes the same point:

    > The entire church is the interpreter, that is, the fellowship of those who believe in Christ, and not only the magisterium. While all the members (including the oldest brother) read and hear the same sacred Scripture and tradition, the word that is heard is first chewed and digested on the individual level, before rumination takes place on the public level of the community.[6]

- The lives of key members of the present African Christian community should motivate other believers to live exemplary Christian lives. Paul makes it clear that African elders should demonstrate the kind of lifestyle that is appropriate for believers. It is easier to follow the examples of believers who have shared the same experiences.

---

[6] Bujo, *Foundations*, 156.

• The redeemed Christian community will have a public witness to an unbelieving world. They are to shine like lights in the surrounding darkness, and to be like cities, standing out clearly on the hilltops.

Questions

1. Which authors cited in Part 1 of this book contributed the most to your understanding of African Christian ethics (or challenged your thinking the most)? Consider seeking out the works of these authors so that you can benefit from direct study of their work in the future.

2. How does your community deal with an ethical issue? For example, how do the people deal with a girl who gets pregnant before marriage? Or with a boy who makes a girl pregnant before marriage?

3. Evaluate your concept of a redeemed community according to the biblical guidelines given in this chapter. Where are you strong? Where are you weak? How will you proceed to make sure that you are strong in each area of this foundational concept of African Christian ethics?

6

APPLYING AFRICAN CHRISTIAN ETHICS

It is now time to move on from the theoretical discussion of ethics to an examination of some contemporary ethical issues facing Christians and the church on the African continent. Before doing so, there are two points that must be made about how we need to apply the principles we have discussed in Part 1.

Real-Life Situations

Generating universal laws, as deontological approaches do, without close and careful examination of their applicability to specific situations is not helpful in dealing with ethical problems. This approach ends in abstractions that are not related to real life.

African Christian ethics must grapple with real-life situations. The Scriptures must be seriously studied and the solutions derived must be relevant. Thus when we confront an ethical problem ourselves or on behalf of someone we are counselling, we must carefully ask and answer the following questions:

1) What is the problem?
2) What does Scripture say about it?
3) What changes are needed in me (him, her), so that I (he, she) may do the right thing?[1]

In the discussion of specific ethical problems in the rest of this book, we shall attempt to follow this sequence, first presenting the problem African Christians face in their own context, then finding out what

---

[1] John Frame, "The Word of God and Christian Ethics" in *Readings in Christian Ethics, Vol. 1: Theory and Method* (eds. David K. Clark and Robert V. Rakestraw; Grand Rapids: Baker, 1994), 184.

Scripture has to say about the problem and finally addressing the issue of what action we are called to take.

Resolving Ethical Conflicts

When we deal with real-life situations rather than with theoretical principles, we sometimes find ourselves faced with situations where two ethical principles are in conflict. For example, abortion is wrong, but what should we do if continuing a pregnancy poses a threat to the mother's life? And should the church promote the use of condoms in order to save lives, even if some may see this as encouraging immorality?

Drs. John and Paul Feinberg have surveyed the possible responses to such conflicts, and suggest a range of options based on different moral theories: [2]

- *Antinomianism* insists that there are no moral norms of any sort, so norms can never conflict. This approach is not only non-Christian, but it also offers no guidance in difficult situations.

- *Generalism* argues that there are no universal norms, only general ones. For example, it is usually, but not always, morally right (obligatory) to tell the truth. The exceptions covered by the "not always" clause provide a way to resolve conflicts between moral duties.

- *Situationism* upholds only one norm as universally applicable, namely the basic duty to do the loving thing, or what brings the greatest good to the greatest number of people. The situation alone determines what is the best and most loving thing to do. Though this rule helps in deciding how to respond in particular situations, it does not relieve the tension that exists because God has given us certain definite and universal rules.

- *Non-conflicting or unqualified absolutism* argues that there are many ethical norms, all of which are universally applicable, and none of which ever conflict. The conflicts we see are only apparent, not real. This position sounds appealing but it flies in the face of our experience that there are indeed real moral conflicts.

---

[2] John S. Feinberg and Paul D. Feinberg, *Ethics for a Brave New World* (Wheaton: Crossway, 1993), 29. See also Norman Geisler, *Ethics: Alternatives and Issues* (Grand Rapids: Zondervan, 1971).

- *Conflicting absolutism* admits the existence of real moral conflicts. In such situations, one has to make a choice of what to do, but will be guilty whichever choice one makes.

- *Graded or hierarchical absolutism* also admits that real moral conflicts do sometimes occur. It argues that in such situations one has to determine which obligation has greater weight and act accordingly. The person who does this is not guilty of sin for breaking the lesser obligation, as long as he or she has genuinely chosen the greater good. For example, if during the Rwanda massacre in 1994 a Hutu Christian was asked, "Are there any Tutsis in your house?", and in fact there were, the Christian would be confronted with the conflict between the absolute norms of truth-telling and life-saving. He or she would have to weigh each moral norm and decide whether telling the truth takes precedence over saving lives, or vice versa. Whichever course of action he or she chose would have consequences. The greater good involves choosing the option that expresses the greater love for others.

In this book, I recommend the approach called graded absolutism, which takes a hierarchical view of ethics. When real moral conflicts occur, one should try to determine which moral obligation has the greater weight and will do the greatest good.

Conclusion

As we embark on the study of particular ethical issues in the rest of this book, we would do well to be guided by the wisdom expressed in the following quotation:

> Christian ethics is not rooted in principles such as love or justice, nor in virtues embodied in the narratives of communities, nor in the existence of social structures deemed to be part of the created order. All of these may be important elements in Christian ethics, but they do not form the foundation of moral thought, character and actions. This becomes clear in the biblical patterns of moral teaching, for many parts of Scripture reveal that moral injunctions have a larger grounding that

forms the basis for their acceptance. Thus, ethics in the Bible is not blind obedience to laws, principles, or virtues but rather a response to the living, all-powerful God of the universe, who is himself the foundation of those moral guidelines. The content of our moral responses are certainly known and shaped by the biblical norms in the various forms, but ultimately they are reflections of God's character, purposes, and actions in the world.[3]

Questions

1. Is your focus properly on both current situations and eternal realities? How might you adjust your focus?

2. Have you or someone you know ever confronted a situation where ethical principles were in conflict? Describe the situation, identify the principles and the consequences of acting on each of them, and indicate what action was decided on and why.

---

[3] Hollinger, *Choosing the Good*, 64–65.

PART TWO

CONTEMPORARY ETHICAL ISSUES

SECTION A
POLITICAL ISSUES

INTRODUCTION TO POLITICAL ISSUES

The terms "state" and "government" are often used interchangeably, as when we talk about the relationship of church and state, but technically they have different meanings. A state can be understood as "a nation in its corporate capacity and organized for civil government."[1] Sudan, for example, qualifies as a state because it has the key elements for statehood, namely a population, a geographical location, a government and is independent.

Government is the form or system by which a state is governed. It can be used to refer to the institutions associated with government or to "the activity or process of governing, i.e. the exercising of control over others; the inducing of certain others to behave in a specific ways".[2] Governments can take different forms and may be monarchical, republican, democratic, totalitarian or military dictatorships. Sometimes these forms are combined when the head of state is a military man while the provincial governors and ministers are civilians. This hybrid form is common in Africa, where many heads of states come to power through a coup but then practise some form of civilian government.

The citizens of a state deserve to have a safe and harmonious context in which to live and raise their families. Unfortunately, this is not often the case in Africa because of serious political problems. Many of these problems spring from the failure of governments to fulfil their key function, which is it to maintain order, justice and freedom.

Justice and freedom are not possible without some kind of order. Thus states seek to enact laws that will support helpful behaviour, restrict harmful behaviour and generally encourage harmonious co-existence. They may have to use physical power or coercion to enforce obedience to these laws. This use of power was supported by the seventeenth-

---

[1] A. R. Vidler, "Church and State", *Westminster Dictionary of Christian Ethics*, 91.

[2] S. P. Finer, "Government", *A Dictionary of the Social Sciences*, 294.

century British philosopher Thomas Hobbes, who believed that, left to themselves, people act in brutal ways. He argued that people should be encouraged to agree to give supreme authority to one person or one institution that can exercise powerful, external control.

Some governments, however, take the power to maintain order to extremes. Their thinking is similar to that of Nicolo Machiavelli, a sixteenth-century Italian statesman and political thinker, who argued that a ruler must be prepared to act unscrupulously and risk being accused of cruelty in order to prevent disorder and bloodshed. It is easy to see how his beliefs can result in the rise of dictatorial and totalitarian states like some in Africa. That is why the state's responsibility to maintain order needs to be balanced against the need to provide justice and freedom to its citizens.

The justice the state must provide goes beyond merely settling disputes and punishing wrongdoers. Justice also involves the way the state functions and the way honours, wealth, burdens and benefits are distributed to individuals and groups. There is much debate in Africa about how these things should be distributed. Should the decision be based on merit, that is, on what someone or some group has accomplished, or should everyone receive exactly the same treatment because everyone has the same intrinsic value, or should the distribution be based on the concrete needs of specific individuals or groups?

Unfortunately, there is often little evidence of justice in Africa. Not only are individuals denied justice by corrupt police and judges, but access to certain opportunities and jobs is unfairly restricted to certain ethnic or religious groups or to members of rich and powerful families.

The marginalization of certain groups and injustice when it comes to economic development and political appointments result in civil unrest and political uprisings, as happened in Rwanda. In Nigeria allegations that the government has not been equitable have led to bloody clashes between Christians and Muslims and between ethnic groups. If is there is to be peace in Africa, people must be protected from exploitation by others.

Freedom from political oppression is also essential if there is to be peace. Freedom allows people to live in accordance with what they believe and to be true to their consciences. When groups feel that their freedom is threatened, there are often rebellions such as those in Nigeria, Sudan, Ethiopia, Morocco, South Africa, Uganda, Liberia and Congo.

Faced with these rebellions, governments often resort to violence and oppression in order to maintain order.

International bodies such as the United Nations and the African Union have been set up to intervene when there are national and international crises. For example, the Nigerian-led Economic Community Monitoring Group (ECOMOG) intervened to end the crisis in Liberia. Such groups insist that governments do not have unrestricted power to oppress their subjects but are answerable to the higher authority of international law.

Christians would agree that the power of state is not absolute but is derived from God, to whom rulers are answerable. But the church has had little to say on political issues relating to order, justice and freedom. What has been said has often been hesitant, ambivalent, incoherent and unpersuasive. One reason for this is that African Christians have been very uncertain about the roles of the church and the state and have questioned whether the church (and individual Christians) should be involved in politics at all. Thus **chapter 7** addresses this issue.

Christians are also not immune to involvement in the civil and religious wars that plague Africa. So **chapter 8** deals with the issue of war and addresses how African Christians should respond in situations where ethnic and religious violence prevent the state from maintaining order, justice and freedom.

Conflict also sometimes occurs between employers and their employees or between citizens and their government. In such cases, there may be a call for a strike in order to make a point about the political or economic situation. Christians have to decide whether it is right for them to join in such protests, and so strikes will be discussed in **chapter 9**.

7
CHURCH AND STATE

The issue of the relationship between the church and state in Africa is complex and controversial.[1] Should the church as a body seek to play a role in political affairs, as the Roman Catholic Church and Anglican churches have often done? Or should the church shun any involvement in politics and concentrate on its spiritual mission? What about individual church members – should they be encouraged to participate in politics or to shun it?

Many of the Western Christian missionary societies in Africa were strongly influenced by the Lutheran pietists who advocated strict separation of church and state. This position carried over into many of the national churches that emerged from these missions. For example, the Sudan Interior Mission (SIM), founded by Canadian and American missionaries, insisted that the church was to be seen as entirely different from the state. In Nigeria, SIM gave rise to the Evangelical Church of West Africa (ECWA), which followed the footsteps of its founders and maintained separation of church and state. Pastors were forbidden to have anything to do with politics because it was deemed dirty and worldly. If they wanted to go into politics, they had to surrender their ministerial licenses. Similar positions were taken by most African churches that grew out of Western missions. They held themselves aloof from politics and were deeply suspicious of it. Christians were discouraged from having any involvement with the state.

In contemporary Africa, the situation has changed dramatically. Professor Cornelius Olowola, the president of ECWA, now proclaims

---

[1] In what follows, the "state" is equivalent to the structure of government and the political system. The "church" include all communities who claim some allegiance to Christian beliefs rooted in Scripture. These communities may be Roman Catholic, Protestant, Evangelical, Ethiopian Orthodox, Pentecostal or African Initiated Churches. Their form of church government may be papal, episcopalian, presbyterian or independent.

that it is the duty of Christians and the church to be actively involved in politics and government. ECWA members and even ordained ECWA ministers are now pursuing politics and careers in government. Other Christian churches in Africa have also renounced their previous positions on the separation of church and state and advocate involvement.

How did this change come about? Which of the two positions, aloofness or involvement, is biblical? As we attempt to answer these questions, we will first consider the African context, before moving on to study what the Bible has to say about the nature of the state and the relationship between God's people and the state.

The Changing African Context

Political, sociological, economic and theological factors have all contributed to the change in the perception of the correct relationship between church and state.

Political factors

In the 1960s men such as Kwame Nkrumah of Ghana, Nnamdi Azikwe of Nigeria, Kenneth Kaunda of Zambia, Julius Nyerere of Tanzania, Jomo Kenyatta of Kenya and Milton Obote of Uganda led their countries to independence from their colonial masters. Given the strong links between the missionaries and the colonial powers, it is not surprising that missionary organizations discouraged believers from participating in politics. Yet the struggle against colonialism resulted in many Africans becoming more politically aware and involved in political activity.

As Christians rose to positions of political power, they drew the church into the political sphere. Some appealed to Christian voters as their major constituency. For example, in 1991 Frederick Chiluba, the former president of Zambia, publicly declared Zambia a Christian nation.[2] Similarly, prior to the 1999 general election, President Obasanjo of Nigeria claimed that while imprisoned by the military he had been

---

[2] On behalf of the Zambian people, Chiluba repented, "of our wicked ways of idolatry, witchcraft, the occult, immorality, injustice and corruption … I submit the Government and the entire nation of Zambia to the Lordship of Jesus Christ. I further declare that Zambia is a Christian nation that will seek to be governed by the righteous principles of the word of God. Righteousness and justice must prevail in all levels of authority, and then we shall see the righteousness of Zambia." Quoted in Paul Freston, *Evangelicals and Politics in Asia, Africa and Latin America* (Cambridge: Cambridge University Press, 2001), 158.

born again. After winning the election, he announced that he would be a Christian president. This gained him considerable favour with the Christian community.

Sociological factors

The population of many African countries is classified as either Christian or Muslim, and these religious affiliations often play a significant role in how people vote. Muslim politicians appeal to Muslims for votes while Christian politicians appeal to the Christian constituency. The extent to which voting mirrors this sociological division is very clear in places like Sudan and Nigeria. During the 2003 elections in Nigeria, Muhammadu Buhari, one of the presidential candidates, allegedly stated that a Muslim should never vote for a Christian candidate. This claim is indicative of the politicizing of religion in Nigeria. The same politicizing is evident in the secret admission of Nigeria to the association of Muslim states known as the Organization of the Islamic Conference and in the introduction of Sharia as the legal code in many states in northern Nigeria. There is a perception that Muslims, who form part of every Nigerian government, have been pushing an Islamic agenda to the detriment of Christian interests. Consequently religion and politics are now seen as bedfellows, with political power offering opportunities to enhance the status of one's religion.

However, the heated debate roused by Buhari's comment also shows that it is no longer possible for any group to isolate itself from other religious or ethnic groups. Buhari needed the support of Christian voters if he wished to be elected president.

Economic factors

Christians have come to realize that politics affects economic development, for it is in part the process of persuading governments to act in certain ways and is thus a means of getting things accomplished. It encompasses all the activities of "negotiation, argument, discussion, application of force, persuasion, etc, by which an issue is agitated or settled."[3] Many political issues have a direct effect on local communities. Failure to get involved in politics may result in economic deprivation,

---

[3] J. Gould, "Politics", *Dictionary of the Social Sciences*, 516.

while involvement may help to improve their community's infrastructure, education and lifestyle. Improvements in the economic situation of the community also improve the economic situation of the church. The church has also realized that having church members in government makes it easier to get responses from officials and to have requests met.

Religious factors

Christians no longer see politics as unchristian and dirty, which is how it was perceived before the 1970s. Since then, the founding of many Christian organizations such as the Christian Students Social Movement of Nigeria (1977), the Christian Social Movement of Nigeria and the Christian Association of Nigeria has brought a new appreciation of politics and government.

During the 1970s Christians in Nigeria began to express concern for the nation, which was believed to be under the forces of darkness. All-night prayer meetings, fasting and prayers for the nation were common in churches and parachurch organizations. Christian student organizations like Scripture Union (SU), the Nigeria Fellowship of Christian Students (NIFES) and the Fellowship of Christian Students (FCS) played a key role in these prayers for revival. There was much quoting of verses like 2 Chronicles 7:14, "If my people, who are called by my name, will humble themselves and pray and seek my face and turn from their wicked ways, then will I hear from heaven and will forgive their sin and will heal their land" and Proverbs 14:34, "Righteousness exalts a nation, but sin is a disgrace to any people".

Christian organizations and Christian students continue this interest in political matters. Prayer and fasting are still considered key elements in the effort to bring political healing to the nation. Even Christian leaders are now involved in politics. The president of the Pentecostal Fellowship of Nigeria (PFN) has said that:

> God expects us to reach a situation whereby we will decree
> that there will be no rain in Nigeria (and it will not rain). As

> Proverbs 28:2 says, "when the righteous are in authority, the
> people rejoice"... And how are we going to get someone
> who is righteous in authority? ... Thieves will never vote for a
> policeman ... only the righteous will vote for the righteous ...
> So... it is by winning the masses to Jesus ... PFN will become
> PFA. We will take over the whole of Africa.[4]

Pentecostals had once been very opposed to any link between the church
and politics, yet in the 2003 general elections in Nigeria, a Pentecostal
preacher, Rev. Chris Okotie, ran for the presidency.

The once radical distinction between church and state no longer
stands. In its place, the church is now seen as an important and necessary
ingredient of society that must be actively involved in the political
realities of its context in order to maintain its relevance.

Christian Theology and the State

Christian thinking about the relationship between the church and the
state cannot be based solely on individual proof texts. It has to take into
account the broad sweep of Christian theology, the contents of both the
Old and New Testaments, and the church's interpretation of these texts
over the centuries.

Our theological presuppositions affect our understanding of the
relationship between church and state. For example, those who make
a radical distinction between body and soul and between spiritual and
material matters favour a radical separation of church and state. Those
who have a more holistic view based on their understanding of God's
involvement in a sinful world argue that the church needs to be involved
in the world. Thus the following statement is true:

> Our understanding of the function of the church in society
> and its relation to the community and to the state depends
> in the last resort on our doctrine, or our undefined and
> unconscious assumptions, regarding the relation of the church
> to the world.[5]

---

[4] Freston, *Evangelicals and Politics,* 186.
[5] W. A. Visser 't Hooft and J. H. Oldham, *The Church and Its Function in Society* (London: Allen
& Unwin, 1937), 108.

John Stott points out that four main areas of doctrine are important when thinking about this topic:[6]

- *Doctrine of God*. God is the Creator, and the world that he created is good (Gen 1:1, 21, 25). We should thus reject the Greek dualistic notion that matter is evil and only the spiritual is good. We have a mandate to be concerned with how God's world is governed.

- *Doctrine of man*. God's world has been corrupted by sin (Rom 5:12–21) and is full of dangers and temptations to sin (Eph 6:12, 1 John 2:15–17). There is thus a need for laws to restrain people from committing evil acts and to encourage them to work together. Christians are warned not to love the world or the things that are in it (1 John 2:15–16). They are to set their minds on the things above and not on the things on earth (Col 3:1–5). Thus while we are right to be concerned about how God's world is governed, we must not focus solely to earthly concerns. We must not be surprised when human sin and corruption circumvent laws and derail political plans. Looking at ourselves, we must be aware that our own political thinking is affected by our own sinfulness and that we too are vulnerable to the temptations that come with political power.

- *Doctrine of salvation*. There are demonic forces that are totally opposed to the kingdom of God and seek to control the world (Eph 6:12). But God's purpose for this world is to save it. He sent his Son to die and rise from the grave to provide salvation for his creation (John 3:16; Rom 8:19–22). God's commitment to saving the world means that we too must be concerned to fight the inroads of evil. However, we must acknowledge that we cannot win this battle without divine intervention.

- *Doctrine of God's kingdom*. Those who have experienced salvation though faith in Jesus Christ are called to be the salt and light of the world (Matt 5:13–16). As God's ambassadors, Christians are to represent him in all that they do to his glory (Phil 3:20; Col 3:23). Ultimate victory is assured when Christ comes back to set up his kingdom (Rev 21:1–6; 21:1–5). Meanwhile, Christians are called upon to live a holy life in the world (Rom 12:2; 1 Pet 1:15–16).

---

[6] John Stott, *The Lausanne Covenant. An Exposition and Commentary* (Minneapolis: World Wide Publications, 1975), 26.

While these basic theological presuppositions underlie our thinking about the world in which we live, it is also important to look in more detail at what the Bible has to say about the nature and purpose of government and of the state, and about the way God's people should relate to it. Only then will we be able to formulate biblical answers to questions like: What is the nature of the state? What is the role of government? What are its primary functions?

Many people have set out to answer these and similar questions, and the answers they reach are often affected by their particular political affiliation and philosophy of government. We should be careful not to dismiss all that is said about the nature and purpose of government by historians, political philosophers and experienced politicians. Our theological understanding of general revelation, in which God reveals truths in reason, nature and history, means that these people may well have valid insights. However, we also have to consider God's special revelation in the Scriptures, which contains explicit and implicit statements relevant to a discussion on church and state.

Biblical Perspectives on the State

When reading the Scriptures to find out what they tell us about the relationship between the church and the state, we need to exercise discernment to tell which statements are meant to be prescriptive (telling us what we should do), and which are merely descriptive (telling us how particular people in a particular situation addressed their political problems).

Church and state in the Old Testament

The church as such did not exist in Old Testament times. But God still had his chosen people, the Israelites. Looking at the record of their history may help up to answer the question: If God were to establish a government, what would it look like? Would it be theocratic (governed by God), monarchical (governed by a king), or democratic (governed by the people)?

At the Exodus from Egypt, the Israelites were led out into the desert by strong individuals like Moses and Joshua. With time, this system of individual leadership developed into a tribal league in which tribal leaders assisted national leaders like Moses and Joshua (Josh 7). After the conquest of the Promised Land, the tribes scattered to settle in cities, towns and other communities. There tribal leaders heard criminal cases, administered civil laws and customs and maintained general law and order in their community. Each tribe was somewhat independent of the others. Particularly strong leaders like Othniel (Judg 3:9) would sometimes rule over several tribes in a region. These "judges" often served as military leaders who responded to external aggression. However, their rule proved unreliable and inconsistent, and led the historians who wrote the book of Judges to complain of anarchy in Israel and lament the lack of a king (Judg 21:25).

During the time of the judges, we also find mention of kingship and an early form of democracy in which the people tried to force Gideon to accept the position of king and start a dynasty. Gideon responded by insisting that the nation was a theocracy: "I will not rule over you, nor will my son rule over you. The Lord will rule over you" (Judg 8:22–23).

Two centuries later, during the time of Samuel, the Israelites again demanded a king (1 Sam 7). Saul became the first king over Israel, and was followed by David, who is described as a man after God's own heart (1 Sam 13:14). This description of him refers less to David's character than to his place in God's plan, which was predicted by Jacob in Genesis 49:10. David's coming to power was no accident, as is clear from the Davidic covenant, which promises that the Messiah will be a descendant of David (2 Sam 7; 13). The government during David's times was more organized and larger than it had ever been before in the history of Israel. Israel existed as God's chosen people, surrounded by many other nations. Yet despite the strong government established by David and Solomon, the kingdom they established collapsed and split in two after Solomon's reign. The years that followed saw ongoing disintegration during the reigns of both weak and strong kings. Eventually Israel was reduced to a vassal state of the mighty Babylonian Empire, and was ruled by governors appointed in Babylon.

So what form of government does God favour? Israel saw many different forms of government over the centuries, and all of them are described as being endorsed by God. God was the one who raised up Moses and Joshua (Exod 3:10; Josh 1:5) and the judges (Judg 3:15; 6:14; 13:5), Saul and David and many of the other kings after them. He was also the one who overthrew the king, and sent the people into exile

(2 Chr 36:17). It seems that God is prepared to use different forms of government to suit his purposes at different times, and that no one form can claim to be perfect.

The Old Testament also makes it abundantly clear that those who are in positions of power in government are not to use their situation to accumulate wealth for themselves (Deut 17:16–17). Their task is to uphold justice and protect the weak (Ps 72:1–4; Jer 21:12). God will judge rulers who support injustice, whether they are leaders of his own people (Mic 3:9–12) or of other nations (Amos 1).

Church and state in the New Testament

In the New Testament, the context of the relationship between God's people (the church) and the state was very different from that in the Old Testament. There was no question of believers exercising political power. Israel was under Roman rule, and Jesus was thus asked questions about how God's people should live (and specifically about whether they should pay taxes) when governed by non-believers. His response to the Pharisees, "Give to Caesar what is Caesar's, and to God what is God's (Matt 22:21), indicates that he saw believers as having a responsibility to both God and the state. This dual relationship was not without tension. Jesus referred to the political ruler, Herod, as a *fox* (Luke 13:32), implying that he was a predator. In Acts we find the apostles disobeying the Jewish religious authorities, who also exercised some civil powers, saying that they would rather obey God than men (Acts 5:29). Still later the state is portrayed as the enemy of the church (Rev 13).

Jesus' teaching on believers' being salt and light indicates that we are not to withdraw from the world and from politics but have a necessary and important role in the world.

The early church began its missionary outreach as a minority in a pagan and hostile state. There are, however, glimpses of what it thought of its relationship to the state. The apostles saw government as divinely instituted with the right to enforce order and restrain certain types of antisocial behaviour (Rom 13:1–5; 1 Pet 2:13–14). Christians were thus to pay their taxes and to show proper respect to the authorities God had set in place (Rom 13:6–7; 1 Pet 2:15–17). They were also to pray for the "kings and all those in authority, that we may live peaceful and quiet lives in all godliness and holiness" (1 Tim 2:1–2). The security provided by government made it far easier for them to carry out their mission.

Guidelines derived from Scripture

The contemporary church is confronted with issues that were never explicitly dealt with in Scripture. For example, how should believers behave in a multicultural democracy where they have duties as voters and citizens? In addressing these issues, we cannot simply cite statements made in biblical times without regard to the context in which they were made. We have to look for broader principles that are implicit in the Bible and allow these to guide our thinking about the relationship between the church and the state. Here are some of the principles that can be extracted:

- *Governments have a divine origin.* God is the one who raises up and deposes rulers. He did that in Old Testament times, and the apostles assert that he is still doing the same thing in New Testament times (Rom 13:1). Prime ministers and presidents cannot boast that they came to power solely through their own effort.

- *Governments function on behalf of God.* Those in government are God's servants (Rom 13:4). God cares for the world he has created and desires to see order and justice for all. Thus in creating order and ensuring justice, governments are carrying out his desires. Rulers may not always be aware of this, or even seem to be carrying out this task, but God can still use their actions to achieve his purposes. He used the Babylonian ruler Nebuchadnezzar to punish Israel. He called Cyrus, a Persian, "my anointed" because Cyrus would allow the Jews to return from exile (Isa 45:1).

- *God's eschatological design sets the standard by which governments ought to operate* (Rom 13). In other words, one day Jesus will return to establish God's government. He will judge justly and will reward the godly and punish the ungodly. His just government should set the standard for all governments.

- *Governments exist for the good of those they rule.* An important function of governments is to do good to those who are righteous and to punish wrongdoers (Rom 13:4–5; see also 1 Pet 2:13–14).

- *Government exists in all spheres of human responsibility.* God not only appointed kings to rule Israel, but he has also given responsibility for the wise use of authority to others, including elders, priests, officials, parents – and even children, who are called to learn how to live as citizens.

- *God's people are called to have an impact on the world.* The Israelites were called to be an example to the nations around them, who should have been asking, "What other nation is so great as to have such righteous decrees and laws? (Deut 4:7). Christians are called to be salt and light (Matt 5:13–14).

Church and State in History

Having seen what the Bible has to say about the relationship between the church and the state, it is worth pausing to see how the church has interpreted biblical teaching over the centuries. Two main positions can be identified, although there are many variations within these streams.

The Catholic position is based on the work of Thomas Aquinas, who had an optimistic view of human nature and thus also of the relationship between church and state. He focused on the goodness of God's creation and argued that the state was an expression of the social nature that God had implanted in people at creation. Thus the state was capable of contributing to the establishment of God's kingdom here on earth, under the guidance of the church.

Protestants are less convinced of the goodness of human nature. They argue that while the world as God created it was good, it has been corrupted by sin and is now opposed to God and all that he stands for. God's kingdom cannot be brought into existence in this world. Martin Luther states his position categorically:

> We must divide all the children of Adam into two classes, the first belong to the kingdom of God, the second to the kingdom of the world. Those belonging to kingdom of God are all true believers in Christ and are subject to Christ and the

gospel of the kingdom ... All who are not Christians belong
to the kingdom of the world and are under the law. Since few
believe and still fewer live a Christian life, do not resist evil, and
themselves do no evil, God has provided for non-Christians a
different government outside the Christian estate and God's
kingdom, and has subjected them to the sword [i.e. to the
coercive power exercised by human rulers] ... For this reason
the two kingdoms must be sharply distinguished and both
permitted to remain; the one to produce piety, the other to
bring about external peace and prevent evil deeds; neither is
sufficient in the world without the other.[7]

Luther's radical distinction between the church and state did not lead him
to object to church participation in the political arena. He saw political
power as falling "within the sphere of God's sovereignty and providence,
and hence the Christian, whether prince or subject, has to serve God in
the political sphere as well as in the Christian community."[8]

However, others took Luther's separation of church and state further
and argued that the church ought not to be involved in politics in any
way. The theological focus shifted away from God as Creator to God as
Saviour, offering salvation through faith in the finished work of Jesus
Christ on the cross. The end result was a very individualistic form of
Christianity "which regards the gospel as having to do only with the
salvation of individual souls and looks on participation in the affairs of
the world as irrelevant or questionable. The church is thought of as an
ark in which saved souls may find refuge from a world that is doomed
to destruction."[9]

Over the centuries, the church has sometimes been closer to the
Roman Catholic position and sometimes to the Protestant position. It
has never fully settled on one or the other. The reason, quite simply, is
that to the end of time, there will be a tension (even a conflict) between
the church and the state. This must be if both realities are to fulfil their
proper God-given roles. Christians are citizens of human and divine
kingdoms, and must live uncomfortably in a world to which they do not
fully belong.

---

[7] Martin Luther, "Secular Authority: To what Extent It Ought to be Obeyed", 1523, WA 11: 249d.

[8] Jose Miguez Bonino, *Toward a Christian Political Ethics* (Philadelphia: Fortress, 1965), 23.

[9] Visser 't Hooft and Oldham, *The Church and Its Function in Society*, 123.

> The Christian can never escape the tension caused by his dual allegiance. He is a citizen of this world which, though fallen and sinful, was created by God and is yet used by God for the realization of His purposes. But the Christian is called to citizenship of another world – and as a church member already belongs to it – the Kingdom whose rule is love. He is led to attempt to apply the rule of the Kingdom to the affairs of this fallen world, his other home, and it will not fit. He may start off with great hopes, but in the end, it is always the same, the application fails. It should not surprise us. Does anything in human experience suggest that love may be institutionalized or legislated for?[10]

It is because of these tensions that two diametrically opposed positions have emerged around the idea of separation of church and state.

Arguments For and Against Separation

It is now time to look at the specific arguments put forward by those who oppose Christian involvement in the state and consider the responses of those who support it.

Jesus distinguished two distinct kingdoms

While there is no disputing the existence of the two kingdoms, the kingdom of God and the kingdom of this world, it does not follow that Christians have no role in the earthly kingdom. Even when he declared, "My Kingdom is not of this world" (John 18:36), Jesus still showed respect for the authority that Pilate had been given by God (John 19:11; see also Rom 13:1–8; 1 Pet 2:17). Moreover, Christ told us to love our neighbours as ourselves. His words indicate that we do have a role in our world.

The believer's chief responsibility is evangelism

Those who support an exclusive focus on evangelism quote verses like "The fruit of the righteous is a tree of life, and he who wins souls is wise" (Prov 11:30) and the Great Commission when Jesus commanded

---

[10] Walter James, *The Christian in Politics* (Oxford: Oxford University Press, 1962), 188.

his followers to go and make disciples (Matt 28:18–20). They argue that the best way to change society is not political involvement but dealing with people's sinful condition. Those who make this argument speak as if

> the church is able to remain angelically pure and free from any contamination of power or geopolitical aims. For them, the church is only the loyal servant of Jesus Christ. It accomplishes the mission it received from Jesus Christ and nothing else. Its actions receive their principles only from heaven, not from earth. The motivation for action is pure obedience to Christ and the Spirit, without any interference from human factors. And indeed, one can imagine an evangelical mission whereby Christians, sent by heavenly inspiration, would go throughout the world to all the peoples, announcing the same message with the same words, indifferent to the different results of their preaching. Is such an evangelization possible? Perhaps in theory, but it certainly does not seem to exist.[11]

Furthermore, those who speak only of evangelism are missing the point that the gospel is to be preached in word and in deed. Though Christ's ultimate concern is for our spiritual needs, his actions during his life on earth show that he was also concerned about people's social and physical needs. Thus Christian involvement in political activity designed to improve people's circumstances does not contradict the command to preach the gospel.

Christian ethics is only for Christians

It is sometimes argued that non-believers are not interested in Christian ethics, which apply only to Christians and do not work when applied to secular society. But the Bible makes it abundantly clear that God is sovereign over the whole world, whether believing or unbelieving. He does not have one set of standards for believers and another for unbelievers.

---

[11] Jose Comblin, *The Church and the National Security State* (Maryknoll: Orbis, 1979), 197,

Christians are called to be holy and separate

Some Christians argue that politics is such a dirty game that it is impossible to avoid being tainted by corruption and unprincipled behaviour that conflicts with the Christians call to holiness. The argue that any Christian who tries to get involved in politics will eventually be put in the unacceptable position of being forced to compromise his beliefs.

> It is spiritually dangerous … to get too involved. There is the sneaking suspicion that it is really unhealthy for a Christian to take too much of an interest in society. To be active in politics, struggling for improvements in the world; active in one's trade union, working for better wages and conditions; active in a local pressure group to protect the community from the big stick of central government – all of this is seen as somehow less than the best in Christian life.[12]

This argument reflects traces of Greek dualistic thinking, with its distinction between the spiritual which is pure and the material world which is evil. It also ignores the fact that it is not politics itself which is dirty but those who practice it. The goal of promoting order, justice and freedom is a noble one. But the human beings who practise politics have sinful natures. They are thus easily tempted by corrupt practices. But the same truth applies to every realm of human activity, whether sex, business, politics or marriage. Politics is, therefore, not dirty in itself; it is those who practice it who can make it a dirty business.

Christ will soon return and solve all social problems

It is argued that Christ's return makes Christian involvement in politics unnecessary. But this argument does not hold water. We do not know exactly when Christ will return, but we do know that he has called believers to be salt and light in the world (Matt 5:13–14) and to continue to live holy lives in society (Eph 5:8; 1 Thess 4:1)

---

[12] John Gladwin, *God's People in God's World: Biblical Motives for Social Involvement* (Downers Grove: IVP, 1980), 24.

The church risks repeating serious mistakes

The corporate church has often made serious mistakes when it has been involved in politics. The merger of church and state during the reign of Constantine resulted in compromise in the church. The church hailed Frederick Chiluba's declaration that Zambia was a Christian nation, and was then embarrassed and split when allegations of corruption emerged. The Dutch Reformed Church in South Africa has had to publicly repent of its support for apartheid. The church in Burundi is alleged to have been passive during the massacre of some ethnic groups in the country. But it is wrong to allow fear of making mistakes to paralyze us and prevent any involvement in politics. By the same logic, the fact that some marriages end in divorce or spousal abuse should discourage Christians from marrying!

Moreover, failure to get involved in cultural, political, social and economic problems in light of Scripture and on behalf of humanity has also often been a serious mistake that has left the church irrelevant and even reproachable. The church in Germany has been heavily criticized for not protesting against the Holocaust. A report on the genocide in Rwanda makes sad reading:

> More than 90 percent of Rwanda's people were baptized Christians (65 percent Catholic, 20 percent Protestants or Anglican, about 5 percent Adventist) … Church leaders, who received patronage and lavish gifts from the ruling party, too often remained silent in the face of injustice, unwilling to exert the authority of their positions in the moral vacuum within Rwandan society in the Habyarimana's last years. Their statements during the genocide and in the chaos that followed were inadequate and insignificant, often sounding as if they had been written by a public relations person for the interim government. For this silent acquiescence and lack of courage, the churches as institutions paid dearly. They will continue to live under a cloud of suspicion for years to come.[13]

---

[13] Hugh McCullum, *The Angels Have Left Us: The Rwanda Tragedy and the Churches* (Geneva: World Council of Churches, 1995), 65.

Further Arguments for Involvement

Some additional arguments are also advanced for why Christians should be involved in politics and government.

The first argument is purely pragmatic: it is impossible for a Christian to be completely uninvolved in the social and political life of the country in which they live. As citizens of this world, Christians enjoy the benefits government offers such as mail service, police protection and maintenance of roads and hospitals.

> Every time we travel on the buses or drive on the roads or visit the health service or take our children to school, we are demonstrating in a practical way that politicians do good and necessary things … If … we maintain that all these different areas of human life are good, then it must follow that they bear some direct relationship to God's care for the world. That being the case it is impossible to deny to Christians involvement in the world.[14]

The church lives in the world and therefore needs the world. If it attempts to deny this, it lapses "into a position of irrelevance and insignificance in relation to the life of the world which is incompatible with its faith in God's sovereignty and fatherly care".[15]

There are also good theological grounds for the church to be involved in politics: "The suffering caused by existing evils makes a claim upon our sympathy which the Christian heart and conscience cannot ignore."[16] The evils that cause suffering are rooted in immoral and unjust structures that result in underdevelopment, oppression, poverty, illiteracy and unemployment. These existing systems and structures must be challenged on moral grounds. The church will be accused of "interfering" when it makes accusations against the economic and social order, but to fail to do so is to betray the trust committed to it, "for the commission given to the church is that it carries out the purpose of God".[17]

---

[14] Gladwin, *God's People in God's World*, 25.

[15] Visser 't Hooft and Oldham, *The Church and Its Function in Society*, 126.

[16] William Temple, *Christianity and the Social Order* (Baltimore: Penguin, 1956), 17.

[17] Ibid., 23.

Without Christian involvement in politics and government, Christians cannot influence society. God can, and often does, put godly men and women in specific political situations to effect changes. The examples of Daniel, Mordecai, Esther and Joseph are persuasive. Even in our age, Christian politicians have had an impact on the political terrain in their countries. The former president of Nigeria Olusegun Obasanjo publicly confessed his Christian faith and gave a positive image of the Christian faith in political engagement. He attracted men and women of integrity into his government.

Finally, involvement in society was central and mandatory for the early Christians. Jesus Christ, the founder of the Christian religion, commands his followers to be salt and light in the world (Matt 5:13–16). These two images indicate that Christians should permeate the world to preserve it and should illuminate it to provide guidance and direction. John Stott highlights other important aspects of these symbols: Christians are fundamentally different from non-Christians, Christians can influence non-Christian society and Christians must retain their distinctiveness.[18]

The Nature of the Church's Involvement

If we accept that the church does indeed have both pragmatic and theological reasons for getting involved in politics, another question arises: What should be the nature of the involvement? How should the church and individual Christians relate to society?

Experience has shown that this is an exceedingly difficult question to answer. Archbishop William Temple summarizes the situation well when he says:

> Either Christians try to act as churchmen in the world, only to find that the world refuses to be ordered on the principles proper to the church; or else they look out for the secular policy most congenial to their Christian outlook, only to find

---

[18] John Stott, *New Issues Facing Christians Today* (London: Marshall Pickering, 1999), 74–76. Stott notes, "On the one hand, we have to permeate non-Christian society, and immerse ourselves in the life of the world. On the other, while doing so, we have to avoid becoming assimilated to the world. We must retain our Christian convictions, values, standards and lifestyle. We are back with the 'double identity' of the church ('holiness' and 'worldliness')."

that their Christianity is a dispensable adjunct of no practical importance.[19]

Guidelines can be suggested to help those wrestling with these issues, but the application of these guidelines will differ in different contexts. Temple provides the following short list of the church's responsibilities:

1) Its members must fulfil their moral responsibilities and functions in a Christian spirit;
2) Its members must exercise their purely civic rights in a Christian spirit;
3) It must itself supply them with a systematic statement of principles to aid them in doing these two things, and this will carry with it a denunciation of customs or institutions in contemporary life and practice which offend against those principles.[20]

The Oxford Conference of 1937 came up with a more detailed outline of the duties of the church to the state:

a) that of praying for the state, its people and its governments;
b) that of loyalty and obedience to the state, disobedience becoming a duty only if obedience would be clearly contrary to the command of God;
c) that of cooperation with the state in promoting the welfare of the citizens and of lending moral support to the state when it upholds the standards of justice set forth in the Word of God;
d) that of criticism of the state when it departs from those standards;
e) that of holding before men in all their legislation and administration those principles which make for upholding the dignity of man who is made in the image of God;
f) that of permeating the public life with the spirit of Christ and of training up men and women who as Christians can contribute to this end.

---

[19] Temple, *Christianity and the Social Order*, 5.
[20] Ibid., 31–32.

These duties rest upon Christians not only as individuals redeemed by Christ who must witness for him in whatever position they may occupy in the state, but also upon the church as a Christian community.[21]

Evangelical churches, who have traditionally opposed any involvement of the church in politics, also issued a strong statement about Christian social responsibility in the Lausanne Covenant of 1974.[22] Article 5 of this covenant reads as follows:

We affirm that God is both the Creator and the Judge of all men. We therefore should share his concern for justice and reconciliation throughout human society and for the liberation of men and women from every kind of oppression. Because men and women are made in the image of God, every person, regardless of race, religion, colour, culture, class, sex or age, has an intrinsic dignity because of which he or she should be respected and served, not exploited. Here too we express penitence both for our neglect and for having sometimes regarded evangelism and social concern as mutually exclusive. Although reconciliation with other people is not reconciliation with God, nor is social action evangelism, nor is political liberation salvation, nevertheless we affirm that evangelism and socio-political involvement are both part of our Christian duty. For both are necessary expressions of our doctrines of God and man, our love for our neighbour and our obedience to Jesus Christ. The message of salvation implies also a message of judgment upon every form of alienation, oppression and discrimination, and we should not be afraid to denounce evil and injustice wherever they exist. When people receive Christ they are born again into his kingdom and must seek not only to exhibit but also to spread its righteousness in the midst of an unrighteous world. The salvation we claim should be transforming us in the totality of our personal and social responsibilities. Faith without works is dead.

---

[21] J. H. Oldham, *World Conference on Church, Community and State* (Oxford: Oxford University Press, 1937), 70–71.

[22] The complete text of the Lausanne Covenant is available online. Cited 13 Nov 2007. Online: www.lausanne.org. Cited 13 Nov 2007.

(Acts 17:26, 31; Gen 18:25; Isa 1:17; Ps 45:7; Gen 1:26–27;
Jas 3:9; Lev 19:18; Luke 6:27, 35; Jas 2:14–26; John 3:3, 5;
Matt 5:20; 6:33; 2 Cor 3:18; Jas 2:20)

This statement contains several very important calls to action: 1) *share* God's concern for justice, 2) *share* God's concern for reconciliation, 3) *share* God's concern for the liberation of men from every kind of oppression, 4) *respect* the dignity of every person, 5) *exploit* no one, 6) *serve* every person, 7) *denounce* evil and injustice, 8) *seek* to exhibit the righteousness of the kingdom of Christ, and 9) *seek* to spread the righteousness of the kingdom of Christ.[23]

Involvement in society is not without its risks, and therefore some cautions are also in order. First, it is important to remember that "the church is a society organized for purposes other than political action. If it enters the political arena it runs the risk of obscuring or compromising the purposes for which it exists". Of course, as shown above, "these purposes may also be obscured and compromised if Christian faith fails to express itself in the political sphere".[24]

Second, the church must not become arrogant, but must be prepared to acknowledge that it does not have the specialist knowledge required to solve particular problems. Its function is to "tell the politician what ends the social order should promote; but it must leave to the politician the devising of the precise means to those ends".[25]

These two points reveal why it is problematic when Christians try to form a Christian political party and try to tie the church to a particular political position or ideology.

Finally, in many situations Christians cannot act in accordance with the principles of their faith without provoking political controversy simply because the ethical witness of the church includes the prophetic denunciation of evil. It is at war with everything contrary to the purpose of God and it is committed to fighting the Lord's battles, scaling "every crag-fortress that bids defiance to the true knowledge of God".[26]

The attacks on the church will come from all sides:

---

[23] Klaus Bockmuehl, *Evangelicals and Social Ethics: A Commentary on Article 5 of the Lausanne Covenant* (trans. David T. Priestley; Downers Grove: IVP, 1979), 17.

[24] Visser 't Hooft and Oldham, *The Church and Its Function in Society*, 200.

[25] Temple, *Christianity and the Social Order*, 50.

[26] Visser 't Hooft and Oldham, *The Church and Its Function in Society*, 198.

It will be told that it has become "political" when in fact it has been careful only to state principles and point to breaches of them; and it will be told by advocates of particular policies that it is futile because it does not support these. If it is faithful to its commission it will ignore both sets of complaints, and continue so far as it can to influence all citizens and permeate all parties.[27]

Key Principles

Three important principles should govern the relationship between church and state: separation, transformation and involvement.

Separation

The church must be separate in terms of values and morality. This is why Jesus said, "You are not of the world" (John 17:16). Paul also said, "Do not conform any longer to the pattern of this world" (Rom 12:2), and "Come out from them" (2 Cor 6:17). The ethics of the church cannot be the same as that of the world. There is to be no compromise in the church. As John V. Taylor notes, "The church must over and over again oppose and repudiate the attitudes and the standards which are accepted in the rest of society, otherwise it ceases to be the Christian church." He adds, "the Christian community is always reluctant to become too different from the rest of society, lest it appear as something alien and out of touch; and yet if the church fails to give a reforming example that is consistent with its preaching, it becomes as salt which has lost its savor."[28]

Transformation

The church must seek to transform the values and morality of the world or state. "This strategy would not reject the world nor identify the Christian ethic with the ethic of the world but would transform the world into the likeness of the Christian ideal."[29] Passages such as Romans 12:2

---

[27] Temple, *Christianity and the Social Order*, 51.

[28] John V. Taylor, *Christianity and Politics in Africa* (Harmondsworth: Penguin, 1957), 54.

[29] William M. Pinson, Jr. *An Approach to Christian Ethics: The Life, Contribution, and Thought of T. B. Maston* (Nashville: Broadman Press, 1979), 201.

and Colossians 3:1–5, among others, encourage the believer to have a renewed mind, a mind focused on eternal matters. Changed lives will have an effect on the choices that believers make and these will have an enduring effect on the world.

> The church as well is called to act as leaven in society. A worshipping, disciplined community, dedicated to Christ's way and honestly attempting to realize His standards in its corporate life, is bound to affect the whole climate of the people among whom it is placed. The church can serve the State best by illustrating in its own life the kind of life which is God's will for society as a whole. [30]

Involvement

The church and every Christian should be active in the world. "The church as a body cannot remain aloof from political life if it is accepted that the Word is intended not simply for the individual but also for the community. This should be openly admitted instead of pretending neutrality and shunning involvement in a delicate issue."[31] John V. Taylor speaks to this issue:

> The church must be rooted in the society within which it has grown up. Its members are a part of that society, sharing its traditional points of view, influenced by its past history, and involved in its strength and its weakness, its rise or fall. A church which is cut off from the rest of society, living a separate, enclosed life of its own, will be ineffectual; and will probably, in the end, become paralyzed or perish altogether.[32]

John Stott discusses the issue of separation versus involvement in terms of escape versus engagement. Escape means "turning our backs on the world in rejection, washing our hands of it (though finding with Pontius Pilate that the responsibility does not come off in the wash), and steeling our hearts against its agonized cries for help." By contrast, engagement means "turning our faces towards the world in compassion, getting our

---

[30] John V. Taylor, *Christianity and Politics in Africa*, 54.
[31] Toivo I. Palo, *Political Engagement as an Ethical and Religious Question* (Publication 25; Tampere: Research Institute of the Lutheran Church in Finland, 1979), 12–13.
[32] John V. Taylor, *Christianity and Politics in Africa*, 5.

hands dirty, sore and worn in its service, and feeling deep within us the stirring of the love of God which cannot be contained".[33]

Conclusion

Politics is a pervasive part of society, affecting individuals and groups, as well as areas like religion and the economy, technology and science. Nobody can claim that politics is irrelevant to their lives. The church in Africa has now recognized the need to fully participate in the political life of the state and seeks to have an impact on education, economics, politics and culture. It has to be involved in the battle to combat HIV/ AIDS and must provide input to politicians on key moral issues such as abortion, euthanasia, sex and marriage. When the church, corporately and individually, has an impact on a nation in these practical areas, the entire political terrain is affected and Christian values permeate the nation.

Questions

1. Describe the political, sociological, economic and religious condition of your culture. Where do these areas overlap? What tensions exist when they overlap?

2. How does your church define its relationship with the state? Evaluate the strengths and weaknesses in this relationship.

3. Evaluate the role of your government (national, state, and local) in maintaining order, justice and freedom. Where are these things being done best? Worst?

4. Using the principles set out in this chapter, evaluate your own, your local church's, and your denomination's relationship to the state. What short-term and long-term steps could be taken to apply Christian principles in this area?

---

[33] John Stott, *New Issues Facing Christians Today*, 18.

8

WAR AND VIOLENCE

History is full of conflicts and wars, some recorded in history books and others almost forgotten. Some of these wars were political: others were sparked by ethnic and religious conflicts. And wars still rage today. The Middle East is racked by conflict between Israelis and Palestinians, and groups within Iraq fight each other as well as the US-led coalition. In Europe, there are conflicts between Protestants and Catholics in Northern Ireland, between Serbs and ethnic Albanians in Kosovo, and between Russians and Chechens. In Asia, there are serious conflicts in Sri Lanka, and between Hindus and Muslims in India.

In Africa in recent years, there have been ethnic and religious conflicts in Rwanda, Somalia, Ethiopia, Eritrea, Angola, Nigeria, Liberia, the Ivory Coast, Sudan and the Democratic Republic of Congo. "The continent of Africa is filled with ethnic conflict, wars over resources and failed states. From south to north, west to east, fighting burns or simmers in Africa."[1]

Consequently the church in Africa has to develop an understanding of the nature of these conflicts and of how Christians should respond to them. It needs to be able to answer questions about its attitude to the use of violence as a means of resolving conflicts, and about how the church and individual Christians should respond to oppression or injustice by the government or other ethnic or religious groups. These are not just theoretical questions, but are questions that face African church leaders, church members, politicians and even schoolchildren.

---

[1] J. Milburn Thompson, *Justice and Peace: A Christian Primer* (Maryknoll: Orbis, 2003), 136.

Ethnic and Religious Conflicts

In Western thinking, war is normally understood mainly in terms of armed hostilities between nations. Thus Western discussions of the ethics of war focus on the responsibilities of citizens in time of war, non-resistance, pacifism, preventive war and what constitutes a just war.[2] But these issues are less important in Africa where war and conflict are seldom international. Instead they involve conflict between factions within a state (civil war), between ethnic groups (ethnic war), or between two religions (religious war).

Most wars in Africa arise from tensions between ethnic groups within the same state. Ethnicity is a characteristic of a group of people, whether a few thousand or several million, who "share a persisting sense of common interest and identity that is based on some combination of shared historical experience and valued cultural traits."[3] It is associated with shared culture, language, religion, social customs, physical appearance and geographic origins, and affects whom people turn to for security and protection. In African countries, which often include a number of different ethnic groups, ethnicity still has great psychological and sociological significance. It can be used as a powerful tool to unify a group against another group of a different ethnicity.[4] Ethnic consciousness and interests often lead to conflict and violence.

These ethnic conflicts are complex and intractable and can only be solved by lengthy negotiation. There is also always the danger that the violence will spill across political boundaries and affect neighbouring countries, as happened when the violence in Rwanda spread to the Congo and when the Liberian crisis transferred itself to Sierra Leone.

Ethnic conflicts can be exacerbated when there are also religious differences between the parties: "Religion is one of the features that can distinguish one ethnic group from another. Since religion pertains to core values, it can inflate the intensity and intractability of ethnic conflict. Religious belief can even be used to legitimate or authorize intolerance toward another ethnic group."[5]

---

[2] Robert G. Clouse, *War: Four Christian Views* (Downers Grove: IVP, 1981) offers an excellent summary of various Christian perspectives on war.

[3] Thompson, *Justice and Peace,* 116.

[4] Some older texts may use the term "tribalism" to refer to the same phenomenon.

[5] Ibid., 121.

In some cases, ethnic tensions are so strong that they eclipse shared religious values, as is happening in the conflict in Darfur where all the parties are Muslim. In other cases, religious tensions override ethnic links, as happened in Northern Ireland, where Catholics battled Protestants, and in India, where the conflict between Muslims and Hindus led to the break-up of the nation into the two states of India and Pakistan.

Sadly, even the churches in Africa have been infected by the cancer of ethnicity. The following observation about the Rwandan situation holds true for much of Africa: "Within the churches of Rwanda, ethnic tensions often surfaced at the time of elections or nominations to senior ecclesiastical positions. Splits were glossed over but never healed; people were elected for their spiritual, administrative or leadership qualities, but along ethnic lines."[6]

These ethnic tensions in Rwanda culminated in a genocide in which church groups and religious leaders participated in the killing of Christian brothers and sisters.

Ethnic and religious tensions and wars are probably the two greatest threats to nations and governments in Africa. They make it impossible for governments to carry out their task of maintaining order, justice and freedom. Instead, there are gross violations of human rights as the conflicts affect the cohesion and stability of nations, shaking them to their very foundations.

Causes of Ethnic and Religious Conflicts

The reasons for the growing tide of ethnic conflicts in the world and in Africa include "a reaction against over-centralized, corrupt and exploitative governments, a search for cultural identity amid the constant changes and confusion of modern society and alienation, which threatens the very roots of community".[7]

In Africa, the conflicts are also being driven by profound forces of change in the economic and political spheres, by increased human migration and by resentment of injustice, both real and perceived.

---

[6] Hugh McCullum *The Angels have Left Us: the Rwanda Tragedy and the Churches* (Geneva: World Council of Churches, 1995), 78.
[7] Ibid., 77.

Economic change

While an economy is growing, people see their lives improving and hope to be able to share in their nation's abundance. However, economic tensions arise if the rate of economic growth slows. When this happens, "ethnic identity will become more salient. This is due to competition over scarce resources, or in this case, a shrinking pie."[8] Economic tension also rises "when new resources, hitherto unallocated, are to be distributed, and … when the new patterns of distribution create alterations in the existing ranking of individuals".[9] The inflation that often accompanies economic change worsens the situation and exacerbates tensions. We see these forces at work in places like the Delta region of Nigeria, where the discovery of oil has led to an explosion of ethnic conflict. The problem is not the booming economy but the distribution of the new wealth. Economic disparity among citizens, where the rich become richer and the poor become poorer, worsens the situation.

In many African societies, competition for power and wealth involves groups that are divided on cultural or religious lines. In Nigeria and Kenya, for example, some ethnic and religious groups are wealthier than others and have more of their own businesses and better access to top government positions. When any ethnic or religious conflict arises, rich people from those groups are targeted and suffer the anger of the poor.

Political change

Because of the prevalence of patronage in Africa, political leaders feel free to use their official positions to amass wealth for themselves or for members of their own ethnic group or class. The result has been social stratification in which "positions of power, status, and prestige are assigned according to one's membership in a particular ethnic group."[10] The resentment this arouses means that when an opportunity for political change arises, there is pressure to align oneself with one's own ethnic group in the pursuit of power.

---

[8] Masipula Sithole, "The Salience of Ethnicity in African Politics: The Case of Zimbabwe", *Journal of Asian and African Studies* 20 (1985): 185.

[9] P. C. Lloyd, "Ethnicity and the Structure of Inequality in a Nigerian Town in the Mid 1950s" in *Urban Ethnicity* (ed. Abner Cohen; New York: Tavistock, 1974), 223.

[10] Sithole, "The Salience of Ethnicity", 187.

> The salience of ethnicity will increase as individuals of lowly ranked ethnic groups attempt to rise into positions hitherto the monopoly of those higher in the ethnic social structure. As the former make a claim to power, status, and prestige, the latter close ranks to defend the same. The ensuing conflict takes on an ethnic flavor because the lines of battle are structured along ethnic lines.[11]

In Nigeria, there has long been a struggle for power between the Hausa-Fulani, who are predominantly Muslim and have occupied key government positions since independence, and the Yoruba and Igbo. Many other smaller groups in the nation are also struggling to gain influence. Similar ethnic struggles are occurring in Kenya, Liberia, Congo, Sudan, Ethiopia and Uganda. These ethnic struggles for power can flare into violence when one group does not get what it desires. The resulting conflict can fragment the state.

Human migration

Tensions arise when ethnic groups from one area move into and settle in areas already occupied by other groups, regardless of whether the area is rural or urban. Africa's cities have not become melting pots, where all groups and cultures mingle. Instead, particular ethnic groups have tended to settle in particular areas of the city. "Just as in the rural area a man turns for help first to the members of his own descent [ancestral] group or small village, so when he comes to the town does he seek the support of those related closely to him by ties of kinship or locality."[12]

Ethnic groups then start to hold their own tribal meetings and to set up political pressure groups, clubs and so on to promote their own interests. The situation highlights the differences between groups and does nothing to encourage national unity.

Real or perceived injustice

Severe injustices exist in many countries and "affect millions of human beings, children of God, reducing them to a sub-human condition".[13]

---

[11] Ibid.

[12] Lloyd, "Ethnicity and the Structure of Inequality", 224.

[13] Helder Camara, *Spiral of Violence* (London: Sheed & Ward, 1971), 25. Cited 29 April 29, 2008. Online: www.alastairmcintosh.com/general/spiral-of-violence.htm.

They lack potable water and endure political oppression and degradation, unemployment, insecurity and a poverty that

> does more than kill, it leads to physical deformity (just think of Biafra), to psychological deformity (there are many cases of mental subnormality for which hunger is responsible), and to moral deformity (those who, through a situation of slavery, hidden but nonetheless real, are living without prospects and without hope, foundering in fatalism and reduced to a begging mentality).[14]

Such injustices are themselves a form of violence and lead to more violence, as the oppressed turn on the oppressors.

Violence as a Solution

When conflicts arise, it is all too easy to resort to violence in an attempt to solve them. This tactic has been used throughout recorded history, right back to Cain's murder of his brother Abel because Abel was enjoying God's favour while Cain was rejected.

Although older people may be the one's inciting violence as a response to conflict, oppression and injustice, it is usually the young who end up doing the actual fighting. There are a number of reasons why they are easily mobilized:

> The young no longer have the patience to wait for the privileged to discard their privileges. The young very often see governments too tied to the privileged classes. The young are losing confidence in the churches, which affirm beautiful principles – great texts, remarkable conclusions – but without ever deciding, at least so far, to translate them into real life. The young then are turning more and more to radical action and violence.[15]

Arguments in favour of violence

The following arguments are advanced by those who claim that it is right to respond to oppression with violence.

---

[14] Camara, *Spiral of Violence,* 26.
[15] Ibid., 33.

- *Violence is the most natural response.* We all want to hit back at our enemies and pay them back in the same coin. If the government uses violence to sustain itself in power, the natural response is to use violence to overthrow it.

- *Violence produces results.* When military force is used to topple a dictatorial government, it produces an immediate change, as happened with the overthrow of Idi Amin of Uganda, Nicolae Ceauşescu of Romania, Samuel Doe of Liberia and even Saddam Hussein of Iraq.

- *Violence communicates.* The message sent by violence is loud and clear and forces a response. It seems to be the only message that some evil and oppressive governments and leaders understand.

- *Violence is the only option when dialogue and diplomacy fail to produce any change.* When all others forms of protest fail, aggressive action is often seen as the most practical way to alleviate suffering. The use of violence in these circumstances has the backing of philosophical and theological traditions:

  > The just-war tradition, rooted in the ethical theories of Plato and Cicero and formulated within the Christian tradition by Augustine, Aquinas and the Protestant Reformers, defends military force as a last resort against grave injustice. According to this view, when the innocent are threatened by an unjust aggressor and all other remedies have failed, Jesus' command for sacrificial love may require us to use lethal force.[16]

Arguments against violence

While the justifications for the use of violence above may seem plausible, it is also important to note the problems related to the use of violence as a response to conflict.

- *Violence begets violence.* To put it another way, violence attracts violence. This principle was clearly illustrated in the Nigerian cities of Jos and Kaduna in 2001 as young men from the church and the mosque took up arms and fought each other. The only result was the destruction of churches and mosques and the loss of many lives.

---

[16] David A. Hoekema, "A Practical Christian Pacifism". *Christian Century* (October 22, 1986): 917–918. Cited 29 April 2008. Online: www.religion-online.org/showarticle.asp?title=115.

The violence solved nothing and simply produced more suffering. As Wink reminds us, "If we resist violence with violence, we simply mirror its evil. We become what we resist."[17] Martin Luther King, Jr. made the same point:

> Returning hate for hate multiplies hate, adding deeper darkness to a night already devoid of stars. Darkness cannot drive out darkness, only light can do that. Hate multiplies hate, violence multiplies violence, and toughness multiplies toughness in a descending spiral of destruction … The chain reactions of evil – hate begetting hate, wars producing more wars – must be broken, or we shall be plunged into the dark abyss of annihilation.[18]

Africa must heed this warning. Violence has never produced peace. It may force a semblance of peace, but violence will eventually erupt again. Governments that come to power through violent revolution will usually end up being overthrown in yet another violent coup d'état.

- *Violence produces more casualties and bloodshed than non-violent approaches that achieve the same result.* The use of violence to accomplish some objective or settle some dispute (religious, ethnic, or political) always results in bloodshed and unnecessary loss of innocent lives and property. The Nigerian Civil War of 1967–70 led to the loss of about one million lives. Many millions more have been lost in the civil and ethnic wars in Rwanda, Sierra Leone, Liberia, Nigeria, Congo and recently Darfur in Sudan. The desired results could have been achieved using non-violent approaches such as dialogue and diplomacy.

Violence is counterproductive and self-defeating; it does not solve conflicts but actually creates more problems than existed before.

Biblical Perspectives on Violence

If we are to come up with a Christian response to injustice and to the pressure to resort to violence, we need to start by examining biblical and theological teaching on the topic.

---

[17] Walter Wink, *Jesus and Nonviolence: A Third Way* (Minneapolis: Fortress, 2003), 76.
[18] Martin Luther King, Jr, *Strength to Love* (Philadelphia: Fortress, 1981), 53.

Violence in the Old Testament

The Old Testament passage most frequently cited in discussions of violence is the *lex talionis,* which is summarized as "eye for eye and tooth for tooth" (Matt 5:38–41; see also Exod 21:24; Lev 24:19–20; Deut 19:21). The same principle of retaliation is enshrined in the famous Code of Hammurabi. This law was not intended to be used as an excuse for personal vengeance, which was specifically forbidden in Leviticus 19:18, but was designed to set a clear limit to the level of punishment. This law provided "the nation's judicial system with a ready formula of punishment, not least because it would decisively terminate vendettas".[19]

The Old Testament mentions many wars, including some that were carried out on God's instruction. For example, the Israelites were commanded to drive out the Canaanites and take over their land (Num 33:50–56; Deut 20:13; Josh 3:10). King Saul was also commanded to completely destroy all the Amalekites (1 Sam 15:2–3). Later, God used the Assyrian and Babylonian armies as tools to punish the nations of Israel and Judah.

Two important points need to be made about these wars that had divine sanction. First, these situations were unique. The commands never suggest that they were intended to be examples of how to achieve objectives. Second, the New Testament, which is the fulfilment of the Old Testament, never even suggests that Christians are to follow these specific commands that were given to a specific group of people at a specific time. Nowhere does the New Testament suggest that it is acceptable to use weapons to settle a dispute.

Violence in the New Testament

Some of Jesus' teaching specifically addresses the issue of violence. It is worth examining each of his statements in some detail.

Matthew 5:38–41   The Sermon on the Mount

In the Sermon on the Mount, Jesus specifically addressed the lex talionis. This passage is the most quoted and, unfortunately, the most wrongly

---

[19] D. A. Carson, "Matthew" in the *Expositor's Bible Commentary* (ed. Frank E. Gaebelein; Grand Rapids: Zondervan, 1984), 155.

interpreted passage of all those that give insight into what the Bible and Christianity teach about violence

> You have heard that it was said, 'Eye for eye, and tooth for tooth.' But I tell you, Do not resist an evil person. If someone strikes you on the right cheek, turn to him the other also. And if someone wants to sue you and take your tunic, let him have your cloak as well. If someone forces you to go one mile, go with him two miles.

Some readers argue that Jesus is thinking of the Old Testament use of the lex talionis and is saying that we should never personally respond to an insult, but should leave that to the law. Carson summarizes this position as "if someone strikes you, don't strike back but let the judiciary administer the just return slap".[20] But it is more likely that what Jesus means when he says that we should "not resist an evil person" is that we should not respond to insults by taking the person to court.

Nor should we respond to violence with violence. The verb translated "resist" is the same one used of a "violent rebellion, armed revolt, sharp dissension, … a potentially lethal disturbance or armed revolution".[21] Jesus is condemning any type of violent response. Romans 12:17–21 reinforces Jesus' words, reminding us not to "repay anyone evil for evil" and to leave revenge to the Lord.

So is Jesus saying that we should passively accept violence and insults and not do anything about them? No. He gives us three examples of how to respond to evil, all of which involve what can be called creative resistance.

The first example involves someone being slapped across the face by an oppressor, possibly a soldier in the occupying Roman army. Instead of cowering away, the one slapped stands his ground and turns the other cheek. This act

> allows the inferior in the relationship to assert her or his equal humanity with the oppressor, and it forces the oppressor to take stock of the relationship and perhaps of the social system that supports such inequality. It is risky, to be sure, and demands courage, but it is a creative way to challenge an

---

[20] Ibid.
[21] Wink, *Jesus and Nonviolence*, 11.

unhealthy relationship and unjust system. Both Gandhi and Martin Luther King, Jr. grasped this well and molded this idea into a tool for resisting social injustice and creating a more just community.[22]

Wink makes the same point:

> This action robs the oppressor of the power to humiliate. The person who turns the other cheek is saying, in effect "Try again. Your first blow failed to achieve its intended effect. I deny you the power to humiliate me. I am a human being just like you. Your status does not alter that fact. You cannot demean me." Such a response would create enormous difficulties for the striker ... Even if he orders the person flogged, the point has been irrevocably made. The oppressor has been forced, against his will, to regard this subordinate as an equal human being. The powerful person has been stripped of his power to dehumanize the other. This response, far from admonishing passivity and cowardice, is an act of defiance.[23]

The second example Jesus gives involves a creditor suing someone for his tunic. Jesus tells him to give the creditor his cloak as well. According to Thompson, giving the creditor both one's inner and outer garments is a form of shock tactics:

> Here, take not only my coat, but my underwear as well. Then, you'll have everything. And walk out of the court naked, leaving the red-faced creditor with a coat in one hand and underwear in the other. The creditor would be embarrassed and shamed – and unmasked. This is not a respectable moneylender but a loan shark who perpetuates a system that has reduced an entire social class of his own people to landlessness and destitution. This burlesque offers the creditor the chance to see the human consequences of these practices and to repent, and it empowers the oppressed to take the initiative and burst the delusion that it is a just system. It is a brave and ingenious form of resistance.[24]

---

[22] Thompson, *Justice and Peace*, 192.
[23] Wink, *Jesus and Nonviolence*, 15–16.
[24] Thompson, *Justice and Peace*, 192–193.

Jesus' third example is that when forced to carry someone's pack for one mile, one should voluntarily go an extra mile. By doing this, the oppressed person

> knocks the oppressor off balance and reveals the injustice of the situation. It also affirms the dignity of the oppressed by allowing the victim to seize the initiative. Without shedding blood or even raising one's voice in anger, the oppressed person has started down the road to liberation.[25]

These examples show that Jesus did not teach passivity in response to evil, as is often suggested. Instead, he taught an active condemnation of the evils of his day.

Luke 22:36–38   Buy a sword

Those who think Jesus was a pacifist are puzzled by the words he addressed to his disciples shortly before his crucifixion. John Ferguson admits that "this is undoubtedly the most difficult passage in the New Testament to reconcile with the general tenor of Jesus' teaching of non-violent love".[26] The words in question are these:

> "Now if you have a purse, take it, and also a bag; and if you don't have a sword, sell your cloak and buy one. It is written: 'And he was numbered with the transgressors'; and I tell you that this must be fulfilled in me. Yes, what is written about me is reaching its fulfilment." The disciples said, "See, Lord, here are two swords." "That is enough," he replied.

The difficulty of this passage is that it seems to contradict other statements Jesus made that seem to prohibit the use of swords (Matt 26:52; John 18:36). Thus some scholars prefer to interpret this passage metaphorically. William Barclay is one of these scholars, and he argues that these words are simply "a vivid eastern way of telling the disciples that their very lives are at stake".[27]

---

[25] Ibid.

[26] John Ferguson, *The Politics of Love: The New Testament and Nonviolent Revolution* (Cambridge, James Clarke, 1973), 31. The German theologian Friedrich Spitta said, "See! Jesus has summoned His followers to armed defence! He was no tender pacifist."(Quoted in G. H. C. Macgregor, *The New Testament Basis of Pacifism and the Relevance of an Impossible Ideal* [New York: Fellowship Publications, 1954], 22).

[27] Quoted in Ferguson, *The Politics of Love*, 33.

But an ordinary reading of the passage suggests that when Jesus instructed his disciples to take a sword, he was simply acknowledging the reality of violence. It helps to remember the historical context in which Jesus was speaking. It was common for men to carry swords in those days.

> It is evident that Jesus had not forbidden the disciples in their journey from Galilee to Jerusalem to carry weapons and that these weapons were nothing but the customary means of protection which travelers have always used when beyond the reach of law and armed protection. In Jerusalem they were under the shadow of the law, Jewish and Roman, and their arms were in abeyance. In the passage quoted, the traveler's sword is like the purse, and the wallet, and the sandals, and the cloak, a symbol of homeless wandering on an urgent and dangerous mission, far more formidable than their shorter and safer errands hither at His bidding. It may be inferred that Jesus had taken no exception to them bearing the ordinary means of self-defense when traveling in bandit-infested country beyond the protection of armed authority.[28]

Jesus is acknowledging that swords may be needed for self-protection. When the authorities provide no proper protection, it is appropriate to protect oneself. It would have been unwise to travel in the mountains where there were robbers and thieves without a sword, and it is right and proper to arm oneself in order to defend oneself, one's family and the weak. Advocating a non-violent response to oppression and injustice is not at odds with self-defence or defence of one's family or even one's church. Thus in Nigeria, where families and churches have been targeted for destruction, it would be appropriate for a Christian to use a weapon to protect himself and his family. It is unwise and irrational not to protect one's household if it is being attacked.

Matthew 26:52   Put down your sword

If we interpret Jesus' command in Luke 22:36–38 as allowing us to use violence in self-defence, how do interpret Jesus' apparent condemnation of the use of violence when he tells Peter, "Put your sword back in its place … for all who draw the sword will die by the sword"?

---

[28] Quoted in Macgregor, *The New Testament Basis of Pacifism*, 23.

This passage is often used to condemn any use of violence or force. However, these words are said in the context of Jesus' arrest. The point he is making is that it is unnecessary and useless to use a sword or any other weapon to accomplish a divine purpose. He had already plainly stated that in the process of fulfilling his mission he would die a violent death. It was not appropriate for the disciples to attempt to prevent this.

It should also be noted that Jesus only tells Peter to put his sword back in its place. He does not tell him to throw it away, or destroy it, or never use it again in any circumstances. In this particular situation, it was wrong to fight, but Jesus was not prohibiting the use of the sword for self-defence, as is clear from his command in Luke 22.

John 18:36   My kingdom is not of this world

Addressing Pilate, Jesus made it clear that the kingdom of God is not to be defended by force of arms, "My kingdom is not of this world. If it were, my servants would fight to prevent my arrest." Some, like Martin Luther, have argued that these words permit earthly nations to go to war if there are adequate reasons. But here Jesus is not discussing the philosophy of war in the abstract. Rather, he is making a specific point about his spiritual kingdom. This spiritual kingdom has enough resources of its own to be victorious if it were ever to engage in an actual physical war with the kingdoms of this world (Matt 26:53).

Matt 22:38–40   Love your neighbour as yourself

Jesus insisted that God's law could be summarized in two commandments, one of which was "love your neighbour as yourself" (see also Lev 19:18). His definition of who this neighbour is includes our political opponents, aggressors and even our enemies – in fact, anyone whom we are in conflict (Matt 5:43–48). We are told to act like the Good Samaritan and show our love for these neighbours through offering care that takes risks, is costly, and shows a commitment to them (Luke 10:25–37). We are not to seek revenge (Rom 12:14–21) but are to pray for enemies who maltreat or oppress us (Luke 6:28).

Applying Christian Principles in Ethnic and Religious Conflicts

The ethnic and religious conflicts that trouble Africa cannot be solved by violence. "Because of their intractable and explosive nature, ethnic conflicts can be resolved only through political dialogue and negotiation. War and violence … serve only to exacerbate them. Nor are political solutions alone sufficient."[29] A true solution will involve actively applying the following Christian principles.

Seek healing and reconciliation

The church has been called to a ministry of healing and reconciliation. When it is the victim of aggression, self-defence is permitted but is not required. Even when Jesus was unjustly arrested by armed enemies and Peter could legitimately have used his sword, Jesus said, "Put your sword back into its place" (Matt 26:52). When others are the victims, the church must demonstrate the caring attitude Jesus commended in the parable of the Good Samaritan. Practising non-violence enables Christians to keep the "door open to reconciliation, and to keep the issues in focus".[30]

Promote justice

It is not enough for the church merely to encourage reconciliation and quote Scriptures like "everyone must submit to the governing authorities", "turn the other cheek", "love your enemies" and "all who draw the sword will perish by the sword".

> When church leaders preach reconciliation without having unequivocally committed themselves to struggle on the side of the oppressed for justice, they are caught straddling a pseudo-neutrality made of nothing but thin air. Neutrality in a situation of oppression always supports the status quo. Reduction of conflict by means of a phony "peace" is not a Christian goal.

---

[29] Gerard F. Powers, Drew Christiansen and Robert T. Hennemeyer eds. *Peacemaking: Moral and Policy Challenges for a New World* (Washington D.C.: United States Catholic Conference, 1994), 329.

[30] William Robert Miller, *Nonviolence: A Christian Interpretation* (New York: Shocken Books, 1966), 168.

Justice is the goal, and that may require an acceleration of conflict as a necessary stage in forcing those in power to bring about genuine change.[31]

The church must be seen to be involved in an active struggle against injustice, ethnocentrism and oppression. Where there is fairness and equity for all ethnic and religious groups in respect of employment, political appointments, school admissions and all the normal amenities in any community, there is greater willingness to accept people from other ethnic groups. Thus promoting justice is the greatest avenue for reducing ethnic and religious conflicts in Africa.

Develop an inclusive church

The church should be a place where there are no ethnic divisions but where all are equally welcome and cared for. Unfortunately, the church in Africa has not always lived up to this ideal. Members do not show adequate care for one another during times of crisis. When selecting church leaders, candidates' ethnicity sometimes seems to be regarded as more important than their spirituality. Some churches even refuse to accept leaders from outside their ethnic group. But the church is not meant to serve any ethnic agenda. It must take note of the Apostle Paul's instructions to the ethnically diverse church in his day: "There is neither Jew nor Greek, slave nor free, male nor female, for you are all one in Christ Jesus" (Gal 3:28). The church is basically a community that has unity in diversity. All are one in Christ and share "a common Creator, Redeemer, and Sanctifier, we are one human family, brothers and sisters and all".[32] The church could even be thought of as a new spiritual ethnic group, with a special awareness of each other's needs for protection and security. There is no place in such a group for old ethnic loyalties and hatred of other groups.

Allow Christian principles to guide our approach to politics

Political opinions should not be shaped by ethnic interests or ethnic prejudices but by Christian principles. The love of God is demonstrated in our love of others, especially those who are different from us. Thus

---

[31] Wink, *Jesus and Nonviolence*, 5.

[32] Thompson, *Justice and Peace*, 119.

Christian politicians should be fair to all ethnic groups, irrespective of their political and religious ideologies. There should be no place in our politics for the type of ethnic loyalty and religious fanaticism that encourages hatred of other human beings.

Practise loving and forgiving our enemies

Christians cannot avoid Christ's command to love our enemies and pray for them if we are to be like the heavenly Father we are called to imitate (Matt 5:44–45). We also need to love them because they, like us, have been created in the image of God (Gen 9:6; Jas 3:9). Consequently no one is so wicked that there is no good element in them; and no one is so good that there is no bad element in them.[33] Stott writes about this "paradox of our humanness":

> We human beings have both a unique dignity as creatures made in God's image and a unique depravity as sinners under his judgment. The former gives us hope; the latter places a limit on our expectations ... the Christian mind, firmly rooted in biblical realism, both celebrates the glory and deplores the shame of our human being. We can behave like God in whose image we were made, only to descend to the level of the beasts. We are able to think, choose, create, love and worship, but also to refuse to think, to choose evil, to destroy, to hate, and to worship ourselves. We build churches and drop bombs ... This is 'man,' a strange, bewildering paradox, dust of earth and breath of God, shame and glory.[34]

Forgiveness may not be easy. It is worth taking note of the words of the great American civil rights campaigner, Martin Luther King Jr., who also had much to forgive. He says, "We must develop and maintain the capacity to forgive. He who is devoid of the power to forgive is devoid of the power to love."[35] King also stresses that "the forgiving act must always be initiated by the person who has been wronged, the victim of

---

[33] Martin Luther King (*Strength to Love*, 51) notes, "An element of goodness may be found even in our worst of enemy. Each of us is something of a schizophrenic personality, tragically divided against ourselves. A persistent civil war rages within all of our lives."

[34] John Stott, *Issues Facing Christians*, 44.

[35] Martin Luther King, Jr. *Strength to Love* (Philadelphia: Fortress, 1981), 50.

some great hurt, the recipient of some tortuous injustice, the absorber of some terrible act of oppression".[36]

Willingness to forgive can even be described as the ultimate test of authentic Christian faith.

> Commitment to justice, liberation, or the overthrow of oppression is not enough, for all too often the means used have brought in their wake new injustices and oppressions. Love of enemies is the recognition that the enemy, too, is a child of God.[37]

Conclusion

Violent means have frequently been employed to try to solve the incessant conflicts around the world. But the current situation in Africa shows that violence is not the answer. Violence produces more hatred and more violence, but never ultimately resolves the conflict.

The answer to the nagging conflicts in the church and in the continent is the non-violence that Jesus practised and instructed his followers to practise. This refusal to accept violence does not mean that we passively accept whatever is done to us, nor does it mean that we cannot use force to protect ourselves when attacked. What it does mean is that we must not accept the use of force as a means of settling conflicts. Instead, we must encourage non-violent but active resistance when dealing with African ethnic and religious conflicts.

The effectiveness of non-violent responses to oppression and injustices has been demonstrated worldwide. In South Africa, Steve Biko and Nelson Mandela stood for non-violent but active resistance to the oppressive apartheid regime. In the United States of America, Martin Luther King Jr. was the major spokesman for non-violent but active resistance to racial segregation. Gandhi adopted a non-violent approach to solving the political crisis in India.

Only love for the enemy and the determination not to use force or violence will win conflicts and win the enemy. These attitudes provide a theologically based "framework within which to carry on the vital task of building structures that can eventually eliminate war and its

---

[36] Ibid.
[37] Wink, *Jesus and Nonviolence*, 59.

causes".[38] The only effective remedy against oppression and injustice is the replacement of evil structures that have been institutionalized with good and just structures:

> The only true answer to violence is to have the courage to face the injustice which constitutes violence … The privileged and the authorities will come to understand that common sense obliges one to choose between bloody and armed violence, on the one hand, and on the other the violence of the peaceful: liberating moral pressure.[39]

Questions

1. Describe the role of the factors identified in this chapter (decline in economic growth, political change, spatial mobility and injustice) in wars or ethnic and religious conflicts in your own country. Were these issues addressed in the ending of the conflict?

2. Ask several people, Christian and non-Christian, to explain when it is justifiable to resort to violence. Evaluate their responses according to the biblical and theological guidelines in this chapter.

3. Should Christians participate as soldiers in ethnic or civil disputes or war?

4. Provide some practical suggestions for how Christians individually and the church collectively can help prevent future religious/ethnic conflicts and mediate current conflicts?

---

[38] Hoekema, "A Practical Christian Pacifism", 919.

[39] Camara, *Spiral of Violence*, 55.

9

STRIKES

Ethnic and religious conflicts are not the only types of conflicts that can cause serious disruptions in society. So can strikes, which have been used since the emergence of the labour movement in the late nineteenth and early twentieth centuries to protest against working conditions or certain government policies. When a strike is called, all the workers employed by a company or in an industry refuse to return to work until their demands are met or a negotiated settlement is reached. Sometimes strikes extend beyond individual work stoppages and become general strikes, that is, mass work stoppages by the entire labour force in a country or region. A general strike can be described as "Labor's natural reaction to a system of society based upon the private ownership of the machinery of production. It is Labor's ultimate attitude in the class struggle. It is Labor's answer to the problem of economic disorganization."[1]

Strikes are common in Africa, where workers are often underpaid and poorly treated. It is not that there is no money to pay them adequately; rather, their treatment reflects poor management of resources, with the poorest suffering the most. When these workers take their grievances to their employers and the government, they are often ignored. To get attention, they may decide to go on strike.

Discussion of the ethics of strikes is complicated by the fact that workers in different contexts embark on strikes for different reasons. Moreover because strikes are often directed at correcting economic injustices and political wrongs, they have extensive emotional, legal, political, economic and social ramifications.

---

[1] Industrial Workers of the World, *The General Strike for Industrial Freedom* (Montague, Mass.: Acacia Press, 1946, republished 1996). Cited 2 April 2008. Online: www.crocker.com/~acacia/text_gsif.html.

In this chapter, we shall be talking about strikes in general. In a later chapter we will consider the specific question of whether medical workers are justified in going on strike.

The Nature of Strikes

Strikes always involve two camps: the employers and the employees. Labour leaders or trade unionists usually speak for the employees. They articulate the reasons for the strike and give some justification for believing that such unified action is necessary. Thereafter, they issue deadlines and ultimatums to the government or employers, making it clear that if their demands are not met, there will be a strike. Some countries specify how long in advance this ultimatum must be given; for example, in Nigeria unions must give fifteen days notice before embarking on a strike.

It is important to remember that strikes are a legal option. The constitutions of most countries allow working people to go on strike to protest against poor working conditions when all other attempts to resolve a problem have failed. The reason that constitutions allow strikes is that participating in a strike is a democratic right. It may be the only way for workers to make sure their pleas are heard. In democratic countries, the voice of protest is proper and accepted, and even dictatorial governments sometimes need to hear voices of dissent.

Advantages of Strikes

Strikes have been adopted as a bargaining tool for a number of reasons. The first has already been mentioned. When workers' requests and pleas fall on deaf ears, a strike may be the only way to force employers to enter into meaningful dialogue with their employees (usually represented by labour leaders). Such dialogue can be a valuable learning experience for both groups, as each side gains insight into the realities faced by the opposing side.

The second reason that strikes are popular is that they are sometimes effective in bringing about change. During a well-organized strike, few or no services continue to operate. Even workers who may be reluctant to strike can be coerced into joining in. The disruption caused is often effective in pressurizing employers to improve conditions of service and workers' salaries. The disruption caused to an entire society by a general strike can bring down a government or persuade authorities to revoke or change bad policies.

Strikes are also beneficial in that they encourage an ethic in which people are prepared to endure hardship in the present in order to gain future benefits, not only for themselves but for other workers too. The short-term sacrifice as work is halted and wages are not paid is compensated for by achieving goals that will be for the long-term benefit of all.

Disadvantages of Strikes

Despite the benefits just mentioned, strikes are also associated with serious problems that may overshadow any positive results achieved.

Rather than promoting productive dialogue, strikes can lead to a breakdown in communication. Labour leaders often believe that the goals of employees are diametrically opposed to those of employers. Thus they issue statements like this: "The working class and the employing class have nothing in common. There can be no peace so long as hunger and want are found among millions of working people and the few, who make up the employing class, have all the good things of life."[2]

This belief can harm negotiations because differences are exaggerated and positions misconstrued. Moreover, labour leaders may be eager to strike because they believe that strikes are the only means of bringing about change. Instead of trying to negotiate agreements or using the ballot to change political authorities, they adopt a confrontational attitude from the outset.

When leaders start out with this attitude, it is easy for a strike to turn violent. This is even more the case when strike leaders encourage the use of illegal methods such as throwing tear gas at police officers, intimidating workers, and using hoodlums to harass innocent citizens. Some leaders seem prepared to go to almost any lengths, including holding a country to ransom, in order to achieve their goals. Their actions can cause psychological, political and economic stress.

---

[2] Industrial Workers of the World, *The General Strike.*

Some strikes may even be intended to subvert and bring down a democratically elected government. This accusation was levelled at the Nigerian Labour Congress when in 2003 it attempted to launch a general strike during the All-Africa Games in Abuja, Nigeria. Its aim was to embarrass the government and force it to change its policy on deregulation of the oil sector. Invitations by the government to engage in dialogue fell on deaf ears. The president of Nigeria declared that the movement was acting like "an opposition political movement rather than a labour organization".[3]

The second advantage of strikes is that they can be effective. But this is by no means always the case. Many strikes are dismal failures. Often the workers' sacrifice of wages and time is fruitless and they have to return to work with their demands unmet. The consequences of a failed strike can be drastic. Workers often lose their jobs, thus increasing unemployment, suffering and poverty.

Even a successful strike can cause severe economic harm to the employer or the government. The financial losses resulting from the strike are often passed on to consumers in the form of higher prices. Some companies may even go bankrupt, ending the supply of the product and the jobs of the workers.

Although it can be argued that strikes promote ethical living in that they teach solidarity with others and the need to suffer hardship in order to achieve success, they also undermine other ethical principles such as the need to care for the poor and weak. The poor, who have the fewest resources, often suffer the most during strikes. For example, when a general strike is called because the price of petroleum has gone up, the supply of petrol and products like cooking gas is disrupted. People have to buy these essentials on the black market, where they are sold at exorbitant prices. The high price of petrol raises the cost of transporting food to markets, and thus food prices also rise. Similarly, when doctors and nurses go on strike, it is the weakest members of the community, their patients, who suffer.

Those who lead strikes may also sometimes be praising ethical principles that they do not live by themselves. They may have been bought by special interests or may have yielded to government pressure.

---

[3] President Olusegun Obasanjo in a national broadcast on 8 November 2003. Cited 3 April 2008. Online: www.dawodu.com/obas17.htm.

Corrupt leaders sometimes allow the workers to suffer while they benefit.

Ethics of Participating in a Strike

When deciding whether to participate in a strike, it is important to weigh the advantages and disadvantages just discussed. People with different approaches to ethics will reach different conclusions about whether it is morally right to join in.

Some people will not recognize any ethical problems in going on strike. If a strike will be successful and give them power, it is right. Unfortunately, Africa has seen too much of this type of might-is-right morality, as manifested in military dictators like Sani Abacha of Nigeria, Idi Amin of Uganda and Jean-Bedel Bokassa of the Central Africa Republic.

Those who take a teleological approach to ethics will focus on what is achieved by the strike, rather than on the rightness or wrongness of individual actions associated with it. According to this approach, the end justifies the means. If a strike achieves something that will benefit many people, then it is right to take part regardless of the cost to individuals.

A variant of teleological ethics is utilitarian ethics, which claims that the right thing to do is the thing that provides the greatest happiness to the greatest number of people. Thus if the majority of the workers are happier because their working conditions have improved, it does not matter if a few people suffer or die as a result of the strike.

Traditional African communities often have a group ethic, in which the tribal, political, religious or economic group decides what is right and wrong. According to this ethic, if the group decides to go on strike, the individual must act in solidarity with them. The problem with this approach is that communities can easily come to honour immoral behaviour provided it benefits them. Thus an individual who commits violence during a strike or steals from an employer may be a hero to his community. There is no external authority to adjudicate between one group and another on matters of right and wrong, and it is easy to end up in a "might is right" situation.

Many African Christians opt for a form of situation ethics when deciding whether it is ethical to join a strike. In other words, they argue that it is impossible to have a general rule on whether Christians should or should not participate in strikes and prefer to make their decisions on a case-by-case basis. In reaching their decision, they examine the particular situation and the probable consequences of this particular strike. The focus on results means that this approach is very similar to the teleological approach.

Situation ethics must be applauded for taking specific situations seriously and trying to determine how a Christian should respond to them. But the problem is that in determining what is the most practical action in a particular situation, those who follow this code are guided by pragmatism (what works or satisfies) and relativism (the belief that nothing is absolutely right or wrong or universally binding). Thus teachers might argue that it is acceptable for them to strike and not educate this years' students so that future students will receive a better education from better paid teachers, who are not worrying about how they are going to feed their families.

The above example demonstrates that how one defines "the right thing to do" is very easily affected by one's own needs and the needs of one's family. Rather than having to puzzle out this swirl of conflicting ethical requirements in every situation, the Christian should be committed to obeying the law of God as expressed in Scripture. Their actions should be governed by a deontological approach to ethics, which states that we have a duty to act in certain ways because certain principles like non-malevolence and beneficence are universally binding. Christians' duty is to obey God through a proper reading and interpretation of Scripture, in which he reveals his moral laws. These laws are binding on all peoples at all times and in every place. Situation ethics is right to point out that one of these laws, commanded in both the Old and New Testaments (Lev 19:18; Luke 10:27), is to love our neighbours. But love for one set of neighbours, our fellow-workers, does not mean that we are at liberty to tell lies about or harm another neighbour, our employer or the poor. Ethical behaviour is not what the Christian wants to do for his or her own purposes. A Christian must seek to do what pleases God.

Alternatives to Strikes

The serious disadvantages of strikes can outweigh their advantages. Christians in particular must be careful of taking part in actions that will harm others or violate God's commands. But do workers have any other options when it comes to obtaining fair wages and acceptable working conditions?

Some will argue that we should take a laissez-faire approach, and not attempt to change the status quo. According to these people, we should simply leave it to God to sort out our problems. This approach may appear to be very pious, but it is unacceptable. God does not expect us to ignore injustice and exploitation (Isa 1:16–17; Amos 5:15; Matt 23:23). We must speak out if we are dissatisfied with the state of affairs. If conditions or services are unsatisfactory, we must attempt to change them.

Many will choose to express their dissatisfaction by means of a strike, but industrial action is not the only alternative to passivity. We can also work to achieve our goals through persuasive arguments that confront folly, deceit and wickedness with truth. Truth is a powerful tool when it is argued, and becomes even more powerful when it is also backed up with facts relating to the situation.[4] Rational arguments will, in the long run, bring more positive fruit than strikes, which solve the problem of the day but leave tomorrow's problems unsolved. We need to remember that the power of the pen is stronger than the power of the gun.

Some Specific Questions

The bulk of this chapter has been devoted to discussing the ethics of strike action in general. There are, however, some specific questions that often arise:

Should someone be permitted to refrain from joining in a strike because of religious or moral objections?

When a labour union organizes a strike, all who belong to that union are expected to join in. This position is perfectly legal. However, just because something is legal does not mean that it is ethical. Abortion and

---

[4] John Stott, *Issues Facing Christians Today* (Grand Rapids: Zondervan, 1984), 59.

euthanasia are legal in many countries, but this does not mean that they are ethical for Christians.

Some Christians may feel that it would be wrong for them to participate in a strike (for example, medical personnel may believe that they owe a duty of care to their patients). In such cases they should be able to be recognized as conscientious objectors. "In conscientious objection, the agent claims that the refused act, if undertaken, would violate his or her conscience and would result in a loss of integrity and wholeness in the self, along with heavy guilt and shame."[5]

Religious beliefs and convictions are very important in most African nations. Labour leaders should thus recognize that it is improper to pressure members of the union to join in strike action that contradicts their fundamental moral beliefs. Members should have the freedom to be guided by their consciences if they are to practise their profession with integrity.

What if refusing to participate in a strike results in my becoming a victim?

Actions always have consequences. Those who participate in industrial action will face one set of consequences; those who do not will face a different set. The consequences may be unpleasant. But we should not let consequences be the primary factors in determining how we will act. The question for the Christian is: Is it better to go along with the crowd and have a guilty conscience before God or to obey God and suffer some loss? Like the apostles, we should choose to obey God rather than men (Acts 5:29).

Should someone who refuses to participate in a strike be allowed to enjoy the benefits achieved?

When a strike is successful the benefits achieved by those who endured financial hardship during the strike are available to everyone, even those who refused to join in the struggle. Some will argue that this is unfair. However, we may get a clearer perspective on this question if we think of it in a broader context. If a country goes to war, should those who

---

[5] James F. Childress, "Conscientious Objection". *Westminster Dictionary of Christian Ethics,* 118.

do not participate in the fighting, either because of some disability or because they do not believe in the cause being fought for, be prevented from experiencing any benefits produced by the war? No one would argue that people should be excluded from benefits that come to the country as a whole. In the same way, those whose consciences led them to refuse to participate in a strike should not be excluded from the benefits gained by the strike.

Conclusion

Though strikes have definite advantages and often promote just causes such as the improvement of working conditions, they raise many complex economic, political and ethical issues. Christians must understand the ramifications of involvement in actions that will bring their ethical and moral judgment into question.

Questions

1. Consider a general strike in which you took part or which you witnessed and answer the following questions:
   a) What were the underlying reasons for the strike?
   b) How was it conducted?
   c) What was accomplished?
   d) What were the costs of the strike? What damage was attributed to it?
   e) What goals were left unaccomplished?
2. Distinguish between a Christian's approach to a general strike and that of a non-Christian.

SECTION B
FINANCIAL ISSUES

INTRODUCTION TO FINANCIAL ISSUES

The African continent is racked with financial problems. Poverty is endemic. As the rest of the world is progressing, getting richer and enjoying a better standard of living, Africa is deteriorating rapidly. The population grows poorer, hungrier and sicker. Countries are consumed by war and ravaged by diseases like HIV/AIDS, and the number of widows and orphans increases daily. Yet in the midst of this suffering, a few individuals accumulate immense wealth.

This situation raises questions about why there are so many very poor people and why a few have such riches. These issues are addressed in **chapter 10**, which encourages us to listen humbly to the reality of poverty in Africa and to listen attentively to God as he speaks to us in order to be able to bring the good news to the poor in Africa. The chapter also examines some popular but ineffective approaches to addressing the problem of poverty.

The root causes of Africa's poverty include rampant corruption. From ordinary people to government officials, all use bribery and extortion to achieve their ends. The result is that a few individuals grow richer and richer while others become impoverished. Not only does corruption distort the economy, it also impedes economic development by discouraging donations and investment. Individuals and companies are well aware that any funds they provide are likely to be diverted into the pockets of a few powerful individuals. It is thus important that Christians think seriously about the issue of corruption, which is addressed in **chapter 11**.

In a context permeated with poverty, corruption, and a lack of transparency and accountability, it is likely that ethical questions will arise with regard to how funds are raised for various projects. Churches and Christian organizations need to be sure that any methods they use are in accordance with biblical principles. Thus **chapter 12** is devoted to the ethics of fund-raising.

10
POVERTY

"We are very, very, very poor" Harber Sabane, the elected mayor of Timbuktu, Mali, said a few years ago.[1] This 1995 description of one of Africa's oldest cities could equally apply to the whole African continent. According to the United Nations' 2005 Human Development Report, the five poorest countries in the world are Niger, Sierra Leone, Burkina Faso, Mali and Chad – all located in Africa.[2] Over the last decade, the quality of life for most Africans has steadily but surely declined: "Africa is the only part of the developing world where living standards have fallen over the past decade."[3] As an article in the Chicago Tribune pointed out, "Falling living standards, environmental degradation and high population growth rates risk pushing already impoverished communities to the brink of their capacity to survive, and into competition for scarce resources."[4]

Take Nigeria as an example. In 1992 some 41.8% of Nigeria's population subsisted on less than $1 per household per day. By 1996, this number had grown to 46.3%, and by 1999 to 65%.[5] UNICEF points out that Nigerian children born in 2005 have a life expectancy of only 44 years, and that of every 1000 children born, 100 die before their first birthday. Some 38% of children under five suffer from stunted growth due to malnutrition or disease. Only 48% of the population have access to safe drinking water.[6] Some 43% of the population are illiterate.

[1] Liz Sly, "Africa: Metamorphosis of a Continent" *Chicago Tribune*, 9 July 1995.
[2] United Nations Development Programme *Human Development Report 2005* (New York: United Nations, 2005), 222.
[3] Ibid.
[4] Liz Sly, "Africa: Metamorphosis".
[5] Economic Intelligence Unit. www.eiu.com.
[6] Unicef: "At a glance: Nigeria". Cited 30 April 2008. Online: www.unicef.org/infobycountry/nigeria_statistics.html.

Poverty manifests itself in many ways. Some of the most common are "prostitution, exposure to risks, corruption, robbery, street life, increased unemployment, living in squalor, shanties, shackles, high infant mortality, acute malnutrition, short life expectancy, human degradation, living in overcrowded and often poorly ventilated homes."[7]

Most other African countries can sing the same song. From the tip of the horn of Africa to Namibia, poverty is pervasive. Television viewers are bombarded with pictures of weak, hungry and emaciated human beings all over the continent. Beggars roam the streets of most of our cities, laying siege to car owners and begging for coins in order to feed their families and their stomachs.

What should the Christian do in light of these grim statistics? Is there good news for the poor of the African continent? What hope does the gospel offer the poor in Africa? To find an answer to this question, we need to practise what John Stott calls double listening:

> We listen to the Word with humble reverence, anxious to understand it, and resolved to believe and obey what we come to understand. We listen to the world with critical alertness, anxious to understand it too, and resolved not necessarily to believe and obey it, but to sympathize with it and to seek grace to discover how the gospel relates to it.[8]

First, it is necessary to look at the world and consider some of the harsh realities facing the African continent. As was said at the Uppsala Assembly of the World Council of Churches, we must hear "the cry of those who long for peace; of the hungry and exploited who demand bread and justice; of the victims of discrimination who claim dignity; and of the increasing millions who seek for the meaning of life".[9] Second, we must examine the biblical material, for it is the starting point for meaningful Christian discussion of these issues. Third, we should critically examine some approaches to the problem of poverty in Africa before making recommendations for addressing it.

---

[7] *Nigerian Human Development Report*, 199, 6:31.
[8] John Stott, *The Contemporary Christian: Applying God's Word to Today's World* (Downers Grove: IVP, 1992), 27–28.
[9] World Council of Churches, 1968, 5

Africa's Needs

A number of factors have contributed to the problem of poverty on the African continent. These include overpopulation, inadequate health care, illiteracy, war and civil unrest, corruption and famine. The continent thus has the following needs.

Need to develop resources

Though Africans are poorer than people in other continents, they have more children to feed. The average woman in sub-Saharan Africa gave birth to 5.3 children, whereas her counterpart in the United States averages 2.1 births. And Africa's population is growing faster than its current resources can sustain. The saying is true: the rich continue to get richer while the poor continue to have children, and to get hungrier and poorer. There is a desperate need to harness Africa's vast resources so that there is work and food for all its people.

Africa's governments do not always make wise decisions when it comes to developing and distributing the continent's resources. Sometimes they favour ambitious, attention-getting projects rather than projects that will contribute to economic growth. For example, the N149 billion (over \$10 billion) that Nigeria spent on hosting the 1999 FIFA World Youth Championship (WYC) could have been used to pay civil servants their salary. Failure to pay these salaries almost paralyzed the nation's workforce for months.

Need for better health care

Inadequate health care means that infant and maternal mortality are high on the African continent. HIV/AIDS claims hundreds of thousands of lives. Others die from tropical diseases such as the deadly Ebola fever, or from malaria and tuberculosis. Inadequate health care means that many workers are in poor health, which has a negative effect on their productivity.

Need for better education

Many African adults are illiterate and can neither read nor write. Their poor education restricts their opportunity to seek for meaningful employment. Women are at an even greater disadvantage than men, for men have easier access to schooling while women are mostly restricted to domestic duties.

Need for food

Droughts and other natural calamities often afflict African countries. These disasters make it impossible to cultivate the land and result in the loss of livestock. Famine and starvation follow with deadly results. The loss of many young adults to HIV/AIDS has also reduced the food supply, for children and the elderly lack the strength required for farming.

Need to inhibit warfare

Poverty both fuels and is fuelled by wars and internal strife. The article in the *Chicago Tribune* puts it well: "The potential for sudden outbursts of violence exists in most African countries as rising populations meet falling living standards and weak governments confront regional or ethnic movements."[10]

Nearly a third of sub-Saharan Africa's 42 countries are embroiled in international strife or civil wars, and more and more African rulers are seeking military solutions to political problems. At least thirteen have sent troops to neighbouring wars. There is also much ethnic strife within nations. The Hutu and Tutsi people of Rwanda and Burundi are quite literally at each others' throats and are likely to remain so for years to come. Ethiopia and Eritrea have been fighting for over thirty years.

Billions of dollars are spent on weapons that kill young men and women, leaving behind orphans, widows and devastated economies. Gangs of armed criminals, who can be as disruptive as political rebels, plague many countries. The cost is alarming:

> Around $300bn since 1990 has been lost by Algeria, Angola, Burundi, Central African Republic, Chad, Democratic

---

[10] Sly, "Africa: Metamorphosis".

Republic of Congo (DRC), Republic of Congo, Côte d'Ivoire, Djibouti, Eritrea, Ethiopia, Ghana, Guinea, Guinea-Bissau, Liberia, Niger, Nigeria, Rwanda, Senegal, Sierra Leone, South Africa, Sudan and Uganda.

This sum is equivalent to international aid from major donors in the same period. If this money was not lost due to armed conflict, it could solve the problems of HIV and AIDS in Africa, or it could address Africa's needs in education, clean water and sanitation, and prevent tuberculosis and malaria.

Our research estimates that Africa loses around $18bn per year due to wars, civil wars, and insurgencies. On average, armed conflict shrinks an African nation's economy by 15 per cent, and this is probably a conservative estimate. The real costs of armed violence to Africans could be much, much higher.[11]

The cost of the armed violence is heavily felt by civilian populations:

Most of Africa's wars are fought between a national army and guerrillas representing different groups, including those representing particular ethnicities. The tactics are to deny resources to the other side. Food is stolen, towns looted and roads mined. Villages are often burned; the young men are forced to become fighters, the women and children porters. Hearts, minds and welfare are rarely matters of no concerns. Thousands flee to seek survival in the bush or in camps supplied by aid agencies.[12]

These same tactics were used in the DRC, where militiamen reserved food for themselves and their families and controlled the distribution of aid so as to maintain their power over the other refugees.

Need for honest government

Corruption has infected politics and government in Africa. In 2001 Transparency International identified Nigeria as one of the most corrupt

---

[11] Oxfam International *Africa's missing billions: International arms flows and the cost of conflict* (Briefing paper 107; IANSA, Oxfam, and Saferworld, 2007), 3. Cited 18 Nov 2007. Online: www. oxfam.org/en/files/bp107_africas_missing_billions_0710.pdf.
[12] *The Economist*, 16 November 1998.

countries in the world.[13] The country's ample resources are being wasted. Despite earning billions of dollars as an oil producer, there has been almost no development. Instead, corruption has been elevated to an art form.

Nigeria is not alone in this. Cameroon also ranks among the world's most corrupt countries. General Mainasara of Niger broke and abused political promises and allowed workers' salaries to go unpaid for five months. Assassinated by his personal bodyguards, he left behind a very depressed economy with the citizens unable to provide for their basic needs. Niger is now one of the five poorest countries in Africa. Sierra Leone, although endowed with natural resources whose proper use could transform the nation's economy, is still struggling with poverty. The Republic of Guinea is also plagued by abject poverty due to corruption.

Need for Christians to live out their faith

Sadly, Christians are also implicated in some of the factors that contribute to keeping Africa in poverty. Historically, Liberia has believed itself to be a Christian nation, and in the Liberian civil war from 1989–95 all the various political leaders, including Charles Taylor, Samuel Doe and Prince Johnson, called themselves Christians. Yet these leaders encouraged brutality and devastated their country. Christians, and even pastors, became involved in these wars, just as they did in Rwanda. Christians are also complicit in the corruption that plagues many African countries and inhibits development.

Biblical Perspectives on Poverty

If Christians are to be salt and light in Africa, they need to understand what the Scriptures have to say about poverty and what this means for how they should live.

When God created Adam, the ground was good and produced in abundance as he cultivated it. But the fall changed all this. Adam's sin led God to curse the ground so that farming was no longer easy: "through painful toil you will eat of it all the days of your life. It will

---

[13] Transparency International. Cited 20 Nov 2007. Online: www.transparency.org/policy_research/surveys_indices/cpi/2001

produce thorns and thistles for you, and you will eat the plants of the field. By the sweat of your brow you will eat your food until you return to the ground" (Gen 3:18–19). Sin is thus the ultimate cause of poverty in our world.

The poverty that results from sin is both spiritual and material. Thus when Jesus says "Blessed are the poor in spirit" (Matt 5:3) he is referring to those who recognize their spiritual poverty and are humble and meek.[14] The writers of Psalms also use the word "poor" to refer to spiritual poverty. However, due to the vastness of the subject, I shall here limit myself to dealing only with the material poverty of those who are "destitute of wealth and material goods, lacking in even the necessities of life".[15]

Poverty in the Old Testament

In the Old Testament, many references to the poor specify that this group includes orphans, strangers, aliens and widows (see, for example, Exod 22:21–24). These people were dependant on others for their livelihood.

A number of different words are used to describe the poor. The word *ani* (used 71 times), denotes a person "who occupies a lowly position. He has to look up to others who are higher than him. He is the man bowed down under pressure who finds himself in a dependent relationship.[16] *Dal* (used 48 times) comes from the Hebrew root *dalal*, meaning to be thin, weak and sickly, and refers to physical and material poverty. *Ebhyon* (used 61 times) means "one who begs". Such a person is so poor that he has been reduced to begging.[17] The word *rush* means "the needy". It indicates not only a need, but also an expectation and a request (Exod 23:6–11).[18]

Before Israel went into the promised land, God had assured them of prosperity if they would obey him: "There should be no poor among you, for in the land the Lord your God is giving you to possess as your

---

[14] U. Wolf, "Poor" in *The Interpreters Dictionary of the Bible*, 844.

[15] Ibid., 843.

[16] Albert Gelin, *The Poor of Yahweh* (trans. Kathryn Sullivan; Collegeville, Minn.: Liturgical Press, 1964), 10.

[17] Augustin George, "Poverty in the Old Testament". *Gospel Poverty: Essays in Biblical Theology* (trans. Michael D. Guinan; Chicago: Franciscan Herald Press, 1977), 4.

[18] Gelin, *The Poor of Yahweh*, 20.

inheritance, he will richly bless you, if only you fully obey the Lord your God and are careful to follow all these commands I am giving you today" (Deut 15:4–5).

However, since they were rebellious, there were many poor and needy in the land who needed help. God in his love and mercy made provision for them. In the books of Deuteronomy and Leviticus, which set out God's laws, he insists that the poor are to be treated fairly. They should not suffer injustice because they are poor (Exod 23:2, 6, 7). If they borrow money, the lender is not to charge interest on the loan (Exod 22:25; Lev 25:36; Deut 23:20). If a poor person's cloak is taken as a pledge that a loan will be repaid, the cloak is to be returned before nightfall (Deut 24:12–13). The laws on gleaning required the Israelites to leave some of their harvest for foreigners and the poor (Lev 19:9–10; 23:22). Farmers did have the power to grant "gleaning rights to certain of the poor and sometimes favored an especially deserving person, as Boaz did Ruth".[19] The laws regarding the jubilee and the Sabbath year (Exod 23:10–11; Lev 25:1–55; Deut 15:1–11) dealt with situations in which Israelites who were in debt sold themselves as slaves to fellow Israelites. Such slaves were to be well treated and were to be paid for their services when they were released from slavery.

These laws would have prevented people from falling deeply into poverty. But by the time of the monarchy, the laws seem to have been disregarded as the nation experienced dramatic political and economic changes. An urban civilization began to arise, with kings amassing wealth and enlisting people into the army. Wealthy landowners took advantage of hard times and wars to oppress the poor.[20] Colin Brown notes that during the monarchy "the economy changed from one of barter to one using money, and many of the farmers became financially dependent on townsmen".[21] The story of Ahab and Naboth, in 1 Kings 21, illustrates the injustices that were practiced against the poor by the rich.

During the time of the prophets, being poor became synonymous with being oppressed. In his condemnation of oppression, Amos uses all the Hebrew words for "poor" except *rush*: "They sell the righteous for silver and the needy (*ebhyon*) for a pair of sandals. They trample

---

[19] Rousas John Rushdoony, *Institutes of Biblical Law* (Phillipsburg: Presbyterian and Reformed, 1973), 248.

[20] Gelin, *The Poor of Yahweh*, 16.

[21] Colin Brown. "Poor" in *The New International Dictionary of New Testament Theology*, 2:822.

the heads of the poor (*dallim*) as upon the dust of the ground and deny justice to the oppressed (*anawim*) (Amos 2:6; see also Amos 4:1; Isa 10:1–2; 11:4). The most prominent cause of poverty was injustice and exploitation of the poor by the rich (Isa 3:14; Jer 5:27–28; 6:13; 22:13–17). The prophets also spoke out against traders who exploited their customers (Hos 12:7; Amos 8:5–6; Mic 6:10–11), corrupt judges (Isa 5:23; 10:1–2; Ezek 22:29; Amos 5:7; Mic 3:9–11), and the seizure of property (Mic 2:1–3).

But not all who were rich exploited the poor. Job, who was an exceedingly wealth man (Job 1:3) had no hesitation in claiming that he had been compassionate to the poor and needy. He responded to their pleas (Job 19:12), comforted widows (29:13) and helped the handicapped (29:15). He could even be described as having been "a father to the needy" (29:16).

In the Wisdom literature, "virtue was linked with poverty, wealth with wickedness" (19:1; 28:6; 19:22). However, the writers of Proverbs recognized that poverty could also be caused "by laziness (10:4; 19:15, 24; 20:13; 21:17), foolishness (11:14; 10:14–16; 13:18) and shortsightedness (21:5)".[22]

In Psalms, the enemies of the poor are referred to as the wicked (10:4–7; 140:4, 8), despoilers (35:10), creditors (109:11a), plunderers (109:11b), and perjured witnesses (35:11; 109:31).[23] In their suffering, the poor turn helplessly and humbly to God and seek his help (Psalm 72:2, 4, 12–14).[24]

This brief survey shows that the Old Testament testifies that God cares for the poor and that oppression arouses his anger. He formulated special laws to enable his people to care for the poor. "A compassionate and caring attitude to the poor was regarded as the will of God, the virtue of kings, and the duty of the common people."[25]

---

[22] E. Calvin Beisner, *Prosperity and Poverty: The Compassionate Use of Resources in a World of Scarcity* (Westchester, Ill.: Crossway, 1988), 195.

[23] Ibid., 116.

[24] Brown, "Poor", 2:822.

[25] F. Charles Fensham, "Widow, Orphan and the Poor in Ancient Near Eastern Legal and Wisdom Literature". *Journal of Near Eastern Studies* 21 (1962): 137.

Poverty in the New Testament

While the New Testament does not contain such detailed instructions regarding the treatment of the poor as the Old Testament does, much attention is still given to their needs. Two Greek words are used to refer to them. The first, *penes* (used 34 times), refers to a labourer, the type of person who is not a wealthy landowner but who has to work hard to earn a living. Such people were often economically and legally oppressed. Jesus himself was among the poor in this sense, for "foxes have holes and birds of the air have nests, but the Son of Man has nowhere to lay his head" (Matt 8:20; Luke 9:50).

The other word used is *ptochos* (used 34 times), mostly in the gospels (24 times). Luke in particular uses it ten times. It refers to people who are beggars, utterly dependant on others. This is the word Jesus uses when he says "Blessed are the poor in spirit" (Matt 5:3; see also Luke 6:20). It "served as a particularly apt metaphor for those who had no hope except in God."[26]

The poor had a prominent place in Jesus' ministry. Compassion and care for the needy is a central theme in many of his parables. A rich man is condemned not because of his riches but because he neglected the poor man (Lazarus) who lay at his gate (Luke 16:19–31). When others decline the invitation to the Great Supper, it is enjoyed by the maimed and the poor (Luke 14:10–24). Jesus also noted the behaviour of the poor, and praised a poor widow's generosity, contrasting it with that of the scribes who exploited the poor (Mark 12:38–44). He advised the rich young ruler to sell his possessions and give to the poor (Mark 10:21; Luke 18:22). His conversation with Zacchaeus prompted the tax collector to give half his possessions to the poor as a sign of his conversion (Luke 19:1–10).

Jesus not only taught about the need to help the poor; his actions provided an example of compassionate care. As Peter later said, "he went around doing good" (Acts 10:38). Thus he raised the only son of the widow of Nain, a woman who would have been left destitute with no husband and no son to care for her (Luke 7:12–15). He was aware of the physical needs of those who came long distances to hear him speak (Mark 8:1–9). To drive home the need to care for the poor, he declared

---

[26] Leslie J. Hoppe, *Being Poor: A Biblical Study* (Wilmington, Delaware: Michael Glazier, 1987), 155.

that caring for the sick, needy, and homeless was actually caring for him, and that failure to care for them was equivalent to neglecting him (Matt 25:31–36).

It is true that shortly before his death, Jesus did say, "The poor you will always have with you, and you can help them any time you want. But you will not always have me" (Mark 14:1–9; Matt 19:16–21). This statement is not meant to encourage callous disregard for the poor; it was simply a statement of fact that echoed Deuteronomy 15:11: "There will always be poor people in the land". This statement in Deuteronomy was written in the context of God's desire that "there should be no poor among you" and of an exhortation to generosity (Deut 15:4–10).

After Jesus' ascension, the early church that formed in Jerusalem also took care of the poor and needy (Acts 2:44–45; 4:33–35). The same habit continued as the church spread beyond Jerusalem. Paul wrote to the churches about collections being made for the needy (1 Cor16:1–2; 2 Cor 8:1–4; 9:1–2) and urged them to remember the poor (Rom 12:13). James also condemned the unfair treatment of the poor (Jas 2:1–6).

Summary of the biblical data

The consistent teaching of Scripture is that God cares for the poor. The Old Testament position can be summed up in the words of Proverbs 14:31: "He who oppresses the poor shows contempt for their Maker, but whoever is kind to the needy honours God". The New Testament considered disregard for the poor a sin. The Scriptures therefore bear consistent testimony to God's compassion and care for the poor and to his command that individual believers and his church care for them.

Mistaken Assumptions about Wealth and Poverty

Given the abundant biblical teaching on the subject, one would expect Christians to agree about how to approach the problem of poverty. Unfortunately, this is not the case. Some approaches, while sincere, are unacceptable because they misrepresent biblical teaching.

Before we examine such approaches, it is important to be aware of our own biases and theological prejudices when it comes to the problem of poverty: [27]

- If we are authoritarians or fatalists, we blame the state of the poor on fate;
- If we are hierarchists, we may be uncertain whom to blame, but tend to assign responsibility to the inept poor who must be re-educated;
- If we are individualists, we think that people are poor because of bad luck or personal incompetence;
- If we are egalitarians, we blame the corrupt system for promoting poverty. The poor are deprived by evil systems which oppress them and deny them privileges.

These biases affect not only whom we blame for poverty but also our perspective on the factors that make for economic growth, our assumptions about how to manage resources, and our willingness to take risks in order to bring about change.

We cannot discuss all the mistaken approaches to poverty at length, and so will focus on only a few points, particularly those raised by Ronald Sider, an evangelical scholar who is well known for fighting for the cause of the poor.

God sides with the poor

Christian literature on poverty is unanimous that God is concerned for the poor. However, some authors go still further and say that God actively sides with the poor. Sider has this to say:

> In a mysterious way that we can only half fathom, the sovereign of the universe identifies with the weak and destitute (Proverbs 14:31). Even more moving is the positive formulation, "He who is kind to the poor lends to the Lord" (19:17). By contrast with the way you and I, as well as the comfortable and powerful of every age and society, always act toward the poor, God seems to have an overwhelming bias in favor of the poor. But he is biased only in contrast with our sinful unconcern …

---

[27] Judith Lingenfelter, "Why Do We Argue over How to Help the Poor?" *Missiology* 36 (1998): 154–166.

God is not neutral. His freedom from bias does not mean that he maintains neutrality in the struggle for justice. God is on the side of the poor. The Bible clearly and repeatedly teaches that God is at work in history casting down the rich and exalting the poor because frequently the rich are wealthy precisely because they have oppressed the poor or have neglected to aid the needy.[28]

David Chilton rightly criticizes Sider for this claim that God takes sides and indiscriminately identifies with the poor: "Whose side is God on? Not the rich; not the poor; not any social or economic class; not any race."[29] God does not take sides. He is just and compassionate to all.

Wealth is acquired only by exploiting others

In the passage quoted above, Sider asserts that "frequently the rich are wealthy precisely because they have oppressed the poor". Thus rich nations are seen to be responsible for the plight of the poor. Sider accuses "all the rich and developed countries" of being "participants in a system that dooms even more people to agony and death than slavery did".[30] Similarly Dom Helder Camara, Archbishop of Recife, Brazil, comments on the fact that 20 per cent of the world's population possess 80 per cent of the world's resources, and asks, "The 20 per cent who are keeping 80 per cent in a situation which is often subhuman – are they or are they not responsible for the violence and hatred which are beginning to break out all over the world?"[31]

Colonial empires and richer nations have indeed exploited poorer nations. But this is not the whole story, for nations can become wealthy in other ways. Japan, for example, one of the wealthiest nations in the world, did not acquire its wealth by exploiting colonies or other countries. Moreover, the oppression that poor countries suffer does not always come from another country. As will be discussed in the next

---

[28] Ronald J. Sider, *Rich Christians in an Age of Hunger* (London: Hodder and Stoughton, 1977), 61, 76.

[29] David Chilton, *Productive Christians in an Age of Guilt Manipulators: A Biblical Response to Ronald J. Sider* (Tyler, Tex.: Institute for Christian Economics, 1981), 85.

[30] Ronald J. Sider, "How We Oppress the Poor" in *Christianity Today* (July 16, 1976).

[31] Helder Camara, speech delivered in Geneva in January 1970 to the World Council of Church's Consultation on Ecumenical Assistance for Development Projects. Cited 21 Nov 2007. Online: peaceandnonviolence.blogspot.com/2007/03/fetters-of-injustice-dom-helder-camara.html.

chapter, there is often internal exploitation. Government officials enrich their families and ethnic and tribal factors are allowed to take precedence over any commitment to the economic health of the nation. The result is that

> most Nigerians have come to believe that unless their "own men" are in government they are unable to secure those socio-economic amenities that are disbursed by the government. Hence governmental decisions about the siting of industries, the building of `roads, award of scholarships, and appointments to positions in the public services, are closely examined in terms of their benefits to the various ethnic groups in the country.[32]

This problem is not unique to Nigeria, but is found in many African countries. Ethnic rivalry and a lack of cooperation make it almost impossible for any economic system to succeed.

On the individual level, poverty is not always caused by oppression. Studies have shown that people become poor for a variety of reasons:

> [Some] because of their own lack of discipline and initiative … Other people are genuine victims, suffering from injury, diseases, or catastrophes such as famine and earthquakes … Still others are poor because of economic exploitation. Slavery is a historical example of this; South African apartheid and the East Indian caste system are contemporary versions.[33]

The crucial point is that economic victimization is not the only cause of poverty. Other factors play a role, including the many wars that ravage Africa.

The argument that all wealth results from oppression of others is based on the following assumption:

> Wealth cannot be created but only distributed. The logic goes like this. If there are eight people at a party and a pie is cut in eight pieces, and I take two or three pieces for myself, then I have taken what belongs to the others. The fact that I have

---

[32] Okwudiba Nnoli, *Ethnic Politics in Nigeria* (Enugu, Nigeria: Fourth Dimension, 1980), 176.
[33] Lloyd Billings, "Compassion and the Poor" in *Is Capitalism Christian? Toward a Christian Perspective on Economics* (ed. Frank Schaeffer; Westchester, Ill.: Crossway, 1985), 343, 345.

more to eat proves I took from them and am the cause of their lack.[34]

This zero-sum philosophy does not stand the test of reality. Wealth can indeed be created.

The argument that wealth automatically involves exploitation also cannot stand the test of Scripture, which makes it clear that riches may be a sign of God's blessing. Not all those who are rich are exploiters, as evidenced by the examples of Abraham and Job.

Wealth should be distributed equally

Another misconception is that justice demands the equal distribution of wealth. Jeremy Rifkin, for example, states that, "without a fundamental redistribution of wealth, all talk of lowering energy flow and heeding our planet's biological limits will result in nothing but the rich locking the poor forever into their subservient status."[35] Sider similarly declares, "God sides with the poor because he disapproves of extreme wealth and poverty … The rich neglect or oppose justice because justice demands that they end their oppression and share with the poor."[36]

In arguing that the gap between the rich and the poor is sinful and should be eliminated, Sider appeals to the Apostle Paul: "Our desire is not that others might be relieved while you are hard pressed, but that there might be equality. At the present time your plenty will supply what they need, so that in turn their plenty will supply what you need. Then there will be equality" (2 Cor 8:13–14). Here, Sider claims, "Paul clearly enunciates the principle of economic equality among the people of God to guide the Corinthians in their giving."[37]

But careful examination of the context of Paul's words in 2 Corinthians shows that he is not insisting on equal distribution of wealth among all the churches in Macedonia, Greece, Asia Minor and Jerusalem. Rather than speaking of the funds he is collecting as a compulsory redistribution, Paul speaks of "this grace of giving" (8:7), compares the gift to Christ's gracious gift (8:9), and says that the gifts are "the

---

[34] Randy Alcorn, *Money, Possessions and Eternity* (Wheaton: Tyndale, 1989), 246.

[35] Jeremy Rifkin, *Entropy: A New World View* (New York: Viking, 1980), 194–195. Quoted in John Jefferson Davis, *Your Wealth in God's World: Does the Bible Support the Free Market?* (Phillipsburg, N.J.: Presbyterian and Reformed Publishing Company, 1984), 38.

[36] Sider, *Rich Christians*, 76.

[37] Sider, *Rich Christians*, 81.

proof of your love" (8:24). Their gift is generous (9:5) and voluntary (9:7) and is not motivated by a sense of duty but by their awareness of "the surpassing grace God has given you" (9:14). It is thus safe to say that "the equality envisioned is not that of economic condition but of proportionate giving – giving in proportion to what one has, not what one does not have, and of needs being met".[38]

Paul stresses gratitude rather than guilt as the motivation for helping the poor. This principle is in accordance with the teaching of the entire New Testament that *giving*, not receiving, is the Christian lifestyle. We should not be waiting for others to distribute their wealth to us, but should be actively responding to the needs of the poor among us.

Arguments that God is on the side of the poor and demands for equal distribution of wealth lead logically to calls for violent revolution to overthrow the rich. Such calls find eager audiences in impoverished countries. In Liberia in 1980 the People's Redemption Council led by Samuel K. Doe, who later became Liberia's "unshakable" man, assassinated President William R. Tolbert and executed thirteen of his top government officials because they found the Tolbert government filled with "rampant corruption". Ten years later, Doe's government suffered violence at the hands of Charles Taylor's rebels for similar reasons.

Military coups are often justified on the basis that government officials are enriching themselves while the poor are getting poorer. Generals Babangida and Abacha of Nigeria, for example, took over promising to make life better for all Nigerians, but ended by enriching only themselves. The twenty-nine years of military rule in Nigeria accomplished little for the poor. The Nigerian economy has become worse and the citizens have become poorer, exploited, degraded and dehumanized. In other African countries the story is the same. Once a group gets into power, it too becomes rich and neglects the poor.

Those who recognize that violent revolutions are neither a biblical nor a practical solution to helping the masses may attempt to overcome inequality by confiscating the wealth of the rich and giving it to the poor. That approach has also proved unsuccessful:

> Seldom if ever can poverty be eased by confiscating the wealth
> of the favored … If one seeks to prevent inequality, one almost

---

[38] Beisner, *Prosperity and Poverty*, 72.

inevitably stifles productivity and harms the least favored. At least that has been the universal or all but universal experience of every society that has seriously tried it.[39]

Moreover, the redistributed wealth is unlikely to bring general benefits. This is what the Indian Prime Minister Indira Gandhi found when she changed the constitution and ended the privileges enjoyed by Indian princes. The redistributed wealth amounted to a mere eight *paise* (Rs. 0.08 or about one U.S. cent) per person per year.

Recommendations for Helping the Poor

The mistaken assumptions about the relations between rich and poor all rely on guilt as the motive for action. But at times that guilt is misplaced. If people are not directly or indirectly responsible for the poverty of others, how can they be guilty of what they did not do? Thus the solution to Africa's poverty is not simply to make anyone who is wealthy feel guilty. (This is not to say that those who have accumulated wealth through exploitation of others should not be called to account for their actions.)

Africa urgently needs to recognize that the solution to its economic woes is not simply some change of government or some new political system (important as these may be), but a change in the hearts of the people. Moral and spiritual solutions are basic to any attempt to deal with the problem of poverty.

> If scarcity and want are caused first of all by external conditions, and secondly by defects in human wisdom, character, and desire to deal equitably with one another in sharing this world's limited resources, it is apparent that we cannot hope for a full and lasting solution to the problem of scarcity and resultant poverty unless we have a means to repair those defects. We do have such a means, but it is spiritual, not social, in nature. Social remedies are not worthless, indeed, they can have great value, but they cannot solve the problem in any fundamental way.[40]

[39] Harold O. J. Brown. "The Problem of Poverty", Lecture notes, Trinity Evangelical Divinity School, Deerflield: Illinois, 1992.
[40] Brown, "The Problem of Poverty", 19.

So what does the church have to say to those in our community who are daily oppressed by the economic and political structures? Two thousand years ago, our founder claimed to bring good news to the poor (Luke 4:18). Does the church still have good news for them? Or have we joined the ranks of the oppressors? The final section of this chapter contains some answers to these questions and provides recommendations to help the church be a real source of hope to the poor in Africa.

Be salt and light

Christians in many poverty-stricken countries have failed to obey Christ's call to be salt and light, and have instead contributed to the exploitation of the poor. We need to hear John Stott's reminder of what Christ's call means: Christians are to be fundamentally different from non-Christians; we must permeate non-Christian society; we must influence non-Christian society; we must retain our distinctiveness.[41] We cannot bring good news to the poor unless we ourselves are good. When Christians are involved furthering the rottenness, darkness, degradation and deprivation of others, it is indeed grievous.

In 1997 Christians in Nigeria felt so strongly that they were responsible for the moral decay in society that they met in the capital, Abuja, for a historic meeting known as the Congress on Christian Ethics in Nigeria (COCEN). At the end of a five-day meeting, they came up with the Nigeria Covenant, a powerful pledge and tool for halting Nigeria's downward moral spiral. The pledge is a promise before God and each other to be distinct, to be righteous and to make a difference.

Christians in other African countries should study the moral impasse that is affecting their country and come up with similar covenants to which all Christians, whether in government or in private life, should commit themselves. If the church in Africa were to covenant before God and before each other to be uncompromisingly honest, to defend the poor, and to do all it can within its power to better their lives, it would indeed be a source of good news to the poor.

---

[41] John Stott, *New Issues Facing Christians Today* (London: Marshall Pickering, 1999), 66–68.

Uphold human dignity

The poor, though lacking in material possessions, are created in the image of God. Thus God loves and cares for them, and believers should take care to treat them as persons, not things.

Follow Jesus' example

Jesus' ministry demonstrated God's concern for the poor and needy. His primary mission was to die for the sins of many (Mark 10:45), but he also demonstrated God's mercy and compassion by healing the sick, casting out demons, and providing for people's physical needs. He defined his own mission as preaching good news to the poor, prisoners, the blind and the oppressed (Luke 4:18–19). "The poor understand bondage enough to appreciate the concept of deliverance … Though he himself had little, Jesus made a regular practice of giving to the poor (John 13:29)."[42]

Jesus also taught his disciples to love their enemies (Matt 5:44), an extension of the second great commandment in the Old Testament, which is that we should love our neighbours as ourselves (Lev 19:18). Love in this context is not essentially a feeling but is taking concrete action to meet someone's need. Christ's entire ministry could be characterized as dedicated to serving the true needs of men and women.

> Giving to the poor and helpless and caring for them is so basic to the Christian faith that those who don't do it are not considered true Christians. Indeed, Christ himself says if we feed the hungry, give drink to the thirsty, invite in the stranger, give clothes to the needy, care for the sick, and visit the persecuted, we are doing those things to him" (Matt 25:34–35).[43]

Peter's teaching to the household of Cornelius could be used to summarize this point. "Jesus … went around doing good and healing all who were under the power of the devil, because God was with him" (Acts 10:38).

---

[42] Randy Alcorn, *Money, Possessions and Eternity* (Wheaton: Tyndale House, 1989), 250. Some of the passages include Luke 14:12–14.
[43] Alcorn, *Money, Possession and Eternity*, 251.

NIGERIA COVENANT

We, the Christians of Nigeria, believe that God in Christ is the master of our lives and that He has revealed His will in the Holy Bible. Therefore, we pledge to submit to the lordship of Christ, leadership of the Holy Spirit, and authority of God's Word in every part of life.

We believe the family is the first and most important social institution God created. Therefore we pledge to develop and maintain our families according to the principles of God's Word which prescribe marriage of one man to one woman for life. We will practice faithfulness and fidelity by forsaking fornication, adultery, homosexuality and all other forms of sexual abuse. We further pledge to rear our children in the fear and admonition of the Lord.

We believe the legitimate ownership of property is recognized and commended in the Holy Scriptures. Therefore, we pledge to acquire property only in legitimate ways and refrain from stealing or defrauding.

We believe positions of leadership and responsibility are given by God for service. Therefore, we pledge not to use our positions to give unfair preference to the members of our family, clan, tribe, ethnic or religious group or use our positions in any other way to gain unfair advantage over others.

We believe Jesus Christ is Truth Incarnate and that the pursuit of truth is mandatory for Christians. Therefore, we pledge to uphold and defend truth, regardless of its source and to resist lying, cheating or other distortions of truth. Furthermore, we pledge to reject all attempts to pervert education through examination fraud, falsification of documents, cultic activities and exploitation of students in all its forms.

We believe that without justice, there can be no peace in any human society. Therefore, we pledge to be just in all our dealings with others and to resist all forms of injustice and corruption in society including giving or receiving bribes of money, positions, material possessions, sexual favours or intangible assets. We will also resist any form of injustice or unfairness in the law enforcement or judicial systems. We further pledge to discourage others we see practicing such things.

We believe that public assets including church property and the environment are a trust given to us to be used for the glory of God and the benefit of mankind. Therefore, we pledge not to exploit, abuse, steal, misuse or mismanage any of these public assets.

We believe that God has ordained governments to safeguard the well-being of their peoples and resources. Therefore, we commit ourselves to respect our leaders and live by the laws of the Federal Republic of Nigeria unless these conflict with the Law of God. We further pledge to work for a moral turnaround in the politics and governance of Nigeria through education and active participation.

We believe the Church is the united body of Christ and that it has a sacred duty to provide the moral foundation and be the conscience of the nation. Therefore, we reject sectarianism, commercialism, extravagant lifestyles, neglect of the needy and all other evils that weaken the testimony and purpose of the Church.

We solemnly pledge to fulfill these commitments, no matter the price, and to support all others who join us in our stand for Christian ethics.

In the Name of Jesus Christ. Amen.[44]

Present the whole gospel

A proper response to the poor involves presenting the whole gospel. Too often, the gospel has been presented only in part. Some theologically conservative Christians can rightly be accused of preaching "pie in the sky by-and-by when you die" for they focus only on evangelism and neglect the present needs of the poor. Such an approach involves an understanding of salvation that is rooted in Greek rather than Christian thought:

> Salvation in Scripture is no liberation from the body – as in Platonic thought and much eastern religion – but salvation of the whole person, body and soul. For the sake of our salvation the Word was made flesh (John 1:14) – the Son of God assuming our true and entire human nature, while at the

---

[44] Nigeria Covenant. Cited 27 Nov 2007. Online: www.cdfafrica.org/nigeria_covenant.htm.

same time retaining His divine essence. The Christian hope beyond this life is for the resurrection of the body, not merely for the immortality of the soul. God made us as whole persons, redeemed us as whole persons, cares for us as whole persons, and will finally glorify us as whole persons.[45]

We need to take seriously the social implications of Jesus' Great Commission in Matthew 28:19–20: we are not only to preach to people and to convert them, but are also to teach them how to live in a way that pleases God. As John Stott reminds us, "We have to beware of magnifying faith and knowledge at the expense of love … For saving faith and serving love belong together. Whenever one is absent, so is the other. Neither can exist in isolation."[46]

Paul demonstrates this combination of evangelism and discipleship. He not only made sure that the young Christians in the early church were strong spiritually, but he also taught and modelled the importance of working in order to feed themselves:

> Keep away from every brother who is idle and does not live according to the teaching you received from us. For you yourselves know how you ought to follow our example. We were not idle when we were with you, nor did we eat anyone's food without paying for it. On the contrary, we worked night and day, labouring and toiling so that we would not be a burden to any of you. We did this, not because we do not have the right to such help, but in order to make ourselves a model for you to follow. For even when we were with you, we gave you this rule: If a man will not work, he shall not eat. We hear that some among you are idle. They are not busy; they are busybodies. Such people we command and urge in the Lord Jesus Christ to settle down and earn the bread they eat. And as for you, brothers, never tire of doing what is right (2 Thess 3:6–12).

This passage warns against laziness and encourages hard work, which prevents poverty. We, too, should encourage believers to develop a mature understanding of work. This has been done in the past. The

---

[45] Davis, *Your Wealth in God's World*, 64.
[46] Stott, *New Issues Facing Christians*, 48.

missionaries did not only preach spiritual salvation. They also taught our parents how to work and improve their crops. They were presenting a whole gospel, affecting both our spiritual and physical lives.

However, it is not enough just to encourage people to work hard; we must also encourage their employers to pay a living wage. Labour is so cheap in Africa that it is said that many Africans work like elephants but can only afford to eat as little as ants. There should be laws requiring employers to pay a minimum wage, as is the case in many Western countries.

Give to charity

Scripture clearly teaches that believers, whether rich or poor, are to give to charity from a willing and generous heart. Such giving is not done by compulsion. The New Testament includes several references to regular, systematic giving by congregations to meet the needs of the poor (Acts 4:34; 1 Cor 16:2; 2 Cor 8–9). If there is one thing that can be learned from the early church, it is that Christians should respond to the needs of the poor, especially those in their own midst. Galatians 6:10 states this very explicitly: "Therefore, as we have opportunity, let us do good to all people, especially to those who belong to the family of believers."

We would do well to meditate on the words of the African church father, Augustine:

> That bread which you keep belongs to the hungry; that coat which you preserve in your wardrobe, to the naked; those shoes which are rotting in your possession, to the shoeless; that gold which you have hidden in the ground, to the needy. Wherefore, as often as you are able to help others, and refuse, so often did you do them wrong.[47]

"Every church and individual Christian must ask, 'What are we doing to feed the hungry and help the poor? What are we doing to secure justice for the poor? What are we doing to uphold the cause of the needy?'"[48]

---

[47] Alcorn, *Money, Possession and Eternity*, 223.
[48] Ibid., 255.

Implement policies that help the poor

Government policies can weaken the economy and hurt the poor. In Nigeria the mismanagement of the economy and the subsequent introduction of the structural adjustment programme led to a sharp increase in the cost of goods and services while the income of the Nigerian worker dropped. The imposition of programmes like these has had a negative effect on many African economies:

> The stabilization and adjustment policies advocated by the IMF and the World Bank and widely adopted in Africa have not succeeded in restoring growth in most countries; indeed, they have often been accompanied by continued economic deterioration. Moreover, in many respects, the policies are pushing African economies away from a desirable long-term structure especially because they are dampening comparative advantage in non-traditional agriculture and industry.[49]

National governments should be encouraged to introduce programmes that will reduce economic hardship. These programmes should be targeted to groups such as the rural poor, civil servants, widows and orphans. In Nigeria, for example, the government has established a Family Economic Advancement Programme (FEAP) to provide loans to families to start small businesses. A Women's Rights Advocacy and Protection Agency (WRAPA) has also been established to protect the rights of women, who are usually degraded and abused in Nigerian society. Programmes like these are excellent ways of obeying God's command to care for the poor. Neither programme sets out to produce an artificial equality, but each seeks to alleviate suffering and to give the poor an opportunity to find relief.

Policy initiatives should also extend beyond the national level to the international community, which should offer debt relief to impoverished countries. There is biblical precedent for the rich assisting the poor by writing off debt.

---

[49] Francis M. Stewart, "Short-Term Policies for Long-Term Development" quoted in Bello's *Dark Victory: The United States, Structural Adjustment and Global Poverty* (London: Pluto Press, 1999), 33.

Support programmes run by churches and non-governmental organizations (NGOs)

Programmes run by churches and non-governmental organizations (NGOs) play an important role in helping the poor. In most African countries, mission agencies have long operated the only development programmes designed to combat poverty. They have provided education and medical care and have improved agricultural production so that the farmers are able to take care of themselves and their families.

Christian NGOs that aim to raise the living standards of the poor include:

• The Christian Rural and Urban Development Association of Nigeria (CRUDAN), which has the goal of promoting "Christian wholistic development by enabling the church in Nigeria to empower the poor in the name of Jesus Christ".[50]

• People Oriented Development (POD) of ECWA aims "to promote improved and sustainable living conditions through effective community mobilization and capacity building of the underprivileged communities in Nigeria".[51] It has provided sustainable water supplies, encouraged sustainable agricultural practices, improved community health care and sanitation, and focused on the economic empowerment of women and young people.

• The Almanah Rescue Mission helps widows who are often abused and exploited by their family and society.[52]

• The Daughters of Abraham Foundation (DOAF) reaches out to the many prostitutes in Abuja.[53]

What is exciting about these programmes is that they have identified target groups to whom they direct their efforts. Churches and Christian NGOs across Africa should attempt to do the same, and their efforts should be supported by richer churches overseas.

---

[50] CRUDAN: Our Vision. Cited 1 May 2008. Online: www.crudan.org/visionmission.htm.

[51] POD of ECWA: Mission. Cited 1 May 2008. Online: podecwa.org/mission.html.

[52] Almanah Rescue Mission. Cited 1 May 2008. Online: www.almanahrescuemission.org.

[53] Daughters of Abraham Foundation. Cited 1 May 2008. Online: www.doafnigeria.com/home.html.

Conclusion

The Bible clearly establishes that God cares for the poor and wants believers to do the same. In fact, failure to care for the poor brings God's judgment. We must thus be careful to maintain a compassionate attitude. We should not allow ourselves to become insensitive and callous to the plight of the poor or to pretend that their condition isn't all that bad, or regard them as irresponsible, or rationalize that our small contribution is enough. Each of us must, as Jacques Ellul states, "face up to the poor. We must either do so now, or when we stand before the Judge."[54] Caring for the poor as God does is announcing the good news to Africa.

In order to know how to care for the poor, we need to look closely at poverty and its effects, which are real, pervasive, degrading and dehumanizing. We also need to look closely at the types of solutions to poverty that we propose. A coerced equal distribution of wealth seems a simple solution, but confiscation of wealth, whether by peaceful political processes or by violent revolution, is not biblical and creates more problems than it solves. Any effective solution to the problem of poverty must involve not only economic remedies but also spiritual and moral solutions.

We ended this chapter with a list of biblical and Christian principles that we need to bear in mind as we respond to poverty. These include a call to the church to live up to its spiritual and social responsibilities, to give generously, to encourage governments to help the poor by relieving heavy debts, and to work with church-sponsored agencies or non-governmental organizations to start programs and projects intended to help specific target groups.

The church ought to arm herself with these theological and practical principles for serving the poor in her midst. Then she can be like her Master and Lord in proclaiming the good news to the poor in Africa.

---

[54] Jacques Ellul, quoted in Sly, "Africa: Metamorphosis".

Questions

1. Describe the poverty in the area where you serve. Compare it with the poverty in nearby regions or elsewhere in the country. How serious is poverty in your area? Are their particular groups you could be called to target?

2. How have the factors that contribute to poverty been manifested in your area?

3. Which passages of Scripture (and which scriptural principles) speak most powerfully and directly to your situation?

4. Which of the various approaches and recommendations made in this chapter have you seen attempted in your area? How did they work? Which recommendations do you think are most important in your area?

11
CORRUPTION

Corruption is a feature of African social, political and even religious life, with disastrous consequences. As discussed in the previous chapter, it not only impedes economic development but also increases poverty by making a few individuals richer and many poorer. The BBC was not exaggerating when it observed

> Corruption is illegal everywhere in Africa, but everywhere it is woven deep into the fabric of everyday life. From the bottle of whisky slipped under the counter to speed a traveller's way through customs, to the presidents and ex-presidents living way beyond their declared means, it results in an assumption that no business will ever get done without a present changing hands.[1]

Although Africans know that corruption in all its forms is illegal and undesirable, it seems to have a hold on them everywhere they go. Even mortuary attendants need to be bribed to provide services. Officials require bribes before they issue foreign exchange and import and production licences. A bribe can reduce one's taxes or one's bill for water or electricity. "Even the police, who are supposed to be guardians of the law, also receive bribes to obstruct the administration of justice."[2]

---

[1] Elizabeth Blunt, "Corruption 'costs Africa billions'". BBC News, Wednesday, 18 September, 2002. Cited 21 Nov 2007. Online: news.bbc.co.uk/1/hi/world/africa/2265387.stm.
[2] Eric E. Otenyo, *Ethics and Public Service in Africa* (Nairobi: Quest and Insight Publications, 1998), 60.

Defining Corruption

Corruption can be defined as making someone morally corrupt or becoming morally corrupt oneself. Some of the ways in which it seeks to pervert integrity are defined below.

- *Bribery* is giving money or favour to someone who is in a position of trust, in order to pervert their judgment or corrupt their conduct. It is intended to make a person act illegally, unjustly or immorally. The responsibility for bribery rests with both the giver and the taker (the briber and the bribed).

- *Extortion* comes from a word that means "to squeeze; and refers to "the act of obtaining something, such as money from an entity (whether a person, group, corporate or institution) through threats, violence or the misuse of authority.[3]

- *Fraud* includes financial crimes such as forging cheques and inflating costs. It also occurs when "funds raised for such activities as famine relief, bursary funds for poor children's school fees, and funds to assist the disabled within society are not put to the intended use".[4]

- *Nepotism* occurs when someone appoints relatives and friends to positions of authority or awards them contracts. It often leads to the dominance of one ethnic group over another, which has negative implications for nation building, as discussed in the earlier chapter on war and violence.

Corruption also manifests itself in outright theft, match-fixing, examination fraud, kickbacks, illegal awarding of contracts and the like. In the political sphere, it manifests itself in vote rigging, the purchase and sale of votes and the falsification of election results. In fact, corruption takes so many forms that it is impossible to discuss all of them in this book. We will thus focus primarily on bribery and extortion, investigating their links to traditional culture, their effects on society and what the Scriptures have to say about them.

---

[3] Stanley J. Grenz and Jay T. Smith, *Pocket Dictionary of Ethics* (Downers Grove: IVP, 2003), 38.
[4] Otenyo, *Ethics and Public Service*, 59.

Traditional Gifts and Bribes

Those who hold public office are supposed to perform their duties without any external inducement. They should not have to be given gifts to persuade them to act. In some parts of the world, officials are even forbidden to accept any gifts. But giving gifts to superiors was common in African traditional societies. Were such gifts in effect bribes, extorted by them before they would perform their duties, or were they intended to get them to do something illegal and immoral? In other words, was the giving of gifts in traditional communities equivalent to paying a bribe today? To answer that question, we need to examine the circumstances in which gifts were traditionally given.

- *When approaching the gods.* One had to approach the gods with a gift in hand to appease them for some wrongdoing or to thank them for such things as a good harvest, the birth of a child or the coming of the first rains. Such a gift could never have been considered a bribe to induce a god to do something immoral, for the gods could do no wrong.

- *When appearing before a chief or king or the elders of the community.* It was considered disrespectful and improper to appear before one's superiors empty-handed. The gift was not a bribe because the elders, who often acted as the judges, were expected to be just in their utterances and in the performances of their duties.

- *When consulting diviners and priests.* Diviners and priests were regarded as intermediaries who would carry out the will of the gods. Bribing them to misconstrue what the gods were saying was unthinkable! Any attempt to do so would bring judgment. It is said that when someone did bribe a priest to help him obtain possession of some land, both the man and the priest who took the bribe died in a mysterious fire.

- *When consulting medicine men and women.* A gift was often necessary to ensure the effectiveness of the medicine prescribed. Given that some of these medicine men and women were prepared to use unorthodox and evil methods, the gift could well constitute a bribe to persuade them to use their powers to drive someone mad, kill someone or make someone fall in love.

These examples show that the motive for giving something is important when determining whether it is or is not a bribe. Anything is a bribe if it is intended to make someone act dishonestly or unfaithfully. However, if the motive for giving a gift is not to gain a favour or impose some obligation now or in the future, then it is morally permissible.[5]

Given that it can sometimes be difficult to define motives clearly, gift-giving often bleeds into the desire to extract obligations and favours. Eric Otenyo, who has studied the ethics of the public service in Africa, observes that "public service gifts have turned out to be bribes or inducements to the extent that a 'no gift no service' rule prevails in many public offices in Kenya, Nigeria, Ethiopia, Zaire, Tanzania and other African countries".[6]

Consequences of Corruption

Some may be inclined to accept corruption, saying that this is just the way things are in Africa. But corruption has serious consequences that we should not ignore.

- *Erosion of moral values.* Corruption perverts a nation's sense of right and wrong. In corrupt societies, the right becomes the wrong and the wrong becomes right.
- *Increased social evils.* Corruption provides fertile soil for tribalism, nepotism, fraud, dishonesty and selfishness, and may even lead to murder.
- *Lack of transparency.* Corruption encourages those in authority to shun transparency and accountability. Calls for public officials to be transparent and accountable elicit defensive and vindictive responses.
- *Disregard for the rule of law.* Corruption encourages individuals, entities and institutions to cut corners and ignore legal requirements. It can be difficult to obtain justice.
- Oppression of the weak. In corrupt societies, the weak and powerless suffer because only the rich and powerful have access to the courts.

---

[5] Grenz and Smith, *Pocket Dictionary of Ethics*, 15.
[6] Otenyo, *Ethics and Public Service in Africa*, 42.

- *Loss of public trust.* Corruption makes people cynical as they do not believe that the truth will come out or that the right thing will be done. They have no confidence in the government and the system.

- *Adoption of a utilitarian ethic.* Corruption encourages people to believe that the end justifies the means. They then feel free to use immoral methods and to abuse other people's trust in the pursuit of their own interests. Some may even become so ruthless that they are prepared to indulge in ritual murder in order to ensure their own success.

- *Destruction of the moral fibre of society.* Corruption deadens people's consciences and results in a loss of respect for life and property.

- *Poor productivity and incompetence.* In corrupt societies, officials do not take pride in the quality of the service that they provide, and consequently poor service becomes the order of the day. Standards of education fall as teachers allow students to cheat in examinations and unqualified students bribe their way into class. People's safely is compromised as building inspectors and the police accept bribes. Manufacturing quality is sacrificed as inspectors agree to ignore defects in a product. Commercial contracts are awarded on the basis of who pays the largest bribe. Poor quality supplies or even the wrong supplies may be ordered because a clerk has been bribed by a contractor. Banks collapse and bank officials enrich themselves with people's savings. Government officials launder money for criminal gangs.

- *Ineffective development and administration.* Corrupt governments do not develop their countries. Instead they allow the rich to evade taxes and pilfer funds intended for subsidies and pensions while medical institutions and the transportation infrastructure deteriorate. While accepting bribes to reduce the taxes or fees paid by some, they extort money from other individuals and institutions. Funds meant for development are diverted to their personal accounts.

- *Limited foreign and domestic investment.* Both domestic and foreign investors are reluctant to invest in corrupt countries because of the political and economic instability that accompanies corruption. Negative media reports regarding corruption signal that money invested in such a country will be wasted.

- *Undermining of democracy.* Although many African countries have adopted democratic systems, corruption threatens the very existence of democracy. Polls are rigged, leaders imposed, heads of state and presidents refuse to resign. The corruption present in supposedly democratic systems has often been used to justify military takeovers.

- *General underdevelopment.* Although Nigeria is a major producer of crude oil, corruption has affected its development. More than 60 per cent of its citizens still live below the poverty level. Under Mobutu Sese Seko, Zaire (now the Democratic Republic of Congo) suffered underdevelopment due to various forms of corruption. Similar underdevelopment is found in Liberia, Ghana and many other African countries.

Christian Complicity

Many Christians seem to accept or even benefit from corruption. For example, although some 50% of the Nigerian population (140 million) claim to be Christian, corruption is still rampant. Christians in high places in government have been accused of corruption and a number of Christians have been found guilty of corrupt practices. A panel report indicated that between September 1988 and June 1991, $12.4 billion in Nigerian oil revenues disappeared into dedicated and special accounts.[7] The late head of state General Abacha and his cronies stole billions of naira. Many Christians were implicated in this naked theft and ruin of the Nigerian economy.

Although it is estimated that 96 per cent of the DRC's population are Christian, the Congolese church appeared helpless as Mobutu Sese Seko and his aides plundered the country's resources until he was one of the richest men in the world and his country one of the poorest.

Despite its high Christian population, Kenya is one of the most corrupt countries in Africa. Similarly, although the Ivory Coast is more developed than most African countries and had a devout Catholic president in Félix Houphouët Boigny, it is very corrupt.

One might conclude that the church has lost its ability to be salt and light in the world.

---

[7] *The Economist*, 22 October, 1993.

Biblical Perspectives on Corruption

The writers of Scripture lived in a world where the situation with regard to bribery was similar to that which prevailed in traditional Africa, for the word translated as "a bribe" in the Old Testament can also be translated as "a reward" or "a gift". It is the intention of the giver, which is normally clear from the context, that determines whether the correct translation is gift or bribe. Thus it is clear that Exodus 23:8 refers to a bribe: "Do not accept a bribe, for a bribe blinds those who see and twists the words of the righteous" (see also Deut 16:18–20; Isa 1:23). When the same root word is used as a verb, the dominant meaning is bribing someone to pervert justice. All such use of bribes is strongly condemned. Justice must be done because the Israelites are called to be holy, like their Lord: "The God of gods and Lord of lords, the great God, mighty and awesome, who shows no partiality and accepts no bribes. He defends the cause of the fatherless and the widow, and loves the alien, giving him food and clothing" (Deut 10:16–18; see also 2 Chr 19:7).

Extortion, which is the demanding of a bribe, is also strongly condemned: "Extortion turns a wise man into a fool, and a bribe corrupts the heart (Eccl 7:7). In Psalm 62:10, extortion is linked with robbery: "Do not trust in extortion or take pride in stolen goods; though your riches increase, do not set your heart on them" (see also Isa 33:15; Jer 22:17).

Other forms of corruption that are condemned include using dishonest scales to defraud purchasers (Hos 12:7; Amos 8:5) and cheating one's neighbours of what is rightfully theirs (Lev 6:2). The Scriptures also condemn the type of abuse of the courts that led to Naboth's wrongful conviction and death and the king's seizure of his vineyard (1 Kgs 21).

Despite the condemnation of bribery, it was still practised. Proverbs mentions an adulterer attempting to pacify an offended husband with a bribe (Prov 6:35). King Asa tried to bribe Ben-hadad to break a political treaty (1 Kgs 15:18–20). In the New Testament, Judas was bribed to betray Jesus (Luke 22:3–5), and the chief priests bribed the guards at Jesus' tomb (Matt 28:11–15). Felix, a corrupt public official, wanted a bribe before he would even consider releasing Paul from prison (Acts 24:26). Those who do what is right without waiting for a bribe are commended (Isa 45:13).

The existence of a culture of bribery led people to assume that everything was for sale. Thus a man called Simon even tried to buy the power of the Holy Spirit. Paul strongly condemned his action, for it is wrong to try to purchase what is unpurchasable and to sell what is unsellable (Acts 8:18–24).

Scripture not only condemns corruption as morally wrong; it also recognizes its harmful effects on those who accept the bribe ("A greedy man brings trouble to his family, but he who hates bribes will live" – Prov 15:27) and on the nation that tolerates bribery ("By justice a king gives a country stability, but one who is greedy for bribes tears it down" – Prov 29:4; see also Mic 3:11). But the primary reason for rejecting any form of bribery is the fact that it violates the basic command that we are to follow God's example. The command "Be holy because I, the Lord your God, am holy" is repeated in both the Old and the New Testaments (Lev 19:2; Matt 5:48). Our God does not take or receive bribes, and neither should we.

The Christian Response to Corruption

The Christian tradition has consistently condemned bribery. At the same time, it recognises that the corruption which manifests itself in bribery cannot be condemned in isolation. It is a reflection of the inherently corrupt state of the human heart (Jer 17:9). No amount of condemnation can change that. It is only God who can effect a complete transformation, which he does through the work of Jesus Christ. As 2 Corinthians 5:17 states, "Therefore, if anyone is in Christ, he is a new creation; the old has gone, the new has come!" Thus the first step in fighting corruption effectively is to pray that God will transform hearts and to proclaim the gospel of the Lord Jesus Christ.

The second step is to publicly proclaim that corruption in all its forms is unacceptable and to call on the authorities not merely to condemn it (as most African countries do on paper) but to take action to prosecute those suspected of practising it and to punish them if they are found guilty. Those punished should not be minor officials, for they are simply imitating the behaviour of their superiors. To send a strong message, a few big fish need to be fried. When senior members of government are punished for corruption, everybody will know that corruption does not pay. This is what the Economic and Financial Crimes Commission of the Nigeria Federal Government has tried to do. The sight of Nigeria's former Inspector-General of Police (the Police Boss) being taken to court in handcuffs and accused of corruption sent shockwaves through the nation. Never before had such a powerful figure been arrested for corruption. His arrest has restored some respect for Nigerian businesses. Because "corruption is a calculated, not impulsive, crime",[8] it has also had a chilling effect on corruption at lower levels in the police force.

Next, we must work to ensure that honesty, competence and hard work are acknowledged and rewarded in our churches and businesses. Individuals' ethnic affiliation should not be a factor in appointing them to positions or assigning rewards. We would do well to apply the tenets of the Nigeria Covenant, quoted in the previous chapter, to all aspects of our church and business life.

On the level of civil society, we must actively apply the principle that all are equal before the law. The law should not favour some and discriminate against others on the basis of their ethnic or religious affiliation. It must apply equally to rich and poor, strong and weak, the powerful and minorities.

Accountability and transparency must be embraced at every level of government, from the local to the national. Church leaders and pastors must model what this means by being accountable to church members and transparent in regard to church finances.

It is important that universal ethical norms be accepted and that everyone recognises that bribery is universally shameful and should never be justified on any grounds. This may mean that certain traditional values have to be changed, for the ethical systems held by some groups within a country may send wrong signals. For example, some traditional groups consider it acceptable to steal from a neighbouring group in order to enrich their own group. Such views continue to have a profound influence through the continued recognition of customary laws and courts. Thus some Nigerian public officials do not see themselves as serving the public in general but rather as serving their own ethnic group. They abuse the federal character of Nigeria by embezzling public funds in order to enrich themselves or their own tribal communities.

Progress will only be made in the fight against corruption if universal principles of right and wrong become part of the national psyche.

---

[8] Chander Mehr, *Corruption: Dealing with the Devil* (Nairobi: Shiv Publications, 2000), 35.

Conclusion

Corruption is a vicious sin and crime that destroys a nation and perverts its sense of right and wrong, good and bad. The fact that corruption costs Africa as much as $150 billion a year shows that society as a whole suffers when this evil is tolerated. The only way forward is to radically reject corrupt practices and adopt a position of transparency and accountability before God and our fellow citizens.

We should follow the example set by those who have stood up and fought against corruption, extortion, bribery, exam fraud and the like. The Rev. William Okoye, the former chaplain to the President of Nigeria, rejected bribes of millions of naira. Some Christian judges and lawyers have refused to accept bribes intended to pervert their sense of justice. Policemen and women who are committed Christians have refused to accept bribes when arresting criminals, political thugs and corrupt public officials. Christian teachers have been known to refuse bribes to inflate or change exam results. Their actions demonstrate that God has never been without a witness. Though corruption is present and has many followers, there are God-fearing men and women, who are transparent and honest and will not soil their hands and hearts with corruption.

Questions

1. How common is corruption in your society? Do you regard it as an inevitable fact of life?

2. Identify and analyse a situation involving corruption that you have experienced. How would you deal with it from a Christian perspective?

3. Identify situations in which gifts are exchanged in your society. Do these gifts constitute unacceptable bribery or acceptable give-and-take?

4. How does the development of Christian character proactively prevent corruption? Cite Scripture to support your answer.

5. What role should Christians and the church play in addressing rampant corruption in society?

6. Identify which elements of the Nigeria Covenant quoted in the previous chapter are relevant to the issue of corruption. Find examples of Christians who have lived up to the ideals set out in this covenant.

12
FUND-RAISING

Individuals, groups and governments all need to raise funds in order to carry out projects. An individual may need to raise funds in order to build a house. A non-governmental organization (NGO) may need to raise funds to erect and equip a clinic or a shelter for people with HIV/AIDS and to pay the salaries of those who work there. The government needs to raise funds to build roads, bridges or housing. Churches too need to raise funds for their projects.

The individual who wants to raise funds to build a house has a number of options. He can take out a loan, or he can work and save for several years before starting to build, or he can embezzle money from his employer, deceive gullible people into giving him money, or take a gun and commit armed robbery. There are many options, but not all of them are ethical.

In the same way a church that wants to build a house for its pastor has a number of options. It can take up a special offering, tax members of the congregation, send out special requests to rich donors or hold a launch or fundraiser. Are all of these methods ethical?

In this chapter, we will look at various approaches to fund-raising and ask questions like these: What does a particular fund-raising technique imply about our theology? How do we evaluate various methods of raising funds? Does the Bible give examples and guidelines that we can follow when it comes to fund-raising?

Traditional Fund-Raising Techniques

Traditionally Africans would invite friends and relatives to contribute material or physical resources to help with large projects such as constructing a road, building a house, clearing virgin land for planting, harvesting crops and so forth. This approach was so common that there are even specific words to describe it. Among Hausa-speaking groups of Northern Nigeria, an invitation to the community to participate in executing a project was called a *gaiya,* among the Yoruba of Nigeria *owe* has a similar meaning. In Swahili the idea of working together on a project is expressed by the word *harambe.* This spirit of mutual help has translated into modern fund raising. Fund-raising is thus not an alien practice in Africa, though it has been transformed to fit our current needs.

Contemporary Fund-Raising Techniques

In recent years, Christian organizations, denominations and local churches have used a number of ways to raise funds for various projects.

Launching has become a very popular way of raising funds. In this method, the church or organization agrees on a fund-raising target. Then an advertising campaign is launched to bring the project and the need for funds to the attention of the public. The advertising may be done on radio and television, as well as by distributing flyers. Celebrities and the general public are invited to contribute to reaching the goal. Large donors are given publicity and the sums donated or pledged are announced.

Another approach is to make a direct appeal to the philanthropy of some rich individual, who may or may not be a Christian. Sometimes additional pressure is applied when a man or woman of God claims to have received a divine revelation that the individual must give a certain amount to God's work.

Organizations or churches sometimes encourage people to make faith promises. In other words, they ask people to consider what amount they are willing to trust God for and then pledge to donate this amount. Some churches ask members to do this annually, so that over the period of a year, they give the amount they have promised. Some also encourage such giving by speaking not merely of spiritual blessings but also of the financial rewards or promotions at work that will come to those who give.

Leaflets, letters and coupons[1] are sometimes used to inform people of financial needs and to solicit donations. At certain times of the year,

---

[1] A coupon is a small page, often looking as if it comes from something like a cheque book, with a heading that names the project and an indication of the amount the donor should give.

young boys representing organizations such as the Boys Brigade may go from door to door or up and down the streets looking for donations for their organizations. Sometimes church members are expected to do the same thing to help their church raise funds for a specific project.

Before we can evaluate the merits of these and other techniques, we need to hear what the Bible has to say about fund-raising.

Biblical Perspectives on Fund-Raising

Both the Old and New Testaments contain many examples of fund-raising, as well as teaching regarding giving and stewardship. Dr Manfred W. Kohl has provided a useful list of how some heroes of the faith have raised resources for the Lord's work:[2]

- *Moses raised funds for building the tabernacle.* The methods he employed included holding large group meetings, collecting offerings and engaging skilled volunteer labour (Exod 20–34; 35:4–36:7).

- *King David raised funds for building the temple.* The methods employed included planning time alone with God, encouraging gifts in kind, holding a leadership meeting and accepting large gifts from leaders and heads of families (1 Chr 28:12, 19; 29:2–9).

- *Nehemiah raised resources for building renovations and the reconstruction of Jerusalem.* His methods included personal prayer, an appeal to a major donor, a request for a government grant, executive planning, a pivotal leadership meeting, use of volunteers, debt counselling and action to reduce debt, reductions in executive salaries, and encouragement of personal gifts by the heads of families, as well as gifts by leaders and the general public (Neh 1:4–11; 2:1–18; 3:1–5, 18; 7:70–72; 10:37–39).

- *Ezra raised funds to rebuild the temple.* He relied on a major donor, free-will offerings and gifts by leaders (Ezra 2:68–69; 7:1–23).

- *King Hezekiah instituted annual funding for projects.* He used the methods of personal giving, announcements by leaders to promote giving, and the establishment of a department of development (2 Chr 31:1–21).

---

[2] The information presented here is a summary of a seminar by Dr. Manfred W. Kohl, "Principles of Giving, Publicity, Marketing, and Accountability", presented at the Institute for Excellence in Global Theological Education, Accra, Ghana, 2001.

- *Elijah had to replenish the general fund if his ministry was to survive.* He used three methods: relying on God's miraculous provision, asking for a donor and teaching on stewardship (1 Kgs 17:1–16).

- *Haggai had ministry and building needs.* He taught stewardship (Hag 1:1–14).

- *Jesus had a general fund.* He maintained it through personal ministry relationships and by stretching the resources provided (Luke 8:2–3; Matt 14:17–21).

- *The apostles needed funds for their benevolent ministries.* They set up foundations and boards, and encouraged personal donations (Acts 4:32–5:11).

- *Paul raised funds for relief ministries.* He employed large group mailings, teaching on stewardship and representatives in the field (1 Cor 16:1–3; 2 Cor 8:1–24).

The variety of methods employed to secure the finances to meet needs demonstrates that there are a great many legitimate approaches to fund-raising. We are free to adopt some of the strategies employed in our contemporary world – provided the approach is compatible with Scripture.

Ethical Issues in Fund-Raising

We will now look at ethical questions that arise in relation to some fund-raising techniques and see what the Bible has to say about them.

Asking non-Christians to donate

The New Testament examples indicate that appeals for funding should focus on the household of faith. But are they the only ones who can be approached? The question of whether unbelievers can be invited to participate in giving is a controversial one. On one side of the debate are those who see absolutely nothing wrong in searching for and securing funds from non-Christians, including even rich Muslims. They claim that God owns everything and everybody, and that if God moves someone to give to a cause that promotes his glory, they will accept it. They also point out that biblical leaders like Ezra and Nehemiah accepted funds from unbelieving people to do God's work.

On the other side are those who fear that accepting funds from non-Christians can cause believers to compromise their faith. Some quote the saying that if you accept money from a leper (a person who is thought of as an unkempt beggar) and give him a haircut, you are under obligation to shave his beard as well. Their point is that you will be tempted to make compromises for the sake of those who have donated. For example, if you accept money from Muslims to build or maintain a church school, you may come under pressure to offer instruction in Islam even though the school is Christian.

In answering this thorny question, we need to consider the motives of the donor. When Nehemiah appealed for and received government funds, he was dealing with officials whose role was to govern all citizens – Jews and non-Jews. Their position was similar to that of a Muslim governor in Nigeria, who governs not only Muslims but all citizens. The government allocates certain funds for communal and religious development, and any religious movements, Muslim or Christian, can legally apply for these funds. In such a case, there does not seem to be anything morally wrong with accepting or even soliciting funds for a Christian project.

But what about approaching an unbelieving person who openly shows contempt for the cause of Christ or Christianity? Or government officials who should be disbursing funds to all but who try to impose their will on the direction or execution of a project? Is it right to seek funds from such people? This time, the answer must be no. We cannot accept funds from donors who specifically ask that doctrinal statements or even the name of a church be changed to reflect a more universalistic outlook. Accepting funds with these conditions attached would endanger the mission of the organization.

Announcing the amounts given

In much of the English-speaking world, the word "launching" is not associated with fund-raising. However, in some parts of Africa the idea of launching something has come to be associated with initiating fund-raising in a very public manner. A launch is a calculated attempt to advertise, market and raise funds (in cash or kind) for a particular project, which could be anything from the construction of church buildings, schools, bridges and roads to the purchase of musical instruments or the production of a musical album.

The amount to be raised, for example, 100,000 naira (or $1,000) is usually stated in the invitation card that is sent out. There then follows an aggressive advertising campaign on radio and television and through personal contacts by the planning committee. Special invitations to the launch are sent out to those chosen to be the master of ceremonies, chairman, secretary, chief launcher, mother of the day, father of the day, etc.

The master of ceremonies (MC) is usually someone with charisma who can motivate people to give or pledge large sums of money. The chief launcher is usually someone who is both rich and generous, for he or she is expected to give the largest sum in order to motivate others to give. This person is the first to donate, and the announcement of the amount given is greeted with delighted applause.

The chairman is also an important figure. He makes a short speech and then gives his own donation – usually a large sum. The special guests are the next to give. They have usually been given special seats up front with all kinds of snacks and beverages carefully laid out on beautifully decorated tables. They are called on one by one to give their donations, and their donations are announced for all to hear.

There is nothing wrong with launching a special project and asking people to support it. There may be occasions on which a special plea needs to be made and people can be expected to give generously. Moses, Ezra and Nehemiah turned to the public to raise resources. However, it is important to note that the contemporary style of launching blatantly disregards some principles that are clearly taught in Scripture. The first of these principles relates to the publicity associated with donations. Even though some donors do not want the amount of their donations to be announced, their wishes are generally disregarded. But the Bible teaches that when we give to God's work our aim should not be to impress other people with our generosity. The Pharisees did that kind of public giving and got no divine commendation. We would do well to heed Jesus' words:

> So when you give to the needy, do not announce it with trumpets, as the hypocrites do in the synagogues and on the streets, to be honoured by men ... But when you give to the

needy, do not let your left hand know what your right hand is doing, so that your giving may be in secret. Then your Father, who sees what is done in secret, will reward you (Matt 6:2–4).

The second objection to this type of launch is that the focus falls on the rich and famous while the poor and unknown are ignored. It can be disgusting to see how rich and famous people who lead immoral lives are given recognition while the poor are driven out of the church – and this despite James' warning against showing favouritism to the rich (Jas 2:1–9). Moreover the focus on the rich misses the point of Jesus' commendation of the poor widow who gave little but gave generously without seeking to impress others (Mark 12:41–44).

It is not wrong to acknowledge and recognize donors, but this should be done privately. Their names and the amount given should not be publicized.

Assuming the end justifies the means

Fund-raisers sometimes seek to embarrass people into giving. One aspect of this is publicly announcing the amount donated or asking donors to show their money so that God and people can see what they give. Another technique is to publicly reject donations when it is thought that a donor should have given more. There is at least one individual who regularly returns the money in public, telling the donor to increase the amount. When confronted about the awkwardness such behaviour arouses and its questionable ethics, he shrugs his shoulders and says that this is the only way to raise money for projects. He sees nothing wrong with it. He has become famous, or infamous, for his fund-raising technique!

Some would agree with him, saying that his methods are acceptable as long as the goal is achieved. In other words, the end justifies the means. But if this argument were taken to its logical conclusion, one could argue that it would be morally justifiable to raise funds at gunpoint!

Bible-believing Christians should never allow themselves to be so consumed with accomplishing a goal that they become blind to the means they adopt to get there. Forcing people to give directly contradicts the biblical principle that giving should be voluntary (2 Cor 9:7). As Tertullian, the early church theologian, noted, "On the monthly day, if he likes, each puts in a small donation; but only if it be his pleasure; and only if he is able; for there is no compulsion; all is voluntary. These gifts are, as it were, piety's deposit fund."³

Promising material rewards

Another technique that is used to manipulate donors is an appeal to greed. Some evangelists and church leaders like to promise donors large financial returns for giving to the cause of God: "If you give God $10,000, you will get $100,000 in a month's time". One evangelist even gave out handkerchiefs as a token that his supporters would be handsomely rewarded for their donations.

When preachers quote biblical passages out of context to support the idea that giving will result in some instant material reward, donors should be cautious. Such teaching contradicts the clear words of Jesus:

> If you lend to those from whom you expect repayment, what
> credit is that to you? Even 'sinners' lend to 'sinners', expecting
> to be repaid in full. But love your enemies, do good to them,
> and lend to them without expecting to get anything back.
> Then your reward will be great (Luke 6:34–35).

We should not expect to get something in return for our gifts. Our primary reason for giving should be to invest in eternity. As Jesus said, "Do not store up for yourselves treasures on earth ... But store up for yourselves treasures in heaven where moth and rust do not destroy ... For where your treasure is, there your heart will be also" (Matt 6:19–21). Paul made the same point when he told Timothy

> Command them [the rich] to do good, to be rich in good
> deeds, and to be generous and willing to share. In this way
> they will lay up treasure for themselves as a firm foundation for
> the coming age, so that they may take hold of the life that is
> truly life" (1 Tim 6:18–19).

When money and materialism become central to our lives, Christians and Christian organizations are distracted from pursuing what is pleasing and honouring to God. Heaven-related matters become secondary or

---

³ Quoted in Eugene B. Habecker, "Biblical Guidelines for Asking and Giving" *Christianity Today* (15 May 1987): 32.

even tertiary concerns. God has warned against this temptation many times. He spoke to the Israelites about it before they even entered the promised land (Deut 8:11–14). But the words of the prophet Hosea show that they did not heed his warning: "When I fed them, they were satisfied; when they were satisfied, they became proud; then they forgot me" (Hos 13:6). May the same not be true of us! [4]

Demanding a gift

In recent years, it has become increasingly common for someone with a reputation as a "man of God" to approach people of substance and tell them point-blank what they must donate in goods or money. For example, a pastor may approach a church member and tell him that God has told him (the pastor) that the member must give him his second car for God's work.

Christians must exercise discernment and caution when presented with such a demand. One of my seminary professors suggested that if somebody claims that God has spoken to him, I have the right to ask the person how I can be sure that it was not the devil who spoke. We need to understand that if God is able to speak to the person who needs the donation, he is also able to speak to the potential donor. Every Christian should be able to hear the voice of God on the matter of giving.

Accepting donations from foreigners

Another sticky issue is whether it is justifiable to raise funds from outside Africa. When discussing this, the first point that must be made is that there is nothing inherently wrong in raising funds from our brothers and sisters in Christian churches worldwide. Scripture includes examples of churches supporting other churches (2 Cor 8). A local assembly can support another local assembly of believers.

But it is worth noting that the Macedonian churches referred to in 2 Corinthians were not wealthy. Paul describes them as enduring "severe trial" and "extreme poverty" (2 Cor 8:2). Yet they pleaded with Paul to allow them to help the church in Jerusalem (2 Cor 8:4). We normally associate pleading with beggars, but these churches were "beggars for

---

[4] A must-read book is Randy Alcorn's *Money Possessions and Eternity* (Carol Stream, Ill.: Tyndale House, 2003).

the privilege of giving – not receiving".[5] In New Testament times, it was not only the rich who gave.

In our contemporary situation, there is fear that the poor church in Africa could become dependent on the rich church in the West.[6] The corrective to this situation is for the church in Africa to be encouraged to give to the church in the West. Poverty should not be an excuse for dependence but should be a motivation to keep giving what one has. This giving does not have to be purely financial. The church in Africa has a lot to offer the West in terms of spirituality and church growth.

Effective Fund-Raising

Having criticized many popular methods of fund-raising, it is now time to consider how organizations and church can go about raising funds in an acceptable Christian way.[7]

Strategy

Study of the biblical examples of fund-raising indicates that there was good planning and development of a strategy to meet the needs. Many African fund-raisers are very vague – they want money for projects but the projects are not always well defined. It is important to think carefully about the needs, the sources from which you will seek funds, and the limitations in terms of time, resources and cost effectiveness.

The first step in developing a strategic plan is to develop a clear understanding of the vision and mission of your organization or church. In other words, you need to be clear about why it exists, what its values are, what it does to fulfil its mission, and what its potential impact could be if funding were available.

Next, you need to set specific goals and objectives for the fund-raising campaign. The goals can be formulated in broad terms, but the objectives must be specific, measurable, attainable, results-oriented and time-determined. Without such objectives it may be difficult to measure the successes and failures of the fund-raising.

---

[5] Schwartz, *When Charity*, 157.

[6] Glen J. Schwartz, has dealt extensively with this subject in his book, *When Charity Destroys Dignity: Overcoming Unhealthy Dependency in the Christian Movement.*   Bloomington, Ind.: AuthorHouse, 2007.

[7] Some of the advice in this section is based on Manfred W. Kohl's paper, "Principles of Giving".

Only at this stage is it time to decide on action steps, which outline the exact activities necessary to accomplish the objectives and goals. For each action step, it is important to define "who will do what by when".

If you wish to appeal for funding from outside sources like an NGO or a national or international organization (or even to develop a flyer to give to potential donors), you will have to provide the following information:

- A description of the organization
- An outline of its mission
- A list of its major achievements
- A summary of the current financial situation
- A description of its goals, major projects and targets
- A statement of the resources needed

Integrity

As believers, we must demonstrate the highest standards of integrity, meaning that there must be no difference between who we appear to be and who we are. Not only is this honouring to God, but it will also encourage people to give us their money and resources because we will have demonstrated that we are trustworthy. The following factors are all important.

- *Pure motives.* The motives of both the donor and the receiver must be honest. King David provides an example of an honest donor, when, after giving materials for the building of the temple, he prays "I know, my God, that you test the heart and are pleased with integrity. All these things have I given willingly and with honest intent" (1 Chr 29:17). Such donors recognize that everything they have comes from God in the first place. Those asking for donations "must be extremely careful that in their asking and in how the gift and the giver are recognized something is not done that contributes to an impure motive".[8]

- *Honesty and transparency.* Always tell the truth. If donors suspect you are hiding something, they will rightly not give at all. This truthfulness extends to all the details of the information we give out.

---

[8] Habecker, "Biblical Guidelines", 32.

The Evangelical Council of Financial Accountability (ECFA) stresses that

> All representations of fact, description of financial condition of the [organization] or narrative about events must be current, complete, and accurate. References to past activities or events must be appropriately dated. There must be no material omissions or exaggerations of fact or use of misleading photographs or any other communication which would tend to create a false impression or misunderstanding." [9]

- *Worthy projects.* Donors want to know whether their money is going to be used for something worthwhile. We should not need to apologize for asking them to donate to our cause.

- *Financial responsibility.* When people give money for a specific purpose, make sure that it is used for that purpose. Do not assume that because you are doing God's work, people should trust you. Donors want to see that you actually spent the money on what you requested it for. Keep accurate financial records, showing all amounts given and all the spending on the project for which the funds were raised. It is a very good idea to have your financial records audited by an independent, professional auditor.

- *Supervised projects.* Money given to even the best projects with the most honest intentions can be wasted if the project is not supervised by competent people. That is why the seminary at which I taught in Nigeria appointed a technical committee consisting of a civil engineer, architect, quantity surveyor, electrical engineer and structural engineer to give technical and professional advice on all building projects. When I presented the details of our projects to potential donors, they were impressed that the work would be supervised by professionally trained people who had integrity and who were committed to the seminary. This information convinced them that the seminary leaders knew the importance of professionals handling projects that require technical skills and made them more likely to donate funds.

---

[9] Evangelical Council for Financial Accountability. "Standard 7: Fund-Raising". *ECFA Standards.* Cited 28 Nov 2007. Online: www.ecfa.org. It is worth looking at all eleven points in the ECFA statement on fund-raising, as well as the accompanying commentary. Among the points made is that organizations should not accept gifts that will "knowingly place a hardship on the donor, or place the donor's future well-being in jeopardy".

- *Frequent feedback.* Donors want to be kept informed about the progress of the work. Keep in touch with them through a newsletter or by inviting them to come and visit you and see for themselves what their donations have accomplished. You could also visit them yourself or write them a personal letter. Responding in this way will encourage donors to give even more.

- *Involvement in your activities.* Invite donors to events, and make them feel important while they are there. Help them to feel part of your organization, as indeed they are.

- *Acknowledge all donations.* Donors want to receive appropriate acknowledgment and recognition.

- *Avoid empire building.* Funds are not raised for our own glory but for building the kingdom of God. As Henri J. M. Nouwen reminds us, "to raise funds is to offer people the choice to invest what they have in the work of God".[10] Those who give are investing for eternity.

Errors to avoid

Just as there are ways to promote giving, so there are things that must be avoided when fund-raising.

- *Avoid pressure.* Donors do not like to be pressured. At all cost, avoid arm-twisting. You should never attempt to force people to give what they do not want to give.

- *Avoid falsifying the truth.* Do not exaggerate or minimize the truth. If the project will cost six million, do not tell them that it will cost ten million or reduce it to five million.

- *Guard against manipulation.* Resist any temptation to exploit people in order to attain goals. Such manipulation includes public announcements about how much people have contributed.

- *Do not make money the end and goal of everything.* Money cannot solve all problems.

- *Do not generate confrontation or antagonism.* Provide an opportunity for donors to give without feeling imposed upon and accept the possibility that they may choose to decline to give.

[10] Henri J. M. Nouwen, *The Spirituality of Fund-Raising* (Upper Room Ministries in partnership with Henri Nowen Society, 2004), 25. Cited 30 April 2008. www.parkerfoundation.org/PDFs/SpiritualityOfFundraising.pdf.

- *Do not embarrass prospective donors.* Some may still be studying you and the projects you are promoting and may not be ready to commit yet.

- *Do not beg.* The Bible does not ask us to beg for God's kingdom. Christians and the church are invited to invest in building God's kingdom.

Conclusion

Fund-raising should be done in a way that is pleasing to the Lord. The techniques and means employed should not conflict with clear biblical guidelines such as voluntary giving, giving to honour God and investing for eternity. "Christian fund-raising, in all its activities (including marketing and advertising), should present nothing but the truth. Word and action, promises and delivery, must be the same (2 Pet 2:3a; Matt 5:37)"[11]

Questions

1. Describe how you have used or have seen others use some of the fund-raising techniques described in this chapter. Was this use in accordance with the biblical teaching on fund-raising? What needs to be corrected in future fund-raising?

2. Have any of the issues presented in this chapter raised controversy in your community? How were they handled?

3. Evaluate a current fund-raising project with which you are familiar in terms of the principles of strategy and integrity presented in this chapter. In what areas were the principles followed (or not followed)? What needs to be corrected in future fund-raising?

---

[11] Manfred W. Kohl, "Principles of Giving".

SECTION C

MARRIAGE AND FAMILY ISSUES

INTRODUCTION TO MARRIAGE AND FAMILY ISSUES

The home is a key institution that shapes individuals and society. If families are distorted, so is the whole of society. Thus it is vital that any study of ethics also deals with ethical issues affecting the family.

Our views on marriage, sexuality and procreation inevitably reflect our African world view and Western influences. But it is vital that we also think about them from Christian and biblical perspectives. It is also vital that we reflect not only on the positive elements of marriage such as love, pleasure, procreation and companionship, but also on negative and sensitive elements such as infertility, divorce, domestic violence and death and widowhood.

Before it is possible to have any meaningful discussion of marriage and family issues, we need to determine what marriage is. Essentially, it is the type of union of a man and a woman that God established at creation. From that ancient union of one man and one woman, various peoples and cultures emerged and populated the world. The different peoples of the world have now come to understand marriage differently in accordance with their own world views, cultural customs, beliefs and core values.

The differences between the Western and African understandings of marriage have led to many misunderstandings and have resulted in many ethical issues relating to marriage not being adequately addressed in Western texts. One area of difference concerns who is involved in a marriage. Westerners tend to forget that marriage is lived out in society and that society has an impact on the meaning, expectations and aspirations of this union.

Given their individualistic world view, Westerners tend to think of marriage only in terms of the man and woman involved. But such a view of marriage is far too narrow for the Africans. At an African wedding, it would not be unusual for the pastor to tell the bride:

"You are married not to your husband Paul, but to his family. That means you have to identify completely with all his relatives, look after them, care for them, go out of your way to make them happy. If you do that, you will have no cause for regret." And to the groom he says. "You, Paul, will have to do likewise with Mapule's relatives. Her people are your people.[1]

The stress on community ties in Africa means that any discussion of the sexual, reproductive and relational ethics of African marriage must take the whole community into account, including the immediate living community – parents, brothers and sisters, uncles and aunts, grandparents, cousins, nieces and nephews, the whole extended family and the entire village – and also the living dead (ancestors) and future members of the family who are yet to be born. Thus John Mbiti can say of marriage: "All the dimensions of time meet here, and the whole drama of history is repeated, renewed and revitalized. Marriage is a drama in which everyone becomes an actor or actress and not just a spectator."[2]

As regards the question of what marriage is for, it is possible to argue from Scripture that there are five possible reasons for marriage:

- *Unity.* The desire for unity is rooted in Genesis 2:24 with its insistence that a man and his wife become "one flesh". This unity was upheld by Jesus in Matthew 19:3–6. This motive for marriage is strong in Africa, where a man without a wife is considered incomplete, not a real man. The same applies to a woman without a husband. The very idea of an unmarried man or woman is inconceivable in most traditional African societies.

- *Companionship.* The desire for companionship is also rooted in the creation ordinance where God states, "It is not good for the man to be alone; I will make a helper suitable for him" (Gen 2:18). This motive, too, is important in African culture, where an unmarried person is regarded as lonely, miserable and helpless. Marriage is imperative if one is to have companionship, love, respect and dignity.

- *Procreation.* In Genesis 1:28, God commanded the couple he had just made to "be fruitful and increase in number" and Psalm 127:3–5 celebrates the joy of having a large family – a joy that Africans share.

---

[1] Laurenti Magesa, *African Religion: The Moral Traditions of Abundant Life* (Nairobi: Pauline Publications Africa / Maryknoll: Orbis, 1997), 111.

[2] John Mbiti, *African Religions and Philosophy* (London: Heinemann, 1982), 133.

- *Love and pleasure.* In Ecclesiastes 9:9, the listener is instructed to "Enjoy life with your wife, whom you love". This motive for marriage has not been prominent in Africa, but there can be no doubt that when there is love and pleasure, a marriage stands a better chance of surviving and being a good environment for raising children.

- *Curbing fornication and adultery.* In 1 Corinthians 7:1–2, Paul advises marriage as a protection against sexual immorality.

These reasons are not listed in order of importance. Differences in customs, beliefs and core values mean that the priority given to each will vary from culture to culture. However, problems can arise when the focus falls solely on one or two of these factors and others are excluded.

Biblical revelation provides insight into not only the blessings of marriage but also into its challenges and problems. The fall (Gen 3) has had a significant effect on marriage. Sin and rebellion against God have turned what had been intended to be a loving permanent and lifelong relationship into one that can produce hatred and divorce. Sin has also affected the whole human body, including its reproductive system. Consequently we now have to deal with painful childbearing, infertility, impotence and barrenness. These are the types of issues that will be discussed in this section of the book, which focuses on issues that arise in relation to procreation and companionship. We will, however, not be dealing with the issues raised by the search for sexual fulfilment outside marriage. Those issues will be dealt with in the separate section on sexual issues.

Given the importance Africans attach to procreation, what happens when a couple fail to produce offspring? This issue is discussed in **chapter 13**, which gives some guidelines for helping couples who are wrestling with infertility. When appropriate, they should be encouraged to seek medical help. However, some medical interventions raise serious ethical issues. Thus **chapter 14** presents a brief overview of some reproductive technologies and the ethical questions they raise.

While childlessness places an enormous stress on a marriage, so does the presence of too many children. Thus it is also important to consider the issue of contraception. Is contraception sinful? Are some kinds of contraception more ethically acceptable than others? These questions are addressed in **chapter 15**. Some desperate women may also attempt to avoid having children by resorting to abortion or by abandoning their newborn infants. However, abortion and infanticide will not be discussed in this section – they are dealt with under the heading Medical Issues.

Moving on from the discussion of procreation, we will deal with the issues that threaten companionship in a marriage. Is it possible to have more than one companion in a marriage? In answering this question, **chapter 16** discusses polygamy. And what happens when a marriage fails to provide companionship because a spouse is abusive? Such domestic violence is addressed in **chapter 17**.

Finally, we have to deal with the end of a marriage. Can a Christian marriage be terminated by divorce? This issue is discussed in **chapter 18**. When a marriage is ended by death, what is the fate of the survivors? Some ethical issues relating to the treatment of widows and orphans are dealt with in **chapter 19**.

13

PROCREATION AND INFERTILITY

In Western societies the procreative purpose of marriage is not as important as companionship and sexual fulfilment. Thus Westerners tend not to understand Africans' urgent need to have children. But for Africans, the lack of children leaves a void in the marriage union: "the chief purpose of marriage is to provide opportunity for the unborn members of the family to spring forth. The person who fails, for various reasons, to have children, is one of the most miserable members of society, since he will be despised and regarded as the cul-de-sac of his family."[1] Examining the subject of procreation in more detail, Mbiti states:

> It is a religious obligation by means of which the individual
> contributes the seeds of life towards man's struggle against the
> loss of original immortality. Biologically both husband and wife
> are reproduced in their children, thus perpetuating the chain
> of humanity … A person who, therefore, has no descendents
> in effect quenches the fire of life, and becomes forever dead
> since his line of physical continuation is blocked if he does not
> get married and bear children. This is a sacred understanding
> and obligation which must neither be abused nor despised.[2]

Africans thus value procreation far more than other aspects of marriage such as love, companionship and sexual pleasure. Infertility is seen as a negation of life, the destruction of the individual and the community. This view is not unlike that of the ancient Hebrews who regarded

---

[1] John Mbiti, "African Concept of Human Relations", *Ministry* 9 (1969), 160.
[2] Mbiti, *African Religions and Philosophy*, 133.

death without offspring as a terrible fate (Ps 109:13). It was part of the suffering of the Suffering Servant that his premature death meant that he had no descendants (Isa 53:8).

Rather than endure the shame of infertility, people will go great lengths to try to conceive. Even Christians will consult witchdoctors and all sorts of medicine men and women in an attempt to solve the problem, regardless of the cost. If these attempts fail, many will resort to divorce or polygamous relationships. It is thus important to look at what the Bible has to say about marriage and procreation.

Biblical Perspectives on Procreation

Some Western Christian couples feel free to decide not to have children. African Christians, however, argue that the command to be "fruitful and increase in number" (Gen 1:28) applies to all marriages. They also point to the fact that God's blessings on his people include fertility: "None of your men or women will be childless, nor any of your livestock without young" (Deut 7:14; see also Exod 23:26). On this basis they insist that

> procreation is the purpose of cohabitation and the primary
> object of marriage. Of him who fears the Lord it is said: "Your
> wife shall be like a fruitful vine …" (Ps 128:3). Only as mother
> of the sons whom she has presented to the family does a woman
> enjoy a certain consideration in society. It is this which makes
> her "fruitful" or not.[3]

Africans also point out that Scripture describes children as the crown of old age (Prov 17:6). Sons in particular are described as being "like olive shoots round your table" (Ps 128:3) – an image that implies that they are the new growth that brings promise of future crops and plenty in days ahead. Children are also described as being "like arrows in the hands of a warrior … blessed is the man whose quiver is full of them" (Ps 127:3–5). These children will defend and provide for their parents in their old age.

Given the traditional emphasis on the procreative purpose of marriage, it is not surprising that the same emphasis is often found in the teachings of the church in Africa. Many Pentecostal and newer churches place

---

[3] D. H. Pretorius, "Childlessness" in *Church and Marriage in Modern Africa* (ed. T. D. Verryn; Groenkloof, South Africa: Ecumenical Research Institute, 1975), 112.

great emphasis on the need for offspring. They believe that barrenness and impotence are the work of the devil and evil spirits and that infertility can be cured by the special prayers of a man or woman of God. In support of this position, they cite examples like Rachel and Hannah in the Old Testament (Gen 30:6, 23–24; 1 Sam 1:8). The Synagogue Church of God in Lagos, Nigeria, for example, has become a place of pilgrimage for Christians from all over Africa and even from countries like Holland. The pilgrims include statesmen like former Zambian president Frederick Chiluba and Nigerian soccer stars like Daniel Amokachi. Its famous pastor, T. B. Joshua, claims miraculous power to heal conditions such as cancer, AIDS, diabetes, hypertension, barrenness, impotence and infertility. He says that he has the power of Jesus to enable infertile women to conceive and bear children. Once or twice every year, the church convenes a special event, televised nationwide, in which hundreds of women show babies, allegedly conceived and born as a result of his prayers.

The assertion that it is God's will that every married person should have offspring is one extreme position found among Christians. At the opposite extreme is the view popularized by Western missionaries and some mainline denominations:

> From a psychological point of view the expression of the oneness of love is the principal end of sexual intercourse in marriage. The biological passion to procreate and the physiological for recreation fade away behind the experience of the psychological urge for the love of union. For instance, as soon as the love of the husband for his wife is overshadowed by his looking forward to fatherhood, the latter has become a threat to love. Marriage can be described as the public acknowledgement and realization of a growing love between a man and a woman. Seen in this light, children are not an essential element of marriage.[4]

This view regards procreation as unimportant. It suggests that childless couples should simply accept their position and find fulfilment in their marriages even though there are no children.

---

[4] Ibid., 124.

Both of these extreme positions are to be rejected. It is dangerous to isolate one purpose of marriage and describe it as the primary purpose when the creation ordinance of Genesis 1 and 2 reveals that marriage is intended for companionship and unity as well as procreation. Those who dismiss the biological urge to procreate need to be reminded that the Bible clearly indicates that the desire to have children is normal and has divine backing (Gen 1:28). The survival of society and humanity in general can only be assured by procreation. Childbearing is to be expected in marriage. It is perfectly normal for couples to be concerned if their union does not produce children.

Those who insist that children are essential to a marriage need to be reminded that a childless marriage can still be full of love, companionship and sexual fulfilment. The presence of children is no guarantee that these other important aspects of marriage are actually present.

Rather than ascribing all infertility to the work of evil spirits, it is important to carefully and prayerfully consider other possible physical and psychological causes resulting from the sin that entered the world at the fall, rather than from some particular sinful action by the couple or directed at the couple. Some of these physical causes of infertility can be cured by modern medicine. The local church should be equipped to deal with the spiritual aspects of counselling Christian couples who wrestle with the problem of infertility, including being able to advise them about the ethics of using different technologies.

Causes of Infertility

Infertility is not necessarily the same as sterility. Someone who is sterile is incapable of procreating; infertility is an impairment of normal reproductive capacity that can sometimes be corrected.

The causes of infertility may be spiritual, physical or psychological (emotional). In this chapter, we will not pay much attention to psychological causes, but will focus on the physical ones. However, before discussing these it is important to point out to those who expect a bride to get pregnant on her wedding night that in medical terms a couple who are having regular sexual intercourse are only considered infertile when pregnancy has not occurred within a year.

It is also important to refute the traditional belief that infertility was always the woman's fault. This belief led to much abuse of barren women. Among the Bajju of Nigeria, such a woman is referred to as *anakwu*, meaning "one who is distressed for a child". The word is closely related to the word *dukwu*, meaning "death", and indicates that she is as good as dead. When she does die, a priest steps between the legs of the corpse and says, "go away, you worthless woman." The Igbo of Nigeria refer to a barren woman as *nwanyi aga*, which literally means that she is unproductive, incapable of bearing a child. She may be insultingly referred to as a "man", implying that this is why she is incapable of bearing children.

Both men and women may suffer from physical problems that cause infertility.

Physical causes of infertility in men

Male infertility is still shrouded in secrecy in Africa because of the intense shame associated with it. Among the Bajju, an impotent man will be buried with the words, "May your type never be born into our community again."

The physical reasons why a man may be infertile can be grouped into the following broad categories:

- *Impotence.* The word "impotence" derives from the Latin word *impotens*, meaning lacking strength. It means that the man either cannot have an erection or cannot keep one long enough for sexual intercourse. Men who have this problem sometime claim that their wives have bewitched them. In saying this, they ignore other possible reasons including psychological ones, physical ones like generally poor health or an inadequate blood supply to the penis, diseases (including sexually transmitted diseases) and even sometimes reactions to medication. Many of these problems can be treated with drugs or surgery, but impotent men often become withdrawn and insecure and are reluctant to seek help, or even to admit to having a problem. They know that many men and women would despise them. There must thus be a deliberate attempt to provide counselling for these men and to change the public perception of impotence, getting people to realize that an impotent man is a complete person and can lead a fulfilled life.

- *Problems with ejaculation.* Some men are infertile because their sperm does not reach their wife's egg to fertilize it. This problem can be the result of premature ejaculation, in which the man ejaculates before his penis has penetrated far enough into the vagina. In some men, the sperm is not even ejaculated from the penis but goes into their bladder instead. This condition can sometimes be a side-effect of certain types of medication.

- *Problems with the supply of sperm.* Some men may have no sperm in their semen, either because of some disorder in the testicles or because the passage of sperm is blocked by some physical defect (sometimes resulting from a sexually transmitted disease). A man with this condition is said to be "shooting without bullets". Other men may have a low sperm count, that is, their semen may have too few sperm to be able to fertilize an egg.

- *Damage to the sperm.* Hormonal problems and some infections can damage sperm, so that even when conception does occur, the fertilized egg does not survive.

Physical causes of infertility in women

There are also a number of physical reasons why a **woman** may be infertile. These, too, can be grouped into some broad categories:

- *Hormonal problems:* Hormonal imbalances mean that some women may fail to release an egg that can be fertilized while others may have only occasional menstrual periods or none at all. These problems can be symptoms of some underlying reproductive disease or of physical problems like malnutrition.

- *Anatomical problems in the uterus, cervix or ovaries.* An abnormality such as a turned uterus, where the cervix is at the wrong angle to the vagina, makes it difficult for sperm to fertilize an egg. Fibroid tumours or scarring on the ovaries can negatively affect conception. Tumours or blockages in the fallopian tubes may prevent the fertilized egg from moving into the womb and developing into a baby.

- *Diseases and vaginal infections.* A number of diseases, some of which are sexually transmitted, can cause infertility in women. The fact that a woman has a disease such as gonorrhoea or chlamydia does not necessarily mean that she has been unfaithful. She may have been given the disease by an unfaithful husband.

Some women are not infertile, because they become pregnant fairly easily, but they have no children because they suffer miscarriages or stillbirths. There are often physical or genetic explanations for their problems, although they are traditionally ascribed to witchcraft and spiritual causes.

Many of the physical causes of infertility in both men and women can be corrected by medical procedures or by medication.

Spiritual causes of infertility

The Western world view generally ignores the spiritual aspect of infertility, but Africans do not. Magesa describes the situation: "God, ancestors, mother and father must all cooperate for conception to take place. Mother and father 'copulate to 'beget' jointly and give birth,' while God intercedes to 'create' and the ancestors assist in protecting the creation from the malevolent powers of destruction."[5]

Africans thus seek to find and deal with the spiritual cause of the infertility. They may blame it on sins against parents or ancestors, or on the breaking of some taboo. A woman may be accused of "eating her eggs" or "eating her children", a metaphor expressing the belief that she has willingly destroyed her own unborn children. The belief that women can do this is supported by the confessions of women who have been accused of witchcraft.

Other women may be said to be the victims of witchcraft. Some groups believe that stillborn babies and those who die shortly after birth were sent specifically to torment their parents, and may be reincarnated and reborn time after time, only to die. The Igbo of Nigeria refer to such babies as *ogbanje*, while among the Yorubu they are referred to as *abiku*.

Scripture, too, recognizes that infertility may have spiritual causes. It was interpreted as a disgrace (Luke 1:25), an affliction sent by God (Gen 16:1–2; 29:31) or as a punishment for sin (Gen 20:18). Infertile women prayed that God would grant them children (1 Sam 1:10–16).

---

[5] Magesa, *African Religion*, 82.

A Christian Approach to Infertility

When helping couples and their families and community deal with the distressing problem of infertility, pastors and counsellors should stress the following principles:

- *The need for a good understanding of marriage.* Marriage is not defined by procreation but by the loving, permanent, committed and trusting union of a man and woman who have come together to live a life pleasing to God. African Christians must indefatigably emphasize unity, commitment, trust and love in marriage. A childless couple still have a fully fledged marriage.

- *The need to understand infertility in the light of the Scriptures.* Children are a wonderful gift from God, but sin in general, not necessarily the couple's own sin, can interfere with this aspect of marriage. Their infertility may be a disease like other diseases and physical problems that came into the world with the fall. They should not respond to infertility in ways that displease God. Instead, they should seek God's grace to help them deal with it, just as they would seek his grace in dealing with other problems in life. Whatever the actual thorn in the Apostle Paul's life was, God did not remove that affliction when he prayed. God's answer to Paul's prayer is relevant to couples struggling with childlessness. "Three times I pleaded with the Lord to take it away from me. But he said to me, 'My grace is sufficient for you, for my power is made perfect in weakness'" (2 Cor 12:8–9).

- *Avoid jumping to conclusions about the causes and cure of infertility.* Both the husband and wife should undergo a thorough medical examination to determine whether a physical problem is preventing conception and child-bearing. Such problems can sometimes be treated by modern reproductive technologies. Any psychological and spiritual causes of infertility should also be examined and dealt with.

- *Do not judge childlessness a curse or assign a stigma to it.* Even the barren can be joyful: "Sing, O barren woman, you who never bore a child; burst into song, shout for joy, you who were never in labour; because more are the children of the desolate woman than of her who has a husband" (Isa 54:1). A couple with a dozen children may be more miserable than a childless couple who have learned to trust God and love each other.

- *Consider other options.* Adopting children is a fulfilling way to deal with the issue of childlessness. In this age in which many children are being orphaned by the AIDS pandemic, Christian couples can adopt children and raise them in a godly context. A couple with adopted children are not childless but are the parents of their adopted children.

Questions

1. "A marriage without children is not a marriage." Is this statement correct?
2. What are the common cultural responses to infertility in your community? How do these responses relate to the biblical and theological perspectives presented in this chapter?
3. How are problems of infertility manifested in your ministry situation? How could you address these needs practically as well as theologically?

14

REPRODUCTIVE TECHNOLOGIES

Some of the medical problems that prevent couples from conceiving can be solved fairly easily. However, in some cases, the standard medical interventions are unsuccessful. What is a couple to do if they are unwilling to adopt a child or to give up their dream of having children? What are the ethics of using reproductive technology? It is impossible to answer this question in full in just one chapter, but it is hoped that this introduction will motivate us to start thinking about this important matter. Although some of these procedures are not yet widely available in Africa or are prohibitively expensive, others are becoming available – and African church leaders, pastors, and scholars need to give careful thought to the ethical issues they raise.

The chapter will also touch on some other moral issues raised by technological advances, including the ethics of screening an unborn child for genetic defects or to determine its sex.

Traditional Solutions to Childlessness

In a traditional African context, when normal sexual relations between a husband and wife failed to produce offspring (or a son), they would turn to medicine men and women for help. If their interventions failed, they would turn to other options. The husband would often be encouraged to take a second or even a third wife in order to have the desired child or son.

We see the same pattern of behaviour in the story of Abraham and Sarah. When Sarah could not conceive and bear a child for Abraham, she told her husband, "Go, sleep with my maidservant; perhaps I can build a family through her" (Gen 16:2). Abraham then had sexual intercourse with Hagar in order to have a child. Scripture does not specifically discuss the ethics of this act, but it can be evaluated in light of its long-term consequences. The jealousies that arose have led to thousands of years of strife in the Middle East (Gen 16:12; 25:18). Moreover we know that this was not the way in which God had intended Sarah to have a child. He had promised Abraham a son through Sarah, not Hagar, and Sarah's child would be the child of promise (Gen 17:19).

If the couple's infertility was the fault of the man, the wife might leave him and seek another husband. Or she might take the route described to me by a student pastor. A couple in his church had wanted to have a child for several years. They had sought medical help several times to see if the condition causing the infertility could be reversed. The husband cooperated for a while, but soon he stopped going for further check-ups. The wife, in frustration, went and slept with another man. She became pregnant, and her husband thought that he was the child's biological father. When it was time to have a naming ceremony for the child in the church, she confessed her adultery to the pastor because her conscience was bothering her.

Another traditional approach, subject to strict ritual laws, permitted an impotent man's brother or cousin to have intercourse with his wife in order to give him offspring. This practice is somewhat similar to the institution of levirate marriage in the Old Testament, although there it only happened after the husband had died without an heir. His brother was to impregnate the widow so that the dead brother could have descendants (Deut 25:5–10). This was why Judah told his son Onan, "Lie with your brother's wife and fulfil your duty to her as a brother-in-law to produce offspring for your brother" (Gen 38:38). Such marriages maintained the property rights and the name of the deceased, and also provided security and status for their widows. By refusing to raise up offspring for his dead brother, Onan displayed a lack of concern for others, and God judged this as so evil that he killed him (Gen 38:10).

Another traditional option would be for the husband's brother to give the couple one or more of his children to be raised as their legal children. The impotent man would then be considered the father of these children.

Technological Solutions to Childlessness

Western technology has greatly extended the range of options open to couples:

> artificial insemination of a wife with her husband's sperm; artificial insemination of a wife with a donor's sperm; artificial insemination of a woman's ovum by her husband's sperm and then implantation into her own uterus; egg transfer from a donor to a woman's womb before fertilization; embryo transfer from a donor to outside of the uterus, also called ectogenesis; cloning, or nuclear transplantation.[1]

Some of these the methods have become so popular that they now seem almost routine. Others are still being perfected. But while these new methods offer couples great hope, they also raise serious moral and ethical dilemmas. That does not mean that they must be rejected out of hand. As Colson reminds us, "While many of the startling strides in biology are frightening if we do not learn how to apply moral restraints, there is never a cause for despair."[2] We need to look clearly at the pros and cons of these methods rather than simply issuing a blanket condemnation.

Artificial insemination by husband

There are a number of possible reasons why a husband may be unable to impregnate his wife. He may be impotent, unable to sustain an erection because of some accident or disease, or he may have such a low sperm count that it is difficult for enough sperm to reach the egg and fertilize it (see chapter 13). Or he may be away from his wife for long periods of time due to his work or a war. In such cases, one option for treatment is artificial insemination, a simple procedure in which the husband's sperm is collected and then inserted into his wife.

Some object to all artificial insemination on the basis that it is unnatural, a departure from God's original plan that children should come through physical sexual intercourse. But it is important to appreciate the effect of the fall on our human bodies. If sin had never entered the world, there

---

[1] George H. Kieffer, *Bioethics: A Textbook of Issues* (Reading, Mass.: Addison-Wesley, 1979), 68.
[2] Charles W. Colson, "Contemporary Christian Responsibility", in *Genetic Ethics: Do the Ends Justify the Genes?* (ed. John F. Kilner, Rebecca D. Pentz, and Frank E. Young; Grand Rapids: Eerdmans / Carlisle: Paternoster, 1997), 226.

would be no illness and no male infertility, and children would always be conceived in the ideal way. But the fall means that our reproductive system, like any other bodily system, may need medical help to remedy an ailment. If we followed the same line of reasoning as these critics, we would not even be allowed to correct defects in our eyesight because God never intended us to wear glasses!

Others object to artificial insemination because the man has to masturbate so that sperm can be collected. Their objection is not absolutely correct, for the sperm can sometimes be collected during sexual intercourse (either by coitus interruptus or a condom) or after intercourse, by taking it from the wife's vagina. In cases where masturbation is necessary, it is important to remember that in this context its purpose is to create life and bring joy and fulfilment to both the husband and wife.

Artificial insemination by donor

A husband may sometimes be sterile, with no sperm with which to impregnate his wife. This condition may be caused by a genetic defect, environmental contamination or some disease. In such cases, some couples resort to using sperm provided by a donor, who is often anonymous. Some have attempted to link this practice to the biblical story of Abraham, Sarah and Hagar or to the story of Onan and Tamar, but these stories are more closely linked to polygamy and widow inheritance. Neither involves artificial insemination of a woman by a donor who will have no part in raising the child.

What the biblical stories do have in common with artificial insemination by donor is that the complicated relationships that result can lead to problems. A few years ago, it was reported that a prominent Nigerian politician and statesmen had played the role of a donor to assist a friend's wife to conceive and give birth to two children. The husband later filed for a divorce on the basis that his wife had committed adultery. It is not clear whether there had been any physical sexual relationship between the man and the woman or whether he had simply donated sperm.

In assessing the ethics of donor insemination, the first point to be made is that any sexual relationship outside of the marriage union is adultery. Having sexual intercourse outside marriage, even with the best of intentions, is clearly condemned in Scripture (Exod 20:14). But is insemination adultery if there is no physical contact between the donor and the wife? Some will insist that it is because the wife is carrying the sperm of a man other than her husband. But this is not a common understanding of adultery.

The German theologian Helmut Thielicke provides two major reasons why donor insemination is not equivalent to adultery. First, the medical doctor involved is focused on procreation as a medical procedure. There is no sexual contact between the woman and the donor, a man she has never met and will probably never meet. Second, doctors will only carry out donor insemination of a married woman if both the husband and wife desire it. Their mutual consent means that neither should accuse the other of infidelity. However, as the example from Nigeria quoted above shows, this consent is sometimes revoked after the pregnancy. The reason for this revocation may be related to the question of the paternity of the child. Thielicke notes:

> The fusion of sperm cell and ovum, however, is not simply a matter of amalgamation in the female organism. On the contrary, in the genesis of the child an independent "third person" comes into being. This is not without its consequences for the mother, but it can ... have an extreme effect upon the father. Even though it need not be so, the possibility is nevertheless there that the father may react in an emotionally hostile way to a child which to him appears to be a constant reminder of his own weakness. This understandable psychological reaction would then be the symptom of a far deeper, "existential" fact, namely, that the psycho-physical totality of a marital fellowship is indivisible.[3]

John Jefferson Davis makes the same point, arguing that donor insemination "introduces an imbalance into the relationship between the husband and the wife. Her maternal functions have been fulfilled, but his paternal function has not. The child remains as a constant reminder of [the husband's] biological failure, and the shadow of an anonymous third party clouds the relationship."[4]

---

[3] Helmut Thielicke, *The Ethics of Sex* (trans. John W. Doberstein; New York: Harper & Row, 1964), 262.

[4] John Jefferson Davis, *Evangelical Ethics: Issues Facing the Church Today* (Phillipsburg, N.J.: Presbyterian and Reformed, 1985), 73.

There can be no doubt that this kind of stress may arise, but the argument that it *must* arise is weak, for exactly the same problem can arise in relation to adoption. An adopted child is also not biologically of one's own body and could also be said to be a constant reminder of failure.

Some critics of donor insemination insist that it is better to adopt a child than to resort to donor insemination. However, most couples would rather have a child that is biologically the wife's:

> The wish to satisfy the will to have children, not by adoption but rather in such a way that the artificially engendered child may be at least 50 percent physically a part of the marriage can undoubtedly spring subjectively from the desire to fulfill one's own marriage and to find a special psycho-physical relationship to the child thus begotten.[5]

Donor insemination using modern technology is clearly preferable to the tradition of having a living brother or cousin sleep with the wife, which is clearly adulterous.

Surrogate motherhood

A surrogate mother is a woman who has been impregnated with the egg and sperm of another couple, so that she is not the biological mother of the child she bears. She carries the pregnancy to term, and when the child is born she relinquishes the baby to the biological mother. A couple might choose to enter into such an arrangement if the wife is unable to conceive, or if she suffers miscarriages and cannot keep a pregnancy, or if she faces serious health problems during pregnancy. In some cases, a grandmother has even become a surrogate for a daughter who could not bear a child

The egg that is implanted in the surrogate mother may be the wife's egg, fertilized by her husband or by a donor. Or the egg may have been donated by some other woman and fertilized by the husband's sperm.

Surrogate motherhood raises numerous legal and ethical problems. Who is actually the legal parent of the child? What happens if the couple who provided the egg and sperm get divorced? And what becomes of a baby rejected by both its legal and biological parents, as can happen if

---

[5] Thielicke, *The Ethics of Sex*, 260.

the child is born with a defect? In the West, there have been many legal battles with regard to the custody of such children.

Another matter of great concern is that this technology often involves fertilizing a large number of eggs, but only two to five of them are placed in the surrogate mother's uterus. The remaining embryos are thrown away – which is equivalent to throwing away human lives, for life begins with fertilization.

These problems warn us to be cautious about the use of surrogates, and to think through the issues ethically as well as well as scientifically.

Disability Screening and Sex Selection

These days it is possible to know a good deal about a baby before it is born. Ultrasound scans and amniocentesis (a procedure in which a doctor withdraws fluid from around the unborn child) can reveal important information about some physical and genetic defects. It is now possible to know whether a child still in the womb has Down's syndrome or spina bifida. Such knowledge can be useful. For example, it is now possible to perform life-saving surgeries on infants before they are even born.[6] However, not all problems that can be diagnosed before birth can be treated.

But the knowledge gained can also be used as an excuse to take life, as when a couple decide to abort a child who will be born with a debilitating ailment. Scripture explicitly condemns murder, including the killing of an unborn child (Gen 9:6; Exod 21:22–25).[7] Rather than being encouraged to seek an abortion, the couple should be given proper counselling to help them prepare to meet the special needs of their child.

Ultrasound images make it possible to know the sex of a child before it is born. This knowledge can help parents as they prepare clothing and select a name for their child. It identifies the child as a particular human being with his or her own identity and can help parents and others in the community to bond with the child as an individual before birth. However, this knowledge, too, can be abused if it is used to abort a baby that is the "wrong" sex.

---

[6] Randy Alcorn, *Pro-Life Answers to Pro-Choice Arguments* (Sisters, Ore.: Multnomah, 2000), 33.

[7] See also the discussion of abortion in chapter 26.

With artificial insemination, it is sometimes even possible for parents to choose whether their child will be a boy or a girl. Research has shown that the sex of the child is determined by the sperm. Sperm with Y chromosomes produce boys, while sperm with X chromosomes produce girls. Medical specialists can separate the two types of sperm and use only the type most likely to produce the desired sex when they fertilize an egg.

Another approach to sex selection involves the woman's eggs being fertilized in a laboratory and then examined to see whether the chromosomes indicate that the offspring will be male or female. The eggs with the desired sex are implanted in the woman's uterus, while the others are either frozen for later implantation or discarded – destroyed despite the fact that they are human life.

Advocates of sex selection procedures argue that they allow for family planning. In Africa, where male children are traditionally preferred, couples may keep on having children until they have a son (although parents with a number of sons may also keep having children in hopes of producing a daughter). Sex selection would make for smaller families. It is also argued that sex selection prevents child abuse. Some babies are abandoned or abused because they are not the sex that their parents wanted. A girl may be given a name like Bvokanbyin ("Another girl") or Nyanang or Nyamindiyi ("who will give me a boy?"). Advocates of sex selection also point out that being able to produce a son will make couples happier in that they will not be mocked because they lack of an heir and so have to fear extinction at death.

But Christians must not fall into the trap of embracing technologies simply because they promise a good end. The end does not justify the means, and there are serious problems with sex selection and genetic screening. First, they lead to the abortion of unwanted babies such as those with genetic defects or those of the undesired sex. They may eventually lead to parents being able to order "designer babies" with the desired height, skin tone and other traits. But in order to have such a child, the parents have to reject – in fact, kill – other offspring who do not meet their requirements. These children are still in the embryonic stage but they are nonetheless living human beings.

An excessive focus on male children has also produced major problems in some countries like India and China, where there are now so few young woman that many young men have great difficulty in finding a wife.

Sexual stereotyping is wrong. Who is to say that one sex is inferior to another? God made them both. It is refreshing to know that the belief that sons are worth more daughters is beginning to change in Africa because parents are beginning to discover that girls are sometimes more helpful to their parents than boys.

Problems with Reproductive Technologies

Modern reproductive technology offers exciting new possibilities for helping those suffering from infertility and barrenness. But because this is a fallen world, technology can also be used in ways that conflict with God's law and promote unethical behaviour. Some of these ethical problems have already been mentioned above. Other problems are already evident in the Western world, and we need to be on our guard against them in Africa.

- The use of technology rather than the traditional marital union as the means to acquire a baby feeds into the transition that has led to sex being regarded as mere recreation in the West.

- The dehumanization of the human person in the earliest stages of life can lead to an increase in abortions. Many (though not all) procedures involve producing a number of embryos and then selecting some and discarding others. Couples may move from wanting a child to assuming that they have the right to the exact child they want. If they do not like the sex of the child or are told that their baby has some defect, they may choose to abort it.

- The number of single parents may increase as men and women who do not want to face the challenges of marriage choose to have a child on their own. Homosexual or lesbian partners may choose to have children by artificial insemination. Children born and raised in such situations will never know the divinely ordained institution of marriage in which they are raised by both a man and a woman.

- The definition of human life will become blurred as scientists seek to use embryos, tiny human beings, for scientific experimentation. Many are already being frozen for such purposes.

- The prostituting of reproductive organs will become common as young men sell their sperm and women rent their wombs and sell their eggs for money.

A Christian Response to Reproductive Technologies

Some Christians suggest that acceptance of any reproductive technology is the first step on a slippery slope. While we may not agree with the extreme position, we need to be aware that newer techniques like cloning, embryo transfer and gene-splicing will present us with even more acute ethical problems. Mitchell reminds us:

> The genetic revolution is upon us. What was once thought to be science fiction has rapidly become science fact ... As with every technology, however, genetic science holds both promise and risk. As Neil Postman has warned, "Technology is not a neutral element in the practice of medicine: doctors do not merely use technologies but they are used by them".[8]

As some scientists are tempted to play God, the church must not ignore what is going on. If we do, we may find that these technologies will be like a genie that has gotten out of the bottle, used without question or careful moral reflection. We need to stay informed about progress in genetic engineering and human reproduction so that we can contribute to the ethical debate on these issues. What do we say to those who advocate using reproductive technology to clone prominent or highly intelligent human beings, alive or dead? Or to those who see human beings as no more than "a complex of chemicals"?[9]

As new reproductive technologies become available in the West, they will increasingly be sought by wealthy African couples, and later by others as the procedures become more routine. How will we counsel church members who may turn to us for advice about whether they should use them to end their childlessness?

Our first step must be is to provide a more holistic and balanced approach to the whole subject of infertility, dismantling myths that prevent couples from having a fulfilled and satisfying marriage in whatever state God has placed them. This will involve education about marriage and about sex.

[8] C. Ben Mitchell, "The Church and the New Genetics" in Kilner, Pentz and Young, *Genetic Ethics*, 230, 233.
[9] John S. Feinberg, Paul D. Feinberg, *Ethics for a Brave New World* (Wheaton, Ill.: Crossway, 1993), 286.

Unfortunately, many African men are afraid of talking about sexuality and human procreation. So they cling to myths, such as the notion that only women are infertile and that it is the woman who determines the sex of the child. They are also hesitant to seek medical help for sexual problems. So pastors, church leaders and community leaders need to be forthcoming in talking about sexual issues. They need to help couples understand that infertility can be caused by treatable physical conditions. They also need to be able to give couples a clear understanding of the processes involved in new reproductive technologies. By doing this they will provide emotional and physical assistance to African Christian couples who are struggling with infertility.

Finally, we may need to ask couples to consider whether their desire to make use of sex selection, donor insemination or in vitro fertilization may indicate a failure to accept God's plans for them. This failure is often based on the unconscious assumption that fertility is a matter that involves only the husband and wife. But God is the one who opens and closes the womb and determines who will live on earth (Gen 20:18; 29:31; Acts 17:26). Human beings have a tendency to try to improve on and correct God's plan for their lives. Christian couples need to be encouraged to seek and find fulfilment in God's will. To be childless or the parents of adopted children is not to be incomplete if that is what God has ordained for a couple.

Questions

1. In what ways might reproductive technologies be beneficial? In what ways might they be harmful?

2. What technological solutions to infertility are available in your area? How do these solutions relate to traditional approaches to childlessness?

3. What are the issues that face the church with regard to reproductive technologies? In what ways is your church or denomination addressing these issues? How should a pastor or a denomination approach issues that are especially complicated and controversial?

15
CONTRACEPTION

We have been considering the situation of couples who want to have children but cannot. But there are also couples who do not want children – or at least, who do not want any more children. So they choose to use contraceptives to protect against unwanted pregnancies. But is this practice biblical? And are all forms of contraception equally acceptable from an ethical standpoint? These questions will be addressed in this chapter.

Traditional Attitudes to Contraception

Traditionally, it was believed that the natural order of things was that sexual intercourse within marriage should result in the conception and birth of a child. The sexual act would lose its meaning and purpose if it did not produce children. That is why intercourse was taboo at times when a woman could not or should not conceive, such as when she was nursing a child. (It was widely believed that if she became pregnant, her milk would be tainted and the nursing baby would die.)

It was considered a great blessing when a newlywed conceived, and a woman who bore many children, especially male children, was highly favoured by her husband, family and society. Families with eight or more children were not uncommon. Any attempt to avoid pregnancy was regarded as not only unnatural but wicked.

The coming of Christianity and the Bible further baptized these traditional beliefs. Bearing children was understood to be fulfilling the divine command to "fill the earth" (Gen 1:28).

Today, this passion for many children has waned, for a variety of reasons. One is that it is much easier to take care of three children than ten children. Whereas in the past children helped on the farm and did not have to be sent to school, today children have to be given an education, and this is quite expensive. Many couples fear they will be reduced to poverty if they do not control the number and spacing of their children.

The change in attitude to family size has been accompanied by a change in attitude towards sex and its relationship to procreation. In the West, sex is now often seen as mere recreation, and even in Africa, it is now commonly assumed that even within a marriage, sex does not have to be procreative. Both Christians and non-Christians make use of contraceptives to protect against unwanted pregnancies.

Methods of Contraception and Birth Control

The terms "birth control" and "contraception" are often used as if they are synonyms, but there is an important difference between them. Birth control refers to preventing the birth of a child, and can even include terminating a pregnancy at an advanced stage. For biblical, ethical and theological reasons, we reject abortion as wrong. Contraception, on the other hand, refers to the prevention of the fertilization of the egg by sperm. It thus prevents a pregnancy; it does not prevent the birth of a child or seek to disrupt an existing pregnancy.[1]

The methods used to prevent conception may be physical or chemical.

Physical methods of contraception

The physical methods of contraception fall into three groups:

*   *Natural methods.* The method most commonly called the natural method is the rhythm method. A woman is only capable of getting pregnant at the time of the month when she is ovulating. If the woman takes care to know which days these are and abstains from sexual intercourse on those days, pregnancy can be avoided. This is the only method of contraception approved by the Roman Catholic Church.

    Another natural method is coitus interruptus, a Latin name that means "interrupted intercourse". It involves withdrawing the penis

[1] John T. Noona, Jr., defines contraception as the "use of physical or chemical means to prevent sexual intercourse from resulting in the conception of a child". ("Contraception". *Westminster Dictionary of Christian Ethics*, 123).

at the point of ejaculation. This was the method Onan used when he "spilled his semen on the ground" after having intercourse with his late brother's wife, denying her the opportunity to get pregnant and give birth to a child for his late brother (Gen 38:9–10).

- *Barrier methods.* In these methods, some barrier is used to prevent the sperm from reaching the egg. A man may wear a sheath or condom of rubber or plastic over his penis, or a woman may carefully insert a special diaphragm into her vagina. The diaphragm covers the cervix and prevents sperm from reaching the egg. The use of a condom provides some protection from conception and from sexually transmitted diseases.

- *Surgical methods.* The surgical method most commonly used for women involves severing the fallopian tubes, thereby preventing eggs from travelling from the ovary to the uterus and preventing sperm from reaching the egg. This procedure is permanent, and normally means that the woman will never conceive again. The equivalent operation for men is a vasectomy, a medical procedure that involves severing the *vasa defentia*, the tube which conducts semen. Once this has been done, the man can still have sexual intercourse but he can no longer impregnate a woman.

Chemical methods of contraception

The chemical methods of contraception fall into two groups:

- An *intra-uterine device* (IUD) is a combination of a physical and a chemical method. The device is inserted into the uterus through the cervix. The material of which it is made causes chemical changes that help to prevent fertilization. If fertilization does occur, the device prevents the fertilized egg from implanting itself in the lining of the uterus, thereby aborting it.

- *Spermicides* in the forms of jellies, suppositories, creams and foams can be inserted into the vagina before intercourse. The chemicals in spermicides kill sperm, while the substance itself acts as a barrier to sperm reaching the eggs.

- The contraceptive pill works by changing a woman's body chemistry so that she does not ovulate, and thus cannot fall pregnant as long as she takes the pill regularly.

- The contraceptive injection operates in the same way as the pill, but one injection lasts for three months.

Biblical Perspectives on Contraception

The Scriptures have very little explicit teaching concerning family planning. Thus an evangelical understanding of contraception must be derived from biblical principles regarding the nature of human sexuality and the divine purposes for the institution of marriage. There are three key elements to be considered.

The command to multiply

After creating Adam and Eve, God blessed them and instructed them, "Be fruitful and increase in number; fill the earth and subdue it. Rule over the fish of the sea and the birds of the air and over every living creature that moves on the ground" (Gen 1:28). After the flood, a similar command was given to Noah and his sons: "Be fruitful and increase in number and fill the earth" (Gen 9:1). This blessing and command was given at critical moments in human history. Adam and Eve were the first and only couple at creation and they needed to reproduce if they were to populate the earth. Noah and his sons were the sole survivors after the flood had destroyed all other human beings. There was an urgent need to repopulate the earth.

A mere glance around indicates that both Adam and Noah fulfilled this command. Their descendants now number more than six billion! But was this same command given to everyone else? Examination of the text suggests that it was directed primarily to Adam and Eve and later to Noah and his sons, not to every one of their descendants. This point is reinforced by the observation that not everyone is capable of fulfilling this command because not everyone is capable of reproducing. Barren women and impotent men, for example, cannot comply with this command no matter how much they want to. This suggests that the words in Genesis 1:28 and Genesis 9:1 cannot be taken as a universal command to procreate. These were particular commands given to particular persons.

A case of sinful contraception

Onan's behaviour is often cited as proof that God is opposed to contraceptives. However, one must take note of the context in which he acted.

> Then Judah said to Onan, "Lie with your brother's wife and fulfil your duty to her as a brother-in-law to produce offspring for your brother." But Onan knew that the offspring would not be his; so whenever he lay with his brother's wife, he spilled his semen on the ground to keep from producing offspring for his brother. What he did was wicked in the Lord's sight; so he put him to death also (Gen 38:8–10).

The reason he used coitus interruptus was clearly to deny his brother any offspring. The thinking at that time was that "each man is born for the preservation of the whole race. If anyone dies without children, there seems to be some defect of nature. It was deemed therefore an act of humanity to acquire some name for the dead from which it might appear that they had lived."[2] His motive for practicing contraception was clearly selfish, and his outrageous and wicked behaviour brought divine judgment on him. This case cannot be cited as a universal prohibition of contraception for it is a particular judgment on a selfish man.

The responsibility to provide for one's family

Paul is not dealing with the issue of contraception, when he says, "If anyone does not provide for his relatives, and especially for his immediate family, he has denied the faith and is worse than an unbeliever" (1 Tim 5:8). Nevertheless, he makes an important point about one's responsibility to one's family. He does not say that conceiving and giving birth to children is one's most important duty. What God is really concerned about is that we care for the families we have. To fail to do so is tantamount to denying the faith, for one is acting even worse than an unbeliever. On this basis, it can be argued that it is better not to bring children into the world when one cannot provide for them, and that contraception is thus a wise option.

---

[2] John Calvin, *Commentary on the First Book of Moses called Genesis: Volume 2* (trans. John King, 1847; repr. Grand Rapids: Baker, 2005), 281.

Opposition to Contraception

Those who oppose any use of contraception offer some strong arguments that we should not ignore because they contribute to our understanding of the ethical issues involved.

- *The use of contraceptives is contrary to natural law.* Natural law is understood to dictate certain types of behaviour for all human beings. Such behaviours are understood to be consistent with the nature and the structure of the universe, and thus with the law of God. For example, God created human beings with reproductive organs so that they could procreate. To use these reproductive organs for any purpose other than procreation is to go against nature. Thus natural law requires that each and every marriage act must remain open to the transmission of life. But this argument is flawed, and not even in accord with the natural order that it appeals to. A woman can only conceive on certain days of the month. There are thus days on which conception cannot take place. Furthermore, as a woman ages she loses the ability to conceive, although she can continue to have sexual pleasure after her childbearing days are over. And a barren woman can have sexual relations even though she cannot have offspring. Thus we cannot say that nature proves that all sexual relations have to be associated with conception.

- *Contraceptives can encourage promiscuity.* The knowledge that the risk of pregnancy is low may make it easier for married and unmarried men and women to engage in irresponsible sexual behaviour.

- *Some products called contraceptives actually cause abortions.* Any device that prevents a fertilized egg from attaching to the uterus or forces the mother's body to abort the embryo once implanted is just another form of abortion.

- *Contraceptives can have negative side effects.* Some contraceptives can increase the medical risk of blood clots (although researchers point out that these dangerous side effects are less common than the dangerous side effects of pregnancy). Indirectly, by encouraging promiscuity, contraceptives can contribute to the spread of venereal disease.

- *Contraceptives can make people devalue one another.* Without any need to be accountable to one another, sex loses its intimacy and commitment. Sexual partners are treated as means to an end, rather than as fellow human beings.

Marriage and Contraception

While the above arguments against contraception are strong, the fact that something can be abused does not mean that it should not be allowed in any circumstances. We need to reflect on the profound questions that contraception raises with regard to the meaning of marriage, sexuality and love.

In the introduction to this section on marriage and family issues, we listed some reasons for marriage. The first was companionship (Gen 2:2). Adam was lonely and needed a suitable companion, and God made Eve to fulfil that need. But the marriage relationship goes beyond mere companionship, and thus the second reason for marriage is to enter into a unique and special relationship in which the man and woman become one flesh (Gen 2:24). A third reason for marriage is procreation (Gen 1:28; 9:1). Having children is the natural expectation of marriage. Not bearing children is not natural and must be considered the exception rather than the rule. For the Christian especially, marriage provides an opportunity to raise godly children.

In Africa, companionship and procreation have been the main motives for marriage. But Scripture also supplies other reasons which should not be neglected. One of these is that marriage should be a source of love and pleasure (Eccl 9:9). Thus sexual relations can legitimately be focused on love and pleasure, and not solely on having children.

Paul did not emphasize procreation as the reason for marriage when he was writing to the Corinthians. Some of them were struggling with sexual temptations, and so he advised them to marry in order to have their sexual needs met (1 Cor 7:1–9). He did not even mention children. There is thus no need for a couple to try to abstain from sex in order to avoid having children. They can use morally justifiable forms of contraception without being in conflict with Scripture, which recognizes their sexual needs.

Conclusion

Contraception raises many moral issues for Christians, and couples should not take the issue lightly. They should seek professional advice and counselling on the issues involved and should weigh the ethical as well as the medical merits of different methods of contraception. But they should have no doubt that from a biblical, theological and ethical point of view, contraception is morally justifiable.

Questions

1. Why are contraceptives becoming more prevalent in Africa? How is their availability affecting society?

2. How well are the risks of certain contraceptives understood? What misunderstandings are common among the people you serve? (e.g., Is there excessive confidence that condoms will prevent all forms of sexually transmitted diseases?)

3. How can you provide instruction, guidance and advice regarding contraception? What other sources of information are available? How can you ensure that those who you serve are getting the best, accurate information?

4. What are your convictions regarding various methods of contraception? How would you advise couples about the available options?

16
POLYGAMY

It was once assumed that the practice of polygamy would decline as economic forces raised "the cost of living and the cost of bride wealth".[1] But this has not happened. Instead, David Barrett's 1968 prediction holds true:

> Polygamous society will not disappear for some time to come. Even if future economic and social changes virtually remove its practice, it by no means follows that it will no longer be a point of conflict … In the 580 tribes who practice it (78% percent of all tribes south of the Sahara), the polygamous past will certainly be defended strongly.[2]

In Africa, polygamy is not dying out. It is still practised by old and young, educated and uneducated, religious and pagan, Christians and non-Christians. It is therefore very important that Christians come to understand it, and in particular come to understand the biblical position with regard to the polygamist who contracted his marriages before conversion. Is he an adulterer, as the church has traditionally asserted? Should polygamists be admitted into the church?

In this chapter, we will examine the history of the church's interaction with polygamy in Africa as well as the biblical data and will attempt to formulate an African Christian ethic in regard to polygamy.

---

[1] Aylward Shorter, *African Culture and the Christian Church* (Maryknoll: Orbis, 1974). See also G. C. Oosthuizen *Post-Christianity in Africa: A Theological and Anthropological Study* (Grand Rapids: Eerdmans, 1968), 174, which states that the "modern economic situation counteracts polygamy".

[2] David B. Barrett, *Schism and Renewal in Africa: An Analysis of Six Thousand Contemporary Religious Movements* (Nairobi: Oxford University Press, 1968), 241. Based on extensive research in East Africa, he maintains that cultural heritage, polygamy, the ancestor cult and traditional religion will persist for a long time in Africa.

Polygamy in Africa

Before discussing the reasons why polygamy has long been widely practised in Africa, it is important to dismiss one false reason that shallow thinking often suggests: polygamy is not driven by unrestrained sexual impulses.[3] Those who suggest this have very little knowledge of African society and are influenced by the Victorian notion that primitive societies are more sexually active. Polygamy actually fulfils a number of functions:

> [Polygamy] ensures the bearing of many children so that the status and property may be passed on and the family may become extended in space and time … [It] serves the prosperity and growth of the extended family and provides status and support for women in societies where they have no vocation other than marriage and the bearing of children to their husband's lineage … [It is] a way of catering for unsupported women in a society which does not tolerate the independent woman, … [and it provides] a solution to a wife's infertility.[4]

Many of these functions are similar to the functions played by polygamy in the Old Testament, particularly as regards the system of levirate marriage.

Traditionally polygamy was not regarded as in any sense equivalent to adultery. In fact, adultery, that is, sexual relations with anyone other than a legal spouse, was regarded as bringing disgrace not just on the individuals involved but on the whole clan. Special cleansing rituals were required to remove the shame and guilt of such behaviour. In one Nigerian tribe, an adulterer would be made to drink the excreta from a black dog, after which the testicle of a he-goat (a symbol of promiscuity) would be hung around his neck. He would then be paraded through the village so that all could see his shame.[5] John Mbiti noted that, "when adultery is discovered, it is severely dealt with. In some societies the guilty person (particularly a man) would be whipped, stoned to death,

---

[3] Ralph D. Winter, "Polygamy: Rules and Principles," *Church Growth Bulletin 3* (March 1969): 355.

[4] Shorter, *African Culture,* 173.

[5] A lengthy discussion of these purification rituals can be found in Carol McKinney, "The Bajju of Central Nigeria: A Case Study of Religious and Social Change" (Ph.D. diss., Southern Methodist University, 1985).

made to pay compensation or have his head or other part of his body mutilated."[6]

Reactions to African Polygamy

The history of missions and church planting in Africa strongly suggests a lack of appreciation of the social justifications of African polygamy. Due to the missionaries' own cultural practice of monogamy, they generally saw polygamy as a state of adultery that was in conflict with both natural and divine law. The World Missionary Conference at Edinburgh in 1910 labelled polygamy one of "the gross evils of heathen society which, like habitual murder or slavery, must at all cost be ended."[7] Thus it was declared to be

> unlawful within the Church of Christ even though commenced in ignorance. 1) Because it has been pronounced adultery by Christ. 2) Because it has been declared by God to be contrary to the divine institution of marriage. 3) Because it is written "Let every man have his own wife, and let every woman have her own husband."[8]

Consequently the first missionaries to Africa required polygamists to forsake all their wives except one. When Kasagama, the Omukama (king) of the Toro Kingdom in Uganda converted to Christianity, he had to send away eleven of his wives and retain only one.[9]

This rigid and unsympathetic view of polygamy has persisted. As recently as 1964, Kenneth Taylor reported on an incident that occurred when he met with a group of keen evangelical missionaries in Africa. One of them shared how a local chief had received the Lord Jesus as his Saviour and how he had carefully pointed out to the chief that the very first thing to do after disposing of his idols or fetishes must be to

---

[6] John S. Mbiti, *African Religions and Philosophy* (London: Heinemann, 1982), 147.

[7] Benezeri Kisembo, Laurenti Magesa and Aylward Shorter, *African Christian Marriage* (London: Geoffrey Chapman / Nairobi: Pauline Publications Africa, 1977), 104.

[8] W. Knight, "Missionary Secretariat of Henry Venn, D. D." 1880, p. 353, quoted in Adrian Hastings, *Christian Marriage in Africa: Being a Report Commissioned by the Archbishops of Cape Town, Central Africa, Kenya, Tanzania, and Uganda* (London: SPCK, 1973), 12.

[9] Christopher Byaruhanga, *Bishop Tucker of Uganda and the Africanization of the Church* (Nairobi: WordAlive, 2008), 135.

dispose of all but one wife. All the other missionaries praised the Lord when they were told that the chief had done this.[10]

The issue of polygamy has begun to receive serious study by Western and African scholars.[11] Some even contend that it is legitimate. Robert Holst, a missionary among the Ipili people of Papua New Guinea, states that "There is no reason why one man and several wives would not be one flesh."[12] Such voices are unhelpful and confusing when dealing with the serious problem of polygamy.

Biblical Perspectives on Polygamy

The starting point for our analysis of polygamy must be the biblical ideal of marriage as presented in the opening chapters of Genesis. Thereafter, however, most of the biblical material is descriptive rather than prescriptive; in other words, it simply describes what people did in particular situations rather than making statements about the morality of their actions. The Bible has no clear-cut statements condemning or prohibiting polygamy as practised in the Old Testament. We are thus faced with the standard problem of "whether it is possible to move from statements of fact to statements of value, and vice versa. That is, can one derive statements of *ought* from statements of *is*?[13]

Different scholars have drawn different conclusions from descriptive passages. However, since God does comment on some of the incidents recorded, we can hope that any conclusions we reach will reflect God's intention for marriage and acknowledge the effects of sin, which is the root cause of polygamy.

Most of the biblical data on polygamy comes from the Old Testament. This raises the question of how Christians should use Old Testament passages when thinking about ethical issues. This point cannot be

---

[10] Kenneth N. Taylor. "Is Polygamy Ever Permissible?" *Eternity* (July 1964): 25.

[11] Some representative scholars include Eugene Hillman, *Polygamy Reconsidered* (Maryknoll: Orbis, 1975); Adrian Hastings, *Christian Marriage in Africa*; Stephen Duncan, "An Enquiry into the Biblical Data on Polygamy" (Th.M. thesis, Western Conservative Baptist Seminary, Portland Oregon, 1986); Nathaniel G. Inyamah, "Polygamy and the Christian Church" *Concordia Theological Monthly* (March 1972): 138–143; I. Gaskiyane, *Polygamy: A Cultural and Biblical Perspective* (Carlisle: Piquant, 2000) and William F. Luck "The Morality of Biblical Polygamy" in *Divorce and Remarriage: Recovering the Biblical View* (San Francisco: Harper & Row, 1987).

[12] Robert Holst, "Polygamy and the Bible". *The International Review of Missions*, 56 (April 1967): 209.

[13] John S. Feinberg and Paul Feinberg, *Ethics for a Brave New World* (Wheaton, Ill.: Crossway, 1993), 19.

discussed at length here, but the basic principle we shall adopt is that "where the content of the Mosaic Law ... and the Law of Christ overlap, appeal to the OT is proper. In fact, appeal to the OT may give a fuller explanation of a principle and God's reasoning for it than one finds in the NT."[14] For example, when questioned about marriage and divorce, Jesus appealed to the creation ordinance in Genesis 1 and 2 and affirmed God's plan for marriage (Matt 19:2–9; Mark 10:2–11). We can thus refer to this same ordinance when discussing polygamy.

As Christians, we should also pay attention to the example set by the apostles. Paul instructed his readers: "Join with others in following my example ... and take note of those who live according to the pattern we gave you" (Phil 3:17; see also 2 Thess 3:7). The "we" referred to here must include the church leaders, who had to meet the requirement of having only one wife (1 Tim 3:2; Titus 1:6).

The biblical ideal for marriage

Monogamy is, without a doubt, God's ideal for marriage. God created only one wife for Adam (Gen 1:28; 2:24). Had he wanted polygamy to be the norm, he would have made more than one woman. John Stott summarizes the concept of marriage set out in Genesis 2:24 as "an exclusive heterosexual covenant between one man and one woman; ordained and sealed by God, heralded by a public leaving of parents in exchange for a permanent mutually supportive partnership, normally crowned by the gift of children."[15] This is the type of relationship that Jesus endorsed in Matthew 19:4–6. The church must stand by this position.

Because the monogamous and indissoluble union of one man and one woman is God's ideal, it follows that polygamy, like divorce, is a deviation from this norm. A polygamous marriage is thus a "form of marriage which is less satisfactory than monogamy and one which cannot do justice to the full spirit of Christian marriage, but in certain circumstances individual Christians can still put up with it, as they put up with slavery, dictatorial government, and much else".[16]

---

[14] Ibid., 39.

[15] John Stott, *Involvement: Social and Sexual Relationships in the Modern World, Vol. II* (Old Tappan, N.J.: Fleming H. Revell, 1978), 163. For a more detailed discussion of the purposes for marriage, see the introduction to this section on Marriage Issues.

[16] Kisembo, Magesa and Shorter, *African Christian Marriage*, 105.

Polygamy in the Old Testament

The study of polygamy in the Old Testament involves close scrutiny of the circumstances in which it was practised and the individuals who practised it.

Lamech (Gen 4:19–25)

The first polygamist mentioned in the Bible is Lamech, who married two wives. He was a vengeful man who followed in Cain's footsteps and killed to avenge a mere wound. His bad character has traditionally been interpreted as an indication of moral depravity in other areas of his life as well. Thus the nineteenth-century commentators Keil and Delitzsch accused him of lust, arguing that the fact that he had two wives shows that he was "the first to prepare the way for polygamy by which the ethical aspects of marriage, ordained by God, were turned into the lust of the eye and lust of the flesh". They insisted that even the names of the wives of Lamech are indicative of "sensual attraction, for Adah ('the adorned'), and Zillah ('the shaking' or the 'twinkling')".[17] But is it correct to interpret the reference to Lamech's polygamy as a moral judgment on the practice of polygamy?

To answer this question, we need to look at this passage in context. In Genesis 4 and 5 the godless descendants of Cain are contrasted with the God-fearing descendants of Seth: "The Cainite line culminated with the portrayal of the violent and arrogant Lamech, paralleling his violent ancestor Cain … Lamech, the sixth generation from Adam in Cain's line, has a contrasting counterpart in Enoch, the sixth generation from Adam in Seth's line."[18] John Calvin stated: "The Lord therefore willed that the corruption of lawful marriage should proceed from the house of Cain and from the person of Lamech, in order that polygamists might be ashamed of the example."[19]

Some theologians assume that anything associated with Cain's line must be condemned. The problem with this argument is that some good things also came from this line, including musical instruments and metal work (Gen 4:21–22).

---

[17] C. F. Keil and F. Delitzsch, *Commentary on the Old Testament in Ten Volumes, Vol. I. The Pentateuch* (1866; repr., Grand Rapids: Eerdmans, 1988), 118.

[18] Duncan, "An Enquiry", 226.

[19] John Calvin, *Commentaries on the First Book of Moses called Genesis, Vol. 1* (1554; repr., Grand Rapids: Eerdmans), 217, quoted by Duncan in "An Enquiry", 25.

Another problem with basing our denunciation of polygamy on the evil character of Lamech is that "for each instance of the bad sort of polygamist, one could cite a righteous man who had more than one wife – Abraham, Jacob, David to name but a few."[20] Given that the moral character of a number of other polygamists in Scripture is very different from that of Lamech, it is clear that we cannot use the polygamist's overall character as a criterion for judging whether polygamy is right or wrong. To do so would be to make polygamy right for some and wrong for others.[21]

It thus seems that the reference to polygamy in Genesis 4:19 should be properly interpreted as a mere statement of fact, "without comment or moral judgment".[22] If the polygamy of Lamech is to be judged, the judgment should be based on the fact that it is a deviation from the prescribed norm (monogamy).

People before the flood (Gen 6:1–7)

The association of polygamy and lust in the words of Keil and Delitzch quoted above is also present in the writing of another nineteenth-century commentator, Dwight. He notes that "the second and only remaining account of polygamy before the deluge is found in Genesis 6:1–7",[23] a passage which is traditionally interpreted as dealing with lust. It says that as the population increased, men married any women they chose. Kaiser also mentions this passage, saying that it was because of "man's autocratic and polygamous ways that God destroyed the earth with the flood".[24]

The problem is that this passage in Genesis is very difficult to interpret. We should be very hesitant to suggest that polygamy was the sin that prompted the flood.

Abraham's family (Gen 16–17; 28–30)

The next occurrence of polygamy is found in Abraham's family. Abraham himself was probably born into a polygamous family: "Since Abraham married his half-sister Sarah, the daughter of his father, but not the

---

[20] Luck, *Divorce and Remarriage*, 234.
[21] Duncan, "An Enquiry", 28–29.
[22] Robert Davidson, *Genesis 1:1–11* (Cambridge: Cambridge University Press, 1973), 56, quoted in Duncan, "An Enquiry", 30.
[23] Sereno Edwards Dwight, *The Hebrew Wife* (New York: Leavitt, Lord & Co., 1836), 5.
[24] Walter C. Kaiser Jr. *Toward Old Testament Ethics* (Grand Rapids: Zondervan, 1983), 183.

daughter of his mother (Gen 20:12), it is probable ... that Terah had concubines or multiple wives."[25]

When Sarah proved barren, she became desperate for a child and encouraged Abraham to have a child with Hagar, her Egyptian slave (Gen 16:1–16). Some commentators deny that this is an example of polygamy. Dwight, writing in the nineteeth century, stated that "it proves merely that a husband who was childless might lawfully, with the consent of his wife, connect himself temporarily with his female slave; but obviously this is not polygamy".[26] Kaiser similarly claims that Sarah talked Abraham into having "a temporary sexual relation" with Hagar.[27]

But this position is not tenable, for the whole context indicates that this was more than just a temporary sexual relationship. Hagar became pregnant, and her pregnancy seems to have affected her status. Whereas previously she had simply been an Egyptian slave, now she insists on being treated as a concubine. She sees her pregnancy as giving her a higher status than her mistress. "She is lifted up to the place of a legally recognized concubine, even a wife with the rights of such. That means that she has to be cared for ... concerning food, clothing and marital rights (Exod 21:8–11)."[28] There can thus be no doubt that Abraham maintained a polygamous household for at least some period of time.

God is not shown as condemning Abraham's behaviour as immoral. Rather, God simply insists that Ishmael is not the child he had promised. That child would be born to Sarah (Gen 17:15–21). If God does not condemn Abraham's action, neither should we (which, incidentally, is not the same as saying that he was right to give in to his wife's demands).

Abraham's twin grandsons followed his example and were also polygamous. Esau married two Hittite (Canaanite) women, much to his parents dismay (Gen 26:34) as well as Ishmael's daughter (Gen 28:9). Yet Isaac and Rebekah were not upset by the number of Esau's wives but by the fact that they were Canaanites (Gen 28:1–9).

---

[25] Duncan, "An Enquiry", 31.

[26] Dwight, *The Hebrew Wife*, 7. Dwight argues that polygamy, though sanctioned by the custom of the time, was never authorized by divine law.

[27] Kaiser, *Toward Old Testament Ethics*, 183.

[28] Gerhard Jasper, "Polygamy in the Old Testament", *African Theological Journal*, 2 (Feb. 1969): 40. He argues that "polygamy is a possible way of family life sanctioned by the example of the patriarchs Abraham and many of Israel's heroes".

Jacob married two sisters and also had children with their maids (Gen 29:1–30:22). Interestingly, some of those who condemn the polygamy of men such as Esau and Lamech do not condemn Jacob's polygamy. Dwight, for example, explains that "Laban and his children were idolaters, yet polygamy was not part of Jacob's plan of life. Leah was put upon him by a fraud, to which he must submit, or hazard the loss of Rachel."[29] Kaiser is at least consistent in condemning the practice of polygamy by both Jacob and Esau.[30]

Levirate marriage (Gen 38:6–10; Deut 25:5–10; Ruth)

Levirate marriage, which has already been mentioned in the chapter on procreation, was the custom whereby a dead man's brother or next closest relative was obliged to marry the widow and raise up children for the deceased brother. Its general purpose was to prevent a man's name from being blotted out and to prevent the dissipation of family property.[31] Given that most men would probably already have had a wife, this practice amounts to "a mandated form of polygamy".[32]

The first levirate marriage recorded in the Bible predates the Mosaic law. Judah's son Er had died, and his brother, Onan, was expected to marry Er's widow, Tamar, so that she could have a son who would keep Er's name alive and inherit his property. However, Onan, "while outwardly pretending that he was fulfilling this law, regularly spilled his seed and thereby prevented the conception from taking place (Gen 38:8–10)."[33] Onan's refusal to impregnate Tamar led to his death.

The formal statement of the levirate law is found in Deuteronomy 25:5–10. It makes it clear that anyone who refused to impregnate his brother's widow and raise up children for his brother would be perpetrating a grave social injustice and would incur a stigma and a severe penalty: "If he persists in saying, 'I do not want to marry her,' his brother's widow shall go up to him in the presence of the elders, take off one of his sandals, spit in his face and say, 'This is what is done to the man who will not build up his brother's family line'" (Deut 25:8–9).

---

[29] Dwight, *The Hebrew Wife*, 7.
[30] Kaiser, *Toward Old Testament Ethics*, 183.
[31] Ibid., 191. The term "levirate" comes from "the Latin *levir*, which is translated from the Hebrew word *Yavam*, 'brother in-law' (p. 190).
[32] Duncan, "An Enquiry", 36.
[33] Kaiser, *Toward Old Testament Ethics*, 191.

The second case of levirate marriage recorded in the Old Testament involves Ruth. In her situation, there was no surviving brother-in-law whom she could marry. She turned to Boaz as her "kinsman-redeemer" (Ruth 3:9), for "the aim and effect of kinsman-redeemer marriages were the same as those of the levirate marriage".[34]

> Thus Boaz married Ruth, the widow of one of his cousins by the name of Elimelech, after a more closely related kinsman declared openly before the elders in the gate of the city that he felt unable to fulfill this duty. Yet as Boaz apparently had already received his heritage, we have to think that he was already married. Ruth then was his second wife without any shame or blame; on the contrary, the hardship of the life of a lone widow was taken away from her and her mother-in-law Naomi.[35]

Kaiser is disturbed by this apparent endorsement of polygamy. He suggests that "this is the single exception since it aids in fostering the goal of godly families. God can and did permit and bless such exceptions. Only he can modify his own directives for his good purposes."[36]

Some crucial observations must be made here. If levirate marriage was a "frequent cause of polygamy",[37] it follows that being polygamous was not equated with committing adultery. If polygamy were adulterous before God, it would contradict his holiness to permit it at all, even in the case of levirate marriage. It thus seems that polygamy was not adulterous, but rather a legally and culturally accepted form of marriage that God permitted and even sanctioned.

David (2 Sam 11–12)

King David's relationship with Bathsheba, the wife of Uriah the Hittite, involved coveting, adultery and murder. All three of these sins were specifically forbidden in the Ten Commandments (Exod 20:13–14), with adultery and murder being punishable by death (Lev 20:10; Deut 22:23; Num 35:31). Even David, an absolute monarch, could not

---

[34] Ibid.
[35] Jasper, "Polygamy", 39.
[36] Kaiser, *Toward Old Testament Ethics*, 192.
[37] Geoffrey Parrinder, *The Bible and Polygamy: A Study of Hebrew and Christian Teaching* (London: SPCK, 1958), 23.

escape punishment.[38] As a result of his adultery, his concubines were sexually abused in broad daylight and there was constant bloodshed in his household (2 Sam 12:9–11).

God's response to David's sins also throws light on the relationship between adultery and polygamy, for there is an explicit reference to polygamy in the message communicated to David by Nathan the prophet:

> This is what the Lord, the God of Israel, says: 'I anointed you king over Israel, and I delivered you from the hand of Saul. I gave your master's house to you, and your master's wives into your arms. I gave you the house of Israel and Judah. And if all this had been too little, I would have given you even more' (2 Sam 12:7–8).

Those who reject the morality of polygamy argue that when God says "I gave your master's house to you, and your master's wives into your arms", he was not sanctioning David's marrying Ahinoam, the mother of David's wife Michal (1 Sam 14:50), and Rizpah, Saul's concubine (2 Sam 3:7). In fact, if David has married Ahinoam, he would have broken the law against marrying a wife's mother and would have been condemned to death for incest (Lev 18:17, 29). We also have no evidence that David actually married Rizpah. Thus God's words may simply mean that he had given David possession of everything that had been Saul's – including even his wives. Kaiser thus interprets it as meaning that God had given all Saul's women into David's care.[39]

But we are still left with the question of why God even brings up the topic of additional "wives" or "women" in the context of David's adultery and punishment. It is not as if these were the only women in David's life, for he already had more than one wife (2 Sam 3:1–5). Yet God does not condemn David for being polygamous, but for his adultery – "David committed adultery, not with his many wives, but with the wife of another man."[40] This understanding of what constituted

---

[38] Kaiser, *Toward Old Testament Ethics*, 183, quotes Dwight Edward to the effect that "nine of the thirteen [polygamists in the Old Testament] were absolute monarchs, whom no earthly tribunal could call to account, or punish, for their conduct." While this is true, it does not matter that no earthly tribunal can punish a monarch because God surely can.

[39] Ibid., 188.

[40] Kenneth N. Taylor, "Is Polygamy Ever Permissible?" *Eternity* (July 1964): 25.

adultery in David's situation is in keeping with the concept of adultery as understood in the Old Testament.

If God did not punish David for his polygamy, why should we punish polygamists today? The negative treatment of polygamists is contrary to the spirit of the Old Testament. It is David's adultery, not his polygamy, that was severely punished.

However, the Bible also clearly shows the negative effects of David's polygamy. The result of having more than one wife was rivalry for the throne, dividing the nation during the days of Absalom's rebellion (2 Sam 15–18) and again at the end of David's life, when there was rivalry between the son of David's first wife and Solomon, Bathsheba's son (1 Kgs 1).

Solomon (1 Kgs 11)

According to 1 Kings 11:3, Solomon had "seven hundred wives and three hundred concubines". These multiple foreign marriages were the result of his "practice of sealing political alliances by marriage"[41] and are clearly condemned in 1 Kings 11:1–13 and in Nehemiah 13:26. But why was Solomon's polygamy immoral while that of David was not?

The answer is that the sheer number of Solomon's wives was in direct violation of God's command that the king should not take many wives (Deut 17:17). "If ever there was a clear case of violating the prohibition against multiplying wives, Solomon's case was it."[42] As predicted in Deuteronomy, the foreign wives led Solomon astray and turned his heart to other gods.

Conclusion

The Old Testament passages that we have examined indicate that polygamy was an aberration from the principle laid down in Genesis 2:24. However, its practise by Lamech, Abraham, Jacob, Esau and David was not condemned as immoral or adulterous. Moreover, levirate marriage was a form of marriage sanctioned by God that often resulted in polygamy. Adultery, by contrast, was a serious violation of God's law and brought divine judgment. God also prohibited the multiplication of foreign wives by kings since they would lead them away from the living God, as happened when King Solomon violated his law.

---

[41] Duncan, "An Enquiry", 51.

[42] Ibid., 51.

In general, it would seem fair to say that even if polygamy is wrong because it falls short of the ideal of monogamous marriage, we cannot equate it with adultery. Jasper is right when he says:

> A polygamous marriage is for the Old Testament a marriage in the full sense of the word with all the protection which the law and the elders of Israel could give to it. An Israelite who had two wives was by no means considered as one who had fallen in his faith or in the necessary obedience in faith.[43]

Polygamy in the New Testament

While there are many examples of polygamy in the Old Testament, no case of polygamy is recorded in the New Testament. However, there are some passages that indirectly address the issue.

Jesus' teaching on divorce and remarriage (Matt 19:9; Mark 10:11; Luke 16:18)

In response to a question from some Pharisees, Jesus states, "Moses permitted you to divorce your wives because your hearts were hard. But it was not this way from the beginning. I tell you that anyone who divorces his wife, except for marital unfaithfulness, and marries another woman commits adultery" (Matt 19:8–9). Some have applied these words not only to divorce but also to polygamy. Thus Johann Gerhard, writing in the seventeenth century, reasoned that "if it is adultery to dismiss one's wife and marry another, how much is it a sin to marry another while the first is retained?"[44] Dwight, writing in the nineteenth century, put it like this:

> But in what does the adultery, thus committed by the husband consist? Not in the mere putting away. That might be cruelty but it is not adultery … It consisted in the fact, that, having one wife, he marries another and has intercourse with another before the first is dead or lawfully divorced. By the Original Law of Marriage, therefore, as thus explained by Christ, the man, who having a wife, marries another, before the first is

[43] Jasper, "Polygamy", 41.
[44] *Loci Theologici*, Berlin: Gust. Schlawitz, 1869W VII, 1211ff., quoted by William Bruce, "Polygamy and the Church" *Concordia Theological Monthly*, 34 (April 1963): 224.

lawfully divorced, is guilty of adultery. But every polygamist does this: every polygamist, therefore, is guilty of adultery. Of course polygamy according to the Original Law of Marriage is adultery.[45]

By contrast, William Luck argues that this passage is irrelevant to the debate about polygamy and insists that "Jesus means only to reaffirm the Old Testament's condemnation of a man who would divorce his wife in order to marry another woman (Mal 2)."[46]

While I disagree with those who say that this passage brands polygamy as adultery, I also disagree with Luck. The principles taught in this passage are indeed relevant to the discussion of polygamy. However, it must be noted that the main focus of this passage is divorce, and that any applications of it to the issue of polygamy are inferences. We must take care to ensure that any inferences we draw are valid and true to the context of the original.

For detailed discussion of the dispute in which Jesus was involved and of the issue of divorce, see chapter 18. The main point that needs to be made here is that Jesus insists that God's norm for marriage is one husband and one wife in a union that is indissoluble, apparently until the death of one of the parties. Divorce issues from disobedient hearts and is sinful because it goes against God's command in Genesis 2:24 (Matt 19:5–6).

Applying this same principle to polygamy, we can safely say that it is also sinful because it, too, violates the divine norm that marriage involves one man and one woman.

Jesus brands remarriage as adultery in Matthew 19:9 "because the Jews rid themselves of the wives for the purpose of marrying another".[47] Thus it is also appropriate to say that he clearly condemns successive polygamy through easy divorce.

But is he also here condemning simultaneous polygamy of the kind which is common in Africa, in which culture, rather than lust or wilful disobedience to a known law, leads a man to marry more than one woman? In answering this question, we need to remember that the Pharisees to whom Jesus was speaking were familiar with the creation

---

[45] Dwight, *The Hebrew Wife*, 12.

[46] Luck, *Divorce and Remarriage*, 234.

[47] R. C. H. Lenski, *The Interpretation of St. Mathew's Gospel* (1932; repr. Minneapolis: Augsburg, 1961), 733.

ordinance in Genesis and thus with the concept of monogamy. However, they were also familiar with the practice of polygamy and divorce. They would also have known that levirate marriage, which often produced polygamy, was commanded in the law. In this context, it does not seem that Jesus' comments on divorce would naturally be interpreted as a condemnation of all forms of polygamy. To say that Jesus' words here mean that polygamy is "unlawful within the church of Christ even though commenced in ignorance, because it has been pronounced adultery by Christ"[48] is to draw an inference that goes beyond what the text warrants.

Monogamy and eldership (1 Tim 3:2, Titus 1:6)

In 1 Timothy 3:2 and Titus 1:6, Paul specifies that "an elder must be the husband of but one wife". But if it was necessary to specify that church leaders must be monogamous, it seems likely that some of the members of the early church were polygamous. These people "must have contracted their polygamous marriages prior to conversion, in their Judaic or heathen ignorance, and had been permitted to enter the church without renouncing any of their wives".[49]

These polygamists in the early church were clearly not considered adulterers. The sin of adultery is repeatedly condemned in the New Testament. Paul states that adulterers will not inherit the kingdom of God (1 Cor 6:9–10). So does the writer of Hebrews, who insists that "God will judge the adulterer and all the sexually immoral" (Heb 13:4). John, writing in Revelation, also speaks of the immoral being consigned to the second death (Rev 21:8; 22:14–15). But the epistles to Timothy and Titus nowhere imply that the salvation of polygamous church members is in doubt; all they specify is that they should not be in positions of leadership.

Remaining in the condition in which one was called (1 Cor 7)

The question arises, if polygamy is sinful because it is less than God's ideal for marriage, how can someone be forgiven that sin while continuing to be a polygamist? Doesn't forgiveness require renunciation of sin? The answer to this question can be found in 1 Corinthians 7:1–40. Paul

[48] Knight, "Missionary Secretariat", 12.
[49] James E. Karibwiji, "Polygamy and the Church in Nigeria: A Study of Various Christian Positions" (M. Div. thesis, Trinity Evangelical Divinity School, Deerfield, Illinois. June 1984), 210.

is addressing certain questions about marriage that had arisen in the Corinthian church. One of them is the problem of a believer married to an unbeliever. Paul tells those in this situation that "each one should retain the place in life that the Lord assigned to him and to which God has called him. This is the rule I lay down in all the churches" (1 Cor 7:17). He repeats the same principle in 7:20 and 7:24, applying it to believers' socio-economic and physical circumstances as well as their marital circumstances. "The entire verse implies that in whatever state we are when we come to the Lord, we should function faithfully in that state without immediately seeking to change it."[50]

Some may object that the examples Paul uses in 7:18–19 are circumcision and slavery, both circumstances which an individual cannot change, and neither of which represents a sin on the part of the one circumcised or enslaved. Such critics argue that Paul is not saying that someone should remain in a sinful state like polygamy.

But we also need to take into account Paul's opinions on marriage in 7:25–27. He states, "Are you married? Do not seek a divorce" (7:27). This principle underlies all the preceding instructions regarding marital relations.[51]

It is contextually appropriate for us to infer from this passage that marriages that are contracted in terms of culturally accepted norms should be tolerated in the church. The polygamist who married his wives before his conversion should not seek to divorce them when he becomes a Christian. Rather he should remain faithful to the marital condition in which God called him.

Summary of the biblical data

The indissoluble monogamous union of a man and woman is God's ideal for marriage. Even after the fall, this ideal of marriage is to be maintained. The practice of polygamy issues from a sinful heart because it violates God's command at creation. However, neither the Old nor the New Testament depict polygamists as living in adultery.

Polygamy was less common in New Testament times, but it seems safe to infer, that there were polygamists in the churches who were not

---

[50] Craig L. Bloomberg, *1 Corinthians* (NIV Application Commentary; Grand Rapids: Zondervan, 1994), 145.

[51] R. C. H. Lenski, *The Interpretation of St. Paul's First and Second Epistle to the Corinthians* (1935; repr., Columbus, Ohio: Wartburg Press, 1955), 298.

considered adulterers but were baptized on the basis of their repentance and faith in Jesus Christ. They may well have been full-fledged members of their local congregations. We can also infer that Christians should not seek to change their marital situation.

Our study of the biblical teaching on polygamy has made it clear that we do not have clear answers regarding polygamy in the revealed word of God. Where the Scriptures are silent, we have to be very careful in drawing conclusions that may suit our cultural inclinations and contradict the spirit of the Scriptures.

Treatment of Polygamists in Churches

The intolerance of polygamy by the missionaries and some contemporary church leaders has created many ethical and social problems and has left a legacy of embittered wives and children, who were sent away without anyone to provide for them. Some have even had to resort to prostitution in order to survive. This situation raises the question, "Is it morally right to require that a man who has contracted marriages to more than one wife renounce them on conversion?" Which is a greater evil; polygamy or divorce?

Adrian Hastings' observations are appropriate:

> A non-Christian has accepted a lifelong obligation by plural marriages from which he is not entitled to withdraw. To do so is frequently to cause very real injustice and misery to wives and children. To impose this upon other defenceless people is a strange way of preparing for baptism. It is the women and children, not the men, who … suffer in enforced separations of this kind. To end a polygamous marriage in the name of Christ, who said nothing explicitly to condemn it, at the expense of effecting divorce, which Christ explicitly forbids, is to pay too high a price to achieve a theoretical conformity with one part of the Christian pattern.[52]

And what happens to the children? In Africa being without a parent causes serious social problems and has long-lasting psychological implications. The children of a rejected wife have no one to provide

---

[52] Adrian Hastings, *Christian Marriage in Africa* (London: SPCK, 1973), 77.

for them and are considered illegitimate. The grandson of a polygamist who had seventeen wives and many children expresses his anger and frustration when he writes:

> It is my opinion that legislation against polygamy has done more harm than good. The church's position is neither warranted by Scripture nor sanctioned by apostolic example nor justified by common reason. Whenever the church breaks up legitimate family ties, it creates bastards out of legitimate children, and indirectly promotes adultery or whoredom; it is failing in its mission to bring the gospel of Jesus Christ to a sick world.[53]

Again the question might be asked: "Would Jesus or St. Paul have demanded that polygamists send away their wives and children in order to become Christians?"

Another consequence of the requirement to divorce all but one wife has been the splintering of the church as polygamists have founded their own churches that will accommodate their way of life. Today many African initiated churches allow, and even encourage, polygamy. Such groups include the Cherubim and Seraphim Movement Church in Nigeria, the United Native African Church (now the First African Church Mission Inc., some branches of the Methodist church, and the African Greek Orthodox Church.[54] This splintering would likely not have come about if the church had helped people to remain in the truth without demanding that polygamists separate from additional wives.

The church's opposition to polygamy has also led some people to completely refuse to accept Christ and instead remain pagans or embrace Islam. The Yoruba chiefs of Nigeria could not reconcile themselves to a God who would tear their families apart.

The issue of how to respond to polygamy is especially crucial in northern Nigeria where many people are polygamous, but are coming to know the Lord Jesus. Should the church require these polygamists to forsake their wives before being accepted? In one of the larger towns

---

[53] Nathaniel G. Inyamah, "Polygamy and the Christian Church", *Concordia Theological Monthly* (March 1972): 142.

[54] G. C. Oosthuizen, *Post-Christianity in Africa: A Theological and Anthropological Study* (Grand Rapids: Eerdmans, 1968), 181. In this scholarly work, Oosthuizen observes that polygamy is common and is encouraged in African independent churches.

(with a population 45,000) more than two-thirds of the population were lost to Islam when one man of considerable influence was denied church membership because his home was polygamous. The young man in charge of the parish where the man lived applied a strict interpretation of the ideal of "one wife" when the man accepted the Christian faith and desired baptism. Unwilling to reject his wives, he ran into the warm embrace of Islam, the religion in which his family remains to this day.[55]

The above story is not intended to imply that Christians must sacrifice the truth in order to retain converts in the church. The point is that there is great need for tact and understanding concerning the issue of polygamy, especially when there is no clear biblical statement that equates it with adultery.

Conclusion

Polygamy violates God's norm of a monogamous and indissoluble marriage. From this point of view it fails to meet God's intended plan for marriage. However, the biblical material on polygamy indicates that God in his sovereign will tolerated polygamy as a form of marriage. More than that, polygamists in the Old Testament were full members of the people of God. The inference in the New Testament strongly indicates that polygamists, though disqualified from positions of leadership, were also full members of the Christian church.

In light of this, the past and present ecclesiastical perception and treatment of polygamists as adulterers is unbiblical, unethical and harmful. Polygamists who contracted their marriages before conversion should not be required to divorce their wives but should be accepted as full members in the body of Christ. To do otherwise is to obscure the central gospel of justice, mercy and love.[56] Divorce is harmful, even in polygamous situations, and has severe consequences for wives and children.

We should heed the opinion of Professor Danfulani Kore, a Nigerian who is a respected conservative Evangelical theologian:

---

[55] T. A. Adejumobi, "Polygamy" in *African Independent Church Movements* (ed. Victor E. W. Hayward; New York: Friendship Press, 1963), 58.

[56] Hastings, *Christian Marriage in Africa*, 79.

> When those [with a] polygamous background become believers, the church must not command that the husband divorce the second wife before they are saved or become church members. This is unbiblical. Divorce is a sin. In addition, such an action will harm the woman and her children. No one can deny a polygamist salvation in Christ if they put their faith in Him. They should be allowed baptism in obedience to Christ's command (Matthew 28:19–20) ... It follows then that believers from polygamous backgrounds should be allowed to take part in the Holy Communion.[57]

In their zeal to "give the gospel in its purest form along with the highest Christian ideals [missionaries] often forget that principles of the Word of God often take time to work themselves out as ideals".[58] Thus the church in Africa should "tolerate polygamy but undermine it by promoting it to the superior ideal of monogamy".[59] As the church teaches a biblical theology of marriage, it can be hoped that by the second and third generations, the problem of polygamy in the Christian church will be minimized and hopefully eradicated.

Questions

1. Describe the state of polygamy in an African community with which you are familiar. What circumstances encourage the practice?

2. In what ways did the review of the biblical data inform, change or reinforce your perspective on polygamy?

3. What church issues are you facing with regard to polygamy? How have these situations been handled in the past? Are they currently being handled in accordance with biblical teaching?

---

[57] Danfulani Kore, *Culture and the Christian Home* (Jos: ACTS, 1995), 94–95. See also comments on 1 Corinthians 7:17–27.

[58] Ralph D. Winter, "Polygamy: Rules and Principles," *Church Growth Bulletin 3* (March 1969): 356.

[59] Hastings, quoted in Kisembo, Magesa and Shorter, *African Christian Marriage*, 105.

17
DOMESTIC VIOLENCE

Most of us condemn violence as a great evil, yet we fail to recognize how prevalent it is in our own homes. This point is true regardless of our culture, race, ethnic group, religion or social class. Many of us have experienced domestic violence either as a spouse or as a child. Even if we have not suffered physical violence ourselves, we have probably witnessed a mother, aunt or a neighbour's wife or child being physically, verbally or psychologically abused. A recent study conducted by the Kenyan Women's Rights Awareness Program found that 70 per cent of those interviewed knew neighbours who beat their wives.

Domestic violence is thus a serious matter that must be dealt with as an illegal and immoral practice. Yet many cases of domestic violence are unreported, so that it is often described as one of the world's best-kept secrets. Even the church is complicit for, by and large, churches around the world have remained silent about violence against women.[1]

The Nature of Domestic Violence

Domestic violence involves the abuse of power in intimate relationships within a household. On the simplest level, a man is guilty of violence when he beats his wife with his hand or with a stick or belt. But domestic violence is also "linked to control and manipulation of the victim by the perpetrator and there are a whole range of ways he can accomplish this without resorting to a physical assault."[2] Thus a man is also guilty of violence if he forces his wife to carry heavy burdens and take on a totally disproportionate workload, or if he infects her with a sexually transmitted disease such as HIV/AIDS, or forces her to endure

---

[1] Aruna Gnanadason, *No Longer a Secret: The Church and Violence Against Women* (Geneva: WCC, 1997), 1.

[2] Helen L. Conway, *Domestic Violence and the Church* (Carlisle: Paternoster Press, 1978), 6.

numerous pregnancies. Men may also practise psychological abuse, a form of violence in which the husband shows no appreciation for his wife and instead makes her fear his physical violence and his humiliation of her in public and before the family. Violent husbands control their wife's movements and what she can and cannot do. Desertion of a wife is another form of violence, for it leaves her destitute.

Domestic violence does not only occur between husbands and wives, but can also be perpetrated against children. According to the American Psychological Association, some 40 to 60 per cent of men who abuse women also abuse children.[3] Adults (parents and relatives) may beat, neglect or sexually abuse children in the home. Older children may abuse their younger siblings. Babysitters may maltreat infants whom they are supposed to be taking care of. The violence against children may not only be physical, but can also include teasing, bullying, intimidation and psychological and sexual harassment.

Female violence against men is rare. When it does occur, it often takes the form of verbal or physical retaliation after repeated attacks on the woman or her children. This is sometimes referred to as violent resistance, in which a trapped victim sees violent retaliation as the only escape from further violence.

Causes of Domestic Violence in Africa

The following are the major reasons for the domestic violence in Africa:

- *Demonstration of power and control.* African traditional beliefs often hold that a woman is a man's property. In order to prove this and to uphold his image as the "lion" in the family, a man will not permit any insubordination by his wife or children, and resorts to physical and verbal violence to assert his control over them.[4] This situation is not unique to Africa.

- *Denial of sex.* Because the woman is often assumed to be the man's property, he assumes that he has a right to have sex with her any time

---

[3] American Psychological Association, *Violence and the Family: Report of the American Psychological Association Presidential Task Force on Violence and the Family* (Washington: APA, 1996), 8.

[4] Karen Burton Mains, *Abuse in the Family* (Elgin: David C. Cook, 1987), 15. Mains states that the motive for wife beating is to maintain women in a dependent and submissive state.

he wishes. Should the wife show any resistance or unwillingness, she may be verbally abused or beaten (see also chapter 20 on rape).

- *Jealousy and possessiveness.* Some men are so jealous and possessive that they do not want to see their wife even talking to another man. Any exchange with a man, no matter how innocent, will result in a confrontation. If the wife's responses are judged unsatisfactory, she will be battered.

- *Learnt behaviour.* Children learn how to behave by watching their parents. If a boy grows up in an abusive home, he is likely to be abusive himself. The environment he grew up in is perpetuated in his own adulthood and marriage, maintaining the vicious circle.

- *Polygamous marriages.* Jealousy, lies and misrepresentation abound in polygamous situations where the wives compete for the husband's favour. For example, a wife may claim that her rival has stolen a yam from her farm or is trying to poison her husband. Such accusations often lead to confrontations and beatings or verbal abuse.

- *Social tolerance of violence.* Family members such as parents, uncles and aunts do not encourage women to leave violent and abusive relationships. Instead, they urge them to stay in the marriage, particularly when there are young children, for they would not be allowed to take the children with them.

- *Lack of sanctions on those who perpetrate domestic violence.* Many communities have no measures for controlling or punishing those who abuse their wives. Their behaviour is simply explained away as a character flaw involving bad temper or lack of self-control.

- *Physical and emotional weakness of women.* Men are regarded as physically strong while women are characterized as passive, dependent and physically and emotionally weak. This characterization makes it difficult for women to resist abuse.

- *Alcohol abuse.* Some men abuse alcohol and other drugs. In their drunken state, they are unable to tolerate any disagreement from their spouses or children and are liable to interpret any action as insulting or insubordinate, and they respond to this with violence.

Effects of Domestic Violence

Domestic violence is enormously destructive of its victims, who live in a climate of fear and intimidation. The constant insecurity with which they live may even lead to problems in sleeping. Some abused wives will immerse themselves in activities outside the home, such as church meetings, weddings, funerals, and the like in order to avoid having to be at home with their abusive spouse.

When a wife flees a violent marriage, she may have to leave her children behind, to be raised without the loving care of their mother. If she is allowed to take the female children with her, they will grow up without a father. But even if the mother stays and endures the violence, the children will be scarred by the home environment. Children learn from what they see happening around them. They will learn violence as they watch their fathers beat and molest their mothers. Children who have been abused often become delinquent and abusive in their relationships with other children. The bullies in the streets are often those who have been physically abused at home. Some children may even end up fearing marriage itself. Many young men have expressed their fear that they will become like their fathers in terms of wife battering, while young girls have expressed fear of marrying an abusive man.

Biblical Perspectives on Domestic Violence

Much domestic abuse arises from a man's determination to prove that he is the head of his household. The Bible does not deny him this position, for it asserts that "the husband is the head of the wife" (Eph 5:23). However, the biblical definition of what it means to be the head of the house does not allow the husband to beat his family into submission. Rather, he is to be their servant and is to love his wife, "just as Christ loved the church and gave himself up for her" (Eph 5:25).

Some will also argue that the Bible gives parents the right to physically abuse their children. They may quote Proverbs 13:24: "He who spares the rod hates his son, but he who loves him is careful to discipline him." We must be careful when we read this verse with modern eyes. In some Western cultures, the use of a rod, stick or belt in discipline is associated with extreme violence. But in many African cultures, this is an acceptable means of discipline, applied in moderation. This tradition has a long history; there is even an ancient Egyptian proverb, "The ears of a boy are set on his back, and if you beat him he will listen".

But the focus of Proverbs 13:24 is not on "the rod" but on the principle of loving correction. It is making the point that a parent demonstrates love for a child by directing him in the right path. Loving discipline is very different from the unrestrained beating meted out by a drunken father or a man who merely wants to prove that he is the "lion" in the house.

The same focus is found in Hebrews 12:5–11, a passage in which a loving God is presented as our model when it comes to discipline: "the Lord disciplines those he loves, and he punishes everyone he accepts as a son" (Heb 25:6). The same attitude to discipline is found in Paul's words: "Fathers, do not exasperate your children; instead, bring them up in the training and instruction of the Lord" (Eph 6:4). Physical beating often produces only fear, rebellion and exasperation; loving discipline involves the hard work of training and instruction.

The final argument against any biblical support for child abuse is found in Jesus' attitude to children. He showed deep concern and love for them (Matt 21:16; Mark 10:16; Luke 18:15–16). He even taught that to show love to children is to show love to him (Matt 18:5–6). Abusing a child would thus also be equivalent to abusing Jesus.

A Christian Response to Domestic Violence

The starting point for our response to domestic violence must be the recognition that all violence against women and children is morally unjust. They are human beings created in the image of God, and as such they are not inferior to men. They are entitled to be treated with respect.

This truth needs to be communicated to boys and girls at a young age. Boys need to be educated about the fact that they are in no way superior to women. They need to be taught that women are to be respected and treated with dignity. Young girls, too, need to be trained to know that they are not inferior to their male counterparts. They must be taught to assert their equality to men and to report acts of aggression against them and their children.

Reporting involves recognising that domestic violence is not a private offence but a criminal one. As such, it must be reported to the police, who must act to restrain the perpetrator and prevent future violence. In a traditional setting such as a village, it should be reported to the elders who can easily and effectively restrain the man from abusing his children or wife. It is advisable to also report the matter to the pastors and elders of the church. Violence is perpetuated by silence. When reported, it can be monitored and checked.

Men must be taught that Jesus is to be their example when it comes to the way they treat women and children. Where wives are loved as Christ loved the church, there can be no scope for physical and psychological violence against them. When children are treated in the same way that Jesus treated them, there will be no child abuse, but only the same loving disciplines that God metes out to us.

Not only the government and institutions but also all of us must work hard to break the vicious circle of domestic violence that breeds hatred and more violence. Loving and caring families will produce loving and caring members of society.

Questions

1. What forms of domestic violence are found within your community? Which ones seem to pose the most significant problem?

2. What factors seem to lead to the forms of domestic violence that you have identified above?

3. Is Scripture sometimes abused to justify domestic violence? How would you respond to those who justify abuse in the name of obedience to God?

4. How can your church become a leader in the prevention of domestic violence?

18
DIVORCE AND REMARRIAGE

Many of the topics discussed in earlier chapters – infertility, polygamy, abuse – can put great strain on a marriage. So can situations where one partner is diagnosed with HIV/AIDS or some other illness. What should the Christian response be when the unity that should be present in a marriage cracks and one or both parties seek a divorce? And what is the status of the Christian who is divorced? Can he or she be a full member of the church? Can he or she be permitted to marry again? These questions are becoming increasingly urgent as African societies are being affected by Western values, with their easy acceptance of divorce and what could be called "serial polygamy".

Traditional Views on Divorce

Divorce must be understood in the context of the purposes of marriage. In Africa, the most important reason for getting married has traditionally been procreation. A marriage that fails to produce children is thus in crisis. Danfulani Kore underscores this point. His study of 34 ethnic groups in Africa showed that "the greatest single factor that causes a quick divorce … is childlessness".[1] No matter how satisfactory a wife may be in all other respects, if she does not produce a child, her husband will either divorce her or will marry additional wives in order to have children. Sometimes, he will take these steps simply because the wife has failed to produce a male child. "It appears that having children is of higher importance than even the marriage union itself".[2]

Another scholar who has studied Christian marriages in Africa insists that "the church needs to insist very strongly that a childless marriage should not be regarded as an invalid marriage, and those within such a

---

[1] Danfulani Kore, *Culture and the Christian Home* (Jos: ACTS, 1989), 88.
[2] Ibid.

union should be given every help to persevere. It would be very wrong to make sterility a ground for nullity".[3] But he also concedes that "the production of children is such a central part of marriage, it should be easier for the church to accept the dissolution of a brief childless union than one in which children have been born".[4]

Early Christian missions in Africa also permitted divorcing an unbelieving partner and remarrying a believing partner. And many African Initiated Churches permit divorce and remarriage, as well as polygamous marriages.

Biblical Perspectives on Divorce and Remarriage

God's original plan for marriage envisaged such a fundamental unity between the man and his wife that they would enjoy a loving, trusting and happy married life (Gen 2:24). However, with the fall, sin and hatred became part of the human condition, and thus divorce came into our world.

Two key biblical passages are referred to in any Christian debate about divorce. The first is Deuteronomy 24:1–4:

> If a man marries a woman who becomes displeasing to him because he finds something indecent about her, and he writes her a certificate of divorce, gives it to her and sends her from his house, and if after she leaves his house she becomes the wife of another man, and her second husband dislikes her and writes her a certificate of divorce, gives it to her and sends her from his house, or if he dies, then her first husband, who divorced her, is not allowed to marry her again after she has been defiled.

This passage does not require, recommend or even sanction divorce. Its primary concern is not with divorce at all, nor even with certificates of divorce. What it says is that "if a man divorces his wife, and if he gives her a certificate, and if she leaves and remarries, and if her second

---

[3] Danfulani Kore, *Culture and the Christian Home* (Jos: ACTS, 1989), 88.
[4] Adrian Hastings, *Christian Marriage in Africa* (London: SPCK, 1973), 90.

husband dislikes her and divorces her, or dies, then her first husband may not marry her again".[5]

However, because this passage is the main reference to divorce in the Pentateuch, it became central to the Jewish debate on the subject, with attention focusing on the exact meaning of the Hebrew word *ervah*, which indicates the grounds for divorce. Literally, it means "nakedness" or "shameful exposure", but the NIV translates it as "something indecent", the KJV as "some uncleanness", the NRSV as "something objectionable", and the NASB as "some indecency".

The second biblical passage cited involves Jesus' words to the Pharisees when they questioned him about his position on the famous controversy between the school of Hillel, which interpreted Deuteronomy 24:1 as allowing divorce for any reason, and the school of Shammai, which only allowed divorce if the wife was guilty of sexual sin. In Matthew 5:31–32, Jesus quotes the passage in Deuteronomy, and then adds a further clarification:

> It has been said, 'Anyone who divorces his wife must give her a certificate of divorce.' But I tell you that anyone who divorces his wife, except for marital unfaithfulness (porneia), causes her to become an adulteress, and anyone who marries the divorced woman commits adultery.

The same idea is repeated in slightly different words in Matthew 19:9.

Once again, the bone of contention is the exception clause, "except for marital unfaithfulness". The Greek word *porneia*, is variously translated as "fornication" (KJV and Living Bible) "unchastity" (REB, NRSV), and "immorality" (NASB). The variety of words used to translate it indicates that it is difficult to pin down the exact meaning of the word. This difficulty accounts for the controversy it generates. The debate focuses on whether divorce is justifiable in exceptional cases.

Instead of trying to repeat all the exegetical and theological expositions of these passages in Deuteronomy and Luke, I will summarize the key positions.[6]

---

[5] John Stott, *Involvement: Social and Sexual Relationships in the Modern World. Vol. II* (Old Tappan, N. J.: Fleming H. Revell, 1978), 165.

[6] There are excellent treatments of these passages in many commentaries on both the Old and New Testaments as well as in books such as John and Paul Feinberg's *Ethics for a Brave New World* (Wheaton: Crossway, 1993), 306–319; Benezeri Kisembo, Laurenti Magesa and Aylward Shorter, *African Christian Marriage* (Nairobi: Pauline Publications Africa, 1977), 56–83; William F. Luck,

No divorce at all

Some hold that marriage is for life and can only be terminated by death. Those who take this view hold that the words translated "except for marital unfaithfulness" in Matthew 19:9 should actually be translated "not even in the case of marital unfaithfulness". In their view, nothing justifies divorce. Even when there has been a separation and the couple have no physical contact, proponents of this view maintain that the marriage is still intact. In support of their position, they quote the analogy that Paul uses in Romans 7:2–3:

> For example, by law a married woman is bound to her husband as long as he is alive, but if her husband dies, she is released from the law of marriage. So then, if she marries another man while her husband is still alive, she is called an adulteress. But if her husband dies, she is released from that law and is not an adulteress, even though she marries another man.

Although the topic of Paul's argument is not marriage, the analogy he uses implies that a marriage endures as long as a spouse is alive. Any remarriage before one of the spouses dies is branded adulterous. Paul makes the same point in 1 Corinthians 7:39: "A woman is bound to her husband as long as he lives. But if her husband dies, she is free to marry anyone she wishes, but he must belong to the Lord."

This approach does justice to the creation ordinance in Genesis 1:27 and 2:24, which Jesus referred to in his comments on divorce, and also has Jesus agreeing with Malachi 2:16, where God says, "I hate divorce". However, its major weakness is that it fails to deal completely with the question that Jesus was being asked in Matthew 9:7, which was about why Moses permitted divorce:

> Jesus taught that Moses' concession reflected not the true creation ordinance but the hardness of men's hearts. Divorce is not part of the Creator's perfect design. If Moses permitted it, he did so because sin can be so vile that divorce is to be preferred to continued "indecency". This is not to say that the person who, according to what Moses said, divorced his spouse was actually committing sin in so doing, but that divorce could even

Divorce and Remarriage: Recovering the Biblical View (San Francisco: Harper & Row, 1987) and William A. Heth and Gordon J. Wenham, *Jesus and Divorce* (Nashville: Thomas Nelson, 1984).

be considered testified that there had been sin in the marriage. Therefore any view of divorce and remarriage (taught in either Testament) that sees the problem only in terms of what may or may not be done has already overlooked a basic fact – divorce is never to be thought of as a God-ordained, morally neutral option but as evidence of sin, of hardness of heart.[7]

Divorce but no remarriage

Some argue that the "indecency" referred to in Deuteronomy 24:1 cannot be adultery because the law laid down that adultery was punishable by death, not divorce. They admit that in Matthew 19:9, Jesus was permitting divorce on the grounds of adultery, but deny that he would permit remarriage. They, too, argue that remarriage is adulterous as long as the other partner is still alive. Churches holding this position will admit a person who has divorced an adulterous spouse to the fellowship of the church. But if that person remarries, he or she is immediately subject to church discipline. Someone who has remarried cannot become an official member of any group in the church, cannot be elected to any leadership position in the church and is not permitted to participate in Holy Communion. They lose all their membership rights.

The major problem with this position is that it isolates adultery as the unforgivable sin. It is also very controversial to limit the meaning of porneia in Matthew to adultery and nothing else.

Divorce and remarriage

Some argue that Jesus explicitly permitted divorce on the basis of adultery. Others extend this permission to cover other grounds for divorce such as mental illness, desertion, abandoning the faith (particularly when the person becomes involved in witchcraft or joins a secret society), conviction of a crime, and imprisonment for a serious crime like murder. They also allow the innocent party to remarry.

Some theologians take the matter still further and argue that, in a metaphorical sense, marriages themselves die and that this "death" dissolves both the marriage covenant and the marriage union. A legal

---

[7] D. A. Carson, "Matthew" in *Matthew, Mark, Luke*. Vol. 8 of The Expositor's Bible Commentary (ed. Frank E. Gaebelein; Grand Rapids: Zondervan, 1984), 413.

marriage may still exist, but in reality the marriage is nonexistent. The couple may be living together, but there is no love, no sex, and no intimacy of any kind. Or, as often happens in Africa, spouses who were married in a church or in a traditional wedding end up living apart. They may be living with another man or woman and having children with them. In such a case, remarriage is allowed for both partners.[8]

The major weakness of this position is that it fails to emphasize the permanence of the marriage union and stresses the justifiability of divorce. This position can be a slippery slope, as has been amply demonstrated in Western countries where adultery, incompatibility, desertion or a lack of love are all considered legitimate grounds for divorce. In the United States divorce has even been granted on grounds of sexual incompatibility because the wife claimed that sexual intercourse with her husband made her sick.

A Theological and Pastoral Perspective

Though divorce and remarriage are not as common in Africa as in the West, there is a need to face up to the realities of marriage and divorce, and all their related problems. Christian leaders need to have a biblical, theological and pastoral perspective on marriage so that they can offer humane teaching and counselling to those in their congregations who are dealing with marital problems. It is hoped that the following points will contribute to their developing such a position.

Christian marriage is for life

• The Christian ideal is that marriage is the lifelong union of a man and woman. Christian marriage is monogamous and indissoluble and is intended to be enjoyable and fruitful (Gen 2:24; Matt 19:5–6; Rom 7:2–3). Divorce is the antithesis of marriage and God's reaction to it is succinct: "I hate divorce" (Mal 2:16).

Divorce will happen

• Jesus saw divorce as a result of the hardness of the human heart (Matt 19:8). This hardness is not limited to unbelievers but is also a reality

---

[8] Kisembo, Magesa and Shorter, *African Christian Marriage*, 75.

among the believing community. Any theological or counselling position that fails to acknowledge this is doomed to frustration and will fail in dealing with the human needs surrounding this tragedy. Our approach to marriage counselling must be simultaneously biblical, realistic, holistic and therapeutic.

Divorce is harmful

• Divorce is undesirable, psychologically traumatic and socially disruptive. Divorce means disunity, the separation of two parties who were formerly united. As Danfulani Kore notes, "The damage of divorce is irreparable. It is one of the worst tragedies in human life. It shatters the hopes and aspirations of many families."[9] John Stott makes the same point: "Marital breakdown is always a tragedy. It contradicts God's will, frustrates his purpose, brings to husband and wife the acute pains of alienation, disillusion, recrimination and guilt, and precipitates in any children a crisis of bewilderment, insecurity and often anger."[10]

General rules are not helpful

• Setting general rules for all divorce and remarriage situations is not helpful. The context of each marital crisis is different. Rather than having a one-size-fits-all approach, we need wisdom and insight in order to respond to each case with caution, care and discernment. We need to remember that "hard cases make bad laws, but hard laws make bad Christians".[11] We should not issue harsh rulings that disregard the spiritual care of the divorced and remarried. Thus we may need to acknowledge that "inadequate understanding or insensitivity to the cultural values, beliefs and practices of a spouse can also destroy marriages".[12] So can a case in which a spouse has become mentally ill and chooses to be homeless in another part of the country. In one such situation, the wife had not been seen by her husband and family for quite some time. The church insisted that he could not divorce her and remarry because she had not committed adultery. This is overstretching the argument. We need to imitate Jesus'

---

[9] Kore, *Culture and the Christian Home*, 91.

[10] John Stott, *New Issues Facing Christians Today* (Grand Rapids: Zondervan, 1999), 320.

[11] Kisembo, Matesa and Shorter, *African Christian Marriage*, 79.

[12] Kore, *Culture and the Christian Home*, 90.

gracious response to the woman at the well who had been married to five husbands (John 4) and to the woman caught in adultery (John 8:1–11). When Jesus forgave her, he did not lay down any hard rule about what she was to do or not do, but simply said "leave your life of sin". He did not deny that there were moral principles involved, but compassion and mercy triumphed over a harsh judgment.

There is hope after divorce and remarriage

• Divorce should not be seen as ending all privileges of membership in a local church. Divorce and remarriage should not be seen as the supreme sins that cut people off from all spiritual or ecclesiastical privileges, although Paul's letter to Timothy indicates that certain functions in the church such as leadership may not be open to polygamists and divorcees (1 Tim 3:6). The sad irony of divorce and remarriage is that, though we are challenged by the reality of sin and the horror of divorce and its consequences, we remain unsympathetic and uncompassionate to this group of suffering people. John Stott's advice though, written in the context of Britain and the USA, is worth noting:

> We continue to be caught in the tension between law and grace, witness and compassion, prophetic ministry and pastoral care. On the one hand, we need the courage to resist the prevailing winds of permissiveness and to set ourselves to uphold marriage and oppose divorce. The state will continue to frame its own divorce laws, but the church also has its own witness to bear to the teaching of its divine Lord, and must exercise its own discipline. On the other hand, we shall seek to share with deep compassion in the suffering of those whose marriages have failed, and especially of divorcees. We may on occasion feel at liberty to advise the legitimacy of a separation without divorce, or even a divorce, without remarriage, taking 1 Corinthians 7:11 as our warrant … Wisdom, righteousness and compassion are all found in following him [Jesus].[13]

Karl Lehmann gives us some valuable recommendations to be borne in mind when considering whether to admit divorced and remarried people into fellowship.

---

[13] Stott, *New Issues*, 344.

(i) The obligatory, basic form of an indissoluble marriage must in no way be called into question. The parties concerned and the community as a whole must be made thoroughly aware that the situation is exceptional and that help is only given in clearly circumscribed emergencies. (ii) Any fault or responsibility for the breakdown of the first marriage must be acknowledged and repented, and any possible wrong or damage inflicted must be made good as far as possible. In certain circumstances this might even include a return to the first partner. (iii) If a return to the first partner is impossible, it must be convincingly shown that, with the best will in the world, the first marriage cannot be restored. Particular attention must be paid to whether the first marriage has broken down for both partners. (iv) A subsequent contracted marriage must have stood the test of considerable length of time, as an indication of a determination to live together permanently, and must have proved itself as a moral reality. It must also be considered whether the maintenance of this second union has not become a new moral obligation in relation to the partner and to children that have been born. The partners must demonstrate that they are trying to live by the Christian faith and are asking to share in the sacramental life of the church for religious reasons and after serious examination of conscience. (v) Both parties and the pastor responsible for them must see to it that no justified scandal is caused in the congregation and that the impression is not created that the church no longer takes the indissolubility of marriage seriously."[14]

These recommendations are worth serious reflections. In particular, we should pay attention to the following basic ideas:

• The permanence of marriage is an essential Christian truth that must be taught and obeyed in the Christian community.

• Sin in marriages must be acknowledged, confessed and forsaken. Failure to deal with sin in marriage is one of the major causes of divorce.

---

[14] Karl Lehmann, quoted in Kisembo, Magesa and Shorter, *African Christian Marriage*, 82–83.

- Couples must cultivate the spirit of forgiveness without which a marriage will not survive.
- When a marriage cannot be salvaged, the whole Christian community must be aware of the cause or causes that led to its breakdown. This information must be carefully recorded and stored for future reference. Broken marriages and remarriages tend not to go away but continue to haunt the church and the individuals.
- Divorce is always a last resort and remarriage should not be rushed into.

Conclusion

Issues related to marriage, divorce and remarriage will continue to dominate the life of the church and community in Africa. Marriage is a fundamental human institution ordained by God, who intended it to be a loving and permanent relationship between a man and woman in which godly children are born and raised. Problems associated with marriage thus deserve serious examination and reflection.

Questions

1. Do you and your church have a solid commitment to the foundational principles of marriage? What areas need to be addressed before you will be able to address issues of divorce and remarriage appropriately?
2. What practical, pastoral issues do you face with regard to marriage, divorce and remarriage? How have you addressed them? How might your response have been different based on the information of this chapter?
3. Does Paul's statement that we are not to be yoked together with unbelievers (2 Cor 6:14) give a Christian license to divorce a partner who converts to Islam?
4. Is divorce a legitimate option in cases of spousal abuse, insanity, irreconcilable differences, excessive sexual appetite, HIV/AIDS or possession by an evil spirit?

19
WIDOWS AND ORPHANS

Widows and orphans have always been the most vulnerable and helpless group in Africa, and their vulnerability is increasing. So are their numbers as wars, ethnic conflicts, epidemics like HIV/AIDS, disease and natural disasters kill millions. The World Bank estimates that by 2015 some 35 million children in Africa will have lost either one or both parents to HIV/AIDS. This number doubles if children orphaned by other causes are included.

In a continent where there is high unemployment and the husband is commonly the sole breadwinner, a man's death means that his widow and orphaned children are plunged into poverty. Their problems are compounded by the breakdown of traditional ways of caring for them, the illiteracy of many women and the difficulty of paying for any education for the orphaned children. Many endure unimaginable emotional turmoil, deprivation, sorrow, anguish and abuse at the hands of their relatives and society.

It is thus vital that we reflect on the ethical question raised by the treatment of widows and orphans. What should be done to meet their needs today?

Traditional Treatment of Widows and Orphans

Traditional African societies had ways of providing for widows and orphans. Practices like widow inheritance meant that a widow could easily be remarried within a matter of months. Children were not solely the responsibility of their parents but were regarded as belonging to everybody in the community. The children of my brothers, uncles, aunts and cousins, whether born in or out of wedlock, were also my children.

That is why traditional African societies did not have words for "uncle", "aunt" or "cousin". It was considered wicked and immoral to maltreat a child just because he or she lacked a mother or father. An orphan would be adopted by family members and integrated into the community.

Widows and orphans may sometimes have suffered injustice and maltreatment in traditional communities, but this was the exception. They were not subjected to the same inhumane and immoral treatment that often occurs today, as reflected in Coleta Khamete Aduod's testimony:

> I was widowed almost three decades ago. My properties were taken away by clan members in what was referred to as property inheritance, not minding that I had four sons and four daughters to be taken care of. I had dropped my job with the police force to take care of our children but after the death of my husband I was forced to look for another job. Though I did not manage to get back to the force, luckily enough, having been in medical field, I got a job with a local missionary hospital as a nurse. At the local mission hospital I learned that beside severe poverty there are other major problems facing widows in our rural communities which include domestic violence, sexual abuse, indecent funeral procedures and rites, eviction and homelessness, violation of human rights and freedom, ignorance, to mention but just a few.[1]

Aduod's experience led her to found Widows in Resistance and Against Threats and Harassment in Africa (WRATH_Africa). This is a nondenominational faith-based organization in which widows seek to support and help other widows throughout Africa.

In the quotation above, Aduod refers to "indecent funeral procedures and rites". It is worth looking at what may be required of a widow in some cultures in more detail:[2]

• She may be expected to dress in black for the period of mourning, which can last for many months.

---

[1] Coleta Khamete Aduod, quoted in "Widows in Resistance and Against Threats and Harassment in Africa (WRATH_Africa)". Cited 18 Feb 2008. Online: www.widowsrights.org/wrath.htm.

[2] This list draws partly on work done by the Widows and Orphans Ministry (WOM) in four communities near Bolgatanga in the Upper East Region of Ghana. Cited 18 Feb 2008. Online: widowsrights.org/ghana1.htm. Similar practices are common in other communities throughout Africa.

- She may be suspected of having contributed to her husband's death. To prove her innocence, she may have to perform unhygienic rituals such as drinking the water used to wash her husband's corpse.

- She may be seen as impure, a potential source of danger and defilement. The cleansing ritual may involve being bathed naked before the crowd during the funeral ceremony. It may also involve sexual intercourse with a relative of her husband to prevent "the spirit of the deceased coming to seek sexual union, which is believed to be both possible and dangerous". Only after completing this ritual can "the surviving partner … safely enter new sexual relations with the blessing of the family of the dead relative".[3]

- She may be treated as an outsider, a mere spectator, at the burial of her husband, with no say in what is done. Her only role is to acknowledge condolences and act as instructed by others.

- She may be inherited by a relative, along with her husband's property, or she may have to marry someone from the husband's family so as to continue bearing children in his name. She may be forced into such a marriage regardless of whether she likes the man or whether he already has a wife or several wives.

- She may be forced to immediately surrender all her husband's property to his relatives. Such property includes his cheque books and all household goods such as cars, bicycles, clothes and shoes.[4] In some instances, even the house is taken and the widow is driven away, especially if she has no children or has borne only female children. It is not uncommon to hear a woman testify, "I and my children were beaten and kicked out of our house by the brothers-in-law. We live by begging, in continual fear."[5]

- She may have to allow her young children to be sent to live with various family members.

- She may be required to bear all the financial cost of the funeral rites and ceremonies, including providing food, drink, alcohol and tobacco for the participants, and gifts of food for those performing the rituals to

---

[3] Joe Simfukwe, "Funeral and Burial Rites" in *Africa Bible Commentary* (ed. Tokunboh Adeyemo; Nairobi: WordAlive / Grand Rapids: Zondervan, 2006), 1462.

[4] A widow reported that a brother-in-law started wearing her late husband's shoes just a day after he had been buried.

[5] www.widowsrights.org/stories_eve.htm. Cited 10 March 2008.

take home after the funeral. She may be expected to borrow money to cover these costs. Her financial indebtedness further contributes to her enslavement.

The specific details of these rituals may differ from one community to another. Here is one description of the traumatizing experience of Efik widows in the Cross River State in Nigeria:

> The death of a husband heralds a period of imprisonment and hostility to the wife or wives. The treatment may not be out of malice, but in all cases, women suffer and are subjected to rituals that are health hazards and heart-rending ... The wife's hair is loosened and made very untidy; she is dressed in a very old dress and wrapper. Bathing is a taboo. Verbal attacks keep her weeping all the time and she is expected to cry for her husband three times a day, publicly and audibly, at dawn, noon and evening. The children are taken away by their aunts, who may not take care of them; neither is the mother allowed to take care of them. The widow is forbidden to eat, and she is never to leave the family house until the period of mourning is over, after which she wears a black dress for months ... Since she has no right of inheritance, she can either go back to her family or establish herself on her own if she is an industrious woman. She now assumes the total parental responsibilities for her children, becoming to them both father and mother.[6]

The modern African widow is totally dependent on the goodwill of her husband's family. She cannot even turn to the community for support, for

> although [she] is perceived as someone to be pitied, sympathized with, and helped, she suffers emotional and spiritual violence. The widow is perceived as taboo to living husbands and other males. She is subject to hopelessness, punishment, neglect, contempt, suspicion about her treachery, or lack of good care. She is perceived as threatening to other couples' relationships

---

[6] Rosemary N. Edet, "Christianity and African Women's Rituals," in *The Will to Arise: Women, Tradition and the Church in Africa* (ed. Mercy Amba Oduyoye, R. Musimbi and A. Kanyoro; Maryknoll, N.Y.: Orbis, 2001), 31–32.

and suspected of adulterous living. The result is that a widow
is usually a neglected and deserted lonely woman.[7]

Orphans in Africa have fared no better as the traditional structures
that used to provide for them have crumbled. Today, they not only
lack fathers and mothers but also food, clothing, homes, discipline and
education. Many are abused, abandoned and rejected, with no family to
call their own. The result has been the sad rise in the number of child-
headed homes, child soldiers and street children.

Biblical Treatment of Widows and Orphans

The Bible has much to say about the way widows and orphans should be
treated. It makes the following points:

- *God is a defender of widows and orphans.* He "defends the cause of the
  fatherless and the widow, and loves the foreigners residing among
  you, giving them food and clothing" (Deut 10:18 TNIV). In the
  Old Testament, one of the ways God did this was by setting out laws
  regarding gleaning (Lev 19:9–10; Deut 24:19–21) and by insisting
  that widows and orphans share in religious feasts and offerings (Deut
  26:12). We are to follow God's example and give high priority to
  their needs, as Isaiah 1:17 makes clear: "Learn to do right! Seek
  justice, encourage the oppressed. Defend the cause of the fatherless,
  plead the case of the widow."

- *God punishes those who mistreat widows and orphans.* Those who abuse
  widows will find their own wives widowed: "Do not take advantage
  of a widow or an orphan. If you do and they cry out to me, I will
  certainly hear their cry. My anger will be aroused, and I will kill you
  with the sword; your wives will become widows and your children
  fatherless" (Exod 22:22–24).

- *Godliness involves care of widows and orphans.* This point is stressed
  in both the Old and New Testaments. In the Old Testament, Job
  associates maltreatment of widows and orphans with "sins to be
  judged" and being "unfaithful to God on high" (Job 31:28). He
  insists that he has not "let the eyes of the widow grow weary", but has
  instead shared his bread with the fatherless and "reared him as would

---

[7] Daisy N. Nwachuku, "The Christian Widow in African Culture", in *The Will to Arise*, 61.

a father, and from my birth I guided the widow" (Job 31:16–18). In the New Testament, James reminds us that "Religion that God our Father accepts as pure and faultless is this: to look after orphans and widows in their distress and to keep oneself from being polluted by the world" (Jas 1:27).

Recommendations

God has instructed those who follow him to protect and provide for widows and orphans, and clearly states that he will judge those who abuse them. The church should thus be in the vanguard when it comes to protecting them. But what specifically should the church be doing to help these vulnerable, powerless and defenceless people?

Legislation

One of the ways in which God provided for orphans and widows in the Old Testament was by making laws that would help them to survive. So we, too, should encourage our governments to introduce laws and regulations that will protect widows and orphans. For example, there should be laws that protect their property rights. Unless willed otherwise by the late husband, all his property should remain with his widow and children. They should also be given access to employment, schooling and medical treatment.

We should also strive for laws that forbid anyone from forcing a widow to engage in funeral rituals and practices that go against her religious beliefs. Her participation should be voluntary, not mandatory.

In some places, such laws may already be in place but are widely ignored. We should know what laws are on the books and should be prepared to report breaches of them to the authorities for proper investigation.

Education

The church should be involved in educating communities about how widows and orphans should be treated. We could hold seminars focusing on this topic. Such seminars should also address the fear that making a will is equivalent to signing one's own death warrant. Church members should be encouraged to make wills in which they specify what should be done with their property after their death.

The church should also remind communities that traditionally motherless or fatherless children were seen simply as children needing protection and provision just like one's biological children. The abandonment, rejection and maltreatment of orphans are contrary not only to the Scriptures but also to the African value system. The church should thus work to reorient believers to the need to care for orphans with respect, appreciation and love. Like all other children, they need a home and a family in which to grow to maturity.

Adoption and support of orphans

Teaching about the needs of orphaned children should be followed by practical action. Church members should be encouraged to adopt orphans, not only the orphans of church members but also those from their communities. Families who cannot adopt children should be encouraged to help orphans by supporting them in school and buying them clothes and food. Church members can also be encouraged to support orphanages in their communities. If there is no orphanage, a number of churches should work together to establish one and to set up a school with boarding facilities and full scholarships for orphans.

One of the best examples of such a programme is provided by the Rafiki Foundation, which was established in 1985 to "help Africa's orphaned and vulnerable children become godly contributors to their communities and the world".[8] The foundation has set up Rafiki Villages that "provide living and educational facilities in African countries where there are many orphans ... [These] villages provide a Christian environment for young men and women to develop leadership and life skills that promote their physical and spiritual well-being".[9] The goal is not to have these children adopted by foreigners or educated abroad. Rather, the focus is on raising them within the context of their own

---

[8] www.rafiki-foundation.org/what/what_we_do.html. Cited 10 March 2008.
[9] www.rafiki-foundation.org/about-rafiki.html. Cited 10 March 2008. "Rafiki's goal is to establish one training village in each of the ten following countries: Ethiopia, Ghana, Kenya, Liberia, Malawi, Nigeria, Rwanda, Tanzania, Zambia, and Uganda ... A Rafiki Village consists of eighteen homes for ten orphans each, schools, for these orphans, vocation training day schools for vulnerable teenage girls and boys, medical care for occupants, and facilities for training select African church denominations to replicate Rafiki's efforts."

community. This approach is close to the traditional African method of adoption that raised orphans within the context of family relationships.

Moral and Material Support for Widows

The church also needs to provide moral and material support for widows. For a start, we should demonstrate respect by insisting that a widow be allowed to participate in planning her husband's funeral. Rather than simply listening to the husband's relations, we should consult her about when, where and how he should be buried.

The church must also stand with the widow if her late husband's family come to lay claim to his property. The church, and especially the pastor, should intervene to mediate between the parties and restrain abuses. For example, in a seminary with which I was associated, a student died, leaving behind his wife and four young children. His father soon arrived with a vehicle, intending to carry away everything including the student's bank pass book. It was only intervention by the pastor that stopped him and allowed the widow to retain all the property and the children.

Once these immediate crises are past, the church needs to help widows find some means of earning a livelihood. Many of them may be uneducated and untrained, and therefore unemployable. Some may consent to polygamous marriages in order to be able to care for themselves and children. Young widows may turn to prostitution if they see no other options. The church needs to take deliberate steps to assist these vulnerable women. It should put them in touch with some of the many Christian and governmental agencies that provide soft loans, grants and the like to help widows start small businesses.

Conclusion

The church should be in the vanguard when it comes to protecting widows and orphans. As James 1:27 reminds us, such action is a sign of "pure and lasting religion in the sight of God our Father" (New Living Translation).

Questions

1. Identify the burial and funeral rites that widows are expected to undergo in an African society with which you are familiar. Which of these rites are acceptable in terms of biblical teaching and which are not?

2. How are widows and orphans treated within the culture you have identified? What are the good and bad aspects of their treatment?

3. Identify biblical passages that deal with widows and orphans. How do they relate to the issues faced by widows and orphans in your locality?

4. How is your church meeting the needs of widows and orphans? Formulate a plan that will help your church to deal with the growing need to care for them.

SECTION D
SEXUAL ISSUES

INTRODUCTION TO SEXUAL ISSUES

As we saw in the unit on marriage, sexual intercourse is an important and God-ordained aspect of marriage. It is the primary and natural means of procreation, as well as an expression of love, a means of satisfying sexual desire, and a source of mutual pleasure for a man and woman. Paul's comments in 1 Corinthians make it clear that it is legitimate for some men and women to marry not because they desire to procreate but because of their sexual needs (1 Cor 7:2, 9, 36–37). This emphasis on pleasure does not, however, mean that every type of sexual activity that gives someone pleasure is legitimate:

> Sexuality can be compared with electricity. Electricity, in its pure form, is an unbridled power with both creative and destructive potential. Think of the untamed power of lightning. But men have learned to bridle electricity, to channel it into constructive uses; electricity has become the motor that keeps cities alive. Sexuality, too, is a natural power that, unchanneled, can be destructive. Man, the image of God, has the calling to channel his sexual powers. The point of morality and of human institutions is to channel sexuality so that it will be the power that keeps humanity alive and creative.[1]

The Bible makes it clear that sexual relationships should only be pursued within the bonds of marriage. It is only in this relationship that a man and a woman can truly "know" each other in the same way that Adam "knew his wife Eve, and she conceived and bore Cain" (Gen 4:1). Here the word "knew" does not mean merely an intellectual knowledge of the woman but an intimate knowledge of her being.

---

[1] J. Rinzema, *The Sexual Revolution: Challenge and Response* (trans. Lewis B. Smedes; Grand Rapids: Eerdmans, 1974).

This knowledge is so intimate that some argue that sex is a decisive factor in determining when marriage actually takes place. That is, sexual intercourse between a single man and woman makes them husband and wife. Some would apply this rule regardless of whether the sex was consensual or forced, and regardless of whether the couple in question have any real affection for one another. The problems with this view are among the issues dealt with in **chapter 20** on rape. Rapists are sometimes members of the victim's family, and so in **chapter 21** we deal with the issue of incest.

Women are usually the victims rather than the perpetrators of sexual crimes. This applies even when the crime in question is prostitution and sex trafficking, the topic of **chapter 22**. Women are also the ones who have to endure the suffering associated with the traditional practice of female circumcision, which is discussed in **chapter 23**.

However, both men and women can be homosexual, and this issue which has sparked much controversy is the topic of **chapter 24**.

The topics in this section were not readily discussed in traditional African societies, but in recent years they have drawn enormous attention. It is thus contingent upon Christian ethicists and church leaders to discuss these issues and articulate a Christian ethical position.

In our discussion, we should bear in mind the words of J. Rinzema:

> The sexual question is tied to the question of how human beings relate to each other. To ask about sexuality is to ask what man really is, what his worth is, and how he can live humanely with other men. The sexual problem is more than a biological problem. It is intertwined with issues of faith and a perspective on the whole of life and the world.[2]

---

[2] Rinzema, *The Sexual Revolution*.

20

RAPE

Rape is a topic that is rarely mentioned in male-dominated African societies. At best, a woman who has been raped may tell her mother and maybe a very close friend about her ordeal. If others were to learn what had happened, they might assume that she had actually wanted the sexual encounter. She might find herself labelled as a prostitute and have difficulty finding a man to marry her. This code of silence has meant that men have been able to rape with impunity. It is time to end this state of affairs.

The word "rape" derives from a Latin word meaning "to seize". In rape, the perpetrator seizes the victim's body and engages in sexual activity without his or her consent. Violence is used both for intimidation and for sexual gratification.[1]

The use of "his or her" in the above definition is a reminder that our definition of rape as only something that men do to women is too narrow. It is not only women who are raped. In homosexual rape, men are raped by other men, or women by other women. There are also rare cases in which a woman is the aggressor and a man the victim.[2]

It is possible for a husband to rape his wife when he forces her to have sex against her will. This idea is startling in Africa, where it is generally assumed that a woman is her husband's property and that he has the right to have sex with his wife whenever he wants. But if he does so regardless of her feelings or desires, he is guilty of rape – sex without the consent of his partner. Sex within marriage is supposed to be a loving, shared experience, not something violent, selfish and brutal.

---

[1] A. R. Denton, "Rape" in *Baker Encyclopedia of Psychology*, 973.

[2] A female teacher in the United States has been convicted of raping one of her male students. I have also counselled a man in his late seventies who had been raped by a woman when he was a teenager. He was still dealing with guilt in his old age.

Causes of Rape

Rape happens for a variety of reasons, but before looking at these it is important to dismiss some false explanations for rape. One is the argument that rape is the woman's fault: "If she had been properly dressed, the man would not have been tempted. The way in which she exposed her body was an invitation to a sexual encounter."

The hollowness of this argument becomes clear when we remind ourselves of the many respectably dressed women who have been raped. Tamar, David's daughter, would have been wearing a long robe that covered her body and her legs, yet she was raped by her half-brother (2 Samuel 13:17). Her clothing had nothing to do with her rape: rather, it was the result of his lust for her.

We can also refute this argument by looking at traditional African societies. In such societies, people did not dress 'properly', as we would define it today. Traditional dress covered only their private parts. Yet there is no record that rape was more frequent in such societies. Though women should dress decently and modestly, it is cruel and unacceptable to suggest that the way someone dresses is an invitation to sexual encounter.

Men sometimes also deny rape or blame the woman for it by arguing that when the woman said "no" she was merely challenging them to prove their ardour. Her "no" was interpreted as being a "yes". But this argument is insulting to women. Women are quite capable of communicating their desires and can say "yes" if they want a sexual encounter. When they say "no" they mean "no", and their answer should be respected.

So what are the true reasons for rape? Lust is one of them, as in the case of Amnon and Tamar (2 Sam 13:1–2). But the lust is not always sexual. Sometimes it is a lust to demonstrate one's power over the weak and vulnerable. This is why soldiers so often rape women during wars. Such rapes are a demonstration of the soldiers' contempt for the men and women whom they regard as enemies.

Certain myths also encourage rape. In some communities it is believed that having sexual intercourse with a virgin or a baby will heal one of HIV/AIDS. This belief has led to a surge in rapes against the very vulnerable.

Consequences of Rape

Rape is a clear violation of the victim's body, dignity and self-determination and has enormous consequences physically, emotionally and socially.

- *Physically*, rape causes trauma to the victim's body and transmits sexually transmitted diseases (STDs) including HIV/AIDS. When rape results in pregnancy, there can be strong motivation to abort an innocent baby. Babies who are raped suffer great physical damage.

- *Emotionally*, rape is a traumatic experience that can destroy the victim's self-esteem. Victims are filled with a mix of guilt, rage, anger, shame, powerlessness, anxiety and fear. They often suffer from depression and have difficulty sleeping and trusting others. In an attempt to cope with these emotions and prevent the replay of the assault in their minds, they may resort to alcohol and drugs. The rape can also result in sexual and marital dysfunction.

- *Socially*, the victim may be blamed and ostracized and may have to endure injustice. A desire to avenge the rape can also lead to hatred that results in murder and even war.

Biblical Perspectives on Rape

The Bible does not shrink from dealing with rape. It includes several accounts of rapes in different periods of Israelite history. One involves Shechem, the son of a Hivite ruler, who raped Jacob's daughter Dinah. The NRSV says that "he took her and lay with her by force" (Gen 34:2). The words he "took her" underscore the basic meaning of rape as "seizure", and the words "by force" indicate the lack of consent and unwillingness on the part of the victim. Rape is violent sexual assault on an unwilling person. The end result of Dinah's rape was the destruction of an entire community (Gen 34:25–29).

Another instance of rape in the Scriptures took place in the time of the judges. Some wicked men in Gibeah planned the homosexual rape of a travelling Levite (Judg 19:22). In order to save himself, he gave them his concubine, whom they raped and abused throughout the night (Judg 19:25). The war that resulted from this shameful act nearly annihilated the tribe of Benjamin.

There was also rape in David's time. David's son Amnon grabbed his half-sister Tamar "and said, 'Come to bed with me, my sister.' 'Don't, my brother!' she said to him … But he refused to listen to her, and since he was stronger than she, he raped her" (2 Sam 13:11–14). Again, the basic meaning of rape is emphasized – grabbing or seizing, force, violence and sexual assault without the consent (and even despite strong objections) of the partner. This rape had disastrous consequences, not only for Tamar (2 Sam 13:19–20) but also for David's entire household as it marked the start of his trouble with Absalom, who avenged Tamar's rape by murdering his brother Amnon.

The Bible does not merely mention rapes; it also lays down laws regarding how rapists are to be dealt with: "If out in the country a man happens to meet a girl pledged to be married and rapes her, only the man who has done this shall die. Do nothing to the girl; she has committed no sin deserving death. This case is like that of someone who attacks and murders his neighbour" (Deut 22:26–27). The equation of rape with murder shows how seriously we should take this heinous act of violence against an innocent victim.

The law above relates specifically to a girl who is already engaged to be married. In terms of Jewish custom, she was regarded as married, although the marriage had not yet been consummated. But the Bible also addresses the situation of the girl who is not yet betrothed: "If a man happens to meet a virgin who is not pledged to be married and rapes her and they are discovered, he shall pay the girl's father fifty shekels of silver. He must marry the girl, for he has violated her. He can never divorce her as long as he lives" (Deut 22:28–29).

Some Christians would argue that this passage means that a girl who is raped must marry the rapist. This argument is also rooted in the belief that sex is the decisive factor in determining when a marriage actually takes place. However, it is important to recognize that this is not the only law regarding the subject. Exodus 22:16–17 clearly indicates that sexual relations did not automatically result in a marriage.

The point that is being made by the law on the rape of a young girl who is not engaged is that irresponsible sexual intercourse has serious consequences. The man cannot simply rape the girl and discard her in a society where she would be unlikely ever to be able to marry. Instead he has to assume financial and material responsibility for her.

Before we apply this ruling today, we need to remember that rape no longer disqualifies a girl from marriage and that our society is no longer polygamous, where such a girl might have been able to take a position as one of a number of wives. We are not required to force a raped girl into an unwelcome marriage without love, which is a sure road to a miserable marriage and home life.

A Christian Response to Rape

Rape, like all violence, is a sin against God and a crime against humanity. It dehumanizes the victims and destroys communities. The church should have no hesitation in condemning it in the strongest terms.

But when the church condemns rape, it must not condemn the victims of rape. They should not be stigmatized and blamed. Like the Bible and the great North African bishop St. Augustine of Hippo (AD 354–430), we must argue that "there will be no pollution, if the lust is another's; while the mind's resolve endures, which gives the body its claim to chastity, the violence of another's lust cannot take away the chastity which is preserved by unwavering self-control."[3] Victims need to be assured that they are not guilty of the crime that was committed against them. They also need counselling to help them deal with the physical and emotional consequences of the rape.

The church must encourage the state to put in place laws that protect rape victims from public and societal condemnation and judgment. Then it must encourage rape victims to report sexual assaults. Attempting to deal with rape secretly and privately does not solve the problem, but merely allows rapists to flourish.

Society needs to be educated to support rape victims and to condemn rape and all forms of violence against women. There should also be legislation against all forms of pornography that undermine women's dignity by depicting them as sex objects or as men's property. There should be a deliberate attempt to show respect for women, who are created in the image of God.

Rather than being allowed to get away with their crime, rapists should receive stiff penalties. But the focus must not simply be on punishment. They should also receive counselling to teach them to respect the wishes and desires of others.

---

[3] Augustine, *City of God*, I.18; quoted in *Dictionary of Ethics, Theology and Society*, 715.

Questions

1. Are you able to discuss issues like rape openly among ministry leaders? If not, what inhibits you from doing so? What may need to be changed in order be able to address such crucial issues?

2. How does the description of traditional African perspectives on rape compare to the opinions in your context?

3. What do you think about the changing definition of rape, particularly as regards the raping of a wife by her husband?

4. Who do you think is generally at fault in a rape? Are those who are most at fault held sufficiently responsible for the attacks?

5. How significantly has your local situation been affected by the terrible lie that having sex with a virgin or a baby will cure HIV/AIDS?

6. How do you minister to those who have committed rapes and are now seeking to repent?

7. How can your church minister to victims of rape in your church and community?

21
INCEST

Incest involves forbidden sexual relationships between family members, such as between brother and sister, cousin and cousin, uncle and niece, father and daughter, mother and son, stepfather and stepdaughter, grandfather and granddaughter.

Incest and Traditional Values

In African societies, incest is considered a grievous sin against society, the gods and the family. However, there are some differences between ethnic groups as regards the exact relationships which count as incestuous. Most groups would have strict laws forbidding sexual relationships between those with close blood ties, such as siblings. But some will allow marriages between first cousins (those who share the same grandparent), while others refuse to permit marriages between third or even fourth cousins (those who share the same great-great-great-grandparent).

The prohibitions against incest were once strictly adhered to, and those who violated them either lost their lives or were sent into exile.

Causes and Consequences of Incest

Almost all societies forbid incest, but nevertheless it still happens, and is increasing in prevalence. One reason for the increase is social change. In traditional African societies, related members of the opposite sex were not allowed to discuss intimate sexual matters or even to be alone together, especially after dark. These rules are no longer observed, and there is thus more opportunity for sexual intimacy between close family members.

The sexual permissiveness of the contemporary age has also made people more prepared to disregard the respect they were supposed to have towards members of the opposite sex, including their own blood relations. Stepfathers may seduce their stepdaughters, and even grandfathers may exploit their closeness to their granddaughters to seduce them into sexual intimacy. Women and girls are particularly at risk, as they can be overpowered by male family members, and may be too afraid and threatened to expose them to the rest of the family.

When incest results in pregnancy, there is a danger that the baby will be affected by genetic diseases that would otherwise be latent within the family. But even if there is no pregnancy, incest causes deep spiritual and emotional trauma to the victims. The guilt, shame and other effects are similar to those associated with rape, except that this rape was perpetrated by someone the victim should have been able to trust.

Biblical Perspectives on Incest

Incest has a long history and was known even in Bible times. The Bible records that a drunken Lot unknowingly impregnated his two daughters (Gen 19:30–35), Reuben slept with his father's concubine (Gen 35:22) and Amnon raped his half-sister, Tamar (2 Sam 13). In the New Testament, there is the case of the man who was sleeping with his father's wife, who was probably his stepmother (1 Cor 5:1–5).

The Mosaic laws included strict prohibitions on incest: "No-one is to approach any close relative to have sexual relations" (Lev 18:6). The intention of these laws was to protect the integrity of marriage and family relationships. For this reason, incest was defined in terms of parent and child, half-brother and half-sister, uncle and niece, aunts and nephew, fathers-in-law and daughters-in-law and grandchildren (Lev 18:7–16; see also Lev 20:17–21).

The consequences of incest for the offender, the victim, family members and society at large are vividly demonstrated in the story of Amnon and Tamar, where it resulted in hate, vengeance and murder.

Christian Response to Incest

Incest is morally wrong both by biblical standards and societal laws. It distorts the integrity of marriage and family relationships, exploits the weak and vulnerable, and is degrading to those involved. But we should not pretend it does not exist. We must be prepared to talk about incest in public and openly discuss the shame and trauma it causes, as well as the danger of passing on genetic diseases. Nor should our discussion of this topic be limited to adults. Children should be taught to know the boundaries of what is acceptable in relationships.

We should encourage governments to pass laws against incest and then to implement them by prosecuting offenders. However, it is no use simply imprisoning offenders, for when they are released they may repeat the same crime. They must be offered counselling and rehabilitation – recognizing that the gospel is an effective tool for effecting transformation. Their victims, too, should receive counselling to help them overcome their shame.

The community as a whole must be taught to accept victims of incest and not reject them, much as it must be taught to accept victims of rape without suggesting that they are responsible for what was done to them. At the same time, we must encourage a return to the traditional values which protected girls from situations of unnecessary intimacy that left them vulnerable to incest.

Harrison sums it up well: "The abhorrent crime of incest, which often arises from complex family situations, demands the full weight of legal, moral, medical, and religious sanctions in order to secure the proper punishment of the offender and the rehabilitation of the victim."[1]

Questions

1. What are the traditions regarding incest in your situation? How do they compare with the laws of your country?

2. Which of the possible reasons for incest explain why it continues in your situation?

3. How can you apply biblical teaching about incest to your situation?

---

[1] R. K. Harrison, ed. *Encyclopedia of Biblical and Christian Ethics* (Rev. ed.; Nashville: Thomas Nelson, 1992), 199.

22

PROSTITUTION AND SEX TRAFFICKING

In this chapter, our focus will be on the ethics of prostitution and sex trafficking, that is, on their moral status. We will not be discussing whether prostitution should be criminalized or whether it should be accepted as a profession on a par with, say, engineering. Nor will we be discussing whether prostitution and the sex industry are really an attempt by men to control women, nor whether prostitution should be banned because it promotes the transmission of HIV/AIDS, nor the relationship between prostitution, pornography, violence, rape and organized crime. These are all legitimate topics for discussion and have been dealt with at length by feminists, human rights organizations, ethicists and theologians. However, our focus here will simply be on prostitution and sex trafficking as social evils that affect the lives of millions of women and children in Africa and throughout the world. There is, of course, also male prostitution, but this is less common than female prostitution and so in what follows we will speak of prostitutes as female.

Prostitution in Traditional Africa

Prostitution and sex trafficking were almost unknown in traditional African societies. While there were loose women in every community, they did not sell sex as a way of making money.

One of the reasons why there were no professional prostitutes was that girls were often married off at a young age. They did not have the option of staying unmarried. Another was that there were no restrictions on the number of wives a man could marry.

The rise of prostitution and sex trafficking in contemporary Africa is traceable to changing attitudes towards sex and marriage, the emergence of towns and cities, unemployment and poverty, the breakdown of traditional values, cross-cultural contacts and international travel.

Prostitution and Sex Trafficking

The word "prostitution" is derived from the Latin *prostituere*, which means to expose something for public sale. Prostitutes sell sexual pleasure in exchange for a reward, which may be financial or some special favour. Proverbs 6:26 expresses this well when it states: "A harlot may be hired for a loaf of bread" (RSV). A more comprehensive definition of prostitution is that it is "the practice of engaging in sexual activity for immediate compensation in money or other valuables, in which affection and emotional investment are minimal or absent, and in which the selection of sexual partners is relatively indiscriminate".[1] This definition emphasizes three important points. First, prostitution involves immediate compensation. Second, there is little or no affection or emotional involvement between the prostitute and the client. By contrast, sex within marriage involves love, commitment and responsibility. Third, almost any partner will do. All that the client wants is someone who can provide temporary sexual gratification, and all that matters to the prostitute is that the client pays.

A distinction is sometimes made between "free prostitution", involving women who have freely chosen this line of work, and "forced prostitution", involving women who have been intimidated into working as prostitutes or children who have been coerced or sold into the sex industry by their parents, family members or sexual predators. Those who make this distinction argue that free prostitution is acceptable but that forced prostitution is wrong and should be criminalized. However, the distinction can be difficult to apply in practice. If poverty drives a woman to sell her body for sex, is she really choosing this option freely or are circumstances forcing her into it? If, as I will argue, prostitution always involves the abuse of women and children, there is little point in attempting to distinguish between free and forced prostitution.

---

[1] James Nelson, "Prostitution". *Westminster Dictionary of Christian Ethics*, 513.

A distinction is also sometimes made between local prostitution and international prostitution. The former involves the sale of sex by local prostitutes within a geographical area such as a town or city. International prostitution involves the transporting of prostitutes or clients from one country to another or even from one continent to another. One form of international prostitution involves women and girls acting as temporary wives. They provide sex and perform household chores such as cooking, washing and cleaning for a fixed period, say, two months. At the end of this time, they move on to serve another man.

International prostitution is an industry for it involves a large number of individuals, institutions and whole societies cooperating in the exploitation of women and children. There are those who lure girls with promises of work, often seemingly respectable work, in other regions or countries. They are guilty of sex trafficking, the "process that delivers victims into prostitution. It includes the recruitment, harboring, movement, and methods by which victims are compelled to stay in prostitution, whether by violence, coercion, threat, debt, or cultural manipulation."[2] These victims "may be from the same city or country as the exploiters, or they may be trafficked from other countries or continents".[3]

Forgers and corrupt officials provide the documentation that makes it possible for the victims to travel. Corrupt police can be bribed to ignore the existence of brothels and massage parlours and the plight of the women in them. The operators of these brothels often work in association with criminal gangs, drug pushers and the like. They maintain a network of pimps who offer to provide prostitutes for visiting businessmen, politicians, tourists, celebrities and sports teams. They will even arrange to supply prostitutes of specific ages and races.

And finally there are the clients, all those who buy sex in legal brothels, adult stores, massage parlours, bars, strip clubs, motels and the like. Without them, the industry would be forced to shut down:

> There can be no supply of women and children without the male demand for the sex of prostitution; without the sex industry's commodification of women and children; without

---

[2] Donna M. Hughes, "Prostitution: Causes and Solutions" p.1. Cited 13 March 2008. Online: www.uri.edu/artsci/wms/hughes/prostitution_spain_july04.pdf.
[3] Ibid.

the direct and/or tacit approval of governments in fostering sex tourism, for example, or zoned areas of prostitution; and without the exporting of a Western sexual liberalism that depicts prostitution as sexual pleasure and liberation, calls it work, and tell us that prostitution is about a woman's right to control her body![4]

Factors Promoting Prostitution and Sex Trafficking

The entire sex industry is driven by issues of supply and demand.

Demand for sex

The demand for sex comes mainly from men (although there is also a developing trend in which women pay younger men for sex). The reasons why people patronize prostitutes include the following:

- Desire for temporary sexual pleasure without commitment. Clients have no interest in a permanent relationship but only want to satisfy their immediate desire.

- Compensation for an unsatisfactory sexual relationship with a wife (or husband).

- Separation from a spouse by business travel or war.

- Relaxation while on holiday (often known as 'sex tourism').

- Indulging exotic tastes. In many Western countries, men are now wanting to have sex with "cheaper and more exotic women from developing countries"[5] or with children. These tastes play into sexual trafficking and the child sex trade.

As long as people crave sex and are prepared to pay for it, the sex trade will continue. That is why it is critical that attempts to combat prostitution and sex trafficking do not focus solely on the prostitutes but also on their clients.

---

[4] Janice G. Raymond, co-executive director of the Coalition against Trafficking in Women, in "Prostitution as Violence Against Women: NGO Stonewalling in Beijing and Elsewhere", *Women's Studies International Forum*, 21(1998): 1–9. Cited 13 March 2008. Online: action.web.ca/home/catw/readingroom.shtml?sh_itm=46413d9acb7e9322a28f1df36d75637c.
[5] Ibid.

Supply of sex

Men desire sex and women and girls supply it. If one asks why they do this, the answer is often simple: poverty. Prostitutes tend to come from "marginalized, poor and vulnerable populations ... They may be women and girls who are poor, uneducated, and naïve, and therefore easy to control".[6] They resort to prostitution for the following reasons:

- It is an easy and quick way for young women with no training or education to earn money.

- They may be lured or forced into it through their jobs. Women and girls who go to the cities in search of work often find menial employment as cleaners, waitresses and barmaids in brothels, bars, hotels, restaurants and business and tourist centres. In time, they may be lured or forced into casual sexual encounters with clients for some small financial reward and may ultimately become full-time prostitutes.

- It may be one of the few options available to women whose homes have been broken by death, divorce or abandonment and who are often the sole supporters of their children. Their situation is even worse if their husband's relatives have driven them away, leaving them with nowhere to go and nothing to do except offer their bodies on the streets.

However, it is not only the poor who resort to prostitution. Some prostitutes are "educated, middle-class girls, who, have been sexually abused until their bodily integrity and identities are destroyed and they no longer know how to resist abuse and exploitation".[7]

The same forces that drive women into prostitution lure poor children into it. They may be sent into the cities by parents who overvalue material possessions and insist that their children earn money, or they may be sent there by parents who cannot support them. Or they may have been orphaned or abandoned, without the protection supplied by parents and an extended family. Lacking schooling, they are ill-equipped to get decent jobs. They therefore engage in small trading like selling peanuts, cola nuts and sweets in the street. Before long, they begin to engage in sexual encounters to earn extra money.

---

[6] Hughes, 1.
[7] Ibid.

Biblical Perspectives on Prostitution and Sex Trafficking

Prostitution has been in existence since the earliest times. It is first mentioned in Genesis 34:31, where Dinah's brothers are outraged that Shechem has treated their sister as if she were a prostitute. Their response indicates the extent to which prostitutes were despised. Later, the desperate Tamar pretended to be a prostitute and was threatened with death for having done so (Gen 38:15–24). Samson, one of the judges, is also said to have visited a prostitute (Judg 16:1).

Although prostitutes were despised, some played a prominent role in Israelite history. When the Israelites were spying out the promised land they were helped by the prostitute Rahab, who became an ancestor of David and Jesus (Josh 2:1; 6:17, 22, 25; Matt 1:5). The mother of Jephtha, one of Israel's judges, was a prostitute (Judg 11:1). Moreover, even prostitutes were regarded as entitled to justice. Thus King Solomon was prepared to judge a dispute between two prostitutes over a child (1 Kgs 3:16).

One form of prostitution that was common in Old Testament times was cultic prostitution. The Canaanites believed that having sex with temple prostitutes stimulated the gods into sexual activity, which in turn resulted in the fertility of the soil. God specifically forbad such activities, saying "No Israelite man or woman is to become a shrine-prostitute" (Deut 23:17). Male shrine prostitutes were contemptuously referred to as "dogs" (Deut 23:18).

The Bible sees prostitution in all its forms as morally unjustifiable. Priests were forbidden to marry prostitutes (Lev 21:7). Money or goods earned through prostitution were not to be accepted as gifts to God's sanctuary (Deut 23:17–18). Men are also repeatedly warned against the wiles and waste of prostitutes (Prov 7:10–27; 23:27; 29:3; see also Luke 15:30). However, it is interesting to note that although the penalty for adultery was death, ordinary prostitutes do not seem to have been given the death penalty, possibly in recognition of the fact that they may have been forced into this role.

Sex trafficking was forbidden: "Do not degrade your daughter by making her a prostitute, or the land will turn to prostitution and be filled with wickedness" (Lev 19:29). The Bible clearly recognizes that sex trafficking not only promotes personal immorality but also increases general wickedness through the network of exploitation that it sets up.

In the Bible the word "prostitution" or "harlotry" is used broadly to describe any illicit sex between a man and woman or a man and a man, whether involving a professional prostitute or simply a free offer of sex outside of marriage. Thus it is not clear whether the description of Hosea's wife as a "harlot" (NASB) indicates that she was simply a promiscuous woman or in fact a prostitute (Hos 1:2; 2:2–13). The same word is used to describe the behaviour of God's people when they are unfaithful to him and prostitute themselves with other gods (Exod 34:15–16; Lev 20:5–6; Deut 31:16; Judg 2:17; Jer 3:1).

In the New Testament, prostitutes are grouped with tax-collectors as practising the most despised and immoral professions (Matt 21:31–32; Luke 15:30). Paul explicitly states that male prostitutes will be excluded from the kingdom of God (1 Cor 6:9–10).

Paul also states that sexual encounters with prostitutes make the person one with them in body (1 Cor 6:16). He does not mean that someone who has sexual intercourse with a prostitute becomes married to her, but that "unholy union with a prostitute is a wicked perversion of the divinely established marriage union."[8] To see how we reach this conclusion, you need to read the verse within its context. In 1 Corinthians 6:12–20 Paul is talking about what it means for believers to be united with Christ. He argues that this spiritual union has implications for what they do with their physical bodies. Their bodies now belong to Christ, not to prostitutes! In other words, there is a contradiction between their union with Christ through the resurrection and any union with a prostitute through sexual immorality.

Paul's words make it clear that sexual union with someone is thus more than just a physical act. It also has spiritual implications: "The whole man reveals himself in all that he does. He who unites himself to a harlot has a common existence with her. There is no purely sexual sin. The spirit of the brothel and the Spirit of Christ mutually exclude one another."[9]

---

[8] Kenneth L. Barker and John R. Kohlenberger III. *The Expositor's Bible Commentary: New Testament* (abridged ed.; Grand Rapids: Zondervan, 1994), 624.

[9] Horst Seebass, "Cleave", *New International Dictionary of the New Testament*, 130.

If having sex with a prostitute is immoral and therefore sinful, it follows that what a prostitute does (providing opportunities for sexual sin) is also wrong and unacceptable.

Why Prostitution and Sex Trafficking Are Immoral

Although the point is seldom debated, it may be necessary to spell out the fundamental reasons why there can be no moral justification for prostitution and why those who engage in providing, demanding and sustaining it are acting immorally.

First, Scripture condemns prostitution, and almost all human societies agree with this condemnation. In fact, many of the men and women who participate in prostitution, either as providers or clients, agree that what they are doing is immoral, even though they may try to justify their actions.

Second, though it is true that some women are forced into prostitution against their will, the majority of those working in the sex industry are free moral agents. Prostitutes, pimps and madams have the option of choosing other legitimate employment. Instead they have chosen to be involved in something that is morally evil and to continue working in the sex industry, and thus they incur moral guilt. No such guilt attaches to those whom others have forced to work as prostitutes.

Third, the motives of prostitutes, sex traffickers and those who use prostitutes are purely materialistic, short-lived and self-destructive. Quick financial gain and self-centred pleasure-seeking are their sole motives. These motives are completely at odds with the intended motives for sex within a loving and exclusive marital relationship.

Fourth, prostitution and sex trafficking debase womanhood. The prostitute is seen simply as a tool to satisfy someone's personal needs, and so her value as an individual is minimized. Women become sex objects to be traded as commodities. When they become old, ill or pregnant, they are discarded without any concern for their needs.

Fifth, prostitution and sex trafficking are clear manifestations of underlying social and moral problems. They flourish in areas where there are economic problems, moral decay, a lack of respect for women and a lack of concern for individuals.

Sixth, prostitution exposes women to many other evils. They can easily contract HIV/AIDS and many other sexually transmitted diseases. Moreover, the fact that they are seen as sex objects rather than as individuals means that they are often treated violently. Many are abused, beaten or even killed.

Recommendations

The church has often been shy about addressing the issue of prostitution and the sex industry. But not to do so is to fail to follow our master, who cared for all, including prostitutes and tax collectors. Our approach must be three-pronged:

Legislation

Governments cannot legislate morality, but they can and should control, monitor and punish those found guilty of abusing women. Prostitution and sex trafficking dehumanize and abuse women. We must urge governments to act to rein in the trafficking of women for the purposes of prostitution and to prosecute clients and groups that promote sexual tourism and the sale of sex.[10]

Governments and community groups must also be urged to improve the economic and social situation of young people and widowed, divorced and abandoned women. The poor should not be driven into prostitution and sex trafficking by harsh economic realities.

Education

It is not enough for the church to denounce the evils of prostitution and call on the government to act. The church itself must work to enhance the status of women by clearly teaching that women and girls are not sex objects but human beings created in God's image. As such, they should neither be exploited nor abused.

The church must also promote traditional family values which provide basic security and protection for women and children. Divorce and domestic violence drive many into the hands of sexual predators. Child abuse in particular drives children away from home and leaves them

---

[10] Hughes, 3–4.

vulnerable to the sex industry. When children are protected from sexual predators, the supply of children as sex commodities will be reduced.

The church must also strongly challenge the cultural beliefs that allow parents to sell or send away their children into situations where they can be abused.

Proclamation

The gospel is a tool of change, with the power to change the hearts of those involved in prostitution and sex trafficking. Thus the modern church, like the New Testament church, should reach out to those who are despised by society. Churches should initiate special programmes to reach out to them. For example, several years ago, the Evangelical Church of West Africa (ECWA) became involved in what is now known as City Ministries. Among other projects, this ministry reaches out to prostitutes and other vulnerable girls with the message of the gospel. It rehabilitates them and helps them to go back to school, learn a useful trade and get involved in making a positive contribution to society. Similarly, the Daughters of Abraham Foundation in Nigeria reaches out to prostitutes and vulnerable girls and helps them to recover their dignity and purpose in life by engaging in meaningful and productive activity.[11]

Conclusion

Every society has to deal with the problem of prostitution and sex trafficking. These issues were also present in Old Testament and New Testament times, and both Testaments condemn them as immoral. But the New Testament goes a step further and offers prostitutes the chance to transform their lives through faith in the Lord Jesus Christ. The church cannot afford to do less.

Questions

1. What do you understand by sex trafficking and prostitution? Do you see the effects of these evils in your ministry or environment?

---

[11] For more information about the Daughters of Abraham, see www.doafnigeria.com/home.html.

2. What does the Bible have to say about sex trafficking and prostitution? What relevant principles can we derive from these biblical teachings?

3. What are the areas or places in which prostitution and sex trafficking commonly take place? Is prostitution a problem in rural areas (villages)?

4. How do young girls and children get involved in prostitution? How can the church help them to avoid this?

5. Investigate some non-profit organizations (NGOs) or church-related ministries that reach out to prostitutes. What can you learn from them about what your church can do in your community?

23
FEMALE CIRCUMCISION

Female circumcision is a practice that arouses violent controversy. Those who oppose it insist that it be referred to as female genital mutilation (FGM). This term was officially adopted by the Inter-African Committee on Traditional Practices Affecting the Health of Women and Children at their meeting in Addis Ababa, Ethiopia, in 1990. However, in this chapter, I will not be using this term because those who practise female circumcision do not see it as mutilation but as initiation. They consider it a way of passing on positive values to girls and women. Moreover, as Gachiri points out, "the term female circumcision is today used as a polite term when dealing with affected individuals in order to respect their feeling. No person would wish to be referred to as mutilated."[1]

When our goal is to change people's attitude towards some practice, it is always better to be positive and respectful rather than negative and confrontational.

The Traditional Practice of Female Circumcision

Female circumcision has been practised for centuries in many parts of the world. In much of Africa it is a rite of passage preparing young girls for womanhood and marriage. The United Nations Population Fund (UNFPA) estimates that more than 130 million African girls and women in some twenty-eight countries have been circumcised. In some countries, it is estimated that 98 per cent of the women are circumcised.

---

[1] Ephigenia W. Gachiri, *Female Circumcision with Reference to the Agikuyu of Kenya* (Nairobi, Kenya: Pauline Publications Africa 2000), 32.

The World Health Organization (WHO) defines female circumcision (which it refers to as FGM) as comprising "all procedures involving partial or total removal of the external female genitalia or other injury to the female genital organs for non-medical reasons".[2] The reference in this definition to "all procedures" is an acknowledgement that circumcision can take different forms in different communities. The WHO identifies four broad categories:[3]

- clitoridectomy, involving removal of part or all of the clitoris.

- excision, involving removal of both the clitoris and the labia minora, and sometimes of the labia majora.

- infibulation, the severest form of female circumcision, involving narrowing the vaginal opening. The clitoris and labia minora may or may not be removed, but the surface of the labia are cut and then held together (either by stitching the edges or by tying the girl's legs together) until scar tissue fuses them. Only a very small opening remains for the passing of urine and menstrual blood.

- unclassified, a category that includes "all other procedures to the female genitalia for non-medical purposes, for example, pricking, piercing, incising, scraping and cauterization".

Outsiders tend to react with horror to female circumcision while failing to appreciate the deep religious and traditional values that underlie the practice. Jomo Kenyatta, the former president of Kenya, observed that among the Gikuyu "this operation is still regarded as the very essence of an institution which has enormous educational, social, moral, and religious implications … For the present it is impossible for a member of the tribe to imagine an initiation without clitoridectomy."[4]

What exactly are these educational, social, moral and religious values that Kenyatta referred to? This critical question must be addressed before meaningful progress can be made in understanding female circumcision. The rite involves far more than just the removal of part or all of the female genitalia. It includes teaching positive values about marriage and

---

[2] "Female Genital Mutilation". Cited 12 March 2008. Online: www.who.int/topics/female_genital_mutilation/en/

[3] Annex 2 of *Eliminating Female Genital Mutilation: An Interagency Statement* (Geneva: World Health Organization, 2008), 23. Cited 12 March 2008. Online: www.who.int/reproductive-health/publications/fgm/fgm_statement_2008.pdf.

[4] Jomo Kenyatta, *Facing Mount Kenya: The Tribal Life of the Gikuyu* (London: Secker & Warburg, 1938), 133.

sexuality, hospitability, home-making, a woman's responsibility to her husband and children, community living, solidarity with other women, and chastity. The initiates are taught to avoid a promiscuous lifestyle and virginity is promoted. Kibor points out that girls were traditionally taught that "procreation was only for the mature, the circumcised. Virginity was treasured. Traditionally, the smaller the vaginal opening, the bigger the gift the husband gave to his new bride. The gift served as a key to allow the man to open the wife's birth canal the first night of intercourse."[5]

Supporters of traditional female circumcision feel so strongly about it that they are prepared to resort to violence to defend it. In Cameroon, "associations that have spoken and are still speaking against such practices have met with a lot of hostility from the chief's men, who are usually a gang of thugs living and feeding from the palace and are prepared to do whatever the chiefs demand of them."[6] Pastor John Ayuk lost his life because of his opposition to female circumcision.[7]

Contemporary Opposition to Female Circumcision

Women's rights groups, human rights groups, medical experts, doctors, nurses and midwives have contributed to making people aware of the risks associated with female circumcision. The cause has been taken up by international organizations such as the World Health Organization, Amnesty International and the United States Agency for International Development (USAID). They have campaigned against the practice as brutal, medically risky, repugnant, a form of violence against women, and a public health hazard. The Programme of Action adopted by the International Conference on Population and Development in Cairo in 1994 referred to female circumcision as "a violation of basic rights and a major lifelong risk to women's health"[8] and urged governments to

---

[5] Jacob A. Kibor, "Persistence of Female Circumcision among the Marakwet of Kenya: A Biblical Response to a Rite of Passage" (PhD dissertation, Trinity Evangelical Divinity School, Deerfield, Ill.), 151–152.
[6] Austine Arrey, "Female Genital Mutilation in Cameroon: Man of God Killed by Chief's Henchmen". Cited 12 March 2008. Online: www.fgmnetwork.org/articles/arrey_cameroon.php
[7] Ibid.
[8] "Human Sexuality and Gender Relations: Basis for Action", Programme of Action of the United Nations International Conference on Population and Development, point 7:35. Cited 12 March

"urgently take steps to stop the practice of female genital mutilation and protect women and girls from all such similar unnecessary and dangerous practices".[9]

The health risks associated with female circumcision depend in part on the type of cutting performed. Infibulation, which involves deep cutting of many parts of the female genitalia, obviously has more severe effects than mere piercing of the labia minora. But all forms of circumcision inhibit or terminate sexual feelings during intercourse and can result in infection to the wound, chronic pelvic infections, chronic urinary infections, haemorrhage and shock. If the same knife is used to circumcise a number of girls, HIV/AIDS may be transmitted from one to another during the operation. Female circumcision also causes difficulties during childbirth, increasing the risks to both the mother and the baby.

Women who have undergone female circumcision testify that it is a painful and bitter experience. They endured great anxiety before the circumcision and are left with terrible memories of the circumcision as well as great pain if their wounds failed to heal properly. They also complain of a lack of sexual fulfilment and of the difficulty they have in giving birth.

Obviously, even if those practising this rite mean well and are trying to teach positive values, these negative physical and psychological effects are real and must be dealt with.

The proven health hazards of female circumcision and international criticism of the practice have persuaded sixteen countries, including Eritrea, to ban the practice. However, these bans are widely ignored. The practice continues even among professing Christians: "Examples abound of young Christian women who have been circumcised, even after marriage – especially those married into nominal Christian homes or non-Christian families."[10]

2008. Online: www.iisd.ca/Cairo/program/p07011.html.

[9] "Human Sexuality and Gender Relations: Action", Programme of Action of the United Nations International Conference on Population and Development, point 7:40. Cited 12 March 2008. Online: www.iisd.ca/Cairo/program/p07013.html.

[10] Kibor, "Persistence of Female Circumcision", 2.

Biblical Perspectives on Female Circumcision

The Scriptures are silent with regard to female circumcision. When God commands Abraham to circumcise himself, his son Isaac and all the male members of his household, there is no mention of Sarah and female members of the household:

> This is my covenant with you and your descendents after you, the covenant you are to keep: Every male among you shall be circumcised. You are to undergo circumcision, and it will be the sign of the covenant between me and you. For the generations to come every male among you who is eight days old must be circumcised, including those born in your household or bought with money from a foreigner – those who are not your offspring. Whether born in your household or bought with your money, they must be circumcised. My covenant in your flesh is to be an everlasting covenant. Any uncircumcised male, who has not been circumcised in the flesh, will be cut off from his people; he has broken my covenant (Gen 17:10–14).

Nowhere in all of Scripture or in any of recorded church history is there even a hint that women were to be circumcised.

We can also draw some conclusions about female circumcision from the debate about male circumcision in the early church. The first believers were mainly Jewish and thus practised circumcision. When they found that many Gentiles were being converted, there was much debate about whether Gentile men needed to be circumcised too. The Council of Jerusalem unanimously agreed not to insist on the circumcision of Gentile Christians. They recognized that male circumcision was not a requirement for salvation and membership in the church. Thus there can be no need for female circumcision as proof that a woman is virtuous. Those who are in Christ are cleansed, regenerated and transformed (2 Cor 5:17). To discriminate against uncircumcised women is to fall into the same trap that Peter did (Gal 2:11–21).

The New Testament also makes it abundantly clear that salvation in Christ does not negate traditional values such as hospitality, kindness, hard work, the virtues of womanhood, marriage, sexuality, procreation and love. These universal values that are taught to initiates at the time of circumcision should also be being taught in the churches, for they are fully consistent with Scriptural teaching.

What the New Testament does discourage is any action that harms others. Because female circumcision is indeed medically, physically and psychologically harmful, the church must discourage the practice and urge that it be discontinued.

Finally, from a theological point of view, female circumcision is morally unjustifiable because it negates God's purpose in creating the female reproductive organs. It distorts and mutilates what God created as good and beautiful and denies women God's gift of sexual satisfaction.

Female circumcision must thus be condemned as unbiblical and unethical.

A Christian Response to Female Circumcision

Once we accept that female circumcision is unethical, we need to come up with effective ways of eradicating this practice. The following are some guidelines for how to go about doing this.

Respect those who practise female circumcision

It is important to begin with the positive recognition that "the people who do FGC (female genital cutting) are honorable upright, moral people who love their children and want the best for them. That is why they do FGC, and that is why they will decide to stop doing it, once a safe way of stopping it is found."[11]

Understand the tradition

Scholars and nongovernmental organizations need to study the cultural tradition of female circumcision in every society that practices it. We need more work like that of Gachiri and Kenyatta on the Gikuyu, of Kibor on the Marakwet of Kenya, and of Mackie in Senegal. Case studies of specific ethnic groups will yield a better understanding of the specific cultural values and beliefs underlying the practice. While there are general

---

[11] Gerry Mackie, "A Way to End Female Genital Cutting". Cited 12 March 2008. Online: www. fgmnetwork.org/articles/mackie1998.html.

similarities between groups, there are also unique elements in each local context. This local context needs to be studied and evaluated before recommendations can be made about how to eradicate the practice.

Recognize that change must come from within

Experience has shown that external condemnation and legislation outlawing female circumcision will not necessarily eradicate the practice. If medical personnel are ordered to stop performing circumcisions, the operations will still be performed by others. However, if the community, especially the women who are directly affected, discuss circumcision and decide that it should end, then in all probability the practice will stop. This is what happened in Melicounda, a village with some 3,000 inhabitants in Senegal. Tostan, a non-governmental organization working in collaboration with UNICEF and the government of Senegal, spent two years discussing female circumcision with the women of the village. After serious deliberations, the women themselves decided that the practice should stop. The women then persuaded the community leaders to stop the practice. They then went on to convince neighbouring villages to follow their example.[12]

Educate the community

Community education and awareness are critical for the eradication of female circumcision. Such education must not be seen as attacking positive traditional values and beliefs but as upholding them. So the focus must be on encouraging positive values and not on denouncing female circumcision as a rite of passage.

Circumcision can be thought of as a bag holding positive values. If you insist that people get rid of the bag, they may think that you also want them to discard the contents of the bag, that is, the positive values the rite is trying to pass on to young girls. So any programme to abolish it should actively commend those who demonstrate Christian virtues in their lives and homes while discouraging teasing or disparaging remarks about those who have not been circumcised.

The programme should include teaching by medical experts who can provide information about the many negative medical consequences of

---

[12] Mackie, "A Way to End Female Genital Cutting".

cutting away part or all of the female genitalia. They should discuss infections, problems in childbirth, the inability to enjoy sex, and other psychological and emotional problems associated with circumcision. There should also be Christian teaching, reminding people that God never commanded female circumcision. He created sexual organs for sexual enjoyment, love and procreation. Female circumcision defeats the divine plan and purpose. We should respect, care for and protect the organs that God has so carefully crafted.

Effective means of education and awareness include dramas, talk shows, workshops and discussion of female circumcision in school curricula and church programmes such as Sunday Schools, youth programmes and men's and women's programmes. However, the education programme should particularly target opinion leaders in the community, such as elders, circumcisers, chiefs, older women and women who have been circumcised. They should be given workshops and training sessions at which the issues surrounding circumcision can be dealt with. Once these important groups and individuals have been persuaded of the harmful effects of female circumcision, there is hope that the practice will be discontinued – provided that they can also be assured that positive values will be effectively passed on to the next generation of girls.

Provide effective substitutes

It has been proven over and over again that old practices are not abandoned unless some suitable alternative ritual is put in place. To stop female circumcision without providing an alternative rite of passage would soon lead to a return to the former rite, even if only clandestinely. Thus some communities in Kenya have tried to provide an alternative initiation rite that parallels boys' circumcision rites. Girls can now go through a week-long coming of age program, which marks the transition from girlhood to womanhood. It is called Ntanira Na Mugambo or Circumcision through Words.

There is nothing wrong in having Christian rites that are intended to teach and pass on Christian values on womanhood, sexuality, hospitality, the relationship between husband and wives, the rearing of children, and so forth. In fact, the church in Africa still needs to work out how to celebrate many rites of passage in a way that links them to real life. Baptism, for instance, should not merely be another requirement like attending school or singing hymns in church, but should be a very serious Christian initiation into the body of Christ. Baptismal candidates should be instructed in vital doctrinal truths and the ceremony should be the culmination of an initiation process whereby they move from being babes in Christ to becoming adults who are informed about basic Christian teaching and have been raised anew to live transformed lives.

Introduce legislation

Premature legislation is ineffective and is ignored. All it may do is drive circumcision underground, as happened when the Kenyan government tried to prohibit medical personnel from circumcising females in hospitals. Kenyan communities insisted that the "government has no influence over this customary issue. It is people's way of life".[13] Respect for customary laws and traditions led to the legislation being aborted. As Mackie points out, "unpopular legal prohibitions or harsh propaganda are doomed to meet with resistance. It's just human nature."[14]

However, if the groundwork is first laid through careful education and training of women, village elders and chiefs and religious leaders, legislation will serve to enforce bans that communities are already adopting.

Conclusion

The final remedy to female circumcision is a presentation of the full gospel of Jesus Christ, with its stress that our value and righteousness come from God, regardless of what is done to our bodies. The gospel's stress on doing good, refraining from harm, and thanking God for all his gifts also undercuts all arguments in favour of female circumcision.

Questions

1. Does your ethnic group practice female circumcision? If yes, give reasons why it is done.

---

[13] Kibor, 3.
[14] Mackie, "A Way to End Female Genital Cutting".

2. Is it better to speak of female circumcision, female genital mutilation (FGM), female genital cutting (FGC) or to use some other word or phrase? Which term do you prefer, and why?

3. What are the consequences (positive and negative) of female circumcision?

4. What can we infer from the Bible with respect to female circumcision?

5. How would you go about eradicating female circumcision in your community? What would you recommend as functional alternatives?

24

HOMOSEXUALITY

Homosexuality involves sexual attraction to those of the same sex. Homosexuals may be either male or female (with the latter group sometimes referred to as lesbians). It may be constitutional (or static), in which case it is a "predominant and persistent psychosexual attraction towards members of the same sex".[1] This sexual preference is a fixed reality in the person's life, even though it may or may not be acted on.

Alternatively, homosexuality may be situational (or dynamic). Situational homosexuality tends to occur when someone has a series of homosexual experiences during a specific period, for example, while imprisoned or during a war, but then reverts to heterosexuality when the situation changes.

Much of the modern attempt to justify homosexuality is based on the belief that certain people are constitutionally homosexual, possibly even at the genetic level. Various scientific and biological arguments have been advanced in support of this belief. It is argued that such people have not chosen to be homosexuals any more than other people have chosen to be heterosexual. Their sexual orientation is part of their very nature.

Another distinction closely related to that between constitutional and situational homosexuality is that between a pervert and an invert. A pervert, like the situational homosexual, is someone who is really heterosexual but occasionally indulges in homosexual acts. In other words, perverts distort their actual sexual orientation when they occasionally engage in homosexual sex. An invert, by contrast, is one who is genuinely homosexual. It is argued that homosexual intercourse by inverts is not a perversion or distortion because they are acting in

---

[1] James B. Nelson, "Homosexuality", *Westminster Dictionary of Christian Ethics*, 271.

accordance with their essential nature. They are constitutional or static homosexuals.

Traditional Attitudes to Homosexuality

In traditional Africa, homosexuality and lesbianism, same-sex intercourse and same-sex marriage were not mentioned in public. If they were mentioned at all, it was only in hushed tones. Given the traditional stress on procreation, even the idea of heterosexual intercourse without procreative intent was abhorrent. Homosexual intercourse was considered even more disgusting.

Two African leaders have articulated this strong feeling against homosexuality. Daniel Arap Moi, the former president of Kenya, is reported to have said: "Kenya has no room or time for homosexuals and lesbians. Homosexuality is against African norms and traditions and even in religion it is considered a great sin. Homosexuality is a scourge which runs counter to Christian teachings and African tradition." Similarly, the president of Zimbabwe, Robert Mugabe has said, "I find it extremely outrageous and repugnant to my human conscience that such immoral and repulsive organizations, like those of homosexuals who offend both against the law of nature and the morals of religious beliefs espoused by our society, should have any advocates in our midst or even elsewhere in the world."[2]

Mugabe blames Westerners for introducing homosexuality to Africa. However, it is historically false to assert that there were no same-sex relationships in traditional Africa. While there are no known records of same-sex marriages, homosexual relationships were known. In Northern Nigeria, some cultures had homosexual prostitutes called *yan daudu*. In the 1970s, these male prostitutes would come out annually to dance in the open square. Though female prostitutes were despised, male prostitutes were still more despised and were considered very degenerate.

---

[2] Quoted by Jeremy Seabrook, "Gays and Globalism: Homosexuality and Progress." Cited 14 April 2007. www.gayconspiracy.co.uk/page52.html.

Current Attitudes to Homosexuality in Africa

Over the past decade, homosexuality has moved from being a taboo topic to centre stage. One precipitating factor was the election in 2003 of an openly gay bishop, Gene Robinson, by the Episcopal Church in the United States of America. This action created a crisis, with many African Anglican church leaders threatening to break away from the Anglican Communion. At a meeting of Anglican leaders in Zanzibar in 2007, the Rev. Peter Akinola and six other conservative archbishops refused to take communion with Katherine Jefferts Schori, the leader of the American Episcopalians.

Gay and lesbian rights groups are now speaking up and seeking legislation to protect homosexuals. In response, the governments of countries like Nigeria, Kenya, Zimbabwe and Rwanda have voiced their repugnance and anger at the idea that they should accept same-sex attractions and same-sex weddings. South Africa is the only African country in which such weddings are legal.

What are the main factors, apart from the election of Bishop Robinson, that account for this sudden change?

- *Demands for freedom of speech and human rights.* Today everybody has the right to express an opinion, even if their opinion is that of a minority or is ethically wrong. Taking a cue from their Western counterparts, homosexual advocates have come out of their closets and argue their case in terms of individual freedom and human rights, with the unflinching support of human rights organizations.

- *Desire for morality to be based on empirical and scientific data.* Psychological, social and empirical data have replaced biblical authority and religious conviction as authoritative guides to ethics and morality. In particular, homosexual advocates parade any scientific evidence that suggests that being homosexual is not a matter of choice but of constitution, regardless of whether the evidence is conclusive. Their argument is that if something is innate, it must be acceptable.

- *Erosion and abandonment of traditional values and beliefs.* Africa is experiencing a rapid erosion of the values and traditions that held the community together. A new generation of Africans are rejecting traditional beliefs and practices as backward and unacceptable in this scientific and post-Christian age. The community, which used to be the arbiter of morality, is no longer seen as authoritative. Elders have lost their place in the education and training of the younger generation. Fathers cannot tell their sons what is right and wrong, and mothers cannot do the same for their daughters. The god of individualism has been promoted by the all-powerful media and is the new source of authority and allegiance.

- *Rejection of biblical revelation and ecclesiastical faith and practice.* People's world view is no longer shaped by the Scriptures and the church. Instead it is shaped by secular, humanistic thinking. Such thinking singles out love as the most important factor in marriage, and regards the question of whether those in love are heterosexual or homosexual as irrelevant. It is the presence of love that is decisive. Consequently the very definition of marriage is being challenged. In South Africa, the Marriage Act originally defined marriage as "the union of one man with one woman", but after a legal challenge it was changed to "the voluntary union of two persons". Such a change marks a clear rejection of the biblical and Christian definition of marriage.

- *Advances in reproductive technology.* In Africa, people got married in order to have children. However, these days "technology has broken the link between sexual intercourse and procreation; and this, in turn, has made the connection between intercourse and marriage unnecessary".[3] Homosexuals can now use medical options to have children without committing themselves to heterosexual relationships.

Biblical Perspectives on Homosexuality

Homosexuality has existed for centuries. Plato's *Symposium* makes it clear that love between men was widely known and accepted among the ancient Greeks. The prohibitions against homosexual relations in the Old Testament also indicate that such relationships were prevalent among the surrounding nations.

The first human inhabitants of the world that God created were a man and a woman (Gen 1:27). This first couple set the paradigm for

---

[3] J. Rinzema. *The Sexual Revolution* (trans. Lewis B. Smedes; Grand Rapids: Eerdmans, 1974), 46.

marriage and sexuality, as the narrator of Genesis clearly states: "For this reason a man will leave his father and mother and be united to his wife, and they will become one flesh" (Gen 2:24). This position is endorsed by Jesus in 19:4–5. The relationship between Adam and Eve was clearly sexual, for the very next verse states that "the man and his wife were both naked, and they felt no shame" (Gen 2:25). The sexual relationship between a man and a woman is again endorsed in Genesis 4:1, which states that "Adam lay with his wife Eve, and she became pregnant and gave birth", where the word "lay" clearly refers to sexual intercourse. One can confidently say that Scripture teaches that heterosexuality is the norm. Homosexuality must thus be a deviation from this norm.

In its presentation of homosexuality, Scripture does not discuss whether this condition is innate or situational. What it does do is focus on legislation regarding homosexual acts and incidents of homosexual behaviour. The following are some of the key biblical passages.

- *Genesis 19:1–11.* The men of Sodom who wanted to rape Lot's visitors were homosexuals. Lot told them that such behaviour was wicked, but they refused to listen to him. Their behaviour and their lack of repentance brought divine judgment on their city.

- *Leviticus 18:22; 20:13.* These two verses form part of what is known as the Holiness Code in Leviticus. They strongly condemn lying "with a man as one lies with a woman". They describe such behaviour as "detestable" and prescribe the death penalty for male homosexuals.

- *Judges 19* tells the story of a Levite who ended up in a similar situation to Lot's visitors. He was on a journey and had to spend the night in the town of Gibeah. He was offered hospitality by an old man, but that night "some of the wicked men of the city surrounded the house. Pounding on the door, they shouted to the old man who owned the house, 'bring out the man who came to your house so we can have sex with him'." They were clearly homosexuals bent on raping the male guest, even though the old man described their actions as "vile" and "disgraceful".

- *Romans 1:26–27.* Paul describes male and female homosexuals as idolatrous and wicked, and as acting in a way that is contrary to nature: "Even their women exchanged natural relations for unnatural ones. In the same way, the men also abandoned natural relations with women and were inflamed with lust for one another. Men committed indecent acts with other men, and received in themselves the due penalty for their perversion." He has no doubt that homosexuality is unnatural and a perversion of the heterosexuality that God established at creation.

- *1 Corinthians 6:9–11; 1 Timothy 1:9–10.* Paul groups homosexuality with other sins such as murder, adultery and idolatry. He states that all those who practice these vices, including homosexuals, "will not inherit the kingdom of God".

Clearly, Scripture has a very negative view of homosexual intercourse. It makes it clear that those who engage in such behaviour do not enjoy divine favour and will attract both present and future condemnation and judgment. Any attempt to justify homosexuality and homosexual acts is foreign to the Scripture.

The Christian Response to Homosexuals

Given what Scripture has to say about homosexuality, how should the church and individual Christians respond to homosexuals and to the homosexual agenda?

The first point that must be made is that the church must not abandon the biblical position. Christians must accept that the Scriptures are the final authority in matters of faith and practice and provide the guidelines and qualifications for membership in Christ's church. For example, one cannot call Jesus Lord and also confess that Buddha is Lord because that contradicts the clear teaching of Scripture. In the same way, one cannot approve of same-sex acts when the Bible explicitly condemns them. The Bible must be our yardstick for measuring what is right and wrong.

It follows that we cannot accept same-sex marriage. The scriptural view of marriage is that it is a relationship between a male and a female, and that sex should only take place within marriage. But these days society teaches that sex is purely a biological function, unrelated to marriage, and marriage is assumed to be based solely on love. Thus it is assumed that as long as two people love and care for each other, it does not matter whether they are both the same sex. We need to work to correct this shallow understanding of marriage.

But while we should refuse to condone homosexuality and same-sex marriage, we must be compassionate in our dealings with homosexuals. We do not have to agree with their behaviour or with their argument that it must be accepted, but we should listen to them compassionately and respectfully. Listening does not mean compromising our position.

We must also remember that homosexuality is not the only heinous sin in our world. Besides homosexuality, Paul's list of sins in 1 Corinthians 6:9–10 includes sexual immorality, adultery, greed, drunkenness, slander and fraud. These sins are equally wicked and evil. Yet those who have committed these sins have been accepted into our churches if they turn to Christ and turn away from their evil practices. We should do no less for homosexuals. The church must be willing to extend warm acceptance to those who have changed their ways.

Conclusion

The current debate on homosexuality is complex and troubling. As shown in the discussion above, the issues involved include "the meaning of human sexuality, the interpretation of Scripture, the use of empirical data, and the criteria for evaluation of moral action".[4]

One's position on whether some people are homosexual by nature or choice will affect one's response to the psychological, social and biological arguments regarding homosexuality. So will one's view of science, particularly when it comes to the weight that should be given to empirical data when making judgments about human conduct. Those who have a relativistic view of ethics will tend to view homosexuality as a purely subjective and personal matter.

Christians need to give due weight to empirical and scientific arguments, but should never compromise their basic submission to the teaching of Scriptures. From a biblical point of view, homosexuality is a manifestation of our sinful nature and is contrary to the clear teachings of Scripture. As Helmut Thielicke puts it,

> Homosexuality cannot be put on the same level with the normal created order of the sexes; rather it is a habitual or actual distortion or depravation of it. It follows from this that the homosexual is called upon not to affirm his status or *a priori* to idealize it – any more than any other pathological disorder

---

[4] James B. Nelson, "Homosexuality", 273.

can be affirmed *a priori* – but rather regard and recognize his condition as something that is questionable.[5]

In other words, homosexuality may indeed sometimes be innate, but that may merely reflect the fact that the fall has corrupted our human natures in many ways. We should not naively derive an "ought" from an "is", and so we cannot say that the fact that homosexuality exists means that it ought to be accepted.

Questions

1. Is the view of homosexuality changing in your ministry context? If so, how and why?

2. How ought the African church to respond to international pressure to accept homosexuality, such as the recent actions of the Episcopal Church in America?

3. In what ways is the biblical teaching on homosexuality being twisted and misrepresented by those who claim that it is not a sin?

4. Evaluate your own attitudes and the attitudes of those to whom you minister. Which of the biblical teachings regarding the Christian and the homosexual do you need to develop further? What obstacles keep you (and others) from embracing these teachings?

5. In what ways can you minister effectively regarding homosexuality, both in terms of addressing the act and the person?

---

[5] Helmut Thielicke, *The Ethics of Sex* (trans. John D. Doberstein; New York: Harper & Row, 1964), 201.

SECTION E
MEDICAL ISSUES

INTRODUCTION TO MEDICAL ISSUES

Before the coming of Western medicine, Africans were already practising medicine to cure the sick. Modern medical practice has brought cures for many deadly diseases such as smallpox, measles, infertility, heart problems and malaria. But modern medical care also poses some very serious ethical problems, as we saw in the discussion of infertility and contraception in the section on family issues.

In this part of the book we will explore some of these issues. We will begin in **chapter 25** by looking at ethical issues raised by the HIV/AIDS epidemic. This is not the first plague in history. The Black Death killed between 25 and 50 million people in Europe in three years in the 1340s. Smallpox has been a major killer for centuries. The Spanish Flu killed between fifty and a hundred million people worldwide between 1918 and 1920. In each case, the church has had to respond to the needs of the people. How should we respond today to the needs of millions living with HIV/AIDS? And how should we respond to the needs of those who are not yet infected? Should we be encouraging the use of condoms?

Another epidemic that is killing thousands is abortion, which is the topic of **chapter 26**. The discussion of abortion leads naturally into a discussion of euthanasia and infanticide in **chapter 27**, for all of these issues involve a life that is judged unwanted. Similar principles regarding the value of human life underlie Christian responses to all these issues. Who has the right to make decisions about whether human lives should continue or should end? Does it make a difference if the life concerned is full of pain and suffering?

Our human responsibility to care for one another also comes to the fore in **chapter 28**, which deals with an issue that concerns medical workers whose primary duty is to save lives. Many of these workers are underpaid. Does this justify their going on strike to demand better working conditions?

The final issue addressed in **chapter 29** is the use of drugs and alcohol. This is often not seen as a medical issue, but there can be no doubt that those who have become addicted to these substances need medical help. But should we see addiction as no more than a medical issue? What advice should we give to those who are trying to decide whether to experiment with alcohol and drugs?

25

HIV/AIDS

Acquired Immune Deficiency Syndrome (AIDS) is more than an epidemic; it is a pandemic, a worldwide epidemic. Since it was first diagnosed in 1981, it has killed more than 25 million people.[1] It is still spreading fast in India, China, Indonesia, Papua New Guinea, Vietnam, the Russian Federation, Ukraine, Estonia and Latvia.

Africa has been particularly hard hit. Though Africa has only 10 per cent of the world's population, it is estimated that 70 per cent of those infected with HIV/AIDS are located in Africa. Of the 33 million now living with the disease worldwide, 22.5 million are in sub-Saharan Africa. In 2007, about 1.7 million people in Africa were newly infected with the disease and 1.6 million people in Africa died from it.[2] The AIDS pandemic has also orphaned 11.5 million children across the continent. Given these disturbing numbers, it is no wonder that Kofi Annan, the former secretary-general of the United Nations, refers to the HIV/AIDS scourge as a "weapon of mass destruction". After all, it "is claiming more lives than the sum total of all wars, famines and floods, and the ravages of such deadly diseases as malaria".[3] Those affected come from cities and villages and include men, women and children, the educated and the uneducated.

The reason why AIDS is so often referred to as HIV/AIDS is that the disease known as Acquired Immune Deficiency Syndrome, shortened to AIDS, is spread by a virus call the Human Immunodeficiency Virus, shortened to HIV. Those who have this virus in their bodies are referred to as HIV positive. They may not show any outward sign of illness, but

---

[1] Statistics from "Worldwide HIV and AIDS Statistics. Cited 21 March 2008. Online: www.avert.org/worldstats.htm.

[2] Statistics are taken from the *AIDS Epidemic Update: December 2007* (Geneva: UNAIDS, 2007). Cited 17 March 08. Online: data.unaids.org/pub/EPISlides/2007/2007_epiupdate_en.pdf.

[3] Nelson Mandela, speaking at the 14th International Aids Conference in Paris in 2003.

the virus is slowly damaging their immune and nervous systems and weakening their resistance to all kinds of diseases. When the damage becomes severe, sometimes several years after the person first became infected, the disease known as AIDS appears.

The HIV virus is transmitted in bodily fluids, particularly semen and blood. Thus the most common way of getting infected is through sexual intercourse with an infected partner. Another common source of infection is contact with infected blood. A patient can be given HIV/AIDS during a blood transfusion if the blood has not been carefully screened to make sure it is safe. Intravenous drug users and even nurses can transmit HIV/AIDS from one person to another if they reuse an injection needle that has not been properly sterilized. The disease can even be transmitted during circumcision ceremonies if the same blade is used to circumcise a number of boys or girls.

HIV/AIDS is not the only disease to be transmitted in this way, but it is the most dangerous because it is incurable and fatal. The best current medications can do is prolong the lives of those infected.

This epidemic shows no signs of abating. The battle with HIV/AIDS has yet to be won.

Why the Battle Continues

There are a number of reasons why HIV/AIDS is continuing to spread rapidly in Africa:

- Winning a battle requires knowing the enemy. Unfortunately, when it comes to the enemy known as HIV/AIDS, many people are ignorant about the disease, how it spreads and what can be done to stop its spread. Their ignorance leaves them vulnerable to infection.

- Some governments in Africa do not see the need to invest in the battle against HIV/AIDS. Kofi Annan expressed his frustration at this attitude on the part of African and other governments: "I feel angry, I feel distressed, I feel helpless ... to live in a world where we have the means ... to be able to help all these patients, [but] what is lacking is the political will."[4]

---

[4] Transcript of BBC interview with Kofi Annan, Friday, 28 November 2003 (cited 17 March 2008). Online: www.un.org/issues/calendar/cache/bbc-sg-aids03.asp.

- Companies that develop the life-sustaining drugs needed to treat HIV/AIDS have financial rather than humanitarian motives. The high prices they charge mean that the drugs are too expensive for most Africans. While the rich can travel overseas for treatment or buy the necessary drugs within the country, the poor languish and die.

- Traditional practices contribute to the spread of the disease. For example, some communities still practice widow inheritance even when the husband has died of AIDS. The wife is likely to be HIV positive, and she will infect her new husband, who may in turn spread the infection to his other wives if the marriage is polygamous.

- Traditional attitudes towards sex also contribute to the spread of the disease. A man who is HIV positive or who has sex with someone who is HIV positive (whether his wife or another woman) may refuse to wear a condom. Without this protection, the infection will spread.

- Reluctance to talk about HIV/AIDS makes it difficult to combat its spread. The disease is often seen as a curse that brings a stigma on victims and their families. People refuse to be tested for HIV/AIDS, those who do test positive refuse to acknowledge it, and families do everything in their power to deny that a member of their family has the disease. This same reluctance to confront the disease and talk about it openly is present in churches, many of which do not know how to counsel those who have HIV/AIDS.

Ethical Issues Raised by the Pandemic

HIV/AIDS raises many ethical issues for individuals, their families, society at large, companies and church leaders.

On the individual level, the ethical issue is related to personal choice. If men and women were to refrain from pre-marital and extra-marital sex and not use street drugs and unsterilized needles, the spread of HIV/AIDS would decrease. The disease forces us to acknowledge that our moral decisions and choices about our lifestyle have personal and social consequences.

However, it is important to recognize that although a chain of HIV/AIDS infections may begin with someone who acts unethically, the disease can spread to others who are leading moral lives. AIDS is not like cancer, diabetes, mental illness and other diseases which are not passed on from one person to another. An infected man or woman may pass the disease on to their spouse. Mothers may pass it on to their children, either during birth or while breast-feeding. When children die of HIV/AIDS, the future of the family is in jeopardy. Entire families have already been wiped out by the disease.

The disease also affects family members who are not infected. Grandmothers and grandfathers now have to take on the responsibility of raising their orphaned grandchildren when the parents die. Sometimes children end up as the heads of families, trying to act as parents to their younger siblings.

Nor is the impact of HIV/AIDS restricted to families, for the disease has an impact on entire nations. Most AIDS victims in Africa are between 18 and 35 years old. This age group is usually the major work force of any nation. When hundreds of people in this age group die, the entire economy is affected. Food may also become scarcer as there is a shortage of able-bodied people to tend the crops. Governments and other agencies have to decide how they are going to respond to the ethical obligation to provide compassionate care and treatment for their citizens. Money allocated to helping those affected with HIV/AIDS will have to be taken away from other areas like education or development.

HIV/AIDS also poses ethical questions to businesses. Employers have to decide how to handle employees who are HIV positive or who develop full-blown AIDS. Should they fire them or help provide for them? The pharmaceutical companies who develop and sell drugs are being forced to wrestle with the question of why they do this. Is their goal solely to make money or is it to assist those who are suffering? How much money do they need to make in order to be able to continue to research and develop new drugs?

HIV/AIDS also forces the church to examine its attitude towards sickness, and in particular towards this epidemic. Is this disease a divine punishment? How should the church respond to those infected with HIV/AIDS? Should couples be tested for HIV/AIDS before they can be married? Some churches already insist on this – but should this testing be mandatory or voluntary? What should be done when an engaged couple prove to be HIV positive? Should the church marry them? And what if only one partner is infected? How do our answers to these questions relate to the whole question of confidentiality?

It is impossible to deal with all of these issues in a single chapter. All that can be done is to provide some guidelines addressing a few of the ethical dilemmas posed by the HIV/AIDS epidemic.

Biblical Perspectives on HIV/AIDS

The Bible does not speak of HIV/AIDS because the disease was unknown at that time. But it does speak of sin and suffering, and what it has to say is relevant to our response to the disease. In particular, the Bible must be the basis for our response to the question of whether HIV/AIDS is a divine punishment for sexual promiscuity.

Several years ago, I interviewed about a hundred Christians in Nigeria and found that roughly 80 per cent of them were convinced that those afflicted with AIDS were being justly punished for living a lifestyle that God condemns. It is thus very important to address the question of whether AIDS is a punishment from God.

In answering this question, it is important to correct the mistaken assumption that every case of HIV/AIDS is caused by sexual promiscuity.

> A very large number of those who have died from HIV/AIDS or are living with the disease cannot plausibly be blamed for their fate. Nearly 5 million AIDS victims are children, who obviously did not choose to be born HIV positive. And many other victims are married women who have been faithful to their husbands but became infected anyway because their husbands had unsafe sex with prostitutes. Many wives don't find out that their husbands are infected until they give birth to HIV-positive children.[5]

Moreover, HIV/AIDS is not transmitted only by sex. Millions have been infected by blood transfusions or by injection needles that were not properly sterilized before being reused.

Given these facts, it is impossible to give a simple answer to the question, "Is AIDS a divine punishment?" The answer is both no and yes, as John Stott explains:

[5] David Perry, "The Global Distribution of AIDS Pharmaceuticals", p.1. Cited 18 March 2008. Online: www.scu.edu/ethics/publications/submitted/Perry/aids.html.

No, because Jesus warned us not to interpret calamities as God's specific judgments upon evil people (Luke 13:1–5). No, because there are obviously some people that contracted the disease through no personal sin of theirs. We think here of innocent children who contracted it through their mothers, faithful wives and husbands (usually wives) who have been infected by their unfaithful husbands, even innocent patients who contracted it from careless medical procedures. Yes, because all suffering is related to the Fall. Disease came into the world because man sinned.[6]

At the most basic level, sin is responsible for human suffering. It is at the root of every disease, for if there were no sin, there would be no disease.

When we move beyond this general level to speak of individuals and particular sins, we need to note that while there is a link between sin and suffering, it is not always the individual's own sin that produced the suffering. Exodus 20:5 shows that people sometimes suffer because of the sins of their ancestors, and in 2 Samuel 24:1–17 the nation suffers because of the king's sin.

Yet even allowing for these exceptions, it is also true that people reap what they sow (Gal 6:7). There is a cause-and-effect mechanism at work in many cases where people die from AIDS because of their lifestyle. Thus although we should be very careful about linking HIV/AIDS with divine judgment, ultimately "it will be irresponsible not to see a link".[7] Stott points out that the fact that "evil actions bring evil consequences seems to have been written by God into the universe according to his moral world."[8] Any kind of careless lifestyle is displeasing to God. Such behaviour makes us susceptible to disease and premature death.

But God's punishment of sin is only half the story. It is vitally important for our own treatment of those suffering from HIV/AIDS that we also understand God's grace and mercy. This mercy operates even in his judgment:

[6] John Stott, *New Issues Facing Christians Today* (London: Marshall Pickering. 1999), 353–354.
[7] D. A. Carson, *How Long, O Lord? Reflections on Suffering and Evil* (Grand Rapids: Baker, 1990), 255.
[8] Stott, *New Issues*, 354.

Many who are guilty of this sin do not get the HIV virus. Many others have been infected only after repeated instances of disobedience. God has been patient, hoping that the sinner would repent. Even when infected, God's presence is promised to those who desire it and repent. God blesses the afflicted even amidst the affliction; moreover, Christ's death paid for the eternal consequences of this sin.[9]

Regardless of whether someone contracted HIV/AIDS through their own sinful behaviour or was infected by others, God still extends his love, mercy and forgiveness to them. Thus the Christian and the church must follow Jesus' example. Along with our Lord, we must say "neither do I condemn you" (John 8:11). We are not called to judge others (Luke 6:37). As an American AIDS patient called Jerome said, "I am living under my own judgment. What I need is for you to walk with me."[10] We should be reaching out to those suffering from HIV/AIDS with an attitude not of condemnation but of acceptance and forgiveness, love and care.

Ethical Dilemmas

The Christian response to HIV/AIDS must be multifaceted, focusing both on the church and the community. This response will inevitably involve us in various ethical dilemmas, some of which are discussed below.

Church members with HIV/AIDS: The pastor's dilemma

The belief that HIV/AIDS is associated with immorality has led some to speak as if HIV/AIDS is only a problem for those outside the church. It is assumed that pastors will not be ministering to members of their own congregations who have this disease. But one pastor in South Africa has reported that he conducts funeral services for between seven and eight members of his church *a week*. In a small town in Nigeria, one church buries about three members each week. Yes, there is AIDS in the

---

[9] John S. Feinberg and Paul D. Feinberg, *Ethics for a Brave New World* (Wheaton: Crossway, 1993), 205.
[10] Stott, *New Issues*, 354.

church. A newsletter from the ECWA AIDS Awareness Program bears this out:

> At Evangel Hospital we have recently seen a number of church people falling sick with AIDS. We only fool ourselves if we imagine it is not going to devastate many of our church communities. Then the problem is automatically a problem for the church. Children left parentless. What does the church do? Does it leave them to become street children? No. A Christian community cannot do that.[11]

Medical personnel should educate church leaders on how to relate to the AIDS victims in their congregations and their families. Sadly, out of ignorance there are many pastors and church leaders who have unconsciously hurt more members than they have helped. Though promiscuity may be a major cause of AIDS, that is no excuse for shunning or neglecting AIDS victims. Rather than condemning them, pastors and churches should reach out to those who have contracted the disease with love and care.

The church should even encourage HIV/AIDS testing, not only for engaged couples but for all church members, including church leaders. Such testing will reduce the suspicion and tension that often arise when the church insists on testing prior to marriage. A good example was set at the Eighth Assembly of the All Africa Conference of Churches in Cameroon in 2003, when more than 800 church leaders representing more than 150 churches and 39 countries were tested for HIV/AIDS. Any of them who tested positive were encouraged to reveal this fact in order to help fight the stigma associated with the disease. The leaders promised that they would give their HIV-positive brothers and sisters the loving support that Christians should give to each other.[12] This gesture encouraged others to be tested, normalized the concept of testing for HIV/AIDS and demonstrated how Christians should react to fellow-Christians with this disease.

---

[11] ECWA Aids Programme Newsletter, March 1998 (ECWA stands for the Evangelical Church of West Africa).

[12] BBC News, "African church leaders take HIV test". Cited 20 March 2008. Online: news.bbc.co.uk/1/hi/world/africa/3239926.stm.

Condoms: The educator's dilemma

There is great ignorance when it comes to HIV/AIDS. Some people deny the reality of the disease and continue with lifestyles that contribute to its spread. Even prominent leaders like President Thabo Mbeki of South Africa question the fact that AIDS is caused by HIV. Church members do not understand the theological and religious implications of HIV/AIDS and how to relate to those affected and to the epidemic as a whole.

To win the war against this disease, we need to mobilize an army of health educators to teach church members, citizens, children and students about this disease and combat the many myths that surround it. Education is the most humane and moral way to combat ignorance, prejudice, fear and promiscuous behaviour. The education programme must provide accurate basic information about HIV/AIDS, presented in a way that encourages people to discuss their beliefs about this disease and how it is spread. Such discussion demonstrates respect for those being taught and provides the educator with an opportunity to address their specific concerns. As people describe their beliefs and sometimes their experiences with those infected, the education programme will also promotes awareness of how HIV/AIDS is affecting the community and the need to take active steps to prevent it from spreading further.

The programme must include information about how to prevent the transmission of HIV/AIDS. This is where matters become controversial. Some programmes urge the use of condoms to prevent the spread of the disease. This position is strongly supported by medical scientists, public officials and political figures. However, some in the church argue that encouraging the use of condoms is tantamount to encouraging promiscuity.

The Roman Catholic Church has taken the strongest stand against the use of condoms. In taking this position it is heavily influenced by the views of Augustine (354–430 AD), the first bishop of Hippo in North Africa. He insisted that the sole purpose of sex is procreation, not pleasure. Thus he labelled any technique intended to avoid procreation as sinful. Because condoms prevent conception, the Roman Catholic Church rejects their use, along with that of all other contraceptives. Against this view, Kofi Annan has argued that what is at stake in Africa is not one's beliefs about sex and procreation but the saving of human lives. If condoms will save lives, they are legitimate. After all, religion can only reach out to the living and not to the dead.

How should we respond to this debate? A number of points can be made. First, the church should not be judged too harshly for raising concerns about the promotion of condoms. In certain situations the use of condoms does raise serious moral questions. Religious leaders fear being accused of double talk, preaching against sexual immorality while at the same promoting it. So careful thought needs to be given to when, how, where and to whom the use of condoms is promoted. Is it proper for priests or pastors to promote their use by members of their congregations?

A second point that can be raised concerns the effectiveness of condoms. They have not been shown to be 100 per cent safe even when used properly, which is often not the case. Not one of the manufacturers of condoms guarantees with anything remotely close to 99 per cent certainty that they will even prevent conception, much less the transmission of viruses and bacteria. Thus entrusting one's life and health to a condom is rather like playing Russian roulette. Even if the odds favour one's being safe, the risk of contracting the disease is too high.

The Christian view is well put by Patrick Dixon: "Condoms do not make sex safe, they simply make it safer. Safe sex is sex between two partners who are not infected. This means a lifelong, faithful partnership between two people who were virgins and who now remain faithful to each other for life."[13] The United States Conference of Catholic Bishops makes the same point: "abstinence outside of marriage and fidelity within marriage as well as the avoidance of intravenous drug abuse are the only morally correct and medically sure ways to prevent the spread of AIDS".[14]

Yet even while the church insists on moral faithfulness, we must remember that we live in a sinful world. There are men and women who will not be faithful to their spouses and some unmarried people will continue to commit sexual sin. Their actions will spread HIV/

---

[13] Patrick, Dixon. *The Truth about AIDS: What You Must Know; What You Can Do* (Eastbourne: Kingsway, 1987), 171.

[14] The United States Conference of Catholic Bishops, *The Many Faces of AIDS: A Gospel Response* (Washington: United States Catholic Conference, 1987). Cited 18 March 2008. Online: www. usccb.org/sdwp/international/mfa87.shtml#4.

AIDS to others. In light of this reality, it is important that the church provides sex education so that all members are informed about how the disease is transmitted and ways infection can be avoided. Although latex condoms do not offer full protection, they are certainly better than having unprotected sexual intercourse. Their use could prevent many faithful spouses from getting the deadly disease and could protect sexually active men and women from getting or transmitting the disease to their unaffected sexual partners.

The controversy between governments, public officials, medical experts and the church on the use of condoms is likely to continue. Governments have the right to promote the use of condoms; the church, however, also has the right to promote abstinence and sex education, which may or may not encourage the use of condoms.

Confidentiality: The doctor's dilemma

It is not unusual for ethical norms to conflict, especially when applied to real life. We have looked at this conflict in regard to the use of condoms. Now we need to think of the conflict doctors endure when they have an ethical obligation to maintain confidentiality about a patient's health status and yet know that by remaining silent they are putting the patients' spouse at risk of contracting HIV/AIDS or some other sexually transmitted disease. Doctors will certainly advise their patients to tell the spouse about their condition. But what should they do when patients refuse to do so? Must they respect the patient's right to privacy even when that may endanger the life of another person?

Approaching the question of privacy from another angle: Should a doctor insist that a patient suspected of being HIV positive be tested? Should the doctor get the patient's permission before administering the test, or should the test be given without the patient's knowing what it is? Does failure to gain the patient's consent mean that the doctor has violated the ethical principle of patient autonomy and privacy?

The medical profession has a strong commitment to the tradition of protecting patients' confidentiality. Yet it does recognize certain situations in which other obligations may override this duty. First, doctors have a duty to prevent patients from harming themselves. They can alert others if a patient is threatening suicide. Second, doctors have a duty to prevent patients from harming other people. They can alert others if a patient is threatening to harm them.

Doctors thus have to decide whether the danger posed by a patient with undisclosed HIV/AIDS is sufficiently great to invoke one of these principles and break the rule of confidentiality. But this cannot be done lightly, for it may mean that the patient may never trust a doctor again and may not come for treatment, and it may unleash all sorts of problems in the family.

This type of moral conflict, where two ethical principles clash, is not unique to the world of medicine. As we saw in chapter 6, ethicists have suggested various possible responses in such situations. I recommend the approach called graded absolutism, which takes a hierarchical view of ethics. When there are real moral conflicts, one should try to determine which moral obligation has the greater weight and will do the greatest good. If we apply this to the doctor's situation, we need to determine which principle is more important: preserving the patient's confidentiality or preserving lives.

If we turn to Scripture for guidance, we can see that it can be argued that Scripture supports confidentiality. It certainly strongly condemns gossip, which includes discussing someone's problems with people who cannot help (Prov 18:8; 26:17), talkativeness (Prov 10:19; 29:20) and revealing secrets (Prov 11:13). It also teaches that some duties and responsibilities take precedence over others. Jesus rebuked the Pharisees, saying, "Woe to you hypocrites! For you tithe mint and dill and cumin, and have neglected the weightier matters of the law, justice and mercy and faith; these you ought to have done, without neglecting the others." (Matt 23:23, RSV). The words "weightier matters of the law" indicate that some moral duties and responsibilities far outweigh others. Jesus was referring to passages like Micah 6:8 and Zechariah 7:9–10, which point out that justice, mercy, kindness and faithfulness are moral responsibilities that precede other requirements. Scripture also says that we are to love our neighbours as ourselves (Lev 19:18). Jesus specifically identifies this as the second greatest commandment (Matt 22:39). Because we would certainly wish to be warned if something was endangering our lives, it follows that we have an obligation to warn our neighbours if their lives are threatened. This obligation is more important than the obligation to protect the patient's privacy. Thus if patients with HIV/AIDS reject all their doctors' attempts to persuade them to reveal their physical condition to others who are potentially at risk, the doctors can threaten to do so themselves.

Using the same argument, it is not immoral for physicians to test patients whom they have every reason to suspect of having HIV/AIDS, even without the patients' consent.

Sexual intercourse: The spouse's dilemma

Should an uninfected spouse continue to have sexual intercourse with a husband or wife who is infected with HIV/AIDS? Does the marriage vow, which states that the two are united "for better for worse, in sickness or in health", make it an obligation, an absolute duty, to continue sexual relations with an infected partner? This problem is plaguing many African Christian couples. All such couples should receive intense pastoral and medical counselling.

Unprotected sexual intercourse will expose the spouse to infection with a deadly disease. Sexual abstinence may thus be necessary because this is a matter of life or death. However, abstinence is not the only option. There are ways to have sexual intimacy with minimal risk to the life or health of the spouse. For example, the couple could make use of a strong, thick condom; reduce the frequency of lovemaking while being sensitive to the needs of the other; and avoid deep kissing in which saliva may pass from one mouth to the other. An infected woman should probably avoid pregnancy as there is a significant chance that any child may also be infected.[15]

Unfortunately, the sad fact is that even when couples have been advised to use condoms, the infected partner (usually the husband) often refuses to do so. This is an abuse of the marriage vow. He is not showing the self-sacrificing love for his wife that Scripture commands (Eph 5:25–29).

Marriage: The church's dilemma

Many churches today require that couples be tested for HIV/AIDS before being married in church. Some even extend this testing to cover other sexually transmitted diseases. Is this a legitimate demand?

---

[15] Dixon, *The Truth About AIDS*, 177.

Against this practice, it can be argued that some couples resist taking this test because of fears that it might jeopardize their wedding plans. They postpone taking it until the last moment, often the week before the wedding. If either or both of them prove HIV positive, they have no time to think about how to handle this difficult situation. Overwhelmed by the news, they may cancel their marriage plans at short notice or proceed with the wedding with an attitude of denial.

This argument, however, does not address the question of *whether* testing should be done but only of *when* it should be done. I would urge that the test should be done at least six months prior to the wedding date. The individual who is HIV positive will then have time to work out how to live with this knowledge, and family members will have time to come to terms with the situation. Since marriage in Africa is basically a communal affair, it is appropriate that the family know about the test result (although the couple's confidentiality should not be breached if they do not want to disclose their status because the lives of family members are not at risk). The couple will also have plenty of time for counselling and re-evaluation of their willingness to continue with the marriage before the wedding takes place. Particularly when only one of the two is infected, the marriage is often cancelled.

What should the church do, however, if one member of the couple is infected but both still want to go ahead with the wedding? For example, I know of a young woman whose husband had died of HIV/AIDS and left her HIV positive. Another young man proposed to her and was told her HIV status, but insisted on marrying her all the same. Some pastors would refuse to officiate at such a wedding because it would likely lead to the untimely death of the groom. Others might be prepared to officiate, provided the couple were given full counselling about the risks they were running and about how to have the safest possible sex within marriage (see the previous section).

Conclusion

In closing, I can do no better than quote John Stott: "The HIV/AIDS crisis challenges us profoundly to be the church in deed and in truth: to be the church as a healing community. Indeed, because of our tendency to self-righteousness, the healing community itself will need to be healed by the forgiveness of Christ."[16]

Questions

1. What impact has HIV/AIDS had in the area where you are ministering? What practical problems is it posing for you and your church?

2. How do pastors and people perceive HIV/AIDS in theological terms? Are some parts of Scriptural teaching overemphasized and others overlooked or neglected?

3. Ask several pastors to describe how they and their churches are responding to the HIV/AIDS crisis. What role do they think education should play in their response to it? How do their comments compare to the perspectives given in this chapter?

4. Evaluate the responses to the various ethical dilemmas listed in this chapter. What are the strengths and limitations of each? What is your position on each of the issues raised here?

---

[16] Quoted in Stott, *New Issues*, 355.

26

ABORTION

The statistics on abortion are staggering. It has been estimated that in 1987 there were somewhere between 36 million and 53 million abortions. The range is large because it is impossible to be certain of the numbers as many abortions are not reported. In the fifty-four mainly Western countries where abortion is legal, there were between 26 and 31 million legal abortions in 1987. In the ninety-seven countries where abortion is illegal, there were between 10 and 22 million abortions.[1]

In Africa, only Cape Verde, South Africa and Tunisia allow legal abortions. However, it is estimated that in Africa alone more than 4 million women and girls undergo unsafe abortions annually with 34,000 of them dying as a result. In fact, 44 per cent of all the world's deaths from unsafe abortions occur in Africa.[2] It is likely that these deaths contribute to the very high maternal mortality rates in Nigeria, where there are estimated to be 800 deaths per 100,000 live births.[3]

In this chapter, however, we will not be discussing the issues associated with legalizing abortions or with unsafe abortions, but will be concentrating on the greater ethical issue that all abortions destroy the lives of the unborn.

Defining Abortion

The term "abortion" can be used to refer to different things, which present different ethical problems. Doctors, for example, sometimes speak of *spontaneous abortion*. A spontaneous abortion happens when a

---

[1] Statistics from abortionfacts.com. Cited 20 March 2008. www.abortionfacts.com/statistics/world_statistics.asp.

[2] Statistics from "Ensuring Women's Access to Safe Abortion Care in Sub-Saharan Africa". Cited 20 March 2008. Online: www.ipas.org/Publications/asset_upload_file219_2426.pdf.

[3] Ipas in Nigeria. Cited 20 March 2008. Online: www.ipas.org/Publications/asset_upload_file435_3035.pdf.

fertilized egg fails to implant in a woman's womb and passes out of her body in her monthly period. The woman probably did not even know that she was pregnant. It is estimated that between 30 and 50 percent of all fertilized eggs are aborted in this way. The term "spontaneous abortion" is also used by doctors to refer to a miscarriage, when a developing foetus is expelled from the mother's body before the baby is able to live outside the womb.

This chapter will not deal with any of the ethical or theological issues associated with spontaneous abortion. Instead we will be considering the type of abortion that is called an *induced abortion*, that is, a deliberate action intended to terminate a pregnancy and kill a developing foetus by removing it from its mother's womb.[4]

Abortion in Traditional Africa

It is difficult to know much about abortions in traditional African societies because few records are available. However two points can be made. The first is that many of the factors that lead to abortion today were absent. For example, there was no way of knowing whether a foetus was deformed or the "wrong" sex. Moreover, pregnancies outside of marriage were unlikely because most girls and boys were married young – some were engaged to be married while they were still infants. Most girls were married at around the age of eleven.

The second point is that when a man and a woman had illegal sexual intercourse and the woman became pregnant, it was those responsible for the pregnancy who were punished and not the unborn child. For example, if a married woman became pregnant by a man who was not her husband, both the man and woman had to undergo ritual ceremonies to cleanse the community from such a terrible sin. Similarly, those who committed incest were severely punished. The offenders were publicly condemned, and often cursed by the father of the boy or girl and by the elders of the community. They might be banished, killed or made to undergo rigorous ritual cleansing. A sacrifice might have to be made to appease the gods and avert famine, barrenness, pestilence or some other severe judgment on the whole community. If an incestuous pregnancy

---

[4] Definitions derived from John S. Feinberg and Paul Feinberg, *Ethics for a Brave New World* (Wheaton, Ill.: Crossway, 1993). This book contains a very comprehensive theological, ethical and biblical treatment of abortion.

was discovered early enough, the girl might be forced to drink poison to cause an abortion or she might be married off before the pregnancy became public knowledge.

Reasons for Abortions Today

Women have abortions for a variety of reasons. Some have them because medical complications make it likely that they will die if the pregnancy continues. Others have them because tests have shown that the developing foetus is at high risk of having some severe physical or mental handicap. In this chapter, we will not engage in an in-depth discussion of these therapeutic and eugenic reasons for abortions. Instead, we will focus on the ethical issues associated with abortions performed simply for the convenience of the parents or in response to social pressures.

A large number of abortions are performed because women cannot face the social stigma associated with being an unmarried mother. Many African societies strongly disapprove of pregnancy before marriage. Girls who become pregnant may be rejected by their parents and expelled from school, and unmarried women may be fired by their employer. Their desire to get an abortion is even greater if their relationship with the father of the child is unstable and he is not interested in marriage or in the child.

Even if the couple are planning to marry, they may get an abortion – often in response to church policies on marriage. Many mainline churches refuse to marry a woman who is already pregnant. Some even insist that women take a pregnancy test before the wedding. If the test is positive, the woman is disciplined and the wedding postponed. No wonder some consider abortion a better option than bringing shame on themselves and their families!

The situation is even more stressful when the unmarried daughter of a pastor gets pregnant or his son impregnates a girlfriend. The shame is deeply felt because pastor's families are expected to set an example to the community. The children's failure is taken as a disgrace to the pastor and his calling. An abortion may be seen as the easy way out.

Even some married women abort their pregnancies. They may do so because the baby is a girl, and the father refuses to accept another daughter. Others feel that they cannot cope with another child because of their poverty or may fear losing a job if they have to take time off because of the pregnancy. Others may be overwhelmed by the task of caring for the children they already have. Many of these women would prefer to have used contraceptives to avoid falling pregnant, but did not because of ignorance, misinformation or simply a lack of access to modern contraceptives.

Yet another reason for married women choosing to abort their pregnancies is sexual unfaithfulness. If their adultery were discovered, the husband would seek a divorce, and so they may choose to abort rather than have the baby.

Abortions are also commonly used to end pregnancies resulting from incestuous relationships. Many cultures prohibit sexual relations between close relatives such as cousins, uncles and nieces, aunts and nephews. When an incestuous pregnancy occurs, the immediate response is to attempt to erase the shame by having an abortion.

Abortion Procedures

In order to appreciate some of the ethical issues associated with abortion, it is important to have some understanding of how abortions are performed. There are various options, and the decision about which method to use is often determined by how long the woman has been pregnant.

During the first three months of pregnancy, the following abortion techniques may be used.

- Suction: A powerful instrument is inserted into the uterus, where it tears the developing baby and the placenta apart, allowing them to be sucked out into a jar. Some of the parts in the jar may be recognizable as arms, legs, or a head.[5]

- Dilation and curettage (D&C): The woman's cervix is dilated and a sharp instrument is used to scrape the placenta off the wall of the uterus, in the process cutting the baby to pieces.[6]

- RU 486: A pharmaceutical known as RU486 may either be injected or swallowed. Two days later, the woman is given an injection of prostaglandin to induce labour, expelling the foetus from the body.

---

[5] C. Everett Koop. *The Right to Live, The Right to Die* (Wheaton, Ill.: Tyndale House, 1976), 30–31.

[6] Koop, *The Right to Live*, 30.

If the woman has been pregnant for more than three months, doctors will use other methods:

- Saline method. A long needle is used to inject a strong salt solution through the mother's abdomen into the amniotic fluid which surrounds the foetus. The salt poisons the foetus. A prostaglandin injection is then given to force the uterus to expel the dead foetus.[7]

- Dilation and extraction (D&X). The justification usually given for this procedure, which is performed only in late pregnancy, is concern for the health of the mother. It involves "dilating the cervix and removing the fetus. The head of the fetus is crushed or a catheter is inserted and brain matter removed so the head can pass through the cervix. Opponents say this amounts to partially delivering a live fetus and then killing it."[8] Abortion provider Warren Hern describes the procedure as follows:

> I ruptured the membranes and released the fluid to reduce the risk of amniotic fluid embolism. Then I inserted my forceps into the uterus and applied them to the head of the fetus, which was still alive, since fetal injection is not done at that stage of pregnancy. I closed the forceps, crushing the skull of the fetus, and withdrew the forceps. The fetus, now dead, slid out more or less intact.[9]

It is clear that D&X involves the killing of the unborn baby.

One final method of performing an abortion is hysterectomy, which involves the complete removal of the uterus. This operation is usually only done if there is some urgent medical reason, such as a diagnosis of cancer of the cervix. Sometimes the woman is already pregnant at the time this diagnosis is made. This raises some serious ethical questions as to whether the mother should be encouraged to have the baby before having the operation, or whether she should be encouraged to have the cancer removed as soon as possible in order to increase the chances of saving her own life, even if this will result in the death of the foetus. Another ethical issue arises when the pregnancy is so far advanced that

---

[7] Ibid., 31.

[8] "Abortion Ruling Leaves Ill Women in Quandary". Cited 20 March 2008. Online: www.msnbc.msn.com/id/18204277/.

[9] Warren M. Herm *Did I Violate the Partial-Birth Abortion Ban?* Slate Magazine. Cited 20 March 2008. Online: www.slate.com/id/2090215/.

the baby might be old enough to survive outside the womb but those performing the hysterectomy kill it or allow it to die through neglect.

All the abortion procedures described so far are done by trained medical personnel. But this is not the way that most abortions are carried out in Africa. Instead, women may go to midwives or nurses working illegally outside medical settings. Or they may go to pharmacists who do not warn them of the dangers associated with the abortion pills they provide or tell the women that they should be under medical supervision when taking them. Many women go to traditional medicine men and women and herbalists; others try to induce an abortion by themselves. A sharp object may be poked into the cervix or irritants like ginger, hot pepper, a form of clay called "local chalk" in Nigeria or alum may be inserted into the woman's private parts.

Such abortions are very unsafe. An untrained abortionist can easily perforate or damage a woman's uterus. Such injuries can result in infections, health problems, lifelong disabilities, an inability to conceive, and even death. Here is the pathetic story of young Nigerian girl: "I am a graduate and a banker, but I'm afraid of getting married because I know that medically, I cannot bear children. I lost my womb at 15. I had an unsafe abortion which almost took my life but for God's intervention I survived." Chinyere Amalu, who recorded her story, adds that "this singular act several years ago is today her source of misery and agony. But while she is alive to tell her story of pain, many others are not."[10]

But it is not only those who undergo illegal abortions who run risks. There are also risks associated with legal abortions.

> Under whatever conditions, an abortion is always a potentially dangerous undertaking that can, and not infrequently does, have damaging physical and emotional consequences. … Adverse results of abortions include hepatitis, sterility, tubal pregnancies at a later time, premature births or subsequent spontaneous abortions, and abdominal malaise that can include such things as adherent placental material. These possibilities are present whether the abortion is for the sake of personal convenience or to save a mother's life.[11]

---

[10] Chinyere Amalu, "Whither Women's Health Between Unsafe Abortion and the Law." *Vanguard*, Tuesday, 10 April 2007, p. 50.

[11] R. K Harrison, "Abortion" in *Encyclopedia of Biblical and Christian Ethics*, 2.

Ethical Issues Relating to Abortion

A number of very important ethical issues come up in any discussion of abortion. We will look at some of them here in general terms before proceeding to look at what the Bible has to say about abortion.

The issue of personhood

The way we answer the question "when does human life begin?" affects all our views on abortion. If the unborn child is seen as merely a lump of unwanted tissue (that is, not yet human) or as not yet fully human, then abortion is no great matter. If, on the other hand, the unborn are fully human, abortion becomes a very serious matter indeed.

Those who say that the unborn child is merely a lump of tissue might want to reflect on what medical science has to tell us about the development of the child in the womb.

- 18 days after conception: the baby's heart is beating.
- 2½ months: the baby can squint, move its tongue, and is sensitive to touch.
- 3 months: the baby can suck its thumb and recoil from pain.
- 6 months: the baby can respond to light and sound, and may survive out the womb.
- 7 months: The baby's nervous system becomes more complex.
- 8–9 months: the baby is basically fully developed.

The unborn child is clearly far more than merely a piece of tissue.

There are those who agree with this point, but still insist that the unborn child is less than fully human. In contrast to those who argue that the child is a person from the moment when the male sperm fertilizes the female egg, others argue that it only become a person when the egg is implanted in the mother's womb. (This position obviously has implications for evaluating the way certain contraceptives work – see chapter 15.) Still others argue that the developing foetus only becomes a person when brainwaves can be detected, or when it reaches the point where its human form is clearly recognizable, or when it is capable of surviving outside the womb.

In some societies, it is even held that a baby does not become a person until it is a year old! A similar argument is presented in a more modern form by those who argue in favour of a social, psychological or developmental view of personhood. They say that it is not mere possession of life that makes someone human, but possession of significant life. The issue here is quality of life. To be human, someone must be conscious of both external and internal events, capable of self-motivated activity, have the ability to communicate about contents and topics, and have a self-concept and self-awareness. To those who accept this argument, no foetus can qualify as a person. It is merely a potential person, and its rights are subordinate to the rights of any actual person. The problem with this argument is that the criterion for judging personhood is relativistic and subjective, open to different interpretations. The innocent, weak and defenceless can easily be dismissed as failing to meet the requirements for personhood. Such a view has terrible consequences: deformed babies and the elderly can be put to death without any fear of being charged with murder.

The issue of women's rights

Many in the West would argue that the mother has the right to do as she pleases with her body. If she wants to remove a foetus that is growing in her womb, no one should be able to prohibit her from doing so. This argument is rooted in the Western belief that individual rights trump community rights. Such individualistic thinking is alien to African traditional society. However, Africans are increasingly buying into this mindset where a person does whatever he or she pleases. A girl who gets pregnant now makes her own decision to abort the baby if she does not want it.

The fundamental flaw in this argument is that it fails to acknowledge that the baby does not actually belong to its mother or its father but to its maker: "the unborn child belongs (in the most ultimate sense) not to his parents, not to human society in general, nor to government, but to God."[12]

---

[12] John M. Frame, *Medical Ethics: Principles, Persons and Problems* (Phillipsburg, N.J.: Presbyterian and Reformed, 1988), 89.

The issue of unwanted children

Some argue that it is better for a mother to abort an unwanted pregnancy than to bring an unwanted child into the world. They insist that all unwanted children will endure great suffering because they will not be loved and care for. This would certainly not have been the case in traditional African societies, where no child was dismissed as a "bastard" or neglected, for children were seen as belonging to all. Children were not solely the responsibility of their biological mothers and fathers but belonged to all in the community. If a child's parents could not care for it for some reason, uncles, aunts, grandfathers, grandmothers, cousins, brothers and sisters and stepsisters would take over.

Today, however, community ethics are being eroded, and babies are sometimes being rejected and left to die. Unwanted children now roam the major cities in Africa, begging for money or food. Their situation is often a result of their parents' refusal to accept the responsibility that goes with sexual relationships:

> Since a premarital and extramarital relationship is sought mostly for pleasure and relaxation of tension, as satisfaction of libido, those indulging in it are generally little inclined to make the corresponding sacrifices and accept the responsibility that goes with it. To this extent there is here a denial of one of the essential purposes of sexuality, namely, a personal relationship designed to be permanent and the willingness to accept the office of parent.[13]

The issue of poverty

It is possible that the strongest motivation for abortions in Africa is poverty. It is not that a child is unwanted but that parents who are enduring unemployment and desperate suffering see no way of providing for it. They choose abortion over bringing a child into a home where it will be undernourished, undereducated and doomed to a life of grinding poverty.

---

[13] Helmut Thielicke, *Ethics of Sex* (New York: Harper & Row, 1964), 201. He goes on to conclude that "sexuality loses its essential nature when it is practised outside of marriage with no respect for the personhood of the other partner and refuses to accept parenthood".

Biblical Perspectives on Abortion

As Christians, biblical considerations are critical for our discussion of abortion. Yet there is no explicit teaching on abortion in the Bible. So we have to build our case by looking at what the Bible has to say about related matters. For example, it does say that miscarriages (the death of unborn children) can be part of God's curse on those who disobey him (Hos 9:14) and that those obey him will be blessed with live births (Exod 23:26).

Those who oppose abortion argue that the commandment "You shall not murder" (Exod 20:13) prohibits the taking of human life. But quoting this command does not address the issue of whether the unborn child is fully human, with the same rights and privileges as any other human being. This issue is, however, addressed indirectly in some other places. For example:

> If men who are fighting hit a pregnant woman and she gives birth prematurely but there is no serious injury, the offender must be fined whatever the woman's husband demands and the court allows. But if there is serious injury, you are to take life for life, eye for eye, tooth for tooth, hand for hand, foot for foot, burn for burn, wound for wound, bruise for bruise (Exod 21:22–25).

This passage does not deal specifically with abortion but rather with a premature birth that is brought on by an accidental injury. Abortions are not accidental; they are deliberate acts intended to destroy the unborn baby. Yet oddly enough this passage is sometimes quoted by those who support abortion because they claim it supports their point that an unborn child is less than fully human. The law laid down the death penalty for those who killed another person, as is clear from the reference to "life for life" in the above quotation. Thus if the injured woman dies, the offender must die too. However, the injury is regarded as not "serious" if it is only the baby that dies because the woman miscarries. The offender only has to pay a fine. In terms of this interpretation, the life of an unborn child is worth far less than the life of a person, and the child must thus be less than fully a person.

Those who use this interpretation to support abortion tend to overlook certain flaws in their own argument. The law does not treat the unborn child as worthless. Any injury to it still results in punishment, even if the punishment is reduced, just as the punishment was reduced in cases of unintentional murder (Deut 19:1–13; Num 35:10–34). The mere fact that some punishment is required indicates that what was done was wrong, and that society recognizes that someone was injured.

This argument also fails to notice that the law does not treat the unborn child as merely a part of the mother's own body for her to deal with as she likes. There are two people involved (the mother and the child) and different penalties apply depending on which of them is harmed. Each of the two people involved is unique and important.

Finally, those who interpret the reduced punishment as implying that the unborn child is less than fully human conveniently ignore the law that appears a mere two verses earlier: "If a man beats his male or female slave with a rod and the slave dies as a direct result, he must be punished" (Exod 21:20). This punishment does not appear to be the death penalty – so can we argue that slaves are less than fully human?

So much for the inconsistencies in the argument of those who argue that this verse supports abortion. But there is an even stronger argument against their position: they are misinterpreting the verse. It does not speak about a miscarriage, but about a premature birth that produces a live infant, who may develop severe problems because it was born too early. The literal translation of the original Hebrew is "so that her fruit depart" (KJV). The word translated "fruit" is the same word used elsewhere in the Old Testament to describe a child up to twelve years of age. In Genesis 44:20 it is used of Benjamin and in Exodus 2:6 it is used of Moses. Different words are used to describe a miscarriage (Job 3:6; Pss 58:8; 139:16; Eccl 6:3).

This argument is even stronger if we look at the Hebrew verb that is translated as "gives birth".

> The linguistic evidence of the text itself does not support the "miscarriage" translation, however. The verb *yatza* when used alone, as it is here, refers to a live birth, not a miscarriage (Gen 25:25–26; 38:28–30; Jer 1:5; 20:18). *Yatza* is used of a stillbirth only when accompanied by some form of *muth* "to die," as in Numbers 12:12, and Job 3:11 … There is a specific Hebrew word for "miscarriage", *shakol* (Exod 23:26; Hos 9:14) and this word is not used in Exodus 21:22–25.

Consequently, the better translation of the passages takes it to refer to a premature live birth, not a miscarriage.[14]

The law of retaliation, "eye for eye, tooth for tooth, hand for hand, foot for foot, burn for burn, wound for wound, bruise for bruise" thus applies to both the mother and the child.[15] If either the mother or the newborn child suffers some serious injury, the offender will receive an equivalent punishment.

Psalm 139:13–16 gives us another glimpse of the personhood and worth of the unborn child:

> For you created my inmost being; you knit me together in my mother's womb. I praise you because I am fearfully and wonderfully made; your works are wonderful, I know that full well. My frame was not hidden from you when I was made in the secret place. When I was woven together in the depths of the earth, your eyes saw my unformed body. All the days ordained for me were written in your book before one of them came to be.

The "unformed body" to which the psalmist refers is the embryo or foetus. God created and supervised the psalmist in his unborn state (in fact, even before he was conceived – Jer 1:5; Luke 2:21). There can thus be no doubt that an unborn child is fully human: "From the point of conception, he has a full complement of human chromosomes and is in that respect different from every subhuman embryo or foetus. From the very beginning, he is a human child, and his humanity is verifiable in every cell of his body."[16] He is also already a moral being, in that even in "his embryological state in the closed up chamber of the womb, the moral law was inscribed within his being."[17] He already has a soul that is affected by the sin which taints all human beings. Thus the psalmist can say, "Surely I was sinful at birth, sinful from the time my mother conceived me" (Ps 51:5).

---

[14] John Jefferson Davis, *Evangelical Ethics: Issues Facing the Church Today* (Phillipsburg, N.J.: Presbyterian and Reformed, 1985), 151.

[15] Jack W. Cottrell, "Abortion and the Mosaic Law," *Christianity Today*, 17 (March 16, 1973): 6–9.

[16] Frame, *Medical Ethics*, 90.

[17] E. R. Dalglish *Psalm Fifty-One in the Light of Near Eastern Patternism* (Leiden: Brill, 1962), 124.

As someone who has been created by God, the child deserves our respect. To destroy a foetus is tantamount to destroying a human being, as well as all that he or she would have accomplished. This point is driven home by God's words to Jeremiah, "Before I formed you in the womb I knew you, and before you were born I consecrated you; I have appointed you a prophet to the nations" (Jer 1:5). Paul makes the same point when he speaks of God "who set me apart from birth and called me by his grace (Gal 1:15). These great men recognized that God saw them as fully human even in their unborn state (see also Isa 49:1, 5).

This truth does not only apply to great leaders. Job recognized that God makes everyone, both employers and employees, and stated, "If I have denied justice to my menservants and maidservants when they had a grievance against me, what will I do when God confronts me? … Did not he who made me in the womb make them? Did not the same one form us both within our mothers? (Job 31:13–15; see also Isa 44:24).

The unborn must also not be thought of as merely potentially human but currently emotionless, passive and inactive. Any mother of twins will recognise the description of Rebekah's experience in Genesis 25:21–25, as her twin sons "jostled each other within her". The Lord already knew the destiny of these twins: "two nations are in your womb, and two peoples from within you will be separated; one people will be stronger than the other, and the older will serve the younger." Similarly, in the New Testament, Elizabeth tells Mary: "As soon as the sound of your greeting reached my ears, the baby in my womb leaped for joy" (Luke 1:44). Even an unborn baby can express emotions.

A Christian Response to Abortion

The unborn are God's creation and he is shaping their lives. We should not, therefore, take it upon ourselves to end their lives. Instead, we should encourage those who are seeking abortions to consider others options such as adoption. We should also provide physical and financial help to those who are being driven to abortion by economic need. This help should not only be given when the baby is born, but also as the child grows.

We also need to recognise that a woman seeking an abortion will have to smother her conscience in order to kill her unborn child and will never be able to erase what she has done from her memory. There are many testimonies of women who regret having killed their babies (just as there are many testimonies of women who rejoice that they decided to keep their babies). Nor will it be easy for a woman to admit to having had an abortion. Most Africans believe that the only reason a woman would have an abortion is to cover up shameful behaviour, and so women who are known to have had abortions are stigmatized. Some infertile women are even accused of having had abortions because it is believed that those who have abortions may find it difficult to bear children again.

There are, however, exceptional cases in which we need to think carefully about the advice we give. What should we advise a mother whose pregnancy is endangering her life? Should we risk leaving her young children orphans rather than allowing her to have an abortion? Here again we are in the area of competing moral values. If no other medical option is available, we should not ask the mother to sacrifice her life for her unborn child. But any decision to abort must be made with a real concern for and grief at the loss of life resulting from what Tertullian called "a necessary cruelty".

How should we advise parents whose child is going to be born with some severe deformity? Should they be encouraged to keep the pregnancy, no matter how deeply and painfully disabled their child may be? Once again, we need to turn to medical advisors and counsellors to help us understand the extent of the disability, what if anything can be done about it, and what can be done to support the child and the parents. Certainly, abortion should be the very last option considered, and should only be thought of in the case of the most extreme deformities that are incompatible with life.

A question that is often raised is what should be done about babies conceived by rape or incest. The mothers of these babies have endured great trauma. We should not simply refuse to listen to them if they beg for an abortion. Before making any decision, we should provide counselling. The counsellor should point out that some children born of rape and incest have grown to become powerful witnesses for the Lord. If the woman feels unable to care for a child whose very existence brings back terrible memories, the counsellor may suggest the possibility of her bearing the child and allowing it to be adopted. Increasingly, childless couples are adopting unwanted babies in order to give them a home. Innocent human beings should not be punished for the sins of their fathers and mothers.

Questions

1. How prevalent is abortion in your area? What are you doing to serve women who are considering abortions or who have already had abortions?

2. What difficulties do you face as you try to prevent abortions or help women who have had abortions?

3. What responsibility should men take for the abortion crisis?

4. What strategic ministry decisions must you make related to abortion? For instance, how will you preach on the issue? How will you lead others to care for unwanted babies and the mothers you persuade not to have abortions?

5. Summarize the biblical perspective on abortion. How should this shape your ministry decisions?

6. Investigate the work done by crisis pregnancy centres such as Africa Cares for Life (www.africacaresforlife.org.za/uganda.htm) and Care Confidential (www.careconfidential.com). Could you use any of their ideas in ministering to women with unwanted pregnancies in your area?

27

EUTHANASIA AND INFANTICIDE

The word "euthanasia" comes from two Greek words, one of which means "good" or "well" and the other of which means "death". Thus discussion of euthanasia is literally discussion of how to have a good death and avoid uselessly prolonging the dying process.

Modern medical technologies and techniques have enabled people to live longer and better lives, and can effect almost miraculous cures, but they have also complicated the process of dying. Infants that would once have died soon after birth can now be kept alive. Those who are suffering from ravaging diseases and are in terminal, painful or humiliating conditions can be kept alive for many months or even years. For example, Chantal Sebire, a woman who had a exceedingly painful facial tumour that had eaten away her face and robbed her of the senses of sight, taste and smell, appealed to a French court to be allowed to end her suffering with doctor-assisted suicide. Her appeal was denied, but her death by suicide in March 2008 reignited debate about the ethics of euthanasia or mercy killing.[1]

Euthanasia raises a number of ethical questions, some of which are similar to those relating to abortion. The supreme question is whether euthanasia is ever morally justifiable or whether life should always be preserved in all circumstances. This question has to be answered not only by medical professionals but also by patients, their relatives and even by the entire community.

---

[1] BBC. "Tumour woman's death not natural". Cited 23 May 2008. news.bbc.co.uk/1/hi/world/europe/7308746.stm.

Defining Death and Euthanasia

At one time there would have been no problem in knowing when someone was dead: it was when their heart stopped beating and they stopped breathing. But things are no longer this simple, especially in the West. Patients can be hooked up to artificial respirators which pump air into their lungs to keep them breathing. Those whose kidneys have failed can be kept alive by dialysis. Cardiopulmonary resuscitation (CPR) techniques can restore heartbeat and maintain blood flow after the heart has stopped. Unconscious patients who would once have died can now be kept alive for a long time.

The fact that a body can now be kept functioning by machines has complicated the definition of death. It is no longer enough to say that death occurs when someone's heart and lungs fail. Now death is defined by doctors as "1) Irreversible cessation of circulatory and respiratory functions 2) irreversible cessation of all functions of the entire brain, including the brain stem".[2] Some are pushing to have death defined as the absence of brain activity in the region of the brain known as the neocortex, that is, the area responsible for sensory perception, spatial reasoning, conscious thought and language.

There is no need to go into any long discussion of these various definitions of death because our concern is not so much with the technicalities involved as with some very practical decisions that reflect our values and beliefs relating to death. For example, who makes the decision about when to end life? Should it be the one suffering, in which case we have *voluntary euthanasia*, or should the decision be made by those caring for the sufferer, in which case we have *involuntary euthanasia*. A famous case of involuntary euthanasia was when Terry Schiavo's husband decided to withdraw her feeding tubes after she had been in a vegetative state for fifteen years.

Withdrawing the tubes was an action that can also be described as *active euthanasia*, in which someone deliberately performs an action that causes the person's death. Other examples of active euthanasia would be giving someone an overdose of medication or smothering or shooting them. *Passive euthanasia*, on the other hand, simply requires

---

[2] *Report of the President's Commission for the Study of Ethical Problems in Medicine and Biomedical and Behavioral Research*, 1981, p.2. Cited 28 March 2008. Online: www.bioethics.gov/reports/past_commissions/defining_death.pdf.

that someone does nothing (that is, does not give medical treatment) allowing the patient to die naturally.

Finally, we can also distinguish between *direct euthanasia* and *indirect euthanasia*. In direct euthanasia the person who wants to die takes the action that will cause his or her death, such as deliberately swallowing an overdose of medication or pulling out a breathing tube. In indirect euthanasia somebody else carries out the act, as when a caregiver injects a patient with a lethal dose of morphine.

Euthanasia in Traditional Africa

Today euthanasia is often discussed in the context of hospitals and high-tech medical treatment, but that does not mean that it was not practised in traditional Africa. The whole issue of death in Africa is a complex one. In traditional societies, death involves more than just the separation of life from a physical body. It also involves profound religious, philosophical, social and cultural issues. The causes of death and the whole question of how to handle one's own death and that of others was (and is) associated with superstition, tradition and religious convictions. We cannot deal with this in any depth in this book, but some of these issues are touched on in the chapter on witchcraft.

There is a long tradition of voluntary passive euthanasia in Africa. For example, the very elderly among the Bajju of Nigeria may tell their children and grandchildren that they cannot bear the thought of foreign hands touching them on their last days on earth. Thus they refuse to be taken to hospital when they become sick. For them, the good death is to die at home in the care of their children. Their wishes are respected.

There has also always been involuntary, active euthanasia, which often took the form of infanticide, the killing of babies. Deformed babies were regarded as evil spirits that had taken human form to torment the community. Such babies were abandoned on river banks to be washed away and drowned or in the forest to be eaten by wild animals. Twins were also regarded as evil spirits in Benin, Nigeria, and were routinely killed – a practise horrified the famous Mary Slessor, who worked hard to end it. This type of treatment of disabled infants still continues: not long ago a baby with Down's syndrome was abandoned on a train in Nigeria. Some healthy babies are also abandoned by mothers who do not want them and leave them to die. These practices are not unique to Africa, for infanticide has been practised in many cultures around the world. For example, the Greco-Roman world permitted the exposure of unwanted female infants and weak and deformed male infants.

Traditional societies also resorted to active euthanasia to end the suffering of elderly people who were very sick and had no hope of healing. They might be drowned, abandoned or poisoned.

The methods used to end life may have changed, but the reasons for ending the life of the sick, deformed, weak and unwanted have not changed much since traditional times.

Arguments in Favour of Euthanasia

The arguments in support euthanasia are in many respects similar to those offered in favour of abortion, and face many of the same objections.

Quality of life

The situation ethicist Joseph Fletcher argues that it is wrong to speak of the sanctity of life (meaning that life is a gift from God that should be respected, honoured and protected) and says that we should instead focus on the quality of life (meaning the value of life to a patient and the community). He insists that it is a fallacy to maintain that all life is valuable and to be maintained no matter what the cost. Grossly deformed infants, comatose adults and those who have been severely maimed by accidents or disease may still be clinically alive, but neither they nor their families experience any joy, value or meaning in their lives. It is pointless to continue to spend money and resources to maintain a life that would be better terminated.

The issue of personhood

The question of what makes someone a person was discussed in the previous chapter on abortion. The same question is critical to our view of euthanasia. If we define personhood in terms of quality of life, achievements and economic contribution to society, it is easy to dismiss a deformed baby, comatose patient, severely mentally retarded person, or an aged man as less than fully human and pull the plug. If, however, personhood has a larger definition and such people are seen as fully human, the decision to pull the plug is far more difficult.

Freedom of choice

It is argued that people ought to be able to choose what kind of death they die. Though such an argument may seem to spring from Western individualism, it is also found in traditional African societies. As mentioned earlier, the very elderly may insist on dying at home surrounded by their families.

Economics

While provision of basic medical care (common drugs, food and fluids) is important, there comes a time when the cost of treatment becomes prohibitive. Should a family be expected to bankrupt themselves to send an elderly parent overseas for surgery though he or she may live for only a few more months or years? If the family does not pay for this treatment, are they guilty of passive euthanasia?

Complicating this debate is the rapid change in what counts as extraordinarily advanced or expensive treatment. What was extraordinary fifty years is now ordinary. Kidney transplants were extraordinary thirty years ago, but are now far more common and can give the recipient many more years of life. Nevertheless, they are still very expensive and beyond the reach of most people in Africa.

The Bible and Euthanasia

The Bible does not address the question of euthanasia directly. Nevertheless, it understands the desire for death. Job expressed it well in his lament: "Why is light given to those in misery, and life to the bitter of soul, to those who long for death that does not come" (Job 3:20–21).

Some incidents recorded in the Bible might be taken as examples of euthanasia in that individuals requested someone to kill them. For both Abimelech (Judg 9:54) and Saul (1 Sam 31:4) death was immanent and neither wanted to die in disgrace and humiliation. Others ended their own lives (Samson – Judg 16:29–30; Saul's armour bearer – 1 Sam 31:5; Ahithophel – 2 Sam 17:23; Zimri – 1 Kgs 16:18). Most commentators identify all these cases as suicides rather than as examples of mercy killing as it is understood in contemporary debate. They were "desperate acts by deeply troubled individuals who went against the will of God."³ The Bible regards such suicide as self-murder, a contradiction of the commandment "you shall not murder" (Exod 20:13).

The Bible also understands the desire of family members, patients and even health care professionals to end someone's suffering. Psalm 31:6 is not talking about killing someone when it states "Give beer to those who are perishing, wine to those who are in anguish", but it does reflect a clear desire to relieve suffering. Even the Romans allowed criminals about to be crucified a special drug to reduce their suffering. It was for this reason that Jesus was given a cup of wine mixed with myrrh, which he initially refused (Mark 15:23). Later, however, just before his death, he accepted a drink of vinegar (Mark 15:36).

A Christian Response to Euthanasia

When the Bible does not give specific guidance on an issue, the Christian must be guided by fundamental biblical principles. The first is that every human being, regardless of his or her external conditions, sickness, poverty or deformity, is created in the image of God (Gen 2:24). No one can be dismissed as worthless.

The second principle is that all life is God's gift. He is the one who decides when to give it and when to take it away, as Job reminds us when he hears of the death of his children: "The Lord gave and the Lord has taken away" (Job 1:21). It is arrogant for us to presume to decide when a life should end. Not only is it arrogant, it is also explicitly forbidden. Economic, social, physical or mental reasons cannot be accepted as good grounds for ending someone's life. Such killing is equivalent to murder, which is condemned in Scripture (Exod 20:13). Millard Erickson summarizes the parallel between euthanasia and murder: It is 1) intentional, 2) premeditated, 3) malicious, 4) contrary to the desire or intention of the victim, and 5) against someone who has done nothing deserving of capital punishment.[4]

We are using the wrong yardstick if we think that the value of a human life must be judged only in terms of its usefulness, happiness or productivity. Life is not important because of what it produces but

³ Robert D. Bergen. *1, 2 Samuel* (New American Commentary; Nashville: Broadman & Holman, 1996), 282.

⁴ Millard J. Erickson and Ines E. Bowers, "Euthanasia and Christian Ethics". *Journal of the Evangelical Theological Society* 19 (Winter 1976): 16–19.

because it *exists*. Moreover there is value in suffering and we should not simply try to run away from it. Suffering is to be expected as a consequence of the fall. It will only end when we reach heaven (Rev 21:4). Through suffering, God teaches us many valuable lessons about himself, the world and ourselves. There is much we can learn about loving and caring for one other as well as about dependence on and trust in God (Jas 1:2–4; 1 Pet 1:6–7). The great Apostle Paul himself, when he had some physical ailment, learnt from the Lord's encouragement, "My grace is all you need, for my power is greatest when you are weak" (2 Cor 12:9, GNB).

Although we oppose euthanasia, it is also important to realize that there comes a time when we must accept the inevitability of death (Heb 9:27). Technology can never totally eliminate death and suffering. When we have done the best we can to help someone, it is not wrong to allow nature to take its course. We are not required to go to extraordinary lengths to prevent death or prolong suffering.

> Life has an end called death. Death is not something we eagerly seek, but it is not something to be avoided at all costs. God has appointed the limits of our life and we must accept them … Part of the recognition of such limits is to allow persons to die when the time has come and not require that they be endlessly attached to tubes and machines.[5]

What we can also do is work to relieve suffering, so that people have no need to plead for death. This is the goal of the hospice movement, which originated among Christians and is a striking example of a response that goes beyond merely condemning an evil and seeks to provide a moral alternative. Hospices provide comfort and pain relief to those enduring great pain. Such care, which can be provided in a hospice building or in a patient's home, greatly reduces the temptation to resort to euthanasia and enables people to die with dignity and with the minimum of pain. We should thus support and encourage organizations such as Hospice Africa, which works with those suffering from cancer and AIDS.[6]

Finally, it is vitally important that we remember that the biblical perspective on death includes resurrection and transformation. According

---

[5] Mark W. Foreman, *Christianity and Bioethics: Confronting Clinical Issues* (Joplin, Miss.: College Press, 1999), 140.

[6] More information about Hospice Africa can be found at http://hospiceafrica.org.

to the Bible, death is an unnatural intrusion into God's good universe. Its presence is a direct consequence of human sin (Gen 2:17; 1 Cor 15:56). But for the Christian, death is not the end. It is merely the last enemy, an enemy that will finally be overcome in the resurrection when Christ returns (1 Cor 15:26–56).

Questions

1. Does your culture have any traditions involving euthanasia and infanticide?

2. What aspects of this traditional understanding of death are challenged by biblical teaching?

3. Are new ideas and technologies affecting the way you and those you serve see euthanasia?

28
STRIKES AND MEDICAL SERVICES

In chapter 9 we discussed the ethical issues raised by strikes in general. Now it is time to look at one particular case: should people in the medical profession, particularly doctors and nurses, go on strike to address problems in their remuneration and conditions of service? Many of the principles set out in this chapter will also apply to those in other emergency professions such as the police and fire service.

Medical Ethics

More than two millennia ago, the Greek physician Hippocrates of Cos (about 460–377 BC) laid the basis for medical ethics. He developed what is today known as the Hippocratic oath. The oath reads in part:

> I swear by Apollo the physician, and Asclepius, and Hygieia and Panacea and all the gods and goddesses as my witnesses, that, according to my ability and judgement, I will keep this Oath and this contract: …

> I will use those dietary regimens which will benefit my patients according to my greatest ability and judgement, and I will do no harm or injustice to them.

> I will not give a lethal drug to anyone if I am asked, nor will I advise such a plan; and similarly I will not give a woman a pessary to cause an abortion.

> In purity and according to divine law will I carry out my life
> and my art.[1]

This oath was adopted by both Christians and Muslims as a guideline for the ethical practice of medicine. It, or some modern variant, is still widely used in Africa and in many countries around the world as a guide for fresh medical graduates.

Although this historic oath has a pagan origin, Christians can identify with its emphasis that a healer is ultimately accountable to the gods, or in our case, to the God of the Bible. As Christians, our idea of right and wrong must be linked to our belief in God. He must be the one who shapes our concept of what is ethical when it comes to medical practice.

Ethics of Remuneration

The question of what medical doctors should be paid for their services, or even whether they should be paid at all, is an ancient and controversial one. Hippocrates, who was a wealthy man, said that since physicians saved people from death, no fee would ever be enough to repay the debt. Whatever the physician received from a grateful patient should thus be regarded as a gift, not a payment. However, he recognized that some physicians might need payment in order to survive, and so he added that if payment was required, the physician should be considerate "kind-hearted and willing to accommodate his fee to the patient's circumstance".[2]

Hippocrates' contemporaries debated the same issue, speaking of it in terms of whether medicine was a trade or a profession. "Aristophanes contended that medicine was an art, but Sophocles asserted that the physician was merely a hired hand, a tradesman." Socrates took a middle road, noting that the issue of money was important: "Unless pay is added to the art ... there would be no benefit for the craftsman, and

---

[1] Translated by Michael North, National Library of Medicine, 2002. Cited 4 April 2008. Online: www.nlm.nih.gov/hmd/greek/greek_oath.html.

[2] David Schiedermayer, *Wages Through The Ages: The Ethics of Physician Income*. Cited 4 April 2008. Online: www.llu.edu/llu/bioethics/prov2_93.html. He also deals with this topic in "The Profession at the Fault Line: The Ethics of Physician Income," in *Bioethics and the Future of Medicine: A Christian Appraisal* (ed. John Kilner, Nigel M. de S. Cameron and David L. Schiedermayer; Carlisle: Paternoster, 1995).

consequently he would be unwilling to go to the trouble of taking care of the trouble of others."[3]

The crux of the matter is how physicians can reconcile their understanding of themselves as healers with their need to earn a living. What should medical workers do if what they receive is insufficient to meet their basic needs? Are they entitled to go on strike for better pay, even if their action harms their patients?

Medical personnel who are tempted to go on strike should reflect on the words of Galen, a second-century physician: "It is not possible to pursue the true goal of medicine if one holds wealth more important than virtue, and learns the technique not to help people, but for material gain."[4] What this boils down to is the issue of priorities: What is primary and what is secondary in medical practice? A careful reading of the Hippocratic oath reveals that medical workers are called first of all to serve God and then humanity – specifically the sick. The goal must be to alleviate human suffering. Remuneration and personal interests must be secondary concerns. Medical workers who join a general strike have abandoned their primary duty in pursuit of secondary matters. They are thus distorting their whole calling.

The Bible and Medical Strikes

The ethical principles we have cited so far have all been based on the Hippocratic oath. But what does the Bible have to say about these issues? As Christians, this must be our ultimate guide to the values that should govern our actions.

There is no specific discussion of strikes in the Bible, and no mention of healers going on strike, but what we do have is the loving example set by Jesus. He is our Lord, the one to whom we are ultimately responsible and the one whose example we must follow. He healed many who came to him and could easily have become a rich man if he had chosen to charge them for his services. But he did not. His goal was to serve, not to increase his own wealth.

The parable of the Good Samaritan also demonstrates how Christian medical workers should behave during a strike. What the Samaritan did went against all the cultural norms and requirements of his society. He

---

[3] Ibid.
[4] Ibid.

went out of his way to do what was right. He not only loved God, but he loved and cared for his neighbour. He provided him with basic medical care and referred him to a doctor (Luke 10:25–37).

The Christian Response

In life-threatening situations Christian doctors and nurses cannot fold their arms, say they are on strike, and watch a patient die. Such an action is antithetical to the Hippocratic oath, unethical and unbiblical. It is a denial of their calling to heal.

This insistence on continuing to serve patients may attract persecution. At such times medical workers need to remember that Jesus, too, was persecuted. Those who want to foster truly Christian personal and biomedical ethics must choose to obey God, regardless of the cost. They must also constantly scrutinize their motives, goals and behaviour to see whether they are obeying God or merely saying that they obey him while still pursuing their own interests.

The goal of all Christians must be to finish our lives with a clear conscience, so that we can stand before God and hear him say, "Well done, good and faithful servant!" (Matt 25:21). It is worrisome that many of us have become unfaithful servants. We have prostituted ourselves to the gods of the land and have chosen to survive or to succeed rather than to obey God. Hence, our lives and our ethics, like those of our non-Christian colleagues, are founded on selfish and temporal values rather than on God and his eternal truths.

Rather than going on strike, or adopting a laissez faire approach that says it does not matter how poorly our medical colleagues are treated, we need to speak out and present the cause of justice in forceful and persuasive arguments that neither bend the truth nor bend to injustice.

Conclusion

One of the problems industrial action raises for medical staff is the failure to treat patients during strikes. Failure to treat a sick person for the sole purpose of improving one's own welfare is selfish and against the Hippocratic oath with its promise to do "no harm or injustice" to patients. We need to remember the question the Bible asks, "What good will it be for a man if he gain the whole world, yet forfeits his soul?"

(Matt 16:26). A general strike may enable one to gain a good salary and an improved lifestyle (material benefits), but one may lose one's professional soul in the process.

Questions

1. Answer the following questions about a medical strike that you may have experienced or witnessed:

   a) What were the underlying reasons?

   b) How was it conducted?

   c) What was accomplished?

   d) What were the costs or damage attributed to it?

   e) What goals were left unaccomplished?

2. Ask several members of the medical profession, both Christian and non-Christian, to give you their opinions about strikes and remuneration in their field. Compare their opinions with the contents of this chapter.

3. What practical suggestions might you give to someone in the medical profession to help them be more biblical in their approach to strikes?

29
DRUG AND ALCOHOL ABUSE

Addiction can take many forms. Some people are addicted to drugs, and others to tobacco, caffeine, food, gambling, shopping, sex or the Internet. In this chapter, however, we shall focus only on addiction to the two drugs most commonly used in Africa: marijuana and alcohol. Many people abuse these drugs and end up becoming addicted to them, with devastating consequences for themselves and others. This problem is not only found among non-Christians but also within the walls of the church.

However, this issue is too broad to discuss comprehensively in one chapter. I will not be able to deal with the question of whether certain drugs should be legalized, nor with the use of alcohol in Holy Communion or at ceremonies such as weddings. Instead, I will focus on the ethical issues raised by the recreational use of alcohol and drugs that often results in abuse and dependency.

Drugs and Alcohol in Africa

Almost all traditional communities worldwide have produced and consumed drugs and alcohol. Africa is no exception. The most common drug was tobacco, which was produced in small quantities to be used and sold to others. It was smoked or chewed mainly by the elderly.

Alcoholic drinks were common in every community and were brewed from cereal crops, herbs, roots, leaves, and even the sap of palm trees. However, the consumption of alcohol was subject to strict community control. The elderly were free to take alcohol whenever they pleased, but younger people were not. Young boys and middle-aged men were prohibited from taking it in the mornings as they were supposed to be farming. The rules were relaxed slightly during the dry season, when there was less to do on the farm. Warriors were also prohibited from taking alcohol, and girls and pregnant women were prohibited from getting drunk.

In general, young people were only permitted to taste alcohol on important occasions such as the naming ceremonies for babies, weddings, funerals and annual rituals like harvest celebrations. In some of these rituals, the consumption of alcohol was and still is considered mandatory. For example, among the Agikuyu of Kenya, the bride's father must take a sip of alcohol to signify that he has accepted the suitor's proposal and has blessed the union between the couple. This ceremony precedes the church wedding. It would also have been unthinkable to plan a traditional wedding without alcohol. The reason for drinking at such ceremonies was not to get drunk but to share in a social celebration. Some people drink only on such occasions and are referred to as social drinkers.

In contemporary Africa, the situation has changed radically. Many new drugs and new alcoholic drinks have been introduced, traditional drinks have been mixed with other substances, and the communal regulations that used to govern the use of drugs and alcohol have been swept aside. Both young and old now use alcohol and drugs without restraint, regardless of time or season. People now drink more for their personal satisfaction than as participants in a social event. Drugs and alcohol have become a social evil.

Defining Addiction

The word "addiction" is derived from the Latin word *addicere,* which was used of being enslaved. An addict is thus someone who is a slave to some substance "though often a willing and a devoted slave."[1] The addict uses drugs compulsively in spite of their harmful effects. Thus a succinct definition of addiction is "repetitive behaviors in the face of negative consequences, the desire to continue something you know is bad for you".[2]

---

[1] Kenneth Leech, "Drugs" in *Dictionary of Ethics, Theology and Society*, 255.

[2] Joseph Frascella, director, Clinical Neuroscience, US National Institute on Drug Abuse (NIDA) quoted in Michael D. Lemonick "How We Get Addicted", *Time* (16 July 2007). Online: www.time.com/time/magazine/article/0,9171,1640436,00.html. He adds: "Addictions occur when behaviors start to become excessive. They are driven by our systems that stand up, shake us and say, 'The brain is saying this is good; we should do it again.'"

Key aspects of any addiction are excessive behaviour, a drive to do it again, persistence in the behaviour, negative health and social consequences, uncontrollable drug-seeking behaviour and a need for increasingly large doses of whatever one is addicted to, regardless of the consequences. It has been pointed out that "addiction is not just about substances but is about disrupting the processing of pleasure; the balance point is shifted so you keep creating more and more urges, and you keep wanting more and more".[3]

Addiction has often been treated as a sin, a vice and a crime. However, there are those who argue that it should rather be treated as a disease. Thus the U.S. National Institute on Drug Abuse (NIDA) states that "Addiction is a chronic, often relapsing brain disease that causes compulsive drug seeking and use despite harmful consequences to the individual that is addicted and to those around them"[4] The recognition that addiction is a disease is why it is included in the medical section of this book.

Yet although drug addicts and alcoholics certainly need medical treatment to deal with the physical consequences of their addiction and to help them break free of their addiction, there is more to the problem than this. Treating addiction as no more than a disease absolves addicts and alcoholics of any moral responsibility for their situation. This disease begins with moral choices made by individuals whose choices affect themselves, their families and society. That is why we need to include the issues of addiction and drug abuse in this book on ethics.

Defining Drugs

A drug can be defined as "any chemical substance used in medicine, in the treatment of a disease, either alone or in a mixture, which is capable of changing the state or functions of cells, organs or organisms".[5] Another definition is that a drug is "any substance in a pharmaceutical product that is used to modify or explore physiological systems or pathological

---

[3] Dr Martin Paulus as quoted in the article on addiction at *romancatholicinfo.com/catholic-answers/addiction/*. Cited 8 April 2008.

[4] NIDA "NIDA InfoFacts: Understanding Drug Abuse and Addiction". Cited 8 April 2008. www.drugabuse.gov/Infofacts/understand.html.

[5] Emma Iheonoye, *Drugs? A Dead-End* (Lagos, Nigeria: Peacegate Publishers. n.d.), xviii.

states for the benefit of the recipient".[6] These definitions make it clear that not all drugs are bad. Doctors prescribe drugs to patients all the time, and patients take them without incurring moral guilt. The appropriate use of drugs for therapeutic reasons restores physical and psychological health and is not an ethical problem.

The problems we are dealing with in this chapter arise from a subcategory of drugs called psychoactive substances. These drugs "exert their major effects on the brain and psychological functioning resulting in such effects as sedation, stimulation, or change in mood or behaviour"[7] Such drugs have valuable medical uses and can restore patients to physical and psychological health. But they can also be habit-forming and can result in some users having a "compulsion to take a drug on a continuous or periodic basis in order to experience its psychological effects or to avoid the discomfort of its absence.[8] Users in this condition are addicted to the drug, and will often develop a tolerance for it, meaning that they start to need higher and higher doses.

The non-medical use of some psychotropic drugs is legal in some countries. Thus the consumption of alcohol is legal in most non-Islamic countries and khat may legally be chewed in Ethiopia and Britain. Many other psychotropic drugs have been declared illegal in most countries. The illegal drugs include marijuana (also known as cannabis, ganja and dagga), heroin, cocaine, amphetamines like Ecstasy, and hallucinogens like LSD. These drugs can be taken in different ways, including drinking, smoking, injecting, swallowing, sniffing and chewing.

Reporting on drug abuse in West Africa, and particularly in Nigeria, Odejide and Morakinyo report:

> the following psycho-active substances are commonly abused ... a) alcohol; b) cannabis; c) hypno-sedatives (e.g., Valium, Ativan, sleeping pills); d) CNS stimulants (e.g., amphetamine-type stimulants, ATS); e) opiates (e.g., heroin, morphine,

---

[6] Word Health Organization. *Drug and Therapeutics Committees: A Practical Guide* (Geneva: Switzerland, 2003). Cited 8 April 2008. Online: www.who.int/medicinedocs/es/d/Js4882e?

[7] Olabisi A. Odejide and Jide Morakinyo "Substance Abuse and Its Socioeconomic Consequences in Nigeria", in J. U. Ohaeri (ed.), *Proceedings of the Mental Health Care Practices in the Gulf (Kuwait)*, 2004, quoting E. M. Burns, "The nature of dependence", pp. 43–52 in J. C. Ebie and E. J. Tongue (eds.), *Handbook of the African Training Courses on Drug Dependence*. Lausanne: International Council on Alcohol and Addictions (ICAA), 1988. Cited 9 April 2008. Online: www.ijma-journal.com/pdf/c01a04.pdf.

[8] World Health Organization, 1974. Quoted in Odejide and Morakinyo "Substance Abuse".

codeine); f) solvents (e.g., glue, cleaning fluids, gasoline); g) mild CNS stimulants (e.g., kolanuts, caffeine, prophis, nicotine); h) synthetic substances (e.g., methaqualone); and i) hallucinogens (e.g., LSD).

Biblical Perspectives on Drugs

The Bible is familiar with the use of drugs for medicinal purposes. For example, in describing the restored Jerusalem, Ezekiel states: "Fruit trees of all kinds will grow on both banks of the river. Their leaves will not wither, nor will their fruit fail. Every month they will bear, because the water from the sanctuary flows to them. Their fruit will serve for food and their leaves for healing" (Ezek 47:12; see also Rev 22:2).

The famous balm of Gilead to which Jeremiah refers when he asks, "Is there no balm in Gilead? Is there no physician there" (Jer 8:22) was a drug used for healing wounds (see also Jer 46:11; Jer 51:8).

The Bible was also aware that drugs had less beneficent uses. Thus when Paul includes "sorcery" in his list of evils in Galatians 5:20, the Greek word he uses is *pharmakeia*, from which we get the modern word "pharmacy". In New Testament times this word could refer to drugs used for medical purposes but also to their use in poisons and witchcraft.

Reasons for and Consequences of Drug Abuse

There are many reasons why people become addicted to drugs. One of the most important is that drugs relieve pain, whether physical or psychological, and provide temporary pleasures such as relaxation, euphoria, excitement, boldness, satisfaction, a sense of peace and serenity. These sensations are highly desirable to those who want to escape from frustration, depression or boredom. As Francis Ter Chia notes, "a drug abuser values the psychological gains of drug abuse more than any other thing".[9]

---

[9] Francis Ter Chia, *Understanding Drug Abuse at a Glance: A Training Manual for Local Government* (Nigeria: Drug Abuse Control Committee, 2006), 6.

Many first start to take drugs because they are adventurous and want to try something new or because of peer pressure. Others may simply use them because they are readily available in their family, environment or culture.

The positive sensations associated with drug use must, however, be balanced against the many negative side effects. Some of these affect the body of the person taking the drugs. Alcohol, nicotine and illegal drugs suppress the immune system and damage organs, raising the risk of diseases of the liver and heart, as well as of lung diseases such as lung cancer and bronchitis. They also decrease the production of male sex hormones.

Drugs interfere with the production of neurotransmitters, resulting in tremors (shaking) and confused thinking. They can also cause "distressing psychological and mental disturbances"[10] such as depression, hyperactivity, restlessness, anxiety and even hallucinations, which may be visual, auditory or tactile. Some drugs can cause permanent brain damage.

The side-effects are not only felt by the users but also by those around them, both their own families and those in the community who suffer as a person's drug use leads to the loss of jobs, moral decadence, poverty, increased criminality and road accidents.

Because it is impossible to deal with all the available drugs in one chapter, in what follows I will focus on just two drugs. In most countries, the first, marijuana, is an illegal drug, whereas the second, alcohol, is legal.

Marijuana/Cannabis/Pot/Dagga/Ganja

Marijuana has been used for therapeutic and non-therapeutic reasons for thousands of years. A list of Chinese medical drugs said to have been produced in about 2500 BC recommends its use to relieve numerous common ailments. In ancient Egypt it was used to treat sore eyes. In India it was known in around 1400 BC and was considered a "holy herb" and referred to as the "soother of grief" the "sky flyer" and the "poor man's heaven".[11] However, due to its negative side-effects (including "inebriation and delirium of decidedly hilarious character, including

---

[10] Norman Shields, *Christian Ethics* (Bukuru, Nigeria: African Christian Textbooks, 2004), 288.
[11] "Marijuana". Cited 8 April 2008. Online: www.answers.com/topic/marijuna?cat=health.

violent laughter, jumping and dancing"[12]) governments and religious institutions started to impose restrictions on its use.

In Africa, where there is so much unemployment and suffering, youth are especially vulnerable to using marijuana to escape from harsh reality. It makes them feel relaxed and cheerful, with heightened senses and altered perceptions. Those who engage in crime may also use it to suppress their consciences.

Marijuana is usually smoked in a pipe or in a roll like a cigarette. However, marijuana can also be baked into cakes and eaten, or drunk as a form of tea. It is often taken in conjunction with other drugs.

Consequences of marijuana use

Some of the effects of marijuana are beneficial. For example, it increases appetite, and so a doctor may legitimately prescribe marijuana to an AIDS patient to help them to eat more and so build up their strength. Marijuana has also been used for patients suffering from glaucoma and for cancer patients suffering the nausea associated with chemotherapy.[13] These therapeutic uses of marijuana do not raise the ethical problems associated with abuse and addiction. The same is true of any drug prescribed under strict medical control.

However, these positive benefits are more often than not offset by the negative consequences of using marijuana. These include "impaired memory and ability to learn; difficulty in thinking and problem solving; anxiety attacks or feelings of paranoia; impaired muscle coordination and judgment; increased susceptibility to infections; dangerous impairment of driving skills; and cardiac problems for people with heart disease or high blood pressure".[14] None of these consequences serve any useful therapeutic purpose.

Even more important than the physical consequences of marijuana use are the destructive consequences that flow from overuse and from the compulsive use of the drug by those who become addicted to it.

---

[12] Ibid. citing the 1856 edition of the *Encyclopedia Britannica*.
[13] "Medical Cannabis". Cited 8 April 2008. en.wikipedia.org/wiki/Medical_marijuana
[14] National Campus Safety Awareness Month: "Marijuana". Cited 8 April 2008. www.campussafetymonth.org/marijuana.

Issues associated with marijuana use

The use of marijuana raises the following psychological, social and religious issues.

- *Slippery slope.* Marijuana is usually not the first drug that people take. They start by drinking alcohol and smoking tobacco, and then move on to marijuana. However, this progression does not end with marijuana; it often "proceeds to the use of 'hard' drugs like hallucinogens, benzodiazepines, amphetamines, sedatives, cocaine, and heroin".[15]

- *Criminal link.* The link between criminal behaviour and abuse of marijuana is very strong. Those who use marijuana and other drugs are often guilty of lying, stealing, vandalism, violence and armed robbery, smuggling and rape. Many end up in jail.[16]

- *Disregard for authority.* Those who use marijuana often reject the authority of parents and teachers. They may drop out of school and choose to listen to their peers rather than their parents.

- *Destruction of one's body.* Scripture speaks of believer's bodies being God's temple (1 Cor 3:16–17). Deliberately taking drugs that cause harm to the body amounts to a wilful destruction of what God has made. Such behaviour is explicitly condemned in Scripture.

- *Destruction of individuals and families.* The abuse of marijuana and other drugs has ruined the lives of many promising young men and women and brought untold grief to their families, friends and colleagues. We have seen this happen in the lives of sports stars, politicians and scholars.

- *Economic and social loss.* Those who use marijuana and other drugs are more likely to be socially and economically disadvantaged than those who do not.[17] They are unproductive workers who undermine morale. The community as a whole loses the benefits they could have provided had they lived up to their promise, and also has to bear the cost of supporting them.

---

[15] "Marijuana". Cited 8 April 2008. www.answers.com/topic/marijuna?cat+health.
[16] Chia, *Understanding Drug Abuse*, 13.
[17] Ibid.

Alcohol and Alcohol Abuse

Alcohol is the most common of all drugs – in fact it is so common that some do not even recognize it as a drug. But it is in fact an addictive psychoactive substance that acts as an intoxicant, depressing the central nervous system. It can cause a temporary loss of physical and mental control.[18] When taken in large quantities, it becomes a poison.

One reason that alcohol is so common is that it can be produced from so many sources, including "grains, like wheat, barley and corn; from fruits, like grapes and apples; from tubers like potatoes; from the sap of palm trees and from a host of other plants and other flowers. The resultant wine or beer usually has an alcohol content of around 15%."[19]

Alcohol has been in use since before recorded history. The ancient Egyptians are known to have used it many centuries ago. The ancient Greeks and Romans were heavy drinkers. However, the wine and beer they drank seldom had an alcohol content of more than 14 per cent. Moreover, in the Mediterranean world the ordinary beverage was a mixture of wine and water. The Roman author Plutarch wrote that

> three parts of water to one of wine was suitable for "grave magistrates sitting in the council-hall", two parts to one left a person, "neither fully sober nor … altogether witless," and three parts to two caused "a man to sleep peaceably and forget all cares" … Half and half or unmixed wine in quantity brought on drunkenness or collapse.[20]

In the early ninth century AD, Arab chemists invented distillation, a process that has made it possible to greatly increase the alcoholic content of drinks and led to the production of strong drinks like whisky, brandy, gin, rum and vodka (which has an alcohol content of between 50% and 60%). In Africa the traditional palm wine is now often distilled to increase its alcohol content. Nigerian drinks like burkutu and goskolo (also known as ogogoro) are made from locally obtained grains, honey and other ingredients and are often fortified with additional alcohol.

---

[18] J. Kerby Anderson, *Moral Dilemmas: Biblical Perspectives on Contemporary Ethical Issues* (Nashville: Word, 1998), 102.

[19] Shields, *Christian Ethics*, 288.

[20] Plutarch as quoted by Evert Ferguson, "Wine" in *Encyclopedia of Early Christianity* (New York: Garland, 1990), 940.

Consequences of alcohol use

When alcohol is consumed in large quantities, it causes major social, economic and public health problems. The ancients were well aware of this, as is clear from this quotation from *The Papyrus of Ani*, written in Egypt about 3000 years ago: "Don't drink yourself helpless in the beer garden. You speak, and you don't know what you are saying. If you fall down and you break your limbs, no one will help you. And your drinking companions will get up and say, 'Away with this drunkard.'"[21]

The Romans also recognized the problem of alcoholism, with the philosopher, Seneca, making a sharp distinction between a man who is merely drunk and one "who has no control over himself ... who is accustomed to get drunk, and a slave to the habit."[22]

These warnings against excessive drinking predate distillation. The effects of alcohol are now even worse because many are drinking distilled liquors.

Alcohol in Scripture

Distilled liquors had not yet been invented when the Bible was written. The wine referred to in the Bible is thus fermented grape juice, although the terms used for it can also mean any type of sweet drink made from fruits or grains. As in the rest of the Mediterranean world, it was probably normally diluted with water before drinking.

There are some positive references to wine in Scripture:

• Wine was included in the offerings made to the Lord (Num 15:5, 7).

• Wine, like food, was regarded as one of the good things that God has given. The psalmist says that it "gladdens the heart of man" (Ps 104:15).

• Wine is mentioned as a medicine for those who are enduring physical suffering: "Give beer to those who are perishing, wine to those who are in anguish; let them drink and forget their poverty and remember

---

[21] Quoted in Weldon L. Witteres and Peter J. Venturelli, *Drugs and Society* (Boston: Jones and Barlett, 1988), 200.

[22] J. R. Cheydleu, "Alcohol Abuse and Dependence" in *Baker Encyclopedia of Psychology and Counseling*, 59.

their misery no more" (Prov 31:6). This verse may explain why Jesus was given sour wine to drink on the cross (John 19:29–30).

- Wine was seen as providing a temporary remedy for emotional suffering. The verse from Proverbs quoted above continues, "let them drink and forget their poverty and remember their misery no more" (Prov 31:7). This advice is similar to Plutarch's observation that mixing three parts of wine to two parts of water caused "a man to sleep peaceably and forget all cares".[23]

- Wine was used as a disinfectant to clean wounds. Thus when the Good Samaritan cared for the wounded traveller he "bandaged his wounds, pouring on oil and wine" (Luke 10:31).

- Wine was used in celebrations and ceremonies. Jesus made wine for guests at a wedding ceremony (John 2:1–11). He also instructed his disciples to take wine in remembrance of him (Mark 14:23–25; 1 Cor 11:25; Luke 22:17–18).

- Wine was used as a medicine. Paul instructed Timothy to take some wine: "Stop drinking only water, and use a little wine because of your stomach and your frequent illnesses" (1 Tim 5:23).

It is worth reiterating that in all these passages the wine being referred to is a simple wine, not a distilled liquor like whisky, rum or goskolo.

But while wine is spoken of positively in Scripture, there are also many places in Scripture where excessive drinking and drunkenness are condemned as a sin (Deut 21:20; 1 Cor 6:9–10). In Galatians 5:19–21 Paul mentions it in the same list as witchcraft and sorcery.

The chapter that deals most extensively with drunkenness is Proverbs 23. It begins with warnings about watching how much one eats and drinks when dining with the powerful (Prov 23:1–3) and carries on to warn about eating with the stingy (Prov 23:6–8). The theme of being careful about what one eats and drinks is picked up again in verses 20–21: "Do not join those who drink too much wine or gorge themselves on meat, for drunkards and gluttons become poor, and drowsiness clothes them in rags." These words clearly show the results of overindulgence or addiction to alcohol.

The writer of Proverbs then moves on to warn against sleeping with prostitutes. The link between drunkenness and sexual immorality is also

---

[23] Plutarch as quoted by Evert Ferguson, "Wine".

recognized by the prophet Hosea, who condemns those who "give themselves to prostitution, to old wine and new, which take away the understanding" (Hos 4:11). Those who are prone to excessive drinking are easily ensnared by seductive women.

Immediately after this warning, the writer gives a vivid description of a drunkard as someone who has woe, sorrow, strife, complaints, needless bruises and bloodshot eyes (Prov 23:29). The end result of addiction is that the drinker loses touch with reality and his only concern becomes where he can find another drink (Prov 23:33–35). No wonder the writer warns those who look longing at wine and find it too attractive (Prov 23:31) that its attraction is like the beauty of a snake, concealing its deadly poison (Prov 23:31–32).

We can summarise the reasons for the condemnation of drunkenness in the Scriptures as follows:

- Drunkenness leaves one prone to disgrace and makes one an object of ridicule, as happened to Noah (Gen 9:20–22).

- Drunkenness can make people commit wrongs they would never have done if sober because "they lose inhibitions (internal rules of conscience that preserve decorum and morality)."[24] Lot, for example, committed incest with his daughters while drunk (Gen 19:31–36).

- Drunkenness often results in physical injuries as people fall or engage in fights (Prov 23:29–35). That is why the writer of Proverbs describes beer as "a brawler" (Prov 20:1). Today, the injuries sustained can be even more serious than in biblical times, for people may use guns when drunk or may kill themselves and others by driving while drunk or by staggering into the path of an oncoming car.

- Intoxicating drink affects judgment. As Isaiah 28:7 states, "The priest and the prophet stagger from beer and are befuddled with wine; … they stagger when seeing visions, they stumble when rendering decisions." It is no wonder that those who are enslaved by strong drink are said to be unwise or foolish (Prov 20:1). Shields comments that "they lose concentration and cannot grasp or remember what is said to them."[25]

---

[24] Shields, *Christian Ethics*, 289.
[25] Ibid.

Christians and alcohol consumption

Over the years, there has been much debate about whether Christians may drink in moderation, providing they avoid drunkenness, or whether they should abstain from any use of alcohol except for medicinal reasons. The temperance movement of the late nineteenth and early twentieth century began by advocating moderation, but soon changed its emphasis and began promoting total abstinence from alcoholic drinks. Both sides in the debate can present plausible arguments, which are summarized below.

Those who argue that it is acceptable for Christians to drink in moderation make the following points:

- The Bible does not condemn the drinking of alcohol; it only condemns drunkenness.
- The Bible commends self-control, not abstinence with regards to alcohol.
- The Bible recognizes that wine can be medicinal.
- Church fathers like Clement of Alexandra and Ambrose supported moderation rather than total abstinence.
- Not everyone who takes a drink gets drunk.
- Those who drink moderately still retain self-control.
- Refusing to drink may be considered anti-social in cultures that require drinking at social functions such as weddings, funeral ceremonies and birth ceremonies.

Those who argue that Christians should never consume alcohol but should practise total abstinence make the following points:

- The Bible warns us about the dangers associated with alcohol.
- Priests were forbidden to drink any alcohol before entering the Tent of Meeting (Lev 10:5–9).
- Those who had taken a Nazirite vow were forbidden to take strong drink while their vow lasted (Num 6:3; 6:20). Samson and John the Baptist, who were Nazirites from birth, were forbidden to drink at all (Judg 13:7; Luke 1:15).
- Drinking can cause others to stumble. Thus Paul asserts, "It is better not to eat meat or drink wine or to do anything else that will cause your brother to fall" (Rom 14:21). For the same reason, one should

not encourage one's neighbours to drink: "Woe to him who gives drink to his neighbours, pouring it from the wineskin till they are drunk, so that he can gaze on their naked bodies" (Hab 2:15).

- The Bible teaches self-control and restraint. Self-control is commanded in Titus 2:2 and 2:6 and is mentioned as a gift of the Holy Spirit in Galatians 5:23.

- Drinking is a slippery slope. Many who start as social drinkers end up as excessive drinkers and drunkards.

- Alcohol kills. Each year hundreds of people die in road accidents because they or the driver who hit them were under the influence of alcohol. Heavy drinkers also undermine their own health.

- Drinking leads to immoral and irresponsible behaviour that can result in loss of employment and poverty.

- Drinking wrecks families, breaks up marriages, and leads to the neglect of children, whose lives may be ruined.

Given the many negative consequences of the consumption of alcohol in our society, the advantages of total abstinence far outweigh the advantages of drinking alcohol. The safest position is never even to start drinking. After all, nobody sets out to become an alcoholic. They begin with social drinking and end up as drunkards, with lives that are physically, emotionally and socially ruined.

The many beer parlours in African towns and villages are testimony to the presence of people who are running away from productive work and seeking pleasure at the expense of their families and themselves. These people risk death, for strong drink is compared to the venom of a serpent or viper (Prov 23:32).

For Christians, total abstinence is the safest position. We should heed the Scriptures' advice not to "get drunk on wine, which leads to debauchery. Instead, be filled with the Spirit" (Eph 5:18).

Conclusion

Drug abuse and addiction destroy their victims and harm their families and society as a whole. Therefore, they are not only morally unjustifiable but also destructive, disruptive and unprofitable. Communities where these problems are rampant earn a bad name locally and even internationally.[26]

Christians who are tempted to use or abuse drugs and alcohol should pause to think about them from a spiritual perspective. These substances have a direct spiritual effect on our bodies, which are the spiritual abode of the Holy Spirit and so should be treated as holy (1 Cor 3:16–17). In a real sense, it is not the drugs and alcohol that are abused, but our bodies.

Questions

1. Define drug abuse and alcohol addiction.
2. How has distillation impacted the nature of alcoholic consumption in your community?
3. What does the Bible have to say about the use of alcohol and drugs? Identify and discuss specific biblical passages.
4. Discuss and evaluate the arguments for moderation in drinking or total abstinence from alcohol.
5. What consequences of drug and alcohol abuse have you witnessed in your neighbourhood or within your family?
6. How would you help someone in your family or neighbourhood who is addicted to drugs or alcohol to overcome this addiction or dependency?

---

[26] Iheonoye, *Drugs?*, 57.

SECTION F
RELIGIOUS ISSUES

INTRODUCTION TO RELIGIOUS ISSUES

Religion and ethics are bedfellows, which is why it is appropriate to end this book with a section that explicitly brings them together. All ethical issues have links to fundamental religious beliefs and values. And the ultimate philosophical and ethical issue is the problem of evil. This problem "haunts those areas of inquiry which deal primarily with the nature and destiny of man: philosophy, theology, literature, art and history. Neither is it surprising that every major worldview, whether religious, ethical or political proposes insight into this vexing problem."[1] Peterson is right to say that "what a religious system says about evil reveals a great deal about what it takes ultimate reality and man's relation to it to be. Hence the credibility of a religion is closely linked to its ability to explain evil."[2]

Reduced to its simplest terms, evil is the human experience of pain, sickness, death and anything that causes discomfort. How do we explain the existence of evil in general and the evil that happens in our own lives? Traditional Africa has long had an answer to the second question: the evils that enter our lives are caused by witchcraft. Is this answer adequate? Is it acceptable to Christian communities in Africa today? **Chapter 30** offers a philosophical and theological perspective on witchcraft as it affects Christians in Africa.

---

[1] Michael Peterson, *Evil and the Christian God* (Grand Rapids: Baker, 1982), 11.
[2] Ibid., 16.

30
WITCHCRAFT

When confronted with pain or sorrow, we are all forced to square our experience with our religious beliefs and understanding. Harold Kushner, a Jewish writer, says,

> None of us can avoid the problem of why bad things happen to good people. Sooner or later each of us finds himself playing one of the roles in the story of Job, whether as a victim of tragedy, as a member of the family, or as a friend/comforter. The questions never change, the search for a satisfying answer continues.[1]

The question that faces believers is whether our faith offers us a satisfactory explanation for the evil we are experiencing. John Hick, who has written extensively on the topic of evil, states the problem:

> Christianity, like Judaism and Islam, is committed to a monotheistic doctrine of God as absolute in goodness and power and as the creator of the universe *ex nihilo*. If God is all-powerful, then he must be able to prevent evil along with the entire human crisis accompanying it. If he is all-good, he must (want to) prevent evil. But evil exists. Therefore, God is either not all-powerful or not all good.[2]

David Hume, who was introduced in chapter 3 on Western ethics, puts the problem like this: "Is he [God] willing to prevent evil but not able? Then he is impotent. Is he able but not willing? Then he is malevolent.

---

[1] Harold S. Kushner, *When Bad Things Happen to Good People* (New York: Avon, 1981), 143.
[2] John Hick, "The Problem of Evil", in *Encyclopedia of Philosophy, Vol. 3 and 4* (New York: Macmillan Publishers, 1967), 136.

Is he both able and willing? Whence then is evil?"[3] He goes on to elaborate on the problem by asking, "Why is there any misery at all in the world? Not by chance surely. From some cause then. Is it from the intention of the Deity? But he is perfectly benevolent. Is it contrary to his intention? But he is almighty. Nothing can shake the solidity of this reasoning, so short, so clear, so decisive."[4]

Our understanding of what kind of god we believe in will affect how we understand evil. For example, we may believe in a living god who is not powerful; though he wants to help, he cannot do so. Evil comes upon his children because he cannot protect them from it. Kushner states this position succinctly.

> I believe in God. But I do not believe the same things about him that I did years ago when I was a theological student. I can worship a God who hates suffering *but cannot* (emphasis added) eliminate it, more easily than I can worship a God who chooses to make children suffer and die for whatever exalted reason.[5]

Chapter 7 in Kushner's book has the title "God Can't Do Everything But Can Do Some Important Things". This title demonstrates his profound belief that though God is loving and caring, he is limited as to what he can do, especially in the prevention of evil and suffering for his children.

Many African Christians hold to a position that is very close to that of Kushner. They believe that God is almighty and that Jesus is the Son of God who provides salvation through his shed blood. At the same time, they strongly believe that evil forces such as witchcraft, secret societies and evil spirits are ultimately responsible for all the suffering, sickness and death that afflict God's children. Thus while they theoretically believe in a supreme God, at the practical level their faith is dualistic. Like Manicheans or Gnostics, their understanding of ultimate reality is that there are two equal competing realities, one good and one evil.

---

[3] David Hume, *Dialogues Concerning Natural Religion*, Part X. This classic text is widely available on the Internet.
[4] Ibid., 91.
[5] Kushner, *When Bad Things Happen*, 134.

Traditional Beliefs about Witchcraft

Almost all African societies believe in witchcraft in one form or another. It is the traditional way of explaining the ultimate cause of any evil, misfortune or death.

> Barren women, people whose children die at birth, women with irregular menstrual flow, accident victims, traders who suffer losses, office workers who fail to get promotions, a political candidate who fails to get elected, a student who fails examinations, a person who notices scratches on his or her body, a hunter or fisherman who fails to bring home meat, a farmer with bad crop yields, a football team that consistently loses matches – all suspect witches as the cause of their misfortune. Even those who are most successful in their business or profession constantly fear being bewitched by envious relatives or friends.[6]

Carol McKinney, who studied the phenomenon of witchcraft among the Bajju of Kaduna State, Nigeria, defines witchcraft as "an inherent capacity to exert supernatural influence over another person. This influence frequently causes harm, and it explains phenomena such as breaches in social relations, anti-social behavior, unexpected occurrences, sickness and death."[7]

This belief is not irrational; rather, it is a serious philosophical attempt to deal with the question of evil. It has its own natural logic: "This explanatory system provides answers to questions of why particular occurrences happen to specific individuals at the time they do. It does not invalidate their understanding of empirical cause and effect of an occurrence. Rather it deals with its ultimate cause."[8]

Natural causes and witchcraft are not mutually exclusive, but complementary. The one supports the other, accounting for what the other does not account for. Africans do not deny the working of natural

---

[6] Daniel A. Offiong, *Witchcraft, Sorcery, Magic and Social Order Among the Ibibio of Nigeria* (Enugu: Fourth Dimension Publishing, 1991), 78; quoted in Paul Hiebert, R. Daniel Shaw, Tite Tienou, *Understanding Folk Religion: A Christian Response to Popular Beliefs and Practices* (Grand Rapids: Baker, 1999), 155.

[7] Carol V. McKinney, The Bajju of Central Nigeria: A Case Study of Religious and Social Change (PhD dissertation, Southern Methodist University, 1985), 59.

[8] Evans-Pritchard, *Witchcraft, Oracles and Magic among the Azande* (Oxford: Oxford University Press, 1976), 71.

causes. They would never deny that a motor accident caused the death of a young man crushed by a car. But they would assert that this was not a complete explanation; things do not "just happen". It must have been witchcraft that put the young man in harm's way.

Belief in witchcraft thus serves a very practical purpose in explaining events and the causes behind them. For example, death is not regarded as a natural phenomenon, and the death of a young man or woman is especially unnatural. Thus any death of a young person was traditionally attributed to witchcraft. Even the deaths of some old people were attributed to witchcraft if they died in ways that were considered unnatural, such as from dysentery, falling off a tree or some form of violence. Those who died in this way were not buried in the usual place inside the compound or inside their room but were instead buried behind the compound or in the backyard. The living did not want someone who had died an accursed death to lie near them.

In the African mind, witchcraft is real and is considered the enemy of life.

> Harmony, order, good neighborliness or good company, cooperation and sharing, propriety and equitableness, honesty and transparency – all of which constitute signs of how the human and created order should be – are denied in the most fundamental way by witchcraft … A witch is a person who does not control the impulses that good members of society must keep in check. Insatiable desires and hatreds account, separately or together, for the deaths witches cause. Witches are morose, unsociable people.[9]

Proofs of Witchcraft

Africans believe that witchcraft is real because they have heard scores of stories about it. They have heard the confessions of perpetrators and the testimonies of victims. There are thousands and thousands of such stories told by old and young, rich and poor, educated and uneducated. I can even share stories from my own family. My grandfather, who contracted smallpox when he was a child, was denied medication until he confessed

---

[9] Laurenti Magesa, *African Religion: The Moral Traditions of Abundant Life* (New York: Orbis Books, 1997), 187.

whom he had supposedly killed through witchcraft. He confessed that he had killed all those who had recently died in the community, and even some who had died before his mother married and he was conceived! My uncle's wife recently confessed that she was responsible for her husband's poverty and that she was planning to kill him using witchcraft. Another seventeen-year-old in my family was accused of being an elder in a secret society. His accuser (who was a member of the society) alleged that he was in charge of administering human blood.

In recent years, even children have been accused of being witches. In one small town in the Delta State of Nigeria, ill-informed and greedy preachers have identified some children as sources of evil and encouraged their parents to get rid of them either directly by burning, beating, poisoning or burying them alive, or indirectly by chasing them off into the bush or chaining them to trees and leaving them to die.[10]

What do we make of these stories? What do we say of the mass hysteria associated with witchcraft and secret societies? Don't they all add up to indisputable proof that witchcraft is real? After all, we hear so much about it!

The first response to this question must be that it is impossible to deny the existence and reality of a *belief* in witchcraft. This belief must be taken seriously because it is very real.[11] For those who hold this belief, "there is no kind of illness or hardship at all that may not be attributed to witchcraft ... When natural or religious explanations fail to satisfy, the social explanation – witchcraft – is invariably invoked."[12]

African Christians who are trying to be relevant to their culture must begin by accepting that there is something such as witchcraft, by which we mean the general power of Satan and his evil cohorts to bring suffering and misery to humanity. It is not unbiblical to accept this. However, belief in witchcraft does not exonerate us from asking serious philosophical questions about it. The two critical philosophical disciplines that are relevant to a study of witchcraft are metaphysics and epistemology.

---

[10] Tracy McVeigh, "Children are targets of Nigerian witch hunt" in *The Observer* Sunday 9 December 2007: 34. Cited 16 April 2008. Online: www.guardian.co.uk/world/2007/dec/09/tracymcveigh.theobserver.

[11] Hiebert, Shaw and Tienou, *Understanding Folk Religion*, 173.

[12] Magesa, *African Religion*, 182.

To take one example, witches are often accused of eating human flesh and drinking human blood. When such an accusation is made, we need to ask a metaphysical question: Was this action metaphorical or literal? The Nupe people of Nigeria, for example, believe that such "eating" is spiritual not physical. Christians, too, admit to a spiritual sharing in the body and blood of Christ each time they take communion. But they do not eat actual human flesh or drink actual human blood.

At the epistemological level, we have to ask ourselves: How do we know whether a story is true? It is generally assumed that if someone has confessed to being a witch, he or she is to be believed. However, such confessions may be false. Moreover, even if the person did perform some actions intended as witchcraft, all that the confession proves is a profound belief in the effectiveness of witchcraft as well as a belief that witchcraft harnesses evil forces.

To underline this point: stories and confessions about witchcraft do not prove the reality and certainty of witchcraft. They simply affirm the belief in the existence of witchcraft. Though the belief in witchcraft attempts to provide a solution to the existence of evil in the world, the solution it offers is inadequate.

As Christians, we need to heed the following warning:

> A principal way in which traditional religions accredit, justify and propagate ideas about the supernatural is through the telling and retelling of stories of the supernatural. These stories are told to accredit an incredible range of beliefs about spirits, beliefs which vary according to the culture and religion of the teller … We are expected to assent to the validity of the stories and of the inferences drawn from them … [However] if we proceed on the mistaken assumption that we can infer truth about spirits from people's beliefs about spirits, we will invariably end up syncretistically incorporating animistic and magical notions of spirit power into our doctrinal understandings of the demonic world.[13]

---

[13] Robert J. Priest, Thomas Campbell and Bradford Mullen, "Missiological Syncretism: The New Animistic Paradigm", in Edward Rommen (ed.), *Spiritual Power and Missions: Raising the Issues,* Evangelical Missiological Society Series, No. 3 (Pasadena, Calif.: William Carey Library, 1995), 13.

Biblical Perspectives on Witchcraft

Our understanding of witchcraft must not be based on stories but on the teachings of the Old and New Testaments, both of which warn the people of God to have nothing to do with any form of witchcraft. Leviticus 19:31 tells the people of Israel, "Do not turn to mediums or seek out spiritists, for you will be defiled by them" (see also Lev 20:6–7; Exod 22:18). Deuteronomy 18:10–12 makes the command even more explicit: "Let no one be found among you ... who practises divination or sorcery, interprets omens, engages in witchcraft, or casts spells, or who is a medium or spiritist or who consults the dead. Anyone who does these things is detestable to the Lord."

The New Testament associates witchcraft with the acts of the sinful nature (Gal 5:20). In Acts 19:18–19 those who came to Christ renounced sorcery along with other "evil deeds".

It is very clear from these passages that witchcraft or any human interaction with demonic activity is detestable to God. Paul says that people must be bewitched when they replace faith in God with faith in anything else, including the Law (Gal 3:1). How much more is it detestable to replace faith in God with involvement in demonic activity or giving verbal support to such activity?

Believers who have dabbled in demonic activities have been hurt and injured. Disobedience to the clear teaching of Scripture concerning witchcraft leads to catastrophic consequences such as defeat, injury and death. The stories of Saul in 1 Samuel 28 and of the sons of Sceva in Acts 19:13–19 demonstrate some of the problems encountered when people dabble in demonic activities of any kind. We cannot align ourselves with two masters; God will not share our service with his enemies.

The testimony of Scripture is that the child of God has complete authority over demonic power; the devil flees from the child of God (Jas 4:7). If there is power in witchcraft, it is overshadowed by the power of the child of God. "Jesus' power is super power and Satan's power is powerless power," as in the chorus children sing in Nigeria.

The basis for this assertion is that Jesus has stripped evil forces of their power: "having disarmed the powers and authorities, he made a public spectacle of them, triumphing over them by the cross" (Col 2:15). According to Fred Dickason,

Satan and demons are no match for Christ, the God-man. In the face of satanic opposition, the cross accomplished God's self-glorification, released the devil's prisoners, publicly routed evil spirits and sealed their judgment so that men would never have to fear or follow them again.[14]

The Bible is often used merely as a source of proof texts to support our traditional opinions and beliefs. However, when properly interpreted, the Bible does not support the kinds of doctrines of demons, evil spirits and witchcraft that are supported, nursed and propagated in Africa. Though African experiences and stories are relevant and should be interacted with, the truths we believe should be based *solely* on Scripture.

Christians and Witchcraft in Africa Today

Witchcraft has nothing good to offer; it encourages disrespect for parents and children, disunity and hatred among families, and even murder. A recent case of witch-hunting led a young man to hack his own father to death after accusing him of using witchcraft to kill his grandchild, the young man's son. This is only one of many atrocities that have been committed because of witchcraft – even within Christian communities, for despite Christians in Africa being warned to have nothing to do with witchcraft, there is a resurgence of belief in it.

There is evidence of "widespread belief in the power of witchcraft and the fear of being bewitched. Christian rituals are often seen as new and more powerful protection against the attacks of one's enemies and those who may be jealous."[15] It is not uncommon to hear mothers "covering" the beds of their children with the "blood of Jesus" to ward off witches and evil spirits before putting them to bed. The blood of Jesus is also "poured out" on roads to provide security against witches who are thought to cause accidents.

What has precipitated this frenzy? Why is there such a resurgence of belief in the powers of witches and wizards *among Christians* in Africa today?

Several factors are responsible for this spiritual epidemic. First, church leaders, and especially expatriate missionaries, have not given

---

[14] C. Fred Dickason, *Angels, Elect and Evil* (Chicago: Moody Press, 1975), 215.
[15] Hiebert, Shaw and Tienou, *Understanding Folk Religion*, 173.

an adequate explanation of evil nor answered the question: What is the ultimate cause of misfortune, sickness and death? As far as Africans are concerned God is our Father and we are his children. He does not cause evil, sickness or death. Consequently, they must be the effects of witchcraft.

Missionaries, early African church leaders and some contemporary leaders have dismissed belief in witchcraft as mere superstition. In doing this, they fail to understand the African worldview. While acknowledging the great contribution of missionaries in bringing the gospel to Africa, I agree with Yusufu Turaki:

> The major pitfall of the pioneering and early missionaries was the way they berated African culture. Their attitude was in the main the basic negation of African culture, custom, religious and social life.[16]

Church leaders are now painfully aware that dismissing witchcraft as superstition no longer carries weight with many members of their congregations. Many Christians admit the existence of witchcraft and even confess to practising it. In the light of such testimony, it is doubtful that churches have seriously responded to the nagging problem of witchcraft from a scriptural and theological perspective.

Because of this failure on the part of church leadership, Christians accept worldly standards and demonic explanations regarding the source of evil rather than seeking biblical and theological explanations. Consequently, though we claim to be Christians, we are quick to suspect witchcraft when someone's child becomes sick or dies. We foolishly cling to this explanation because it satisfies our desire to find answers to our questions. The result is that many young Christians can tell countless stories testifying to the power of witches and wizards, but can hardly tell one story about deliverance from demonic power. As long as Christians have more stories (whether true or false) about witchcraft than about Christ's power, they will feel that witchcraft has a greater degree of power over the child of God.

Nominal Christianity has also contributed to the resurgence of witchcraft. External change without an internal transformation does not affect the whole person. Many Christians have confessed that they

---

[16] Yusufu Turaki, "The Minority Ethnic Group and Christian Missions" Boston: typewritten, 1982, 27.

became Christians because it was the expected thing to do. In most former mission stations, it is normal to be churchgoers. Though at the external level these churchgoers claim to be Christians, they are unbelieving and unchanged and cling tenaciously to deep-seated traditional beliefs and values. As Stephen Neill observes:

> On a deeper level than conduct, and in the end more menacing, is the persistent underground of non-Christian structures and patterns of thought. Those patterns are far more instinctive than rational. They persist in all of us, racially as well as individually ... such deep conviction can remain unspoken and can apparently, in Europe no less than in Africa, be transmitted from generation to generation. This explains the distressing emergence in third and forth generation Christians of old and evil practices such as one would imagine to have long disappeared from the Christian consciousness.[17]

Neill's observation is borne out by John Mbiti, a noted African theologian: "A careful scrutiny of the religious situation shows clearly that in their encounter with traditional religions, Christianity and Islam have made only an astonishingly shallow penetration in converting the whole man of Africa, with all his historical-cultural roots, social dimension, self-consciousness and expectations."[18] In the same vein, Aylward Shorter notes that "at baptism, the African Christian repudiates remarkably little of his former non-Christian outlook. What remains above the surface is, in fact, the tip of an iceberg. The African Christian is not asked to recant a religious philosophy. Consequently, he returns to the forbidden practices as occasion arises with remarkable ease."[19] The resurgence of witchcraft, sorcery and witch hunting among Christian communities illustrates the point.

Ignorance of scriptural truths and theology has also contributed to the resurgence of witchcraft-related beliefs and practices among Christians. A quick survey would show that many professing Christians have no knowledge of the Scriptures and are unaware of what the Bible really teaches on many issues, including witchcraft. Pastors and evangelists are

---

[17] Stephen Neill, *The Unfinished Task* (London: Edinburgh House Press, 1957), 117–118.

[18] John S. Mbiti, *African Religions and Philosophy* (London: Heinemann, 1969), 263.

[19] Aylward Shorter, *African Theology: Adaptation or Incarnation?* (Maryknoll: Orbis Books, 1977), 10.

more prone to issue superficial condemnations than to give systematic teaching on philosophical, religious and theological beliefs and values in the African context.

Stephen Neill again puts his finger on the problem:

> Almost everywhere there has been grave failure in the giving of systematic instruction to the members of the Christian faith. There has been plenty of preaching – almost all simple sermons – but the intellectual content has been small, and the aim is all too often moralistic edification rather than serious instruction. The Bible is a more difficult book than is often realized by those who have been brought up on it.[20]

The same point is made by G. C. Oosthuizen:

> One is forced to ask the question: why does the African, in times of human crisis, revert back to non-Christian practices? This appears to be the rule rather than the exception because the African's past has been ignored and no attempt has been made to penetrate it with the regeneration power of the gospel message, the converted African lives in two levels.[21]

Although many Africans are Christians, their worldview has not been transformed.

Finally, the steady disintegration of traditional structures and values has destroyed the controls and restraints that once surrounded the practice of witchcraft. In traditional African society, one could not simply claim that someone was a witch or wizard. The elders exercised control and were the interpreters and judges of who practised witchcraft. The collapse of the authority of the elders has contributed to the breakdown of law and order, and today even children and young people claim to be experts in witchcraft. In fact, young people and children have become *authorities* on witchcraft. There are no checks and controls to curb the modern mass hysteria of belief in and practise of witchcraft.

---

[20] Neill, *The Unfinished Task,* 130.

[21] G. C. Oosthuizen, *Post-Christianity in Africa: A Theological and Anthropological Study* (Grand Rapids: Eerdmans, 1964), 4.

Theological Approach to Dealing with Witchcraft

As Merrill Unger observes:

> Every spirit-anointed minister should echo the words of the Great Deliverer, the Lord Jesus Christ whose wonderful ministry of liberation was so gloriously foretold, "the Spirit of the Lord is upon me to proclaim freedom for the captive and release from darkness for the prisoners" (Isa 61:1–2; Luke 4:18–19).[22]

But many ministers do not understand what they are fighting against, and so cannot proclaim a message of victory. In order to deal with the problem of evil properly, we must approach it with concepts that are properly rooted in Scripture.

The nature of God

An understanding of some of the attributes of God is necessary if Christians are to have an adequate understanding of evil.

- *The sovereignty of God.* According to Scripture, God is wholly sovereign and independent over creation and all of history. He relies on no one but is self-existent and self-directed (Job 12:13–25; Ps 103:19; Acts 17:24–25; John 5:26–27; Jer 10:10–12). This doctrine "is no mere philosophical dogma devoid of practical value. Rather it is the doctrine that gives meaning and substance to all other doctrines."[23] Arthur W. Pink describes it as "the foundation of Christian faith … the centre of gravity in the system of Christian truth. It is also the Christian's strength and comfort amid the storms of this life".[24] Because God is sovereign, Satan and evil spirits act only when God gives them permission to do so. The story of Job (especially chapters 1–2) clearly demonstrates this truth. Knowledge of the sovereignty of God affords a deep sense of security in a world that is full of misery and trouble (Rom 8:31–39).

---

[22] Merrill Unger, *Demons in the World Today* (Wheaton: Tyndale House Publishers, 1971), 188.

[23] James Montgomery Boice, *Foundations of the Christian Faith: A Comprehensive and Readable Theology, Vol. I: Revelation* (Downers Grove: IVP, 1986), 117.

[24] Quoted in Boice, *Foundations of the Christian Faith*, 117–118.

- *The goodness and love of God.* God's goodness is shown in a real and practical way through his demonstration of his grace, love and mercy towards all his creatures (Ps 84:11; 104:10–30; Jas 1:17). This goodness is far greater than we can understand:

    > God's goodness is a blazing, consuming, awe-inspiring thing, unlike the best that we know among men. It is when we see the Creator standing over against his creation, distinct from it, yet controlling every particle of it; loving his children with infinite love, yet hating evil with infinite hatred, that we see theism in all its glory.[25]

In any human crisis the Christian must cling to the fact that God is indeed good (Lam 3:21–25). His love is still evident even as his children suffer for his glory (Rom 8:38–39). Evil will not endure for ever, but God's love for his children is everlasting (Jer 31:3).

- *The presence of God.* God is always present with us, and this knowledge should transform our worldview (Job 34:21–22). God told Moses: "My Presence will go with you" (Exod 33:14). Elisha could reassure his servant, "Those who are with us are more than those who are with them" (2 Kgs 6:16). The Scriptures do not deny the existence of demons and evil spirits. But they insist that the presence of God and his angels provides security against demons and any other cause for human fear. After all, the Apostle John reminds us, "the one who is in you is greater than the one who is in the world" (1 John 4:4). Our God, who is always with us, is greater, mightier and stronger than the devil. The Christian can rest confidently on Christ's promise that he will be with us to the end of the age (Matt 28:20). The point is not to deny the existence and power of Satan and his agents like demons and witches but to affirm the power of God over those who oppose us.

The nature of evil and suffering

- *The ultimate source of evil.* The believer needs to understand that the ultimate source of evil is sin. The consequences of Adam and Eve's sin include death, pain, domination of the wife by the husband,

---

[25] John Wenham, *The Goodness of God* (Downers Grove: IVP, 1974), 184.

cursed ground and hard labour (Gen 3:16–19). In other words, evil in all its forms is a result of sin (Rom 5:12) and "the wages of sin is death" (Rom 6:23).

- *The effect of moral choices.* Evil and suffering are not just the result of Adam and Eve's sin, in which we all share, but also of our own sin and the moral choices we have made. Our choices set in motion the laws of cause and effect that God has established. For example, those who live promiscuous lives and get infected with HIV/AIDS should not blame any witch or evil forces. They themselves are responsible for contracting this deadly disease.[26]

- *The effect of physical laws.* We are free to act, making our own decisions. But if we decide to jump from a tree, the law of gravity will cause us to fall. We may suffer injury or death. Moreover, the fact that we are mortal means that all of us will have to die from one cause or another (Ps 90:10).

- *The effect of evil forces.* Evil spirits or demons exist and they afflict human beings. The story of Job indicates that the demonic world can be involved in causing disease and even death and in tempting us to sin (Job chapters 1–2).

- *God's purposes.* The story of Job is not only a testimony to the presence of evil forces but also makes it clear that God is in control. He is the one who allows Satan to inflict suffering, but he does it for his special purposes (Gen 50:20; Acts 2:23). Ultimately the goodness of God must be seen from his perspective, not from the human point of view. When he allows evil, it is not because he desires to see his children suffer but because he intends to achieve his goal. Job's affliction tested him and refined his faith (Job 1:22; 2:10; see also Rom 5:3–4). Thus the demonic and divine causes of suffering are not unrelated but interrelated.

God controls evil and he will eventually do away with it. He already sets limits to the extent to which evil can harm his children (Job 1:12; 2:6; 14:5). We must realize that we can be touched by the devil only as God Almighty allows the devil or evil forces to do so, and even in this case God has placed a limit on demonic power. The devil does not compete

---

[26] This statement should not be read as implying that all those infected with HIV/AIDS are promiscuous. For more on this subject, see chapter 25.

with God's power; he seeks God's permission to inflict injury or harm God's people. We must show the same confidence as Job did even in the face of the death of his children and the destruction of his property. Even when we cannot fully understand why God permits us to endure so much pain, we must say along with Job, "Though he slay me, yet will I hope in him" (Job 13:15). When crisis and disaster strike, believers do not deny the existence and potency of demonic spirits, but they do not yield to them. Instead, believers affirm their radical commitment to the sovereign Lord.

The problem of evil in all its forms should also motivate us to live as if we were about to die at any moment. This is what the psalmist meant when he said, "Teach us to number our days aright" (Ps 90:12). God has not promised that we will not die a violent death. That we are to die is certain; that we will die in our sleep is nowhere guaranteed. A Christian may become mentally deranged, may drown, may be killed in a car accident, or may be murdered. As Job 21:22–25 states: "Can anyone teach knowledge to God, since he judges even the highest? One man dies in full vigour, completely secure and at ease, his body well nourished, his bones rich with marrow. Another man dies in bitterness of soul, never having enjoyed anything good."

Conclusion

Confessions, stories and experiences of witchcraft are a clear demonstration of what people believe based on their cultural experience. As Christians, we need to address our culturally postulated reality of witchcraft pastorally with seriousness, sensitivity and respect. We should not live as if there are no evil spirits and witches, but should live with the full conviction that God is in control. We believe wholeheartedly that the devil and his forces have been conquered and that as believers we have no need to fear demonic forces.

Without this affirmation from the Scriptures in our ears, it would not be worth being a Christian. The joy of being a Christian is that our God is sovereign over all evil forces, and that the child of God can proclaim this without fear. This is the clear teaching of the Scriptures. It should provide great comfort and strength in these times when the resurgence of belief in demonic activities produces so much fear and terror. The Christian has victory in Christ over witchcraft and all its forces.

Questions

1. Provide stories from your own experience or from the community around you about how witchcraft is manifested in your cultural background or in the context of your ministry.

2. Evaluate your own understanding of the biblical and theological teaching on witchcraft. What aspects do you need to focus on in order to prepare for ministry in a context where witchcraft is prevalent?

CONCLUSION

True holiness is the fundamental trait required of God's people. He set out the basic framework for our moral life in his command: "Be holy because I, the Lord your God, am holy" (Lev 19:2). The command is then repeated: "Consecrate yourselves and be holy, because I am the Lord your God" (Lev 20:7). It is heard again in the New Testament, when Jesus tells his followers, "Be perfect, therefore, as your heavenly Father is perfect" (Matt 5:48). Peter picks up the thread when he tells those he is writing to, "Just as he who called you is holy, so be holy in all you do; for it is written: 'Be holy, because I am holy'" (1 Pet 1:15–16).

But what does it mean to be holy? Holiness is a concept that is not easily accepted in our times. The word brings to mind the "holier than thou attitude" of someone who makes others very aware that he or she is more pious or righteous than they are. Not surprisingly, people react with indignation when they meet someone with this type of condescending air. But such a person is not really holy. The Bible in fact condemns this type of self-conscious holiness when it condemns the behaviour of some Pharisees.

The abuse of the idea of holiness should not lead us to reject the proper holiness that is commanded in Scripture. At the heart of true holiness is the idea of being separated from the things of the world and totally devoted to God. In other words, we are to be wholly committed to God in every aspect of life and are to show this commitment in our everyday conduct. Our holiness must be apparent in the moral decisions we make or, simply put, in our everyday decisions about what is the right or wrong thing to do in each situation.

But how are we to know what is right or wrong? The answer is that all our decisions should be based on the following principles.

- **God is the ultimate source and model of morality.** The God who is revealed in Scripture through Jesus Christ is the originator and model of morality. He does not have a rival and must be seen as the final judge in matters of right and wrong. He stands over and above tribal gods, evil spirits, witches and other supernatural beings. Morality begins with God.

- **The Scriptures provide the ultimate authority in matters of morality.** Without the special revelation of God in the Scriptures, it would not be possible to know precisely what God requires of his people. The Christian has no other authoritative source apart from the Scriptures, which are the final arbiter in matters of faith and practice.

- **Every aspect of life is subject to the scrutiny of the Scriptures properly interpreted.** Though Scripture does not mention everything under the sun, it provides perspectives on every aspect of life. No aspect of life is free from the searching eyes of Scripture.

- **The community of faith provides support, responsibility and accountability.** When we become Christians, we become members of the body of Christ (1 Cor 12:13). This body inspires and motivates us to live responsibly and to hold each other accountable before God.

- **The world provides the context in which we live out this morality.** As Christians we do not have a separate place to live our lives. We have to make our moral decisions in the same world in which those around us live, and we have to deal with real people and real issues. But at the same time, we need to remember that although we may be in a small town like Madakiya in Kaduna State, Nigeria, we are also part of a wider context. We may be struggling with the problem of witchcraft, but Christians in China, the United States of America, Britain, South America and the Middle East are also struggling with the challenge of explaining evil and suffering. Christians do not seek to run away from this world. They must live in it and transform it.

This book has attempted to provide perspectives that will motivate Christians to be true to God, the Scriptures, their community and the challenge of living ethically in their local context and the world. As we struggle with whatever issues we face, may we all be obedient to God's call to live holy lives.

FURTHER READING

This list of recommended further reading does not include every work mentioned in the footnotes but only books that will be helpful to readers looking for more information. Some are no longer in print but can still be found in many academic libraries. Journal articles and Web pages are not mentioned here, but are included in the footnotes to the chapters.

Do not restrict your reading only to the books mentioned under a particular chapter heading. The general reading on Christian ethics listed under chapters 3 and 4 below deals with a range of ethical topics. So do the general lists at the start of some sections.

The entries within each subsection are in alphabetical order, not in order of usefulness. I do not agree with every author or with every position put forward. However, these books will add to your understanding of ethical issues. As always, you must apply your Christian mind and pray for wisdom and insight as you read.

PART ONE: ETHICAL FOUNDATIONS

Chapter 2   Foundations of Contemporary African Ethics

Bitrus, Daniel. *Legacy of Wisdom: Stories and Proverbs from Africa*. Bukuru, Nigeria: Africa Christian Textbooks, 2007.

Davidson, Basil. *The African Genius*. 2ⁿᵈ ed. Athens, Ohio: Ohio University Press, 2004.

Fisher, Robert B. *West African Religions: Focus on the Akan of Ghana*. New York: Orbis, 1998.

Geertz, Clifford. *The Interpretation of Cultures*. New York: Basic Books, 1977.

Kenyatta, Jomo. *Facing Mount Kenya: The Tribal Life of the Gikuyu*. London: Secker and Warburg, 1938.

Magesa, Laurenti. *African Religion: The Moral Traditions of Abundant Life*. Nairobi: Pauline Publications Africa / Maryknoll: Orbis, 1997.

Mbiti, John. *African Religions and Philosophy*. London: Heinemann, 1982.

———. *Introduction to African Religion*. 2nd ed. London: Heinemann, 1991.

Turaki, Yusufu. *Foundations of African Traditional Religion and Worldview*. Nairobi: WordAlive, 2006.

Chapter 3   Foundations of Western Ethics

Ashby, Warren. *A Comprehensive History of Western Ethics: What Do We Believe?* Amherst, N.Y.: Prometheus Books, 2005.

Bellah, Robert N., Richard Madsen, William M. Sullivan, Ann Swidler and Steven M. Tipton. *Habits of the Heart: Individualism and Commitment in American Life*. 2nd ed. Berkeley: University of California Press, 1996.

Dictionary of the Social Sciences. Edited by Julius Gould and William L. Kolb. New York: Free Press of Glencoe, 1964.

Encyclopedia of Philosophy. New York: Macmillan, 1967.

Frankena, William K. *Ethics*. Englewood Cliffs: Prentice-Hall, 1973.

Rand, Ayn. *For the New Intellectual: The Philosophy of Ayn Rand*. New York: Signet, 1961.

Chapter 4   Foundations of Christian Ethics

Anderson, J. Kerby. *Living Ethically in the 90s: Confronting Key Issues in This Generation*. Wheaton, Ill.: Victor, 1990.

———. *Moral Dilemmas: Biblical Perspectives on Contemporary Ethical Issues*. Nashville: Word, 1998.

Baker Encyclopedia of Psychology and Counselling. 2nd ed. Edited by David G. Benner and Peter C. Hill. Grand Rapids: Baker, 1999.

Birch, Bruce C. and Rasmussen, Larry L. *Bible and Ethics in the Christian Life*. Minneapolis: Augsburg, 1989.

Clark, David K. and Robert V. Rakestraw, eds. *Readings in Christian Ethics Vol. 1: Theory and Method; Vol. 2: Issues and Applications*. Grand Rapids: Baker, 1994, 1996.

Davis, John Jefferson, *Evangelical Ethics: Issues Facing the Church Today*. 3rd ed. Phillipsburg, N.J.: Presbyterian & Reformed, 2004.

Dictionary of Ethics, Theology and Society. Edited by P. B. Clarke and A. Linzey. London: Routledge, 1996.

Encyclopedia of Biblical and Christian Ethics. Edited by R. K. Harrison. Rev. ed. Nashville: Thomas Nelson, 1992.

Feinberg, John S. and Paul D Feinberg. *Ethics for a Brave New World*. Wheaton, Ill.: Crossway, 1993.

Geisler, Norman. *Christian Ethics, Options and Issues*. Grand Rapids: Baker, 1999.

Grenz, Stanley J. *The Moral Quest: The Foundations of Christian Ethics*. Leicester: Apollos / Downers Grove: Intervarsity, 1997.

Hauerwas, Stanley. *The Peaceable Kingdom*. Notre Dame, Ind.: University of Notre Dame Press, 1983.

Hays, Richard B. *The Moral Vision of the New Testament: Community, Cross, New Creation – A Contemporary Introduction to New Testament Ethics*. San Francisco: HarperCollins, 1996.

Hebblethwaite, Brian. *Christian Ethics in the Modern Age*. Philadelphia: Westminster, 1982.

Henry, Carl F. H. *Christian Personal Ethics*. Grand Rapids: Eerdmans, 1957.

Hollinger, Dennis P. *Choosing the Good: Christian Ethics in a Complex World*. Grand Rapids: Baker, 2002.

Holmes, Arthur F. *Ethics: Approaching Moral Decisions*. 2nd ed. Downers Grove: IVP, 2007.

Hughes, Philip Edgecumbe. *Christian Ethics in a Secular Society*. Grand Rapids: Baker, 1983.

Kaiser Walter C. Jr. *Toward Old Testament Ethics*. Grand Rapids: Zondervan, 1983.

McClendon, James William. *Systematic Theology, Vol. 1: Ethics*. 2nd ed. Nashville: Abingdon, 2002.

Mott, Stephen. *Biblical and Social Ethics*. Oxford: Oxford University Press, 1982.

New Dictionary of Christian Ethics and Pastoral Theology. Downers Grove: IVP, 1995.

The New International Dictionary of New Testament Theology. Edited by Colin Brown. Grand Rapids: Zondervan, 1976.

Pocket Dictionary of Ethics. Edited by Stanley J. Grenz and Jay T. Smith. Downers Grove: IVP, 2003.

Ramsey, Paul. *Basic Christian Ethics*. 1953. Reprint; Philadelphia: Westminster, 1993.

Rasmussen, Larry. *Moral Fragments and Moral Community: A Proposal for Church in Society*. Minneapolis: Fortress Press, 1993.

Shorter, Aylward. *African Culture and the Christian Church*. Maryknoll: Orbis, 1974.

Stassen, Glen H. and David P. Gushee. *Kingdom Ethics: Following Jesus in Contemporary Context*. Downers Grove: IVP, 2003.

Stott, John. *Issues Facing Christians Today*. 4th ed. Grand Rapids: Zondervan, 2006.

———. *The Contemporary Christian: Applying God's Word to Today's World*. Downers Grove: IVP, 1992.

Temple, William. *What Christians Stand For in the Secular World*. Philadelphia: Fortress Press, 1965.

Westminster Dictionary of Christian Ethics. Edited by James F. Childress and John Macquarrie. Philadelphia: Westminster Press, 1986.

Wright, Christopher J. H. *Old Testament Ethics for the People of God*. Downers Grove: IVP, 2004.

Chapter 5 Foundations of African Christian Ethics

Bediako, Kwame. *Christianity in Africa: The Renewal of a Non-Western Religion*. Edinburgh: Edinburgh University Press, 1995.

———. *Theology and Identity: The Impact of Culture upon Christian Thought in the Second Century and Modern Africa*. Oxford: Regnum, 1992.

Bujo, Benezet. *African Theology in Its Social Context*. Trans. John O'Donovan. Maryknoll: Orbis, New York, 1992.

———. *Foundations of an African Ethic: Beyond the Universal Claims of Western Morality*. Trans. Brian McNeil. New York: Crossroad, 2001.

PART TWO: CONTEMPORARY ETHICAL ISSUES

SECTION A: POLITICAL ISSUES

Chapter 7   Church and State

Bonino, Jose Miguez. *Toward a Christian Political Ethics.* Philadelphia: Fortress Press, 1965.

Church, State, and Public Justice: Five Views. Edited by P. C. Kemeny. With contributions by Clarke E. Cochran, Derek H. Davis, Ronald J. Sider, Corwin Smidt, and J. Philip Wogaman. Downers Grove: IVP, 2007.

Comblin, José. *The Church and the National Security State.* Maryknoll: Orbis, 1979.

Freston, John. *Evangelicals and Politics in Asia, Africa and Latin America.* New York: Cambridge, 2001.

Palmer, Parker J. *The Company of Strangers: Christians and the Renewal of America's Public Life.* New York: Crossroad, 1983.

Sider, Ronald J. *Non-violence: The Invincible Weapon.* Dallas: Word, 1989.

Wogaman, J. Philip. *Christian Perspectives in Politics.* Rev. ed. Philadelphia: Westminster, 2000.

Chapter 8   War and Violence

Camara, Helder. *Spiral of Violence.* London: Sheed & Ward, 1971. Available online at www.alastairmcintosh.com/general/spiral-of-violence.htm.

Clouse, Robert G. *War: Four Christian Views.* Downers Grove: IVP, 1981.

Ferguson, John. *The Politics of Love: The New Testament and Nonviolent Revolution.* Cambridge: James Clarke, 1979.

King, Martin Luther. *Strength to Love.* Philadelphia: Fortress, 1981.

McCullum, Hugh. *The Angels Have Left Us: The Rwanda Tragedy and the Churches* Geneva: World Council of Churches, 1995

Nnolim Okwudiba, *Ethnic Politics in Nigeria.* Enugu, Nigeria: Fourth Dimension, 1980.

Powers, Gerard F., Drew Christiansen and Robert T. Hennemeyer, eds. *Peacemaking: Moral and Policy Challenges for a New World.* Washington D.C.: United States Catholic Conference, 1994.

Sider, Ronald J. *Non-violence: The Invincible Weapon.* Dallas: Word, 1989.

Thompson, Joseph Milburn. *Justice and Peace: A Christian Primer.* Maryknoll: Orbis, 2003.

Wink, Walter. *Jesus and Non-violence: A Third Way.* Minneapolis: Fortress, 2003.

SECTION B: FINANCIAL ISSUES

Chapter 10 Poverty

Alcorn, Randy. *Money, Possessions, and Eternity.* Wheaton: Tyndale, 1989.

Beisner, E. Calvin. *Prosperity and Poverty: The Compassionate Use of Resources in a World of Scarcity.* Westchester: Crossway, 1988.

Boerma, Conrad. *The Rich, the Poor and the Bible.* Philadelphia: Westminster, 1978.

Chilton, David. *Productive Christians in an Age of Guilt Manipulators: A Biblical Response to Ronald J. Sider.* Tyler, Tex.: Institute for Christian Economics, 1981.

Davis, John Jefferson. *Your Wealth in God's World: Does the Bible Support the Free Market?* Phillipsburg, N.J.: Presbyterian & Reformed, 1984.

George, Augustin. *Gospel Poverty: Essays in Biblical Theology.* Trans. Michael D. Guinan. Chicago: Franciscan Herald Press, 1977.

Griffith, Brian. *Morality and the Market Place: Christian Alternatives to Capitalism and Socialism.* Sevenoaks: Hodder & Stoughton, 1982.

Schaeffer, Frank, ed. *Is Capitalism Christian? Toward a Christian Perspective on Economics.* Westchester: Crossway, 1985.

Sider, Ronald J. *Rich Christians in an Age of Hunger: Moving from Affluence to Generosity.* Rev. ed. Nashville: Thomas Nelson, 2005.

Simon, Arthur. *Bread for the World.* New York: Paulist Press, 1975.

Chapter 11 Corruption

Adams, Patricia. *Odious Debts: Loose Lending, Corruption and the Third World's Environmental Legacy.* London: Earthscan, 1991. Available online at www.eprf.ca/probeint/OdiousDebts/OdiousDebts/index.html

Mehr, Chander. *Corruption: Dealing with the Devil.* Nairobi: Shiv Publications, 2000.

Otenyo, Eric E. *Ethics and Public Service in Africa.* Nairobi: Quest and Insight Publications, 1998.

Chapter 12 Fund-Raising

Evangelical Council for Financial Accountability. "Standard 7: Fund-Raising". *ECFA Standards.* Available online at www.ecfa.org.

Nouwen, Henri J. M. *The Spirituality of Fund-Raising.* Upper Room Ministries in partnership with Henri Nowen Society, 2004. Available online at www.parkerfoundation.org/PDFs/SpiritualityOfFundraising.pdf

Schwartz, Glen J. *When Charity Destroys Dignity: Overcoming Unhealthy Dependency in the Christian Movement.* Bloomington, Ind.: AuthorHouse, 2007.

SECTION C: MARRIAGE AND FAMILY ISSUES

Many of those books listed as general reading on Christian ethics and medical ethics also address the issues discussed in this section.

Chapter 13 Procreation and Infertility

Kore, Danfulani. *Culture and the Christian Home.* Jos: ACTS, 1995.

Thielicke, Helmut. *The Ethics of Sex.* Translated by John W. Doberstein. New York: Harper & Row, 1964.

Chapter 14 Reproductive Technologies

Anderson, J. Kerby. *Genetic Engineering.* Grand Rapids: Zondervan, 1982.

Kilner, John F., Rebecca D. Pentz and Frank E. Young, eds. *Genetic Ethics: Do the Ends Justify the Genes?* Grand Rapids: Eerdmans / Carlisle: Paternoster, 1997.

Ramsey, Paul. *Fabricated Man: The Ethics of Genetic Control.* New Haven: Yale University Press, 1970.

Chapter 15 Contraception

Noonan, John T. *Contraception: A History of Its Treatment by the Catholic Theologians and Canonists.* Rev. ed. Cambridge, Mass.: Harvard University Press, 1986.

Chapter 16 Polygamy

Cairncross, John. *After Polygamy Was Made a Sin: The Social History of Christian Polygamy.* London: Routledge & Kegan Paul, 1974.

Gaskiyane, I. *Polygamy: A Cultural and Biblical Perspective.* Carlisle: Piquant, 2000.

Hillman, Eugene. *Polygamy Reconsidered: African Plural Marriage and the Christian Churches.* Maryknoll: Orbis, 1975.

Chapter 17 Domestic Violence

American Psychological Association. *Violence and the Family: Report of the American Psychological Association Presidential Task Force on Violence and the Family.* Washington: APA, 1996.

Conway, Helen L. *Domestic Violence and the Church.* Carlisle: Paternoster, 1998.

Gnanadason, Aruna. *No Longer a Secret: The Church and Violence Against Women.* Geneva: WCC, 1997.

Chapter 18 Divorce and Remarriage

Luck, William F. *Divorce and Remarriage: Recovering the Biblical View.* San Francisco: Harper & Row, 1987.

Heth, William A. and Gordon J. Wenham, *Jesus and Divorce: The Problem with the Evangelical Consensus.* London: Hodder & Stoughton /Nashville: Thomas Nelson, 1984.

Chapter 19 Widows and Orphans

Kore, Dan. *Defender of Widows and Orphans.* Bukuru, Nigeria: Africa Christian Textbooks, 2007.

Kirwen, Michael, C. *African Widows.* Maryknoll: New York, 1979.

Mamo, Mae Alice Reggy. *Widows, the Challenges and the Choices.* Nairobi, Kenya: Salaamta, 1999.

SECTION D: SEXUAL ISSUES

Rinzema, J. *The Sexual Revolution: Challenge and Response.* Trans. Lewis B. Smedes. Grand Rapids: Eerdmans, 1974.

Thielicke, Helmut. *The Ethics of Sex.* Trans. John W. Doberstein. New York: Harper & Row, 1964.

Chapter 20 Rape

Buckenham, Karen. *Violence Against Women: A Resource Manual for the Church in South Africa.* Pietermaritzburg: PACSA, 1999.

Chapter 22 Prostitution and Sex Trafficking

Bakwesegha, Christopher J. *Profiles of Urban Prostitutiton: A Case Study from Uganda.* Nairobi, Kenya: Literature Bureau, 1982.

Chapter 23 Female Circumcision

Gachiri, Ephigenia W. *Female Circumcision with Reference to Agikuyu of Kenya.* Nairobi: Pauline Publications Africa, 2000.

Kibor, Jacob A. "Persistence of Female Circumcision among the Marakwet of Kenya: A Biblical Response to a Rite of Passage". PhD dissertation, Trinity Evangelical Divinity School, Deerfield, Ill., 1998. Available from UMI Dissertation Services, wwwlib.umi.com
———. *Christian Response to Female Circumcision.* Nairobi: Evangel, 2007.

Chapter 24 Homosexuality

Botha, Peet. *The Bible and Homosex: Sexual Truths for a Modern Society.* Kranskop, South Africa: Khanya, 2005.

DeYoung, James B. *Contemporary Claims Examined: Homosexuality in Light of the Bible and Other Ancient Literature and Law.* Grand Rapids: Kregel, 2000.

Peterson, David, ed. *Holiness and Sexuality: Homosexuality in a Biblical Context.* Carlisle: Paternoster, 2004.

Stott, John. *Same Sex Partnerships? A Christian Perspective.* Grand Rapids: Fleming H. Revell, 1998.

Zuck, Roy B. *Vital Contemporary Issues. Examining Current Questions and Controversies.* Grand Rapids: Kregel, 1994.

SECTION E: MEDICAL ISSUES

Cameron, Nigel M. de S., John F. Kilner, and David L. Schiedermayer, eds. *Bioethics and the Future of Medicine: A Christian Appraisal.* Grand Rapids: Eerdmans / Carlisle: Paternoster, 1995.

Clark K. and Robert V. Rakestraw. *Medical Ethics, Principles, Persons and Problems.* Phillipsburg, N.J.: Presbyterian & Reformed, 1988.

Duncan, A. S., G. R. Dunstan and R. B. Welbourn. *Dictionary of Medical Ethics,* Rev. ed. New York: Crossroad, 1981.

Foreman, Mark W. *Christianity and Bioethics: Confronting Clinical Issues.* Joplin, Miss.: College Press, 1999.

Frame, John M. *Medical Ethics: Principles, Persons and Problems.* Phillipsburg, N.J.: Presbyterian & Reformed, 1988.

Lammers, Stephen E. and Allen Verhey, eds. *On Moral Medicine: Theological Perspectives.* 2nd ed. Grand Rapids: Eerdmans, 1998.

Larson, David E. ed. *The Mayo Clinic Family Health Book.* 3rd ed. New York: Harper, 2003.

Chapter 25 HIV/AIDS

A Report of a Theological Workshop Focusing on HIV- and AIDS-related Stigma. 8–11 December 2003, Windhoek, Namibia. Geneva: UNAIDS, 2005. Available online at http://data.unaids.org/Publications/IRC-pub06/JC1119-Theological_en.pdf

Alcorn, Randy. *Pro-Life Answers to Pro-Choice Arguments.* Sisters, Ore.: Multnomah, 1992.

Dixon, Patrick. *The Truth About AIDS: What You Must Know; What You Can Do.* Eastbourne: Kingsway, 1987.

Dube, Musa W. *Africa Praying: A Handbook on HIV/AIDS Sensitive Sermon Guidelines and Liturgy.* Rev. ed. Geneva: WCC, 2004.

———. *HIV/AIDS and the Curriculum: Methods of Integrating HIV/AIDS in Theological Programs.* Geneva: WCC, 2003.

Carson, D. A. *How Long, O Lord? Reflections on Suffering and Evil.* Grand Rapids: Baker, 1990.

Chapter 26 Abortion

Alcorn, Randy. *Pro-Life Answers to Pro-Choice Arguments.* Sisters, Ore.: Multnomah, 2000.

Koop, C. Everett. *The Right to Live, The Right to Die.* Wheaton, Ill.: Tyndale House, 1976.

Chapter 27 Euthanasia

Koop, C. Everett. *The Right to Live, The Right to Die.* Wheaton, Ill.: Tyndale House, 1976.

Chapter 28 Strikes and Medical Services

Kilner, John, Nigel M. De S. Cameron and David L. Schiedermayer, eds. *Bioethics and the Future of Medicine: A Christian Appraisal.* Grand Rapids: Eerdmans / Carlisle: Paternoster, 1995.

Chapter 29 Drug and Alcohol Abuse

Hanson, Glen, Peter J. Venturelli and Annette E. Fleckenstein *Drugs and Society.* 9th ed. Boston: Jones and Bartlett, 2002.

Ter Chia, Francis. *Understanding Drug Abuse at a Glance: A Training Manual for Local Government.* Nigeria: Drug Abuse Control Committee, 2006.

SECTION F: RELIGIOUS ISSUES

Chapter 30 Witchcraft

Carson, D. A. *How Long, O Lord?: Reflections on Suffering and Evil.* 2nd ed. Grand Rapids: Baker, 2006.

Dickason, C. Fred. *Angels, Elect and Evil.* Rev. ed. Chicago: Moody Press, 1995.

Hiebert, Paul, R. Daniel Shaw, Tite Tienou, *Understanding Folk Religion: A Christian Response to Popular Beliefs and Practices* Grand Rapids: Baker, 1999.

Offiong, Daniel A. *Witchcraft, Sorcery, Magic and Social Order Among the Ibibio of Nigeria.* Enugu: Fourth Dimension Publishing, 1991.

Rommen, Edward, ed. *Spiritual Power and Missions: Raising the Issues.* Evangelical Missiological Society Series, No. 3. Pasadena, Califonia: William Carey Library, 1995.